MANCHESTER
MEDIEVAL
LITERATURE
AND CULTURE

Encountering *The Book of Margery Kempe*

Manchester University Press

Series editors: Anke Bernau, David Matthews and James Paz

Series founded by: J. J. Anderson and Gail Ashton

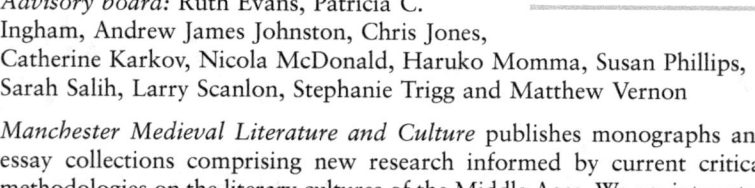

Advisory board: Ruth Evans, Patricia C. Ingham, Andrew James Johnston, Chris Jones, Catherine Karkov, Nicola McDonald, Haruko Momma, Susan Phillips, Sarah Salih, Larry Scanlon, Stephanie Trigg and Matthew Vernon

Manchester Medieval Literature and Culture publishes monographs and essay collections comprising new research informed by current critical methodologies on the literary cultures of the Middle Ages. We are interested in all periods, from the early Middle Ages through to the late, and we include post-medieval engagements with and representations of the medieval period (or 'medievalism'). 'Literature' is taken in a broad sense, to include the many different medieval genres: imaginative, historical, political, scientific, religious. While we welcome contributions on the diverse cultures of medieval Britain and are happy to receive submissions on Anglo-Norman, Anglo-Latin and Celtic writings, we are also open to work on the Middle Ages in Europe more widely, and beyond.

Titles available in the series

32. Riddles at work in the early medieval tradition: Words, ideas, interactions
    Megan Cavell and Jennifer Neville (eds)
33. From Iceland to the Americas: Vinland and historical imagination
    Tim William Machan and Jón Karl Helgason (eds)
34. Northern memories and the English Middle Ages
    Tim William Machan
35. Harley manuscript geographies: Literary history and the medieval miscellany
    Daniel Birkholz
36. Play time: Gender, anti-Semitism and temporality in medieval biblical drama
    Daisy Black
37. Transfiguring medievalism: Poetry, attention and the mysteries of the body
    Cary Howie
38. Objects of affection: The book and the household in late medieval England
    Myra Seaman
39. The gift of narrative in medieval England
    Nicholas Perkins
40. Sleep and its spaces in Middle English literature: Emotions, ethics, dreams
    Megan G. Leitch

Encountering *The Book of Margery Kempe*

Edited by Laura Kalas and Laura Varnam

MANCHESTER UNIVERSITY PRESS

Copyright © Manchester University Press 2021

While copyright in the volume as a whole is vested in Manchester University Press, copyright in individual chapters belongs to their respective authors, and no chapter may be reproduced wholly or in part without the express permission in writing of both author and publisher.

Published by Manchester University Press
Oxford Road, Manchester M13 9PL
www.manchesteruniversitypress.co.uk

British Library Cataloguing-in-Publication Data is available

ISBN 978 1 5261 4661 8 hardback
ISBN 978 1 5261 7158 0 paperback

First published by Manchester University Press in hardback 2021

This edition first published 2023

The publisher has no responsibility for the persistence or accuracy of URLs for any external or third-party internet websites referred to in this book, and does not guarantee that any content on such websites is, or will remain, accurate or appropriate.

Typeset by New Best-set Typesetters Ltd

For our sisters, in kin, friendship, and alliance

Contents

List of figures	page ix
Preface	x
Notes on contributors	xii
List of abbreviations	xvi

Introduction: Encountering *The Book of Margery Kempe* in the twenty-first century   1
Laura Kalas and Laura Varnam

Part I Textual encounters

1. Before Margery: *The Book of Margery Kempe* and its antecedents   23
   Diane Watt
2. The intertextual dialogue and conversational theology of Mechthild of Hackeborn and Margery Kempe   43
   Liz Herbert McAvoy and Naoë Kukita Yoshikawa
3. The prayers of Margery Kempe: a reassessment   63
   Josephine A. Koster

Part II Internal encounters

4. *The Book of Margery Kempe*: autobiography in the third person   83
   Ruth Evans
5. Margery Kempe as de-facement   101
   Johannes Wolf

6. Margery Kempe, oral history, and the value of intersubjectivity — 120
   Katherine J. Lewis
7. 'A booke of hyr felyngys': exemplarity and Margery Kempe's encounters of the heart — 140
   Laura Varnam

Part III Encountering the world

8. Margery Kempe's home town and worthy kin — 163
   Susan Maddock
9. A women's network in fifteenth-century Rome: Margery Kempe encounters 'Margaret Florentyne' — 185
   Anthony Bale and Daniela Giosuè
10. Margery Kempe, racialised soundscapes, sonic wars, and cosmopolitan Jerusalem — 205
    Dorothy Kim
11. The materialisation of Book II: elements of Margery Kempe's world — 234
    Laura Kalas

Part IV Performative encounters

12. Writing performed lives: Margery Kempe meets Marina Abramović — 259
    Sarah Salih
13. Recreating and reassessing Margery and Julian's encounter — 278
    Tara Williams

Select bibliography — 297
Index — 310

Figures

8.1	Map of late medieval Lynn. Created by Susan Maddock	page 165
8.2	Chart of people named Brunham recorded as living or working in Lynn between 1300 and 1440. Created by Susan Maddock	166
8.3	Chart of people named Kempe recorded as living or working in Lynn between 1300 and 1440. Created by Susan Maddock	172
10.1	*Evagatorium: In Terrae Sanctae, Arabiae et Egypti peregrinationen*, vol. 1, 322. Internet Archive, public domain	218
11.1	Wheel of the Four Seasons with connected elements and human characteristics. Isidore of Seville, *De natura rerum*. © Ville de Laon Bibliothèque municipal, ms 422, fol. 6v	238
11.2	The Martyrdom of St Vitalis, *Vies de saints*, Richard of Montbaston and collaborators. Bibliothèque nationale de France, Français 185, fol. 230. © Bibliothèque nationale de France	241

Preface

On 7 June 2014, our paths crossed for the first time in the main building of Birkbeck, University of London. The event was called 'The Birkbeck Medieval Seminar: Margery Kempe at 80', and it marked the eightieth anniversary of the discovery of *The Book of Margery Kempe*. The symposium's aim was to 'take stock of the current state of criticism about Margery Kempe with the aim of discovering promising directions for thought about this unique and marvellous work'. It was indeed an inspiring day. The speakers – Anthony Bale (Birkbeck), Santha Bhattacharji (St Benet's Hall, University of Oxford), Katherine Lewis (University of Huddersfield), and David Wallace (University of Pennsylvania) – shared their own, and the latest, research about Margery Kempe, and the audience engaged with enthusiasm. We found ourselves having lunch together, discussing our research and work, and talking about Margery.

Seven years later, we have become known in medievalist circles, somewhat inevitably, as 'the two Lauras'. We have a firm friendship and an ongoing collaboration that has included the organisation of the 'Margery Kempe Studies in the 21st Century' conference in 2018 (University College, Oxford), the launch of the Margery Kempe Society, and, now, the critical volume *Encountering* The Book of Margery Kempe. It is safe to say, then, that the 'Margery Kempe at 80' seminar at which we first met was most successful in its objective to inspire 'directions for thought' about the *Book*.

Those intervening years of research and productivity have encompassed considerable labour by many people, for which, as editors, we wish to extend our sincere gratitude. First, we are indebted to the conference participants of 'Margery Kempe Studies in the 21st Century'. An overwhelming number of speakers and delegates from around the world converged, and generated a renewed energy in Margery Kempe studies that does not seem to have waned. For this volume we are hugely indebted to our contributors, who have produced chapters which are thought-provoking, rich, and – often – ground-breaking critical responses to the *Book*. The contributors' patience and professionalism during the revision and editing of the volume has been remarkable, particularly in the context of the COVID-19 pandemic. We are grateful to them for their tireless efforts and commitment to the project in spite of the global challenges that we face. Thanks are also due to various individuals who have advised on the volume's content and production along the way, including Kempe experts Anthony Bale, Sarah Salih, Diane Watt, Naoë Kukita Yoshikawa, and especially Liz Herbert McAvoy. We are grateful to Meredith Carroll at Manchester University Press for her enthusiasm for the book from the get-go and to the Series Editors – Anke Bernau, David Matthews, and James Paz – for their ongoing support and advice. Our respective institutions – University College, Oxford, and Swansea University – have provided vital support and the means by which this volume has been possible, and we are immensely appreciative. We owe a debt of gratitude to Anthony Bale, Isabel Davis, and Jess Fenn for organising the 'Margery Kempe at 80' seminar at Birkbeck, from which this book, and these editors, have evolved. Finally, our thanks to our families, for their continuing acceptance of Margery in their team, and for their unfailing support.

Notes on contributors

Anthony Bale is Executive Dean of Arts and Professor of Medieval Studies at Birkbeck, University of London. He edited and translated *The Book of Margery Kempe* for Oxford World's Classics (Oxford University Press, 2015). He is currently completing a short critical biography of Kempe and working on English travellers in the eastern Mediterranean in the fifteenth century.

Ruth Evans has taught at Cardiff University, the University of Stirling, and Saint Louis University, where she is Dorothy McBride Orthwein Professor of English. She is a former President of the New Chaucer Society. Her books include *Feminist Readings in Middle English Literature* (with Lesley Johnson, Routledge, 1994), *The Idea of the Vernacular* (with Jocelyn Wogan-Browne, Nicholas Watson, and Andrew Taylor, University of Exeter Press, 1999), *A Cultural History of Sexuality in the Middle Ages* (Bloomsbury Academic, 2011), and *Roadworks: Medieval Roads, Medieval Britain* (with Valerie Allen, Manchester University Press, 2016). She is working on a monograph, *Chaucer and the Book of Memory*.

Daniela Giosuè is a tenured researcher in English Language and Translation in the Department of Humanities, Communication and Tourism at the Università degli Studi della Tuscia of Viterbo. Her research and publications focus on pilgrimage and travel literature and the translation of works by British authors active between the fifteenth and seventeenth centuries, particularly Margery Kempe, John Capgrave, and Thomas Coryate. She is the author of an Italian translation of John Capgrave's *Ye Solace of Pilgrimes* (*Roma nel Rinascimento*, 1995) which she is currently revising.

Laura Kalas is a Senior Lecturer in Medieval Literature at Swansea University. Her monograph is entitled *Margery Kempe's Spiritual Medicine: Suffering, Transformation and the Life-Course* (D. S. Brewer, 2020). She has published articles on Margery Kempe's spirituality for *Medieval Feminist Forum: A Journal of Gender and Sexuality* (2018) and for *Studies in the Age of Chaucer*, where she revealed the recipe from the back of the manuscript of the *Book* (2019). With Laura Varnam, she is the co-founder of the Margery Kempe Society.

Dorothy Kim teaches Medieval Literature at Brandeis University. Her research focuses on race, gender, digital humanities, medieval women's literary cultures, medievalism, Jewish/Christian difference, book history, digital media, and the alt-right. She is co-editing *A Cultural History of Race in the Renaissance and Early Modern Age (1350-1550)* with Kimberly Coles (University of Maryland, College Park) with Bloomsbury (forthcoming 2021). She has edited a special double cluster on 'Critical Race and the Middle Ages' for Literature Compass (2019).

Josephine A. Koster is Margaret M. Bryant Professor of English Literature at Winthrop University (South Carolina), where she co-founded and directed the Medieval Studies Program. Her scholarship focuses on prayers, prayer books, palaeography, and women's literate practices in the late fourteenth and early fifteenth centuries. She is currently working on a study of the sources of the Passion narratives in *The Book of Margery Kempe*.

Katherine J. Lewis is a Senior Lecturer in History at the University of Huddersfield. She researches later medieval gender, religious, and cultural history. Her publications include *The Cult of St Katherine of Alexandria in Late Medieval England* (Boydell, 2000) and *Kingship and Masculinity in Late Medieval England* (Routledge, 2013). She is also the co-editor of *A Companion to the Book of Margery Kempe* (D. S. Brewer, 2003), *Religious Men and Masculine Identity in the Middle Ages* (Boydell, 2013), and *Crusading and Masculinities* (Routledge, 2019).

Susan Maddock is an honorary research fellow at the University of East Anglia. Formerly Principal Archivist in the Norfolk Record Office, she was responsible for King's Lynn's borough archives for more than thirty years and her current research focuses on the social milieu of late medieval Lynn. Recent publications include 'Society, status and the leet court in Margery Kempe's Lynn', in Richard Goddard and Teresa Phipps (eds), *Town Courts and Urban Society in Late Medieval England, 1250–1500* (Boydell Press, 2019).

Liz Herbert McAvoy is Professor Emerita of Medieval English Literature at Swansea University. She has published widely on writing by, for, and about medieval women; anchoritism and other forms of the solitary life; and medieval gender and sexuality. More recently, she has been focusing on the gendered role played by the walled garden – or *hortus conclusus* – in the medieval religious imaginary and has recently completed a monograph on the topic.

Sarah Salih is a Senior Lecturer in English at King's College London. Her publications include *Versions of Virginity in Late Medieval England* (D. S. Brewer, 2001) and *Imagining the Pagan in Late Medieval England* (D. S. Brewer, 2019) and articles on hagiography, religious lives, and women's writing. She has been reading *The Book of Margery Kempe* for thirty years now and still finds it surprising.

Laura Varnam is the Lecturer in Old and Middle English Literature at University College, Oxford. She is the author of *The Church as Sacred Space in Middle English Literature and Culture* (Manchester University Press, 2018) and a number of articles on Margery Kempe, Middle English literature, and, most recently, medievalism and Harry Potter. With Laura Kalas, she is the co-founder of the Margery Kempe Society. She is currently writing a book on the twentieth-century writer Daphne du Maurier.

Diane Watt is Professor of Medieval English Literature at the University of Surrey. Her most recent book is entitled *Women, Writing and Religion in England and Beyond, 650-1100* (Bloomsbury, 2019). Her previous books include *Medieval Women's Writing* (Polity, 2007), *Amoral Gower* (University of Minnesota Press, 2003), and *Secretaries of God* (D. S. Brewer, 1997). She also edited and translated *The*

Paston Women: Selected Letters (D. S. Brewer, 2004), and has edited and co-edited numerous volumes of essays.

Tara Williams is Dean of the Honors College and Professor of English at the University of Alabama. She is the author of *Inventing Womanhood: Gender and Language in Later Middle English Writing* (Ohio State University Press, 2011) and *Middle English Marvels: Magic, Spectacle, and Morality* (Penn State University Press, 2018). In addition to her work on women writers, gender, and magic in the later Middle Ages, she has published on the scholarship of teaching and learning.

Johannes Wolf is an independent researcher. Since the completion of his 2018 Cambridge University PhD on technologies of subject-formation in medieval devotional texts, he has published on the early Middle English hagiographies known as the 'Katherine Group' in the *Journal of Medieval and Early Modern Studies* (May 2020) and has forthcoming essays on the non-human performances of late-medieval holy women and the uses of *ruminatio* in the twenty-first-century classroom. He is interested in the ways that medieval texts shape their readers to draw conclusions concerning, and associations between, themselves and their worlds.

Naoë Kukita Yoshikawa is Professor of English at Shizuoka University and was a Leverhulme Visiting Professor at Swansea University (2019–20). She is currently collaborating with Professor Liz Herbert McAvoy in the field of Continental holy women's writing and its impact on the literary culture of late medieval England. Her recent publication includes 'Mechtild of Hackeborn as Spiritual Authority: The Middle English Translation of the *Liber Specialis Gratiae*', in *The Medieval Translator*, ed. Pieter De Leemans and Michèle Goyens (Brepols, 2017). She is currently editing, with Dr Anne Mouron, *The Boke of Gostely Grace*, edited from Oxford, MS Bodley 220 (Liverpool, forthcoming in 2022).

Abbreviations

BL   British Library
BMK   *The Book of Margery Kempe*
EETS   Early English Texts Series
KLBA   King's Lynn Borough Archives, King's Lynn
MED   *Middle English Dictionary*
OED   *Oxford English Dictionary*
TEAMS   Teaching Association for Medieval Studies text series
TNA   The National Archives, Kew

Introduction:
Encountering *The Book of Margery Kempe* in the twenty-first century

Laura Kalas and Laura Varnam

A flashback to the proud merchant woman, dressed in 'pompows aray', of Margery Kempe's younger years interrupts the moment of her entry into the city of London in Chapter 9, Book II, of *The Book of Margery Kempe*. Aged sixty-one and recently returned to England after an arduous pilgrimage to northern Europe, Kempe is clad in a coarse sackcloth and in need of a loan. Her notoriety a given, she divulges that many Londoners 'knew hir wel anow', and so she dons a veil as a disguise in order that she might 'gon unknowyn' for the time being. However unexpected this choice of evasive *incognito*, the covering is ineffective and she is recognised nevertheless, a scandalous 'maner of proverbe' reverberating against her through cries on the street of 'A, thu fals flesch, thu schalt no good mete etyn!' (p. 415).[1] This rumoured hypocrisy is based on the false – and, according to Kempe, diabolic – story that she had refused to eat plain herring in favour of fine pike, and rebounds at her again during an event that we have termed *Pike Gate* in homage to its own infamy in Margery Kempe studies.[2] At a feast at the house of a 'worschepful woman' she becomes a victim of mythological construction, quite literally encountering her own public reputation as it is in the process of being made. She becomes a byword and a laughing-stock – an embodied myth – as the proverb continues to circulate as it had before, ventriloquising her reported utterances. Curiously, her identity is not recognised here as it had been on the public street, emphasising further the kind of powerful symbol of her*self* that she has become through a type of auto-mimesis, as she is known widely for her abstruse reputation. In the private feasting room, where she is paradoxically less conspicuous, she boldly stands up and identifies herself: 'I am that same persone to whom thes wordys ben arectyd [imputed]', and lays claim to the person, but not the persona. She is frequently confronted by such reproof – in 'many tymys and in many placys [she] had gret repref therby' (p. 415) – and through these gossiping Londoners in the city streets, at dinner, and in church, Margery Kempe comes face to face with her own image, encountering and refashioning herself in an effort to reclaim her identity in an environment in which she has been reduced to an amusing and entertaining figure of mythology. It is striking, then, that this is the only chapter in the *Book* in which she is fully named as 'Mar. Kempe of Lynne' (p. 415), a nomenclature through which she fluctuates as both legitimate and infamous; existing in and out of 'truth' as the real, and fictionalised, Margery Kempe.

As a particular moment within the 'many tymys and ... many placys' that she is scorned and rewritten by her contemporaries, this episode reveals how Kempe appears to transcend time and space as an un/popular holy woman always already everywhere: in Carolyn Dinshaw's words, Kempe, 'pierced by an eternal *now*, remained an outsider'.[3] But even as the asynchrony of the *Book* makes 'something out of joint' about Kempe, the space of the feasting room in the worshipful lady's house, in which strangers of 'dyvers personys of divers condicyons' encounter each other in an arbitrary locus of otherness, functions as a heterotopia where Kempe herself exists, in Foucauldian terms, as 'simultaneously represented, contested, and inverted'.[4] Forced to confront her own refracted image, like Foucault's mirror, she encounters herself as at once a virtual reality and an undeniable presence: 'From the standpoint of the mirror I discover my absence from the place where I am since I see myself over there. Starting from this gaze that is, as it were, directed toward me, from the ground of this virtual space that is on the other side of the glass, I come back toward myself; I begin again to direct my eyes toward myself and to reconstitute myself there where I am'.[5] Margery Kempe, in the feasting room, exists multiply – as dinner party guest / erstwhile traveller / receiver of charity / holy woman / false hypocrite / honest wretch. Which particular iteration we might find is dependent on something like Foucault's Fourth Principle of heterotopic space, that is, the connection of heterotopias to 'slices in time'; to 'heterochronies', where the heterotopia functions at 'full capacity' when there occurs 'a sort of absolute break with their traditional time'.[6] That Kempe encounters herself in this timeplace as a mythological refiguration of a self that is reappropriated multifariously, even in her own lifetime, gestures towards the very slipperiness of who we might deem her to be, and what our own encounters with her *Book* might, then, mean.[7]

The term 'encounter' is invoked as a central principle in this volume because of such questions of representation and response. As a lexicon of malleability and multiplicity, 'encounter' can signify a physical, metaphorical, casual or accidental meeting of varying sorts, an opposition or dispute, and it can act in the noun or verb form.[8] Encounters can take place in literal time and space, but they can also exist, and operate, in and between texts, across history, and across cultures. Recent developments in medieval studies have sought to explore the active relationship between the past and present, and the field of Margery Kempe studies in particular has been reinvigorated in the light of new theoretical, methodological, and critical approaches. The through-line of 'encounters' as full of dynamic, multiple, reciprocal, and disruptive potentialities thus encapsulates the aim of this volume to foreground and facilitate the multivalence of current Kempe criticism. 'Encounters', as a conceptual framework, has the flexibility and elasticity to underpin a rich variety of approaches whose interactions respond to the current interdisciplinary drive in academia. Whilst the four categories of encounter within this volume – textual, internal, external, and performative – suggest thematic threads, their overlaps, incongruities, tensions, and interlocutions will reveal the way in which *The Book of Margery Kempe* resists categorisation. This fundamental unruliness is a touchstone for the analysis in this volume, whose chapters seek to define but also to destabilise concepts such 'autobiography' or 'feeling', and communities of texts and people, both medieval and modern. Indeed the capaciousness of *The Book* itself shows its ability to generate and sustain multiple, interdisciplinary, overlapping, and exploratory theoretical and creative approaches. As Foucault posits, 'in every culture, *between* the use of what one might call the ordering codes and reflections upon order itself, there is the pure *experience* of order and its modes of *being*'.[9] In prioritising the uncovered histories, (in)congruences, and 'modes of being' in the *Book*, then, this volume itself offers up heterotopic and heterochronic spaces for new, critical encounters.

What *Pike Gate* also shows us is how any attempt to *know* Margery Kempe – in her time and ours – is an ongoing process of communal and shared discourse. Collaboration is a practice at the heart of the production of *The Book of Margery Kempe*, of most medieval writing, and, indeed, of this volume, as our collaborative introduction and the chapters co-authored by Liz Herbert McAvoy and Naoë Kukita Yoshikawa, and Anthony Bale and Daniela Giosuè, demonstrate. Indeed, the significance of 'dalyawns' and 'comown[ing]' together are explored by Tara Williams in Chapter 13 as a testament to the 'complex range of relationships built through verbal exchanges between figures who share emotions, interests, or experiences', as we do, and the shared 'desire for connection as a powerful motivation for and within the *Book*'.[10] Crucially, such collaboration is founded on and sustained by mutual support and affective, as well as intellectual, teamwork and dialogue. The idea for this volume was fostered by our 2018 co-organised conference 'Margery Kempe Studies in the 21st Century' at which delegates received 'Team Margery' badges and we discussed what it might mean to be a 'friend' of Margery, to be her 'avoket' (advocate), like the woman in chapter 60 who speaks up for Kempe to the parish priest who belittles her emotional response to the pietà (p. 286).[11] At the conference Clarissa Atkinson, author of the first monograph on Kempe, *Mystic and Pilgrim* (1983), raised a toast to Kempe and to the collaborative work of the delegates, who came from diverse geographical locations and a range of career stages.[12] Whilst much has been made of Kempe's detractors, within the *Book* and in contemporary attitudes to her exuberant devotional practice, this volume contains a number of chapters that foreground Kempe's supporters, particularly amongst women, including McAvoy and Yoshikawa's reappraisal of Kempe's daughter-in-law's role in the *Book*'s production, Bale and Giosuè's identification of Margaret Florentyne, and Varnam's exploration of female networks of emotional reciprocity. Indeed, the Proem to the *Book* deliberately encourages a supportive encounter based on generosity of spirit, declaring that '[a]lle the werkys of ower Saviowr ben for ower exampyl and instruccyon, and what grace that he werkyth in any creatur is ower profyth, *yf lak of charyte be not ower hynderawnce*' (p. 41, italics ours). Extending a charitable hand to Kempe, and to each other, places us in a direct line of descent from her first twentieth-century 'champion of sorts', as Dinshaw puts it: Hope Emily Allen.[13] In a 1941 letter Allen declared that 'Margery gives me hope' and for us this volume represents a hope for a kinder and more inclusive future in academia, which is open to diverse voices and approaches and which draws strength from Kempe's own persistence in the face of critique.[14] Diane Watt, in her 2004 article 'Critics, communities, compassionate criticism: learning from *The Book of Margery Kempe*' (in Louise D'Arcens and Juanita Ruys's important collection *Maistresse of My Wit: Medieval Women, Modern Scholars*), argued for a criticism that is 'defined by its sensitivity to and respect for its subject matter combined with an overt articulation of personal and political commitments'.[15] Many of the chapters in this volume display their authors' 'personal and political commitments' and are explicit about what is at stake in their interventions in Kempe criticism, from Watt's argument for placing Kempe in the middle of a women's literary tradition to Dorothy Kim's resituating of the *Book* in the context of the Global Middle Ages.

Encountering The Book of Margery Kempe, then, offers a range of new critical approaches to Kempe and her *Book* which include literary analyses, theoretical applications, textual milieux, and historical discoveries that build on and develop the current state of the field. As dynamic encounters themselves – across time, text, theory, and mode – these multiple approaches facilitate an exchange which brings Kempe into conversation with modern and medieval worlds, and allows for a capacious interdisciplinarity that showcases the variety of theoretical, conceptual, and recreative methodologies at work in the individual contributions to the volume. Beyond 'new readings', these 'encounters' operate more broadly: encompassing drawing to the surface, for example, the personal encounters between Kempe and other individuals in her orbit, the textual encounters between the *Book* and contemporary devotional texts and with modern theoretical perspectives, and the cultural encounters between different peoples and geographies. Encounters are dynamic and creative. They can be planned, spontaneous, affirmative, hostile, material and imaginative, but they persistently require negotiation and reciprocity. As the cover image of this volume illustrates, an encounter, such as that between Mary and the saints at the foot of the cross, can also hinge upon a shared experience which nevertheless manifests multifariously. Inside the image, while Mary collapses at the loss of her son, her co-mourners individually withstand, and share, their own grief. Externally, a medieval visual encounter with the painting might figure rather differently to our own, where the affective cues of the iconography of Christ's freshly bleeding wounds and allegorical skull in the foreground foster an urgency in the devotional and eschatological meditations of medieval Christianity. The internal and external encounters with Christ's body, then, signify in myriad ways and offer reciprocal opportunities for the making of meaning. In a similar way the chapters in this volume underscore the ways in which their individual approaches might highlight unexplored areas of interest in Kempe's life and *Book* and also the ways in which an encounter with Kempe studies might offer, in return, fresh perspectives on twenty-first-century modes of engagement with medieval literature. Encountering Kempe and her *Book* is always a multi-way process.

The Book of Margery Kempe (c.1436–38) has gained extensive scholarly attention since the discovery of the only surviving manuscript in 1934.[16] Considered to be the first female autobiography in the English language, the *Book* is now recognised as an important text in the canon of English literature. In 2015 Anthony Bale produced a new translation for Oxford World's Classics, and the *Book* is a staple of undergraduate and graduate courses in the UK and globally. The first international conference dedicated entirely to Kempe and her *Book* was organised by Laura Varnam and Laura Kalas in 2018, at which the Margery Kempe Society was launched.[17] Academic interest in Kempe has significantly increased in recent years. New discoveries have further cemented the *Book* in its historical context, and diverse theoretical models have cast new light on Kempe and her resonance in the modern world. *Encountering* The Book of Margery Kempe showcases such fresh perspectives, building on existing scholarship and offering important new directions for Kempe studies in the twenty-first century as a canonical text. The volume also takes up the urgent academic necessity to diversify, not least by foregrounding the Global Middle Ages. With the *Book* as an important example of the medieval transglobal interactions now being uncovered, this volume sheds new light on the text in its global contexts particularly in the chapters by Watt, McAvoy and Yoshikawa, Bale and Giosuè, Kim, and Kalas.[18]

Introduction

Two critical volumes have preceded the present collection. Sandra McEntire's 1992 volume, *Margery Kempe: A Book of Essays*, remains an important contribution in Kempe studies, not least for several essays which highlight connections between the *Book* and Continental women's devotional traditions. This was a project first posited in 1940 by Hope Emily Allen, who promised a second volume to *The Book of Margery Kempe* which was sadly never delivered, although Allen's ambition to reveal Kempe's rich devotional influences and contexts has since been taken up in scholarship, including in this volume, in the chapters by Watt, McAvoy and Yoshikawa, Koster, and Bale and Giosuè.[19] Katherine Lewis and John Arnold's 2004 edition, *A Companion to The Book of Margery Kempe* (2004) combined literary scholarship with historical analysis in order to contextualise Kempe's devotional, social, and textual lives, and the new archival work in this volume, including by Susan Maddock, Anthony Bale, and Daniela Giosuè, continues this interdisciplinary trajectory.[20] These volumes cemented the *Book*'s canonical status, building on early scholarship which frequently took a sceptical view of Kempe's form of boisterous spirituality. Even Allen, in her Prefatory Note to the 1940 EETS edition, described Kempe as 'largely limited by her constitutional difficulties', as 'petty, neurotic, vain, illiterate, physically and nervously over-strained; devout, much-travelled, forceful and talented'. Allen hoped that the volume would 'aid the professional psychologist who later will doubtless pronounce at length on Margery's type of neuroticism' (pp. lxiv–lxv).[21] Such diagnostic approaches to the *Book* have since been manifold, and myriad retrospective diagnoses offered, from temporal lobe epilepsy to Tourette's Syndrome, hysteria, and depressive psychosis, and Johannes Wolf in Chapter 5 reflects on the consequences of this pathologising for our encounter with Kempe as subject.[22] More recent scholarship has repositioned Kempe's spirituality in its medieval medical context, however, including Laura Kalas's monograph *Margery Kempe's Spiritual Medicine: Suffering, Transformation and the Life-Course* (2020), which adds to a growing corpus of full-length studies about Margery Kempe.[23] Also contesting the early scholarly suspicion of Kempe's religiosity, and her pathologies, are publications that instead assert her exemplarity, or saintliness.[24] Indeed the creation of the *Book* itself, including its authorship, has generated a rich body of scholarship. In 1975 John Hirsh asserted that Kempe's scribe was the author of the *Book*; in 1991 Lynn Staley offered an intervention which distinguished between Kempe, the author; Margery, her fictional creation; and the scribe as a literary trope; and in 2005 Nicholas Watson resituated Kempe as author of her own text in a 'positivistic attitude to some of the text's historical claims'.[25] Recent discoveries have illuminated the *Book*'s historicity, such as Sebastian Sobecki's work on Kempe's son as the first scribe and Laura Kalas's transcription of the recipe in the only existing copy of the manuscript: British Library, Additional 61823.[26] Scholarship has also responded to current trends in literary criticism. Laura Varnam has analysed Kempe's devotional self-fashioning through the lens of performance theory; Rebecca Krug draws on emotions history in her 2017 monograph to consider the *Book* as one of consolation; and Kathy Lavezzo, Jonathan Hsy, and Carolyn Dinshaw have explored the queer potential of Kempe, her *Book*, and its afterlives.[27]

In his 2015 translation Anthony Bale justifiably remarks that '*The Book of Margery Kempe* is a difficult thing to summarize'.[28] Fortunately that is not a task that this volume seeks to attempt. Rather, antithetically, the hermeneutic expanse of encounters enables us to capture some of the capaciousness of the *Book*; to reach across time periods, geographies, and disciplinary boundaries to better understand Kempe's lived experience, the complex production of the *Book*, and its manifold effects on medieval and modern readers. Several chapters practise innovation in their approaches through methodology, collaboration, theory, and technology. Williams analyses modern dramatic performance as a way of interpreting the meeting between Margery Kempe and Julian of Norwich; Kim supports her chapter with an immersive 360-degree video on YouTube that enables readers to use smartphones to explore the Via Dolorosa and the Holy Sepulchre. This sharp encounter between the Middle Ages and the twenty-first century harnesses evolving technologies which provide the mechanism for communication, interpretation, and textual encounter; then and now. Such technologies – reaching back to those of medieval parchment and manuscript production and forwards to the technologies of theatrical spaces and cyber spaces – provide vital conduits for our present interaction with the medieval.[29] The temporal and creative encounters in this volume thus themselves enter into, through their multivalency, something like Dinshaw's zone of *asynchrony*: the 'capacious *now*' of *The Book of Margery*

Kempe, in which 'past-present-future times are collapsed'.³⁰ The following chapters offer various means of 'touching the past' through what Dinshaw might see as 'our efforts to build selves and communities now and into the future'.³¹ What did the *Book* mean then? What does it mean now? And how might we use it to shape a collaborative future as scholars and students of medieval studies in the twenty-first century, when the careful harnessing of the past in the present is more urgent than ever?³² By embracing the interactions of different fields and theories, this volume, like Kempe herself, deliberately resists enforced categorisation. Rather, in the following chapters, theories of psychoanalysis, emotion theory, ecocriticism, autobiography, post-structuralism, and performance theory are used in encounter with the *Book*. The methodologies incorporate the medical humanities, history of science, history of medieval women's literary culture, literary criticism, oral history, the Global Middle Ages, archival discoveries, and creative reimaginings. Deliberately diverse, these rich, multifarious, and often new, approaches capture the necessary hermeneutic capaciousness that the *Book* demands. After all, an encounter is, chiefly, 'a meeting face-to-face', which might be in conflict, unexpected, or accidental as much as sought for, desired, and planned.³³ As we come 'face-to-face' here with the *Book*, the multidisciplinary methodologies of our contributors offer ways of navigating the limitlessness of those possible encounters between Kempe, her *Book*, and ourselves.

Whilst the term 'encounter' will necessarily operate in multiple ways within and between the individual chapters, the four parts of the volume foreground particular types of encounter: textual, internal, worldly, and performative. Part I, 'Textual' encounters, places the *Book* within new explorations of intertextual sources and literary traditions. Opening with the complete repositioning of the *Book* in its historical context, Diane Watt (Chapter 1) examines the literary canon, exploring what happens when we encounter the *Book* not at the beginning but in the middle of a tradition of women's writing. Focusing on the eighth-century letters of Boniface's early medieval women correspondents and Hugeburc of Heidenheim's voyage narrative of St Willibald, *Hodoeporicon*, Watt rereads the *Book* within the context of these earlier texts and thus offers a new way of encountering it. Despite the differences between the women's manner of religious life, Watt's analysis reveals their shared connection of spirituality with the landscape, and a focus on pilgrimage as a tradition that has long enabled women's encounters with devotional travel. Liz Herbert McAvoy and Naoë Kukita Yoshikawa (Chapter 2) next offer an alternative exploration of the literary and devotional context of the *Book*. By pinpointing the 'swech other' texts that Kempe is recorded as having been read by a priest, McAvoy and Yoshikawa argue that one of these texts would have been the *Liber specialis gratiae* of the thirteenth-century visionary nun Mechthild of Hackeborn, probably in its Middle English translation, *The Boke of Gostely Grace*. Regarding the Mechthildian elements within Kempe's *Book* as transforming it into a quasi-devotional compilation like those that the priest was reading with her, McAvoy and Yoshikawa consider evidence of the intertextual materials, or 'conversational theology', inherent in the *Book* as a 'complex process of entangled encounters'.[34] Josephine A. Koster (Chapter 3) then looks both within and without the *Book*'s textuality, first arguing that Kempe's prayers at the end of the text are a neglected but fundamental lens through which its entirety should be encountered by the reader, and, second, that reading the prayers in the context of Middle English prayer cycles enables us to reframe Kempe's self-representation. Unusually for such texts, Kempe's prayers use the first-person singular voice, which both contrasts with the third-person narration of her *Book* and fashions her as a *mediatrix* for her fellow Christians, both lay and ecclesiastical.

Part II, 'Internal encounters', examines how Kempe encounters her*self*, constructing, or destabilising, her identity within the *Book*. Ruth Evans's Chapter 4 on autobiography utilises linguistic and psychoanalytical approaches to ask why Kempe transposed her text into the third person, and to what effect. By analysing the mechanisms through which Kempe's self is represented in discourse – the third person as a play of figures, 'this creatur' as signifying the absence of her own causality, and 'this creatur' as a deictic mode of proximity, space, and temporality – Evans draws upon Philippe Lejeune's work to argue that Kempe's use of the third person both inscribes her divided identity and precludes the reader's encounter with a knowable life. Despite its problematics, Evans argues that we cannot *not* read the *Book* autobiographically; that the split subject in the *Book* is located in its 'constituting division' as both a life and a writing. The narrative encounter, Evans suggests, sees events from Kempe's point of view as 'a shrewd observer of herself', suggesting that there is 'no place in her culture from which she can speak as an I'. Continuing the focus of autobiography, Johannes Wolf (Chapter 5) examines how Kempe's subjectivity is produced in the reader's own encounter with the *Book* through the act of reading itself. Employing Paul de Man's theory of autobiography as a type of *prosopopoeia*, a type of writing that generates 'a voice or face by means of language', Wolf considers the notion of 'de-facement': a concept which undoes the causal assumption that a life (*bios*) precedes the text (*graphē*). An encounter, then, he argues, might be a de-facement whose effects are palpable in both the *Book* and the forms of response it has engendered, such as the sicknesses often ascribed to Kempe. By its resisting of literary and narrative order, Wolf suggests that the *Book* anchors the experience of textuality in a *bios* that governs the rules of its execution and subordinates its effects to a life that is unreachable. In Chapter 6, Katherine Lewis employs the methodologies of oral history to cast fresh light on the relationship between Kempe, her scribes, and her confessors, highlighting both the collaborative nature of the encounter and Kempe's simultaneous, decisive role in determining its content and form. She argues that, before the *Book* was recorded as text, Kempe had already narrated her story orally many times over; repetitions which are fundamentally informed by confession as a mode of self-fashioning that takes place through dialogue. This intersubjectivity extends to the relationship between historian and subject, as Lewis herself reflects at the end of her chapter, and this personal encounter between Kempe, her *Book*, and her empathetic readers is taken up by Laura Varnam (Chapter 7) in the final chapter of this part. Varnam posits that Kempe's interaction with her fellow believers, both within the *Book* itself and in relation to its readers, is predicated on an emotional exchange that takes place in the heart, facilitated by an embedded lyric couplet which draws on well-established devotions to the Sacred Heart, in Middle English lyrics and in the work of Mechthild of Hackeborn. Examining her encounters with her female communities in particular, Varnam argues that the *Book* presents Kempe as an exemplar of heart-felt devotion, modelling a compassionate empathy that we would do well to cultivate in the twenty-first-century academy.

Part III, 'Encountering the world', focuses on social and geographical encounters, from the local to the Continental and global.

Susan Maddock's new archival discoveries (Chapter 8) emphasise the influential status of Kempe's family in Bishop's Lynn and beyond, and her chapter analyses the significant encounters in which she and her kin participated. Maddock reveals the aristocratic connections of Kempe's father, John de Brunham, including with Joan Holland: Duchess of Brittany and Richard II's half-sister. Focusing also on the Brunhams' wealthy merchant-burgess neighbours and friends, the Loks, Maddock posits a possible godmother for Margery Kempe – Margery Lok – and identifies Master Aleyn of Lynn as Alan Warnekyn, who was likely to have been younger than first thought. Not only might Alan Warnekyn's younger age shift our perceptions of the nature of their relationship, Maddock also shows how Kempe's assessment of her husband's status as lower than her own was well founded, suggesting that their marriage was indeed a genuine love-match. In Chapter 9, Bale and Giosuè's new identification of 'Margaret Florentyne' as the Florentine businesswoman and heiress Margherita degli Alberti shows, conversely, how a *chance* encounter not only plays a crucial role in establishing Kempe's spiritual authority in Italy, cemented when she marries the Godhead in Rome, but also deprovincialises Kempe, arguing for her proper place in an Italian cultural environment as a Renaissance woman. This unexpected meeting while on pilgrimage is an encounter that puts Kempe into a specific context of Dominican-influenced spirituality and Dominican-Brigittine patronage circles in Rome and Florence and, moreover, into broader pan-European devotional trends. In Dorothy Kim's innovative piece (Chapter 10), Kempe's tears are examined within the soundscape of fifteenth-century Jerusalem – one of the most cosmopolitan, multiracial or multireligious, and contested spaces in the medieval world – to reframe the *Book* from a global perspective. The chapter is accompanied by a YouTube video which offers an immersive experience of the Jerusalem soundscape.[35] Kim argues that Margery Kempe follows the orthodox devotional 'frameouts' of the Franciscans who led the western Catholic pilgrimage industry in the eastern Mediterranean, and also explores the function of 'the racialised devotional sensorium', and the 'Sonic War' in Jerusalem to demonstrate the ordinariness of Kempe's crying in context. The chapter positions Kempe, regarded by Kim as illegible and 'foreign' in England rather than abroad, as truly international. Laura Kalas concludes this part (Chapter 11) with a critical encounter with Book

II as a distinctive work from Book I, arguing that the dictation of its events more immediately after their occurrence produces a less mythologised account of Kempe's experience. Engaging with Donna Haraway's notion of a 'sympoietic timeplace' with the earth's inhabitants in 'moving relations of attunement',[36] Kalas suggests that the accounts of travel in Book II, and the *Book's* final prayers, illustrate how Kempe's spiritual understanding is predicated much more on encounters with the physical world in Book II, revealing a connection with the universe and Creation that marks her spiritual apotheosis. Two seemingly disparate aspects of the *Book* – the authority and genesis of Book II, and Kempe's maturing encounters *in* Book II with the natural world – the chapter argues, concurrently materialise.

The concluding Part IV, 'Performative encounters', examines and enacts the ways in which theoretical and creative encounters with the *Book* offer a deliberately modern perspective on its archiving of Kempe's own performances. Standing separately as contributions of forward-thinking, recreative possibilities, these chapters explore the ways in which the *Book* continues to be encountered in a postmodern context. Salih's Chapter 12 presents Kempe as a performance artist, an unknowing predecessor to the feminist performance artists of the twentieth and twenty-first centuries whose corporeal displays of pain and pleasure similarly discomfort their audiences and achieve validation through an exploitation of social controversy. In an encounter with Marina Abramović's performance art and her 2016 memoir *Walk through Walls*, Salih presents Kempe's *Book* as a 'performance archive' in which Kempe herself is both performer and curator of that performance. Both Kempe and Abramović repeat and recapitulate their performances and their texts and therefore represent an encounter between past and present selves and a script for future readers to imitate. The final chapter in the volume (Chapter 13), by Tara Williams, focuses on a much cherished encounter, rewritten by modern readers and creative writers: the 'holy dalyawns' between Kempe and her most important medieval counterpart, Julian of Norwich. Williams asks why this particular meeting has attracted such modern, re-creative offerings and shows how it has, at times, overshadowed related but significant religious encounters in Norwich and beyond. Williams begins by showing how female friendship and mentorship is at the heart of modern dramatic performances of Margery and Julian's encounter, from plays such as Dana Bagshaw's *Cell Talk: A Duologue between Julian of Norwich and Margery Kempe* to the Queynte Laydies' *Marge & Jules*, performed at the Margery Kempe Studies conference in 2018.[37] When it is recontextualised in the *Book* itself, however, Williams argues that the encounter shows Kempe visiting Julian as part of a strategic bid for approval from religious authority figures, rather than seeking out a female friend. The modern plays are shown to de-emphasise the diverse and international networks that Kempe builds through travel, and the resulting version of the re-created Kempe appears more embodied, more English, and more isolated than the rest of the *Book* implies. Whilst this final polemical intervention to the volume raises questions about the modern insistence on re-creating this very insular meeting between two holy women, the encounter is shown to form an important part of the 'desire for connection' and meaningful exchange which, Williams concludes, is a 'powerful motivation for and within the *Book*'.

* * * * *

> My life has fashioned me to seize
> what size, what space there is. The words
> burst from me, leaving me open
> like a raggedy split silk; threads all wrenched
> awry. Until my heart is a rip-
> tide of pleasure and remorse.[38]

This extract from Sarah Law's poem 'Margery's Harbour' encapsulates the ways in which the *Book* invites us to engage with the untidy, unruly, uncontainability of Kempe's memoir. However spontaneous the language or how ruptured it leaves her articulated body, it is a self left 'open' for her readers to enter and to encounter anew. Though she might be 'wrenched / awry', in offering up those threads of her fissured self, Kempe gives us the opportunity to weave a new text, in collaboration with her own self-fashioning and with each other.

Law sees lucidly the highly adaptive mode of Kempe's life trajectory: 'My life has fashioned me to seize / what size, what space there is.' This volume shows the myriad ways in which Kempe's life has fashioned her, but also how that fashioning can be viewed in reverse. The *Book* is also Kempe's encounter with her own experience: it is her 'space'. Scholarly encounters continue to debate what *The Book of Margery Kempe* is: its authorship, its historicity, its 'fictionality', and its genre as a life, hagiography, book of consolation, or illness narrative. But as the London sojourn reveals, Kempe was always already negotiating such contestations during her lifetime, and persistently confronted with interpretation, inquisition, and challenge to her authenticity as she was misrepresented, mythologised, and rewritten. In the process of her *Book*'s creation Margery Kempe takes control of this representation. She 'see[s] [her]self over there', in her Foucauldian mirror, reflected through the eyes and words of her interlocutors, and returns 'to reconstitute [her]self there' – in a *Book* which is her own exemplary *Myrrour* – through which she continues to be observed and deciphered; still refracted, backwards, forwards, onward.

Notes

1. All references are to *The Book of Margery Kempe*, ed. Barry Windeatt (Cambridge: D. S. Brewer, 2000, reprinted 2004, 2006), with page numbers provided in the text.
2. This is a term first mentioned in Laura Kalas, *Margery Kempe's Spiritual Medicine: Suffering, Transformation and the Life-Course* (Cambridge: D. S. Brewer, 2020), p. 207.
3. Carolyn Dinshaw, *How Soon Is Now? Medieval Texts, Amateur Readers, and the Queerness of Time* (Durham, NC, and London: Duke University Press, 2012), p. 127.
4. Dinshaw, *How Soon Is Now?*, p. 107; Michael Foucault, trans. Jay Miskowiec, 'Of other spaces', *Diacritics*, 16:1 (1986), 22–7, p. 24.
5. Foucault, 'Of other spaces', p. 24.
6. *Ibid.*, p. 26.
7. Here we employ Donna Haraway's notion of the *Chthulucene*: a term that is derived from the Greek *chthon*, meaning 'earth', and which Haraway refers to as 'kind of timeplace' for living connectedly in the world. See Donna Haraway, *Staying with the Trouble: Making Kin in the Chthulucene* (Durham, NC, and London: Duke University Press, 2016), p. 2.
8. *OED* s.v. encounter (n. and v.).
9. Our emphases. Michel Foucault, *On the Order of Things* (London and New York: Routledge, 2002; first published 1966), p. xxiii.
10. See Tara Williams, 'Recreating and reassessing Margery and Julian's encounter', Chapter 13, this volume.

11 'Margery Kempe Studies in the 21st Century' took place on 5–7 April 2018 at University College, Oxford. The details and programme can be viewed on the conference website, https://margerykempeconference.wordpress.com [accessed 24 June 2020]. See also Laura Varnam's blogpost for initial responses to the conference, '#TeamMargery: collaboration, compassion, and creativity', https://drlauravarnam.wordpress.com/2018/04/29/teammargery-collaboration-compassion-and-creativity/ [accessed 24 June 2020]. We would also like to commend the work of the #medievaltwitter hashtag as an example of online community support and networking.
12 Clarissa W. Atkinson, *Mystic and Pilgrim: The Book and the World of Margery Kempe* (Ithaca: Cornell University Press, 1985).
13 Dinshaw, *How Soon Is Now?*, p. 120.
14 Quoted in *ibid.*, p. 120. On Hope Emily Allen see John Hirsh, *Hope Emily Allen: Medieval Scholarship and Feminism* (Norman: Pilgrim Books, 1988).
15 Diane Watt, 'Critics, communities, compassionate criticism: learning from *The Book of Margery Kempe*', in Louise D'Arcens and Juanita Feros Ruys (eds), *Maistresse of My Wit: Medieval Women, Modern Scholars* (Turnhout: Brepols, 2004), pp. 191–210, p. 191. See also Marea Mitchell's chapter 'Uncanny dialogues: "the journal of mistress Joan Martyn" and *The Book of Margery Kempe*' in the same volume, pp. 246–66.
16 See Diane Watt's online bibliography on Margery Kempe criticism: 'Margery Kempe', *Oxford Bibliographies Online* www.oxfordbibliographies.com/view/document/obo-9780199846719/obo-9780199846719-0034.xml [accessed 8 July 2020]. For a critical assessment of Kempe scholarship see Marea Mitchell, *The Book of Margery Kempe: Scholarship, Community, and Criticism* (New York: Peter Lang, 2005).
17 On the conference see note 111. The Society's website, directed by Kalas and Varnam, is https://margerykempesociety.network/ [accessed 8 July 2020].
18 See, for example, Catherine Holmes and Naomi Standen (eds), *The Global Middle Ages, Past & Present*, 238 (Oxford: Oxford University Press, 2018). Jonathan Hsy began the work to 'decenter the *Book's* "Englishness" *per se* and trace how it explores translingual and intercultural modes of perception and understanding', and he suggests that Kempe's travels and encounters with non-English-speakers means that the *Book* 'pursues non-anglocentric, transnational and multidirectional trajectories'. See *Trading Tongues: Merchants, Multilingualism, and Medieval Literature* (Columbus: Ohio State University Press, 2013), pp. 132 and 134.

19 On Allen see Hirsh, *Hope Emily Allen: Medieval Scholarship and Feminism*, and John C. Hirsh, 'Hope Emily Allen, the second volume of *The Book of Margery Kempe*, and an adversary', *Medieval Feminist Forum: A Journal of Gender and Sexuality*, 31:1 (2001), 11–17. On Kempe's devotional contexts and influences see Nancy Hopenwasser, 'Margery Kempe, St. Bridget, and Margeurite d'Oingt: the visionary writer as shaman'. Alexandra Barratt, 'Margery Kempe and the king's daughter of Hungary', and Julia Bolton Holloway, 'Bride, Margery, Julian, and Alice: Bridget of Sweden's textual community in medieval England', all in Sandra McEntire (ed.), *Margery Kempe: A Book of Essays* (New York and London Garland Publishing, 1992), pp. 165–87, 189–201, and 203–22 respectively. On the influence of European religious women on Margery Kempe see also Liz Herbert McAvoy and Diane Watt (eds), 'Women's literary culture and late medieval English writing', special issue of *The Chaucer Review*, 51 (2016); Gunnel Cleve, 'Margery Kempe: A Scandinavian influence on medieval England', and Susan Dickman, 'Margery Kempe and the continental tradition of the pious woman', both in Marion Glasscoe (ed.), *The Medieval Mystical Tradition in England: Papers Read at Dartington Hall, July 1984* (Cambridge: D. S. Brewer, 1984), pp. 163–75 and pp. 150–58 respectively; and Janet Dillon, 'Holy women and their confessors or confessors and their holy women?: Margery Kempe and Continental tradition', in Rosalynn Voaden (ed.), *Prophets Abroad: The Reception of Continental Holy Women in Late-Medieval England* (Cambridge: D. S. Brewer, 1996), pp. 115–40.
20 John H. Arnold and Katherine J. Lewis (eds), *A Companion to The Book of Margery Kempe* (Cambridge: D. S. Brewer, 2004).
21 For earlier scholarship see Herbert Thurston, 'Margery the astonishing', *The Month*, 168 (1936), 446–56; David Knowles, *The English Mystical Tradition* (London: Burns and Oates, 1961), pp. 138–50; John C. Hirsh, 'Author and scribe in *The Book of Margery Kempe*', *Medium Aevum*, 44 (1975), 145–50; and Wolfgang Riehle, *The Middle English Mystics*, trans. Bernard Standring (London: Routledge and Kegan Paul, 1981).
22 See Richard Lawes, 'The madness of Margery Kempe', in Marion Glasscoe (ed.), *The Medieval Mystical Tradition in England, Ireland and Wales, Exeter Symposium VI, Papers Read at Charney Manor, July 1999* (Cambridge: D. S. Brewer, 1999), pp. 147–68; and 'Psychological disorder and the autobiographical impulse in Julian of Norwich, Margery Kempe and Thomas Hoccleve', in Denis Renevey and Christiania Whitehead (eds), *Writing Religious Women: Female Spiritual and Textual Practices in Late Medieval England* (Cardiff: University of Wales Press, 2000), pp. 217–43. See also Hope Phyllis Weissman, 'Margery Kempe in Jerusalem: *hysterica compassio* in the late middle ages', in Mary J. Carruthers

and Elizabeth D. Kirk (eds), *Acts of Interpretation: The Text in Its Contexts 700 – 1600, Essays on Medieval and Renaissance Literature* (Norman: Pilgrim Books, 1982), pp. 201–17; Maureen Fries, 'Margery Kempe', in Paul E. Szarmach (ed.), *An Introduction to The Medieval Mystics of Europe* (Albany: State University of New York Press, 1984), pp. 217–35; and Mary Hardman Farley, 'Her own creatur: religion, feminist criticism, and the functional eccentricity of Margery Kempe', *Exemplaria*, 11 (1999), 1–21.

23 Kalas, *Margery Kempe's Spiritual Medicine*. For other scholarship that reads Kempe in the light of medieval medical theory see Naoë Kukita Yoshikawa, 'Mysticism and medicine: holy communion in the vita of Marie d'Oignies and *The Book of Margery Kempe*', in Denis Renevey and Naoë Kukita Yoshikawa (eds), 'Convergence / divergence: the politics of late medieval English devotional and medical discourses', Special Issue, *Poetica*, 72 (2009), 109–22; and Diane Watt, 'Mary the physician: women, religion and medicine in the Middle Ages', in Naoë Kukita Yoshikawa (ed.), *Medicine, Religion and Gender in Medieval Culture* (Cambridge: D. S. Brewer, 2015), pp. 27–44. Other monographs about Kempe are Atkinson, *Mystic and Pilgrim*; Karma Lochrie, *Margery Kempe's Translations of the Flesh* (Philadelphia: University of Pennsylvania Press, 1991); Lynn Staley, *Margery Kempe's Dissenting Fictions* (Philadelphia: Pennsylvania State University Press, 1994); Santha Bhattacharji, *God Is an Earthquake: The Spirituality of Margery Kempe* (London: Darton, Longman, and Todd, 1997); Anthony Goodman, *Margery Kempe and Her World* (London: Longman, 2002); Naoë Kukita Yoshikawa, *Margery Kempe's Meditations: The Context of Medieval Devotional Literature, Liturgy, and Iconography* (Cardiff: University of Wales Press, 2007); Julie A. Chappell, *Perilous Passages: The Book of Margery Kempe, 1534–1934* (New York: Palgrave Macmillan, 2013); and Rebecca Krug, *Margery Kempe and the Lonely Reader* (Ithaca and London: Cornell University Press, 2017).

24 On Kempe's authority and exemplarity see Laura Varnam, 'The importance of St Margaret's church in *The Book of Margery Kempe*: a sacred place and an exemplary parishioner', *Nottingham Medieval Studies*, 61 (2017), 197–243; Liz Herbert McAvoy, *Authority and the Female Body in the Writings of Julian of Norwich and Margery Kempe* (Cambridge: D. S. Brewer, 2004); and Carolyn Dinshaw, *Getting Medieval: Sexualities and Communities, Pre- and Postmodern* (Durham, NC: Duke University Press, 1999), pp. 143–82. On saintliness see Gail McMurray Gibson, 'St Margery: *The Book of Margery Kempe*', in Julia Bolton Holloway, Joan Bechtold, and Constance S. Wright (eds), *Equally in God's Image: Women in the Middle Ages* (New York: Peter Lang, 1990), pp. 144–63;

Diane Watt, *Medieval Women's Writing: Works by and for Women, 1100–1500* (Cambridge: Polity, 2007), pp. 116–35; Katherine J. Lewis, 'Margery Kempe and saint making in later medieval England', in Arnold and Lewis (eds), *A Companion to The Book of Margery Kempe*, pp. 195–215; Rebecca Krug, 'Margery Kempe', in Larry Scanlon (ed.), *The Cambridge Companion to Medieval English Literature, 1100-1500* (Cambridge: Cambridge University Press, 2009), pp. 217–28; and Krug, 'The idea of sanctity and the uncanonised life of Margery Kempe', in Andrew Galloway (ed.), *The Cambridge Companion to Medieval English Culture* (Cambridge: Cambridge University Press, 2011), pp. 129–46.

25 Hirsh, 'Author and scribe'; Lynn Staley Johnson, 'The trope of the scribe and the question of literary authority in the works of Julian of Norwich and Margery Kempe', *Speculum*, 66 (1991), 820–38; and Nicholas Watson, 'The making of *The Book of Margery Kempe*', in Linda Olson and Kathryn Kerby-Fulton (eds), *Voices in Dialogue: Reading Women in the Middle Ages* (Notre Dame: University of Notre Dame Press, 2005), pp. 395–434, p. 397 here. For collaborative readings of authorship see Ruth Evans, '*The Book of Margery Kempe*', in Peter Brown (ed.), *A Companion to Medieval English Literature and Culture, c.1350–c.1500* (Oxford: Blackwell, 2007), pp. 507–21; and Felicity Riddy, 'Text and self in *The Book of Margery Kempe*', in Olson and Kerby-Fulton (eds), *Voices in Dialogue*, pp. 435–53.

26 Sebastian Sobecki, '"The writyng of this tretys": Margery Kempe's son and the authorship of her book', *Studies in the Age of Chaucer*, 37 (2015), 257–83; and Laura Kalas Williams, 'The *swetnesse* of confection: a recipe for spiritual health in London, British Library, Additional MS 61823, *The Book of Margery Kempe*', *Studies in the Age of Chaucer*, 40 (2018), 155–90.

27 Laura Varnam, 'The crucifix, the pietà, and the female mystic: devotional objects and performative identity in *The Book of Margery Kempe*', *Journal of Medieval Religious Cultures*, 41:2 (2015), 208–37; Krug, *Margery Kempe and the Lonely Reader*; Kathy Lavezzo, 'Sobs and sighs between women: the homoerotics of compassion in *The Book of Margery Kempe*', in Louise Fradenburg and Kathy Lavezzo (eds), *Premodern Sexualities* (New York: Routledge, 1996), pp. 175–98; Jonathan Hsy, '"Be more strange and bold": kissing lepers and female same-sex desire in *The Book of Margery Kempe*', *Early Modern Women*, 5 (2010), 189–99; and Dinshaw, *How Soon Is Now?*, pp. 105–27.

28 *The Book of Margery Kempe*, trans. Anthony Bale (Oxford: Oxford University Press, 2015), pp. xi.

29 This will be evidenced further by recent stage productions of Margery Kempe's life: John Wulp, *The Saintliness of Margery Kempe* in New York (2018) (see Laura Collins-Hughes, 'Review: In "the saintliness of Margery Kempe", a comically restless mystic', *New York Times*, 1 August 2018 www.nytimes.com/2018/08/01/theater/the-saintliness-of-margery-kempe-review.html [accessed 17 July 2020], and the community production of Elizabeth MacDonald's stage play *Skirting Heresy* in King's Lynn (2018).
30 Dinshaw, *How Soon Is Now?*, p. 107.
31 Dinshaw, *Getting Medieval*, p. 206.
32 Here we refer to the mobilisation of the 'Anglo-Saxon', and later medieval, past as a foundation myth by the right wing, and the misappropriation and misuse of the Middle Ages in modern discourse. For an important study which addresses this see Geraldine Heng, *The Invention of Race in the European Middle Ages* (Cambridge: Cambridge University Press, 2018). See also Andrew Albin, Mary C. Erler, Thomas O'Donnell, Nicholas L. Paul, and Nina Rowe (eds), *Whose Middle Ages? Teachable Moments for an Ill-Used Past* (New York: Fordham University Press, 2019).
33 *OED* s.v. 'encounter' (n.).
34 'Conversational theology' is a term from Laura M. Grimes, 'Theology as conversation: Gertrud of Helfta and her sisters as readers of Augustine' (PhD dissertation, University of Notre Dame, 2004), p. 49.
35 Dorothy Kim, 'Margery Kempe: Jerusalem Pilgrimage,' 10 parts, 21 October 2019, www.youtube.com/channel/UCx5MHU6qbvfadJrzlnq WH2Q [accessed 21 August 2020].
36 Haraway, *Staying with the Trouble*, p. 128.
37 See note 11.
38 Sarah Law, 'Margery's harbour', in *Ink's Wish: Poems for Margery Kempe* (NP: Amethyst Press, 2017; first published Gatehouse Press, 2014), p. 56.

I

Textual encounters

1

Before Margery: *The Book of Margery Kempe* and its antecedents

Diane Watt

Introduction

The Book of Margery Kempe is often one of the earliest texts by a woman encountered by modern-day students of English literature. The status of the *Book* within the literary canon has been confirmed by the publication of Anthony Bale's 2015 Oxford World's Classics translation of the text, and by its inclusion in influential teaching anthologies such as the *Norton Anthology of Literature by Women*, edited by Sandra M. Gilbert and Susan Gubar and the *Norton Anthology of English Literature*, edited by Stephen Greenblatt et al.[1] As its location alongside the works of Marie de France and Julian of Norwich in the Gilbert and Gubar anthology makes clear, the *Book* is positioned at the beginning of the English tradition of medieval women's writing, as a point of origin, whereas, as the Greenblatt volumes indicates, the vernacular English canon more broadly is seen to have a much earlier genesis, dating back to the seventh century and Caedmon's *Hymn*. As a consequence, and despite the widely acknowledged influence of Continental mystical treatises in particular on Kempe's self-fashioning as an English visionary, *The Book of Margery Kempe* is sometimes read as a text without a *pre*-text. Yet even though considerable evidence survives of English women's engagement in a vibrant literary culture in Latin and subsequently French from the early Middle Ages onwards, the relationships between *The Book of Margery Kempe* and its literary antecedents are still relatively unknown or unexplored. This chapter asks what happens if we encounter *The Book of Margery Kempe* differently, not at the start of an English tradition or canon of women's writing, but in the middle of one.

This chapter does not make claims for previously unrecognised textual encounters or for direct influences between Margery Kempe and her *Book*'s literary antecedents. Rather it seeks to unravel intriguing parallels with texts associated with some of the earliest women writers in the English tradition, namely the eighth-century letters of Boniface's early medieval women correspondents and Hugeburc of Heidenheim's *Hodoeporicon* (voyage narrative) of St Willibald (written c.778-80). Of course, as we will see, the religious climate and forms of spiritual devotion changed significantly in the period between the eighth and the early fifteenth centuries. And whereas the early women writers were professed religious, operating within formal ecclesiastical structures, Margery Kempe was a laywoman whose life was not governed by strict rules and regulations, and she consequently enjoyed greater freedom of movement and spiritual expression. Nevertheless, to reread the *Book* within the context of these earlier texts offers a completely new way of 're-encountering' it, not least because these texts anticipate Kempe's own accounts of her journeys around England and Europe and to the Holy Land, and share with her *Book* an emphasis on the connection between spirituality and the landscape. Like the *Book* they also highlight relations between women, as well as between women and men. By paying particular attention to the treatment of pilgrimage in all of these works it is possible to locate the *Book* within an already established tradition of women's experiences of devotional travel.

Women pilgrims

Some of the earliest writings by English women whose names are known (as opposed to anonymous texts that might be attributed to women) are the letters of early nuns found in the collections that have come to be known as the Boniface correspondence.[2] St Boniface (c.675–754) led a Christian mission to what is now Germany. There is a total of ten letters in the surviving correspondence written by nuns and abbesses, some written by nuns in England to Boniface and his supporters, and some by nuns who had joined Boniface on the Continent. Certain subjects recur in the letters both by and to women, most strikingly requests for and offers of spiritual support. Another frequent topic is that of pilgrimage, and perhaps what is particularly remarkable here is that, as is the case in *The Book of Margery Kempe*, it is in this context that close relationships between women become most visible.

The earliest letter by a woman in the Boniface collection is by Ælffled, possibly the second abbess of Whitby (654–714), and is addressed to Adolana or Adela, usually identified as the abbess of Pfalzel (d. 735). It serves as a letter of introduction for a nun, who is travelling to Rome on pilgrimage, and as a request for assistance for her and her companions:

> Quam ob rem iterum iterumque repetendo petimus, ut cum vestris indiculis missisque ad almissimam urbem Romam prospero cursu, suffragante saneto ac signifero apostolorum principe Petro, dirigetur; et, si quando presens Deo volente adfuerit, quicquid viva voce, qualibet occasione stimulante, pro sui iteneris necessitate suggesserit, paratum apud vos invenerit.

> [For which we ask, repeating again and again, that she be directed to the maternal city of Rome on a favorable course with your catalogues and the favor of the holy sign-bearer, Peter prince of apostles; and if she gets to you with God wishing, she find you prepared with whatever she should ask in person, stimulated by the occasion, for the needs of her journey.][3]

By the early eighth century women's monastic houses formed an international network of stopping points for pilgrim sisters travelling along the main pilgrimage routes, providing hospitality and also material and practical help, including guidance and direction.[4] The success of such a journey clearly depended on this support. Indeed, Ælffled's letter suggests that this pilgrimage, which is 'long desired' ('diu desideratum'), is one of several that the nun had embarked upon – 'often begun' ('sepe coeptum') – but been unable to fulfil, presumably because she found herself forced to turn back. In such a context, communities of women provided vital backing that enabled mobility and freedom of movement for nuns, just as informal networks of laywomen, including fellow pilgrims and keepers of lodging houses, would for Margery Kempe, some seven hundred years later. Indeed Kempe was able to undertake her final overseas pilgrimage to northern Europe, recorded in the second part of her *Book*, only because she was accompanying her Prussian daughter-in-law (admittedly against the latter's will) on her return journey home from Norfolk.

If the practice of pilgrimage brought women together, it could also separate them, as a letter written by a nun, Ecgburg, to Boniface illustrates. In this letter Ecburg writes about the loss of her brother, who has recently died, and also of her sister Wethburg who had travelled on pilgrimage to Rome and not returned:

> Et postquam mihi simul carissima soror Wethburg, quasi inflicto vulnere iteratoque dolore, subito ab oculis evanuit, cum qua adolevi, cum qua adoravi idem nutricum sinus; una mater ambobus in Domino et dereliquid; Iesum testor: ubique dolor, ubique pavor, ubique mortis imago. Malui mori, si sic Deo auspice, cui arcana non latent, placuisset, vel tarda Mors non tricaverit. Sed quid dicam nunc? Ante inprovida tandem nos non amara mors, sed amarior divisio separavit ab invicem; illam, ut reor, felicem; me vero infelicem, quasi quoddam depositum, huic saeculo servire permisit, sciens enim, quantum illam dilexi, quantum amavi, quam nunc, ut audio, Romana carcer includit.
>
> [And when at the same time my dearest sister Wethburga vanished from my sight – a new wound and a new grief; she with whom I had grown up, whom I adored and who was nursed at the same mother's breast – Christ be my witness, everywhere was grief and terror and the dread of death. Gladly would I have died if it had so pleased God from whom no secrets are hid, or if slow-coming death had not deceived me.
>
> But what shall I say now? It was not bitter death but a still more bitter and unexpected separation that divided us one from the other, leaving her, as I think, the happier and me the unhappy one to go on, like something cast aside, in my earthly service, while she, whom, as you know, I loved so tenderly, is reported to be in a Roman cell as a recluse.]⁵

This letter is particularly remarkable, because relatively few accounts of close relationships between women survive in the written records of medieval Europe. For the letter writer, Ecgburg, her sister's departure brought anxiety and suffering: 'everywhere was grief and terror and the dread of death' ('ubique dolor, ubique pavor, ubique mortis imago' – the anaphora is sadly lost in the translation). Her torment was only to increase the more when she received the news that Wethburg had decided not to return but to assume a solitary life in the Holy City. At the same time however, Ecgburg acknowledges that her own loneliness and loss are counterbalanced by the greater spiritual satisfaction that Wethburg has achieved in her new existence.

Rome was, of course, a key pilgrimage destination, and Margery Kempe would also choose to stay there for an extended period on her own return from the Holy Land. It is the desire for spiritual fulfilment that also compels other women to travel to Rome, whether in groups or pairs or on their own. Two women, Eangyth and Bugga, wrote a joint letter to Boniface asking his advice about whether or not to undertake the pilgrimage. Eangyth was abbess of a religious house, possibly in Kent, and Bugga was her daughter and a member or joint abbess of the same community.[6] Describing at length the trials and physical hardships that they have had to endure in England, including their overwhelming sense of their own inadequacy and feelings of isolation, they explain that they wish to follow in the footsteps of many of their family and friends in order to seek pardon for their sins. Eangyth and Bugga acknowledge, however, that there exists canonical disapproval of nuns' pilgrimage:[7]

> Sed quia scimus, quod multi sunt, qui hanc voluntatem vituperant et hunc amorem derogant et eorum sententiam his adstipulantibus adfirmant: quod canones synodales praecipiant, ut unusquisque in eo loco, ubi constitutus fuerit et ubi votum suum voverit, ibi maneat et ibi Deo reddat vota sua.

> [We are aware that there are many who disapprove of this ambition and disparage this form of devotion. They support their opinion by the argument that the canons of councils prescribe that everyone shall remain where he has been placed; and where he has taken his vows, there he shall fulfil them before God.][8]

Despite such opposition, both Eangyth and Bugga feel compelled to undertake this journey for their spiritual satisfaction, provided that they can obtain Boniface's approval. For them to remain in England means experiencing an exile that is worse than even the most hazardous sea voyage.

Boniface's response to this request has not survived, and we do not know whether or not the two women did travel to Rome on this occasion, but there is a much later letter from Boniface to Bugga on the topic of pilgrimage. It is apparent that Bugga has once again petitioned Boniface about undertaking the journey. Boniface's response to this request is cautious:

> Notum sit tibi, soror carissima, de illo consilio, quo me indignum per litteras interrogasti, quod ego tibi iter peregrinum nec interdicere per me nec audenter suadere presumo. Sed, quod visum est, dicam.
>
> [I desire you to know, dearest sister, that in the matter about which you wrote asking advice of me, unworthy though I am, I dare neither forbid your pilgrimage on my own responsibility nor rashly persuade you to it. I will only say how the matter appears to me.][9]

Boniface advises Bugga to act in the interests of her soul's health, acknowledging that staying in Rome might provide her necessary freedom from the demands of the world; just as it would for Margery Kempe, when she decided to reside there in voluntary poverty. Boniface cites the example of Ecgburg's sister Wethburg, who was able to find there spiritual peace. Indeed, Boniface informs Bugga that he has on this matter consulted Wethburg, who advises waiting until the threat of Saracen invasion is past but promises to extend an invitation when it is safe to do so. Boniface recommends that Bugga should go ahead and prepare for the journey while she waits to hear from her. It is again clear from this that women pilgrims played a vital role in giving practical as well as spiritual advice on travel, no doubt tailored specifically to the needs of their sex.[10]

Whilst Boniface's letter, although circumspect, is overall encouraging, we do know from elsewhere in the collection that both Boniface and his supporter and successor Lul did come to harbour serious reservations about women travelling abroad, fearing, for example, they might fall into prostitution and vice. In fact Lul excommunicated one abbess, Swithan, for allowing two nuns from her convent in Germany to go abroad 'contra statuta canonum et sanctae regulae disciplinam, sine licentia et consilio meo' [against the statutes of the canons and the discipline of the holy rule, without permission or my advice].[11] The nuns were also excommunicated. Boniface himself recommended to Cuthbert of Canterbury that he consider banning 'mulieribus et velatis feminis' [matrons and veiled women] travelling to Rome because so many have either died or been disgraced.[12] Such disapproval continued in the centuries that followed, and, again, we might be reminded here of the example of Margery

Kempe who set off on her pilgrimage to northern Europe without the permission of her confessor, although, unlike Swithan, Kempe was eventually forgiven.

The circumstances of the pilgrimages of the early English nuns in the Boniface correspondence were of course very different to those of Margery Kempe.[13] Whereas Boniface was leading a missionary campaign to convert the people of Germania, Kempe's remarkable if orthodox spirituality was inevitably shaped by later medieval forms of religious expression and framed on the one hand by the emergence of Lollard beliefs in fifteenth-century England, which typically included objection to the practice of pilgrimage, and on the other by the promotion of the cult of St Bridget of Sweden by the Lancastrians. Rome, in particular, was a key space for experiencing spiritual encounters for all of these women. It is apparent from the letters in the Boniface collection that early medieval women such as Wethburg, Eangyth and Bugga travelled to the Holy City for a variety of reasons, including to escape loneliness, poverty and oppression, to free themselves from the demands of others and the responsibilities of their roles within their communities, as acts of penance, or, more positively, to seek seclusion and quietude. Whilst Margery Kempe may have shared some of these desires, according to her own account in her *Book* she was specifically motivated by 'a desyr to se tho placys wher he was born and wher he sufferyd hys Passyon and wher he deyd, wyth other holy placys wher he was in hys lyve and also aftyr hys Resurrexyon' (p. 101).[14] Margery Kempe's spirituality is of course characterised by visions and conversations with the divine that are peculiarly late medieval, heavily inflected as they are by an affectivity that emerged in the eleventh and twelfth centuries, and this inevitably impacted on her emotional responses to her travels.[15] As will be discussed in the next section, this is illustrated most vividly by her revelations of the Nativity and the Crucifixion that she experienced in her visit to the Holy Land, and which lie at the spiritual centre of her *Book*. Her account of her sojourn in Rome, where she remained for six months in 1414 to 1415, is in contrast marked by two principal events. The first is her mystical marriage to God, which took place in the Santi Apostoli [The Church of the Twelve Apostles] in the presence of divine rather than human witnesses (Chapter 35), in which she mirrors the experience of St Catherine of Siena. The second is her visit to the Casa di Santa Brigida [House of St Bridget], where St Bridget had stayed for nineteen years, and where Kempe spoke at some length with her former maidservant (pp. 203–4). St Bridget's close association with Rome was evidently a major draw for Kempe, and, while she remained in the city, she decided to emulate the Swedish saint and embrace poverty.

The practicalities of travel for the early medieval women pilgrims in Boniface's circle were also rather different from those faced by Margery Kempe. In travelling to sites in England and beyond, including Jerusalem, Rome, and Santiago, Kempe was following well-established routes frequented by both religious and lay people, and she travelled as far as possible in larger mixed-sex groups or with a male guide, staying in hostels or seeking lodgings whenever she could. Indeed, when she set out to the Holy Land, she was initially also accompanied by a female servant who, however, abandoned her en route. Nevertheless, certain parallels do emerge. The concerns of Boniface and Lul for the risks faced by women pilgrims, which are framed in misogynist terms of concerns about prostitution and sexual immorality, are echoed in *The Book of Margery Kempe* early on in the account of Kempe's travels across Europe in 1413, when Kempe's fellow pilgrims turned against her, encouraging her maidservant to desert her: 'thei seyden thei woldyn han awey hyr mayden fro hir, that sche schuld no strumpet be in hyr cumpany' (p. 152). Here, in a reversal of the expected trope in which the lower orders are seen as a potential source of moral corruption, the concern is that the mistress, Kempe, will lead her servant into prostitution.[16] When, later in life, she set off across northern Europe without having first secured the permission of her confessor, Kempe found her journey much more psychologically and physically challenging, and, on being once again abandoned by her companions, she acknowledged her 'drede for hir chastite ... [and] of defilyng' (p. 406), that is, her vulnerability to assault and rape. More positively, like the early medieval women pilgrims, Kempe found that other women (as well as men) sometimes gave her welcome support and assistance, such as providing or finding her lodgings, offering her hospitality, or allowing her to join their company. The most notable of these women is of course 'Margaret Florentyne' (pp. 181 and 200–1), whose identity and friendship with Kempe in Rome is discussed in Chapter 9 by Anthony Bale and Daniela

Giosuè. For both early and late medieval women pilgrims, successful travel depended heavily on being able to draw upon networks specifically of women who could offer companionship, assistance, and advice.

Travellers' tales

If the letters of Ælfled, Ecgburg, Eangyth, and Bugga, alongside those of Boniface and Lul, provide important insights into women's experiences of pilgrimage in the early Middle Ages, then in the hagiographical writing of another English women missionary in Germany, Hugeburc of Heidenheim (fl. 760–80), we find a remarkable full-length pilgrimage narrative. Hugeburc's *Hodoeporicon*, or voyage narrative, is both a life of her kinsman St Willibald and a detailed description of the journey across Europe and to the Holy Land that he undertook in the 730s. According to Hugeburc herself, in 778 Willibald recounted his travels to her and her fellow nuns and she based her text on this account:

> Transacto atque terminato prolixa iteneris meatu Willibaldi, quam ille sagax in 7 annorum indutia lustrando adiebat, illa nunc reperta et ex ritu rimata explanare intimareque conavimus, et non ab alio reperta nisi ab ipso audita et ex illius ore dictata perscripsimus in monasterio Heidanheim, testibus mihi diaconis eius et aliis nonnullis iunioris eius. Ideo dico hoc, ut nullus iterum dicat frivolum fuisse.[17]

> [The long course of Willibald's travels and sightseeing on which he had spent seven long years was now over and gone. We have tried to set down and make known all the facts which have been ascertained and thoroughly investigated. These facts were not learned from anyone else but heard from Willibald himself; and having received them from his own lips, we have taken them down and written them in the Monastery of Heidenheim, as his deacons and other subordinates can testify. I say this so that no one may afterwards say that it was an idle tale.][18]

Hugeburc is careful to establish the truth value of her narrative by emphasising that it is based on Willibald's own words (possibly even taken down from dictation) and that it has been verified as far as possible, and she mentions that the circumstances of its composition can be confirmed by the testimony of male authorities. Hugeburc also wrote a life of Willibald's brother Wynnebald, and Pauline Head suggests that she may have been 'the only woman of her time to write biographies of male saints'.[19] It seems then that she was very aware of the unique nature of the role she was assuming as a female author and keen to deflect criticism, and in this respect she might be contrasted with Margery Kempe, who relied on male scribes not only to write her *Book* for her, based on her own spoken recollections, but also to lend their authority to the text.

In fact it seems Hugeburc found herself torn between wishing to assert her authorship of the text and to apologise for it. Munich, Bayerische Staatsbibliothek, Codex latinus monacensis (Clm) 1086, is the earliest surviving manuscript of Hugeburc's work, and may have been produced at Heidenheim, possibly even in Hugeburc's own lifetime.[20] It is therefore the most authoritative text. On fol. 71v it includes a cryptogram, which, when unencrypted, reads: 'Ego una Saxonica nomine Hugeburc ordinando hec scribebam' [I, a Saxon nun named Hugeburc, wrote this].[21] Hugeburc thus simultaneously hides and preserves her own identity and authorial role. In the text of the *Hodoeporicon* itself Hugeburc also provides a further clue to her own identity, describing herself as an 'indigna Saxonica' [unworthy Saxon woman][22] and also claiming her kinship with Willibald himself.[23] In this context her apology for being 'feminea fragilique sexus inbecillitate corruptibilia, nulla prerogativa sapientiae suffultus aut magnarum virium industria elata' [corruptible by the feminine frailty of the fragile sex, neither supported by the prerogative of wisdom nor elevated by the industry of great strength][24] seems little more than a humility topos, as she is clearly profoundly aware of her status (a member of a family of saints) and proud of her literary achievement.

Some critics have assumed that the *Hodoeporicon* was basically a verbatim account, closely based on the account Willibald gave when visiting Heidenheim, and have even suggested that it is effectively his work, with Hugeburc assuming a passive and purely scribal role.[25] I have argued elsewhere that this is not the case, and have analysed the ways in which Hugeburc shaped Willibald's story, for example by structuring the account in terms of the Ages of Man, and by drawing both explicit and implicit parallels with earlier saints and their lives, most notably Sulpicius Severus's fourth-century *Life of St Martin*.[26] Yet despite framing Willibald's life in terms of its exemplary models, her descriptions of the places to which he travelled are often extremely precise and informative, as revealed in the following description of the Church of the Holy Sepulchre in Jerusalem:

> Et inde venit ad Hierusalem, in illum locum, ubi inventa fuerat sancta crux Domini; ibi est nunc aecclesia in illo loco que dicitur Calvarie locus; et haec fuit prius extra Hierusalem; sed Helena, quando invenit crucem, collocavit illam locum intus intra Hierusalem. Et ibi stant nunc tres cruces ligneas foris in orientale plaga aecclesie secus pariete ad memoriam sanctae cruces dominicae et aliorum qui cum eo crucifixi errant; illa non sunt nunc intus in aecclesia, sed foris stant sub tecto extra aecclesia.[27]

> [Then they came to Jerusalem, to the very spot where the holy cross of our Lord was found. On the site of the place called Calvary now stands a church. Formerly this was outside Jerusalem, but when Helena discovered the cross she placed the spot within the walls of Jerusalem. There now stand three crosses outside the church near the wall of the eastern end, as a memorial to the cross of our Lord and those who were crucified with Him. At present they are not inside the church, but outside beneath a pent roof.].[28]

This short passage, with its geographical and topographical precision, captures what is so distinctive about Hugeburc's account of Willibald's pilgrimage, and, as we will see, what sets it apart for Margery Kempe's later and more affective description of the same locale. Jerusalem is, of course, the centre of the Christian world, and Calvary the centre of the Christian Jerusalem, and it has enormous spiritual significance, but Hugeburc also pays careful attention to the history of the site, detailing how the church was relocated after St Helena's discovery of the True Cross in about 326, and she notes that the crosses that are currently positioned on the exterior of the building are of course mere replicas. Hugeburc, inevitably, shapes the narrative that she recounts, and this description reveals something of her intellectual curiosity. It is possible to imagine from this how she and her fellow nuns must have interrogated Willibald about his journey and the places he visited, places already so familiar to them from their studies of Scripture and holy books.

Much of Hugeburc's travel narrative is naturalistic, perhaps surprisingly so from a modern perspective. For example, she provides a lively account of Willibald's initial sea voyage to the Continent, describing the confusion of sounds of squalls, clamour, and creaking.[29] Later, when she recounts the saint's visit to the Hell of Theodric on the island of Vulcano, she describes it as an amazing phenomenon:

> Statimque Willibaldus curiosius et volens videre, quailis esset intus ille infernus, et volebat ascendere in montis cacumen, ubi infernus subtus erat, et non poterat, qui faville de tetro tartaro usque ad marginem ascendentes glomerati illic iacebant et ad instar nivis, quando de caelo nivans canditas nivalesque cadentes catervas de aereis etherum arcibus arcis coacervareque solet, ita faville coacervati in apice montis iacebant, us ascensum Willibaldo prohibebant. Sed tamen tetrum atque terribilem horrendumque eructuantem de puteo flammam erumpere videbat, ad instar tonitrui tonantis sic flammam magnum et fumi vaporem valde supblime in alto ascendentem terribiliter intuebat.[30]

> [Willibald, who was inquisitive and eager to see without delay what this Hell was like inside, wanted to climb to the top of the mountain underneath which the crater lay: but he was unable to do so because the ashes of black tartar, which had risen to the edge of the crater, lay there in heaps: and like the snow which, when it drops from heaven with its falling masses of flakes, heaps them up into mounds, the ashes lay piled in heaps on the top of the mountain and prevented Willibald from going any further. All the same, he saw the black and terrible and fearful flame belching forth from the crater with a noise like rolling thunder: he gazed with awe on the enormous flames, and the mountainous clouds of smoke rising from below into the sky.][31]

This is very different from the depictions of the otherworld found in other early medieval writing, such as the famous vision of the Monk of Much Wenlock, described by St Boniface in an early eighth-century letter to the abbess Eadburg:

> Inter ea referebat, se, quasi in inferioribus, in hoc mundo vidisse igneos puteos horrendam eructantes flammam plurimos; et, erumpente tetra terribilis flamma ignis, volitasse et miserorum hominum spiritus in similitudine nigrarum avium per flammam plorantes et ululantes et verbis et voce humana stridentes et lugentes propria merita et praesens supplicium; consedisse paululum herentes in marginibus puteorum; et iterum heiulantes cecidisse in puteos. Et unus ex angelis dixit: 'Parvissima haec requies indicat, quia omnipotens Deus in die

futuri iudicii his animabus refrigerium supplicii et requiem perpetuam praestiturus est.'

Sub illis autem puteis, adhuc in inferioribus et in imo profundo, quasi in inferno inferiori, audivit horrendum et tremendum et dictu difficilem gemitum et fletum lugentium animarum. Et dixit ei angelus: 'Murmur et fletus, quem in inferioribus audis, illarum est animarum, ad quas numquam pia miseratio Domini perveniet; sed aeterna illas flamma sine fine cruciabit.'

[He reported further that he saw, as it were in the bowels of the earth, many fiery pits vomiting forth terrible flames and, as the foul flame arose, the souls of wretched men in the likeness of black birds sat upon the margin of the pits clinging there for a while wailing and howling and shrieking with human cries, mourning their past deeds and their present suffering; then they fell screaming back into the pits. And one of the angels said: 'This brief respite shows that Almighty God will give to these souls in the judgment day relief from their punishment and rest eternal.' But beneath these pits in the lowest depths, as it were in a lower hell, he heard a horrible, tremendous, and unspeakable groaning and weeping of souls in distress. And the angel said to him: 'The murmuring and crying which you hear down there comes from those souls to which the loving kindness of the Lord shall never come, but an undying flame shall torture them forever.'][32]

In contrast, although the sight that Willibald beholds is certainly awe-inspiring, even frightening, there is no sense that it is a site of suffering for the sinful on the Day of Judgement and the afterlife. Such horrific visions of purgatory and hell continued in throughout the Middle Ages, and in the early fifteenth century an anonymous woman recluse of Winchester described the purgatorial torments of a nun called Margaret in a series of letters written to her spiritual directors and supporters.[33] Kempe herself seems to have received similar revelations, but she holds back from describing them in any detail in her *Book*, possibly because her revelations concerning the saved and the damned troubled her so much that she feared she was suffering diabolic delusions (pp. 141 and 281).

Hugeburc's pilgrimage narrative resonates in complex ways with *The Book of Margery Kempe*. Both texts have raised questions about authorship – should they be ascribed to the subjects (Willibald, Kempe herself) or to the scribe or scribes taking down dictation, or should they be more properly seen as the product of collaboration?

There are some parallels with the processes of composition: in both cases a scribe who also happens to be a member of the subject's own family or extended kin group is entrusted with the responsibility of testifying to their holiness (Hugeburc herself, and Kempe's son, who, arguably, served as Kempe's first scribe).[34] Of course, to some extent these are artificial parallels, and it should not be forgotten that Hugeburc was also a professed religious and a member of the monastery founded by Willibald's own brother and subsequently governed by his sister, whilst Kempe's son was a layman, a merchant based in Prussia, who would not have had access to the sort of intellectual and cultural resources available at Heidenheim.

More significantly, perhaps, as Aidan Conti observes of Hugeburc, 'as a female hagiographer working on the continent and writing in Latin, her hagiographies fall outside the conventional bounds of English literature, which frequently centres on the English and the island (and particularly England)'.[35] In *The Book of Margery Kempe*, in contrast, Kempe's travels to Rome, Jerusalem, Santiago, and across northern Europe are still framed in terms of journeys to and from England, and embedded within the story of a life very much lived at home rather than abroad.[36] Furthermore Kempe's pilgrimage accounts, although central to the *Book*, are only part of a more diffuse and loosely structured narrative and are profoundly influenced by the later medieval phenomenon of affective piety and overlaid by her visions and meditations. This is vividly illustrated in Kempe's account of her first visit to the Church of the Holy Sepulchre in Jerusalem, which is markedly different from Hugeburc's very topographically specific description. Describing a procession that Kempe attended on this occasion, the *Book* quickly segues into Kempe's violent physical and intense emotional responses to the momentous Biblical event that she sees in her mind's eye.

> [T]he frerys lyftyd up a cros and led the pylgrimys abowte fro [on] place to another wher owyr Lord had sufferyd hys [peynys] and hys passyons, every man and woman beryng a wax candel in her hand … [W]han thei cam up on to the Mownt of Calvarye, sche fel down that sche mygth not stondyn ne knelyn but walwyd and wrestyd wyth hir body, spredyng hir armys abrode, and cryed wyth a lowde voys as thow hir hert schulde a brostyn asundyr, for in the cite of hir sowle sche saw veryly and freschly how owyr Lord was crucifyed. (pp. 162–3)

With its main focus on its subject's inner life and the external manifestations thereof, and in complete contrast to Hugeburc's relation of Willibald's travels, *The Book of Margery Kempe* provides relatively little information about holy artefacts, architectural structures, and geographical locations, but focuses instead on her very physical response to her vision of the crucifixion.

This is not to say however that the *Book* is devoid of the sort of anecdotes that we might expect to find in a pilgrimage narrative. On one occasion when she was making her way to Rome, Kempe is reported to have measured out the dimensions of Christ's tomb for the benefit of visitors to a lodging house in which she was staying (p. 179).[37] Whilst Kempe's accounts include some tantalising details about her journeys, they are also characterised by significant gaps. It *is* possible to trace Kempe's routes across Europe to Venice, from whence she set sail to Jerusalem, and from medieval Danzig in Prussia back to Calais and Dover, but not in the same sort of detail that we can reconstruct Willibald's travels so many centuries earlier. This may perhaps reflect the different purpose of the *Book*, and the different sort of audience that Kempe envisaged for it. Hugeburc expressly wrote to honour her saintly kinsman Willibald, to ensure he would not be forgotten and to encourage his veneration, but it can be no accident that her text effectively maps his journeys, thus enabling his followers to retrace his steps, in a literal sense. Margery Kempe in contrast is concerned with convincing others, and especially both churchmen and laypeople within her own community, of the authenticity of her visionary experiences and of her own blessed state. Indeed, in Chapter 30, she recounts that as she unwillingly left Jerusalem, God reassured her with the words: 'Dowtyr, as oftyntymes as thu seyst or thynkyst, "Worshepyd be alle tho holy placys in Jerusalem that Crist suffyrde bittyr peyn and passyon in", thu schalt have the same parcon as yyf thu wer ther wyth thi bodily presens, bothyn to thiself and to alle tho that thu wylt yevyn it to' (p. 174). It is thus clear that those who choose to support Kempe do not need to go on pilgrimage themselves to share in the spiritual benefits.

Yet whilst *The Book of Margery Kempe* doesn't provide the reader with the sort of detailed textual map found in Hugeburc's narrative, with its focus on her trials and tribulations, Kempe's *Book* tells us much more about her interpersonal relations, such as her conflicts with her fellow pilgrims or the kindness shown by her Muslim guides (p. 174). In contrast, although we are told that he was originally accompanied by his father and his brother, Hugeburc reveals far less about Willibald's travelling companions and those he meets en route. A marked exception is the occasion when Willibald is arrested and imprisoned in Syria and brought before a Muslim leader who is referred to by Willibald as *Myrmumni*, possibly referring to the Umayyad Caliph Yazid bin Abd al-Malik (Yazid II).[38] *The Book of Margery Kempe* also describes its subject being stopped and questioned, most notably by her detractor John Arneby, the mayor of Leicester, although of course in Kempe's case it is during her travels around England that these events occur, and she is suspected of being a Lollard heretic rather than a spy or a smuggler. In both cases the inclusion of these episodes might be seen as characteristic of the genre of hagiography, where the pilgrim saint or would-be saint is put on trial or interrogated by their oppressors. Yet, despite these similarities, and again in contrast to Hugeburc's account, in *The Book of Margery Kempe*, in which visionary experiences play a central role, the pilgrimage narrative is clearly subordinated to the larger narrative about its protagonist's spiritual life and tribulations.

Conclusion

What can be learnt, then, from encountering *The Book of Margery Kempe* differently, from looking back before Margery? Reading *The Book of Margery Kempe* alongside epistolary and hagiographic writing by early medieval English nuns reveals striking parallels in relation to the treatment of pilgrimage and travel. Women across the centuries clearly sought the advice and help of other women, who would understand the particular challenges faced by female pilgrims. They also encountered disapproval and opposition based on their sex and misogynistic assumptions about their vulnerability and susceptibility to sin. Women were motivated to travel on pilgrimage by a desire to free themselves from the demands of their everyday lives and a yearning for spiritual fulfilment, as an act of penance, or, as *The Book of Margery Kempe* reveals, to fulfil an ambition to visit the sites associated with Christ's time on earth. A comparison of the *Book* with Hugeburc's *Hodoeporicon* reveals quite different emphases on itineraries, places and responses, but both texts are clearly concerned with grounding religious devotion within the landscapes of Europe and the Holy Land. No doubt, if the *Book* were read in relation to a different set of texts, for example twelfth- and thirteenth-century French hagiographies written by nuns in England such as Clemence of Barking's *La vie de sainte Catherine d'Alexandrie*, other points of comparison and contrast would emerge.[39] There is much to be gained in taking a long view of the histories of women's writing and women's literary culture and from dismantling the disciplinary boundaries not only between the early and late Middle Ages but also between Latin and vernacular (French and English) texts. Without diminishing its importance in the least, it is crucial that we acknowledge that *The Book of Margery Kempe* is not situated at the beginning of English women's writing, but within a much longer, if often discontinuous, tradition.

Notes

1 *The Book of Margery Kempe*, trans. Anthony Bale (Oxford: Oxford University Press, 2015); *The Norton Anthology of Literature by Women: The Traditions in English*, ed. Sandra M. Gilbert and Susan Gubar, 3rd edition (New York: W. W. Norton, 2007), volume 1; the *Norton Anthology of English Literature*, volume A, ed. Stephen Greenblatt et al., 9th edition (New York: W. W. Norton, 2012).
2 Most of the letters to and from women in the Boniface Correspondence are published in Latin with English translations in *Epistolae: Medieval Women's Latin Letters*, ed. Joan Ferrante, available online https://epistolae.ccnmtl.columbia.edu/letter/354.html [accessed 30 April 2019]. All quotations of the Latin and the modern English translation are from this website.
3 'A letter from Elfled, abbess of Whitby', in *Epistolae*, available online https://epistolae.ccnmtl.columbia.edu/letter/333.html [accessed 30 April 2019].
4 On early medieval women and European pilgrimage see Diana Webb, *Pilgrimage in Medieval England* (London: Hambledon Continuum, 2000), pp. 4–5.
5 'A letter from Egburg/Egburga/Ecburg (716–20)', in *Epistolae*, available online https://epistolae.ccnmtl.columbia.edu/letter/359.html [accessed 30 April 2019].

6 Barbara Yorke, 'The Bonifacian mission and female religious in Wessex', *Early Medieval Europe*, 7 (1998), 145–72, p. 149.
7 See Stephanie Hollis, *Anglo-Saxon Women and the Church: Sharing a Common Fate* (Woodbridge: Boydell Press, 1992), pp. 149–50.
8 'A letter from Eangyth, abbess (719–22)', in *Epistolae*, available online https://epistolae.ccnmtl.columbia.edu/letter/358.html [accessed 30 April 2019].
9 'A letter from Boniface (before 738)', in *Epistolae*, available online https://epistolae.ccnmtl.columbia.edu/letter/342.html [accessed 30 April 2019].
10 A later letter from Bugga's kinsman, Æthelberht II, king of Kent, indicates that Bugga did make the journey to Rome where she spent time in prayer and discussion with Boniface: *The English Correspondence of Saint Boniface*, trans. Edward Kylie (London: Chatto and Windus, 1911), available online at http://elfinspell.com/MedievalMatter/BonifaceLetters/Letters30-38.html#Aethelbert [accessed 30 April 2019].
11 'A letter from Lul (755-86)', in *Epistolae*, available online https://epistolae.ccnmtl.columbia.edu/letter/382.html [accessed 30 April 2019]; Suzanne Fonay Wemple, *Women in Frankish Society, Marriage and the Cloister 500–900* (Philadelphia: University of Pennsylvania, 1981), p. 166.
12 Boniface, *Die Briefe des heiligen Bonifatius und Lullus*, ed. Michael Tangl, MGH Epistolae Selectae 1 (Berlin: Weidmann, 1916), ep. 78, available online at https://www.dmgh.de/de/fs1/object/display/bsb00000534_00361.html?sortIndex=040%3A010%3A0003%3A010%3A00%3A00 [accessed 30 April 2019]; *English Correspondence*, trans. Kylie, available online at http://elfinspell.com/Boniface6.html [accessed 30 April 2019].
13 See, for example, Susan Signe Morrison, *Women Pilgrims in Late Medieval England: Private Piety as Public Performance* (London, Routledge, 2000), pp. 128–41; and Diane Watt, 'Faith in the landscape: overseas pilgrimages in *The Book of Margery Kempe*', in Clare A. Lees and Gillian R. Overing (eds), *A Place to Believe In: Locating Medieval Landscapes* (University Park: Penn State University Press, 2006), pp. 170–87.
14 All in-text references are to *The Book of Margery Kempe*, ed. Barry Windeatt (Cambridge: D. S. Brewer, 2006).
15 See Sarah McNamer, *Affective Meditation and the Invention of Compassion* (Philadelphia: Pennsylvania University Press, 2010).
16 Sharon Farmer, '"It is not good that [wo]man should be alone": elite responses to singlewomen in high medieval Paris', in Judith M. Bennett

and Amy M. Froide (eds), *Singlewomen in the European Past, 1250–1800* (Philadelphia: University of Pennsylvania Press, 1999), pp. 90–1.

17 Hugeburc, 'Vita Willibaldi Episcopi Eichstetensis', in *Vitae Willibaldi et Wynnebaldi Auctore Sanctimoniali Heidenheimensi*, ed. Oswald Holder-Egger, MGH Scriptores 15.1 (Hanover: Hahn, 1887), p. 105, available online: www.dmgh.de/de/fs1/object/display/bsb00000890_00114.html?sortIndex=010%3A050%3A0015%3A010%3A01%3A00andsort=scoreandorder=descandcontext=Vitae+Willibaldi+et+Wynnebaldianddivision Title_str=andhl=falseandfulltext=Vitae+Willibaldi+et+Wynnebaldi+ [accessed 12 May 2019]. All in-text references are to this edition.

18 'The *Hodoeporicon* of St. Willibald by Huneberc of Heidenheim', in *The Anglo-Saxon Missionaries in Germany*, trans. and ed. C. H. Talbot (London: Sheed and Ward, 1954), p. 175. All in-text translations are from this edition unless otherwise stated.

19 Pauline Head, 'Who is the nun from Heidenheim? A study of Hugeburc's *Vita Willibaldi*', *Medium Aevum*, 71 (2002), 29–46, p. 32.

20 Andreas Bauch in his *Quellen zur Geschichte der Diözese Eichstätt, Band 1, Biographien der Gründungszeit* (Eichstätt: Johann Michael Sailer, 1962), p. 20.

21 Head, 'Who is the Nun?', p. 29; the translation is my own. For the identification of Hugeburc see Bernhard Bischoff, 'Wer ist die nonne von Heidenheim?', *Studien und Mitteilungen zur Geschichte des Benediktinerordens und seiner Zweige*, 49 (1931), 387–8. See also Joachim von zur Gathen, *CryptoSchool* (Berlin: Springer-Verlag, 2015), pp. 78–9.

22 'Vita Willibaldi', p. 86; translation my own.

23 *Hodoeporicon*, trans. Talbot, p. 153.

24 'Vita Willibaldi', p. 86; translation my own.

25 See, for example, Rodney Aist, 'Images of Jerusalem: the religious imagination of Willibald of Eichstätt', in Hans Sauer, Joanna Story and Gaby Waxenberger (eds), *Anglo-Saxon England and the Continent* (Tempe: ACMRS, 2011), pp. 179–98; Katharine Scarfe Beckett, *Anglo-Saxon Perceptions of the Islamic World* (Cambridge: Cambridge University Press, 2003), p. 46.

26 See Diane Watt, *Women, Writing and Religion in England and Beyond, 650–1100* (London: Bloomsbury, 2019), pp. 92–103.

27 'Vita Willibaldi', p. 97.

28 *Hodoeporicon*, trans. Talbot, p. 165.

29 'Vita Willibaldi', p. 91; *Hodoeporicon*, trans. Talbot, p. 157. On sea-travel in *The Book of Margery Kempe* see Laura Kalas, Chapter 11 below.

30 'Vita Willibaldi', pp. 101–2.
31 *Hodoeporicon*, trans. Talbot, pp. 171–2.
32 'A letter from Boniface (716/717)', in *Epistolae*, available online https://epistolae.ctl.columbia.edu/letter/353.html [accessed 30 April 2019].
33 *A Revelation of Purgatory*, ed. and trans. Liz Herbert McAvoy (Cambridge: D. S. Brewer, 2017).
34 See the discussion in Diane Watt, *Medieval Women's Writing: Works by and for Women in England, 1100–1500* (Cambridge: Polity, 2007), pp. 118–24; and Sebastian Sobecki, '"The writyng of this tretys": Margery Kempe's son and the authorship of her book', *Studies in the Age of Chaucer*, 37 (2015), 257-83. The identification of this scribe with Kempe's son has been questioned on the basis that Kempe's son was in England for only a month and in a state of great sickness at that time, including by Liz Herbert McAvoy and Naoë Kukita Yoshikawa in Chapter 2 below, who argue that Kempe's daughter-in-law rather than her son might have played a greater role in the first scribal attempt. McAvoy and Yoshikawa draw on an unpublished conference paper by Santha Bhattacharji.
35 Aidan Conti, 'The literate memory of Hugeburc of Heidenheim', in Robin Norris, Rebecca Stephenson, and Renée Trilling (eds), *Feminist Approaches to Anglo-Saxon Studies* (Tempe: Arizona Center for Medieval Studies, forthcoming).
36 Laura Varnam argues for the importance of Lynn and England as Margery Kempe's 'home' and the place to where she returns, in her article, 'The importance of St Margaret's church in *The Book of Margery Kempe*: a sacred place and an exemplary parishioner', *Nottingham Medieval Studies*, 61 (2017), 197–243, pp. 213–14.
37 See Shayne Aaron Legassie, *The Medieval Invention of Travel* (Chicago: University of Chicago Press, 2019), p. 113.
38 'Vita Willibaldi', p. 95; cf. *Hodoeporicon*, trans. Talbot, p. 163.
39 The text is translated in *Virgin Lives and Holy Deaths: Two Exemplary Biographies for Anglo-Norman Women*, trans. Jocelyn Wogan-Browne and Glyn S. Burgess (London: Everyman, 1996).

2

The intertextual dialogue and conversational theology of Mechthild of Hackeborn and Margery Kempe

Liz Herbert McAvoy and Naoë Kukita Yoshikawa

In Chapter 58 of *The Book of Margery Kempe*, Margery is recorded as offering a characteristic rebuke to Christ because of his failure to comply with her request for a suitable cleric out of 'as many clerkys as thu hast in this world' to read to her from the Scriptures and other devotional works.[1] Depicting herself as hungering in spirit for such readings, she calls upon Christ's pity for her devotional starvation, causing him to capitulate quickly and promise her: 'Ther schal come on fro fer that schal fulfillyn thi desyr' (p. 279). As if on cue, a new priest duly appears in Bishop's Lynn some time in 1413, one wholly unfamiliar with Margery, but who is arrested by her remarkable pious behaviour and affective responses as she goes about the streets. As a result he seeks out an introduction and, within days, Margery is invited to this priest's rented accommodation, which he shares with his mother. Soon, the three of them begin reading and discussing Scripture and devotional works together, and Margery punctuates these gatherings with copious tears of compassion, which clearly impress the priest's mother, if not initially the priest himself. Indeed it is this mother who first vouches for Margery's spiritual authority, counselling her son to pursue the acquaintance further (p. 279). Hence Margery begins a six-year period of deeply satisfying religious exchange with the priest – and possibly his mother too – teaching him – or them – much about 'good scriptur and many a good doctor, whech he wolde not a lokyd at that tyme, had sche ne be' (pp. 279–80). In turn the priest provides Margery with 'many a good boke of hy contemplacyon' – some of which are even named in the text: 'the Bybyl wyth doctowrys therupon, Seynt Brydys boke,

Hyltons boke, Boneventur, *Stimulus Amoris, Incendium Amoris,* and *swech other*' (p. 280, our emphasis).

Here we find listed a pretty much predictable array of texts to be read for private devotional purposes *in camera* amongst like-minded people.[2] But what is of particular concern to this present chapter is the 'swech other' texts, of which there must have been a considerable number, given the seven-year period when this priest and Margery read together between 1413 and 1421. Also significant is the fact that these reading encounters are presented as both communal and reciprocal – they are as beneficial to the priest as to Margery, increasing his own 'cunnyng and of hys meryte'. Explicitly, too, they provide him with the spiritual added-value that allows him ultimately to receive a benefice of his own: he 'lykyd hym ful wel that he had redde so meche beforn' (p. 280). The inference here is that Margery and the priest are, in fact, discovering new works to read together, each informing and developing the other's devotional knowledge-base. Between them, we can also infer, they devour many of the devotional 'best-sellers' of the day. Indeed, it cannot be insignificant that, just two chapters later, Margery Kempe's scribe recounts how his faith in Margery was restored and reinforced by his own encounters with Continental women's visionary writing: specifically *The Life of Marie d'Oignies* (d. 1213) and the visions attributed to Elizabeth of Hungary (d. 1231), which recorded similar affective practices (pp. 291–7).[3] No doubt these texts also constituted some of the 'swech other' works read collaboratively by Margery and her priest, demonstrating clearly that female-authored visionary writings were being circulated and read in the milieu in which Margery Kempe was operating at this time. In this chapter, however, we wish to argue that another of these 'swech other' would have been the *Liber specialis gratiae* of Mechthild of Hackeborn (1240–98), a visionary nun and chantress domiciled in the Helfta monastery in Saxony during the second half of the thirteenth century. Margery's access to this text was most likely in its translated form, known as *The Boke of Gostely Grace*, its title probably the result of a scribal error in the Latin manuscript used by the translator, although it is also quite possible that the Latin work could have been summarised or paraphrased for her – or else that one or other of her scribes had also been strongly influenced by it before or during the writing-up of Margery's life.[4]

This suggestion is not entirely a new one: it was first posited by Hope Emily Allen in her Prefatory Note to the Early English Texts Society edition of the *Book* produced with Sanford Brown Meech in 1940.[5] Additionally, in appendix IV of that edition, also prepared by Allen, she argues for the importance of studying Margery's text in the context of Dominican – or Dominican-influenced – visionary women operating in Germany during the thirteenth century, amongst whom Mechthild can certainly be numbered.[6] Indeed, again in her preface, Allen also declared that she would be presenting long extracts from the work of Mechthild and others like her to evidence her assertion of strong influence upon Margery Kempe, who, she also claims, had 'a habit to drop clues useful to the scholar ... sometimes split up in widely separated sections'.[7] As we know, Allen's collaboration with Meech was subject to considerable difficulties, the promised second volume never materialised, and we are still left to a large extent second-guessing what this remarkable and assiduous early twentieth-century scholar would have presented us with.[8] Nevertheless, at the same time, we do have full access to this same series of 'clues' dropped into the text by Kempe and her scribes, which we aim to discuss in this present chapter.

As mentioned, *The Boke of Gostely Grace* is the Middle English translation of the *Liber specialis gratiae*, the latter a seven-book set of revelations compiled collaboratively with Mechthild at Helfta by Gertrude the Great (1256–1301/2) and another unknown nun during the last decade of the thirteenth century. Soon after Mechthild's death, however, it was anonymously abridged from seven to five books and circulated widely throughout Europe.[9] The *Liber*, extant in three manuscript copies of English provenance, is, moreover, the only Helfta text to have been translated into Middle English – probably at Syon Abbey during the same period as Bridget of Sweden's *Liber Celestis* and Catherine of Siena's *Dialogo* were being translated into English, also in a Carthusian or Brigittine milieu.[10] The translation survives in two manuscripts only – Oxford, Bodleian Library, MS Bodley 220, dating from the mid-fifteenth century, and London, British Library, MS Egerton 2006, dating from the last quarter of the fifteenth century – but it is very likely that the two manuscripts share a common Middle English antecedent, now lost.[11] This would mean that a version of the *Boke* was almost certainly in circulation when Margery and the unnamed priest were reading together between

1413 and 1421. Indeed, the clear – and, on occasion, unique – correlations between the *Boke* and the 1422 text, *A Revelation of Purgatory*, attributed to an anonymous female recluse in Winchester, would strengthen the case for the *Boke*'s early circulation in such circles.[12]

In addition to complete manuscript copies of the *Liber* and the *Boke*, there are a number of extant devotional works and anthologies that contain passages taken from Mechthild's revelations in Latin and/or English.[13] Extracts, for instance, were circulating in important devotional manuscripts soon after the foundation of Syon Abbey in 1415. *The Myroure of oure Ladye*, written for the nuns of Syon probably between 1420 and 1448, contains two excerpts from 'Mawdes boke', although, as Rosalynn Voaden has pointed out, it is impossible to discern definitively whether these were based on the *Liber* or the *Boke* because of their largely paraphrastic tenor.[14]

Extracts also appear in the Carthusian-authored *Speculum devotorum*, or *Myrowre to Devout Peple*, written between c. 1415 and 1425. In the prologue its author memorably endorses Bridget of Sweden, Catherine of Siena and Mechthild of Hackeborn as 'approued women', probably for the deemed orthodoxy of their visionary writings.[15] Here again it is difficult to discern which version of Mechthild's writing the extracts were based upon.[16] Extracts attributed to Mechthild are also found in a number of other devotional compilations and anthologies, including British Library, MS Harley 494, an early sixteenth-century manuscript connected with the Syon network that incorporates Mechthild's revelations bilingually as one of its sources.[17] Whether Latin, vernacular, or bilingual, Mechthild's text (in a variety of forms) thus forged predominantly Brigittine and Carthusian connections and was widely disseminated under these auspices.

Given her own Syon connections and those of her supporters, then, Margery was very likely to have had access to Mechthild's work, whether in Latin or in translation. Again in her prefatory note to the *Book*, Allen states that the revelations of Bridget, Catherine and Mechthild had all been translated into English before Margery finally succeeded in getting her own experiences recorded between 1436 and 1438. Here Allen cites the examples of the readership of the so-called '*Mauldebuke*', which was owned by Eleanor Ros of York as early as 1438, and points out that MS Egerton 2006 belonged to 'R. Gloucester and Anne Warwick', that is to say Richard III and his wife, Anne, in the latter part of the fifteenth century.[18] Both of these royal persons were direct descendants of the Lady Westmorland (d. 1440) mentioned in Margery's text (pp. 265–6), also known as Joan Beaufort, legitimated daughter of John of Gaunt and Catherine Swynford, and named as both a close acquaintance and a supporter of Margery Kempe (at least according to Margery's perspective). Indeed, one of Lady Westmorland's daughters, Cecily Neville, duchess of York (d. 1495), is also known to have owned a copy of Mechthild's *Boke*, which formed part of her daily reading; and Cecily, of course, was the sister of the same Lady Greystoke, of whom Margery was accused of persuading to leave her husband in 1417 (pp. 265–5).[19] Such connections and encounters thus point towards a number of other ways in which Margery could have gained access to Mechthild's writing – or, at the very least, oral discussions of it.

Other possible routes for Margery Kempe's familiarity with Mechthild's writings emerge within Carmelite contexts. The Carmelite order was one of the older monastic traditions, and one from which Syon sought help in its early history: as Vincent Gillespie points out, Carmelites were involved in developing Syon's own distinctive form of living as advisers.[20] We know of Margery's association with the Carmelites from the many references to the friars peppered throughout the *Book*.[21] Among others Alan of Lynn, native of Lynn, Carmelite anchorite and doctor of divinity, remained a highly valued spiritual adviser to Margery throughout much of her adult life, having enormous influence on her spiritual education through the highly intellectual Carmelite network within which he appeared to have operated.[22] Indeed a school in the Carmelite Friary in Lynn was almost certainly instrumental in disseminating the latest theological ideas and trends, then shared and discussed by the friars and their associates. The cartulary of the Carmelites, which includes various arrangements for corrodies, suggests that the interchange of personnel between England and the Continent was very frequent, enabling them to maintain the high standard of intellectual pursuit for which they were renowned.[23] We know that Alan was keen on cataloguing works of mysticism and accommodating the demands of the laity seeking access to the Bible.[24] He is also recorded as having made indexes of the revelations and prophecies of St Bridget of Sweden and of the pseudo-Bonaventuran *Stimulus Amoris*, both known to Margery, as mentioned earlier. So, between 1413 and possibly 1428, when Margery interacted regularly with the reading priest and Alan of Lynn, there were any number of opportunities for her to become familiar with Mechthild's writings. Indeed, considering the Carmelites' academic network and close links with the Brigittines of Syon from the Order's early years, we can speculate with some confidence that Alan may well have had a specific interest in Mechthild's *Liber* which, like Bridget's revelations, was circulated from Syon, and would surely have been consulted by him, if the opportunity arose.[25]

There remains one more distinct possibility – that Margery's familiarity with Mechthild's writings could have been influenced – or consolidated – by her son and daughter-in-law, residents of one of Lynn's primary trading outposts in Danzig – or present-day Gdansk – now a Polish city but part of northern German territories during the later Middle Ages.[26] In Book II of her text Margery recounts a visit made to Lynn in 1431 by her son, John, who was at that time living in Danzig with his unnamed German wife, who accompanies him to England (pp. 389–90). With this journey and his subsequent residency in Margery's home having recently been historically verified by Sebastian Sobecki, this son's position as Margery's first scribe has been largely confirmed for contemporary scholarship, although we wonder if it really was that straightforward and simple.[27] Indeed, given that the text also records how pious conversion, followed by marriage to a local woman, had saved the son from a dangerously dissolute lifestyle, it is very likely that he – and, perhaps more importantly, his wife – brought back with them to Lynn knowledge of the renowned holy women of northern Germany, amongst whom Mechthild of Hackeborn was a dominant figure. Indeed, in an important unpublished conference paper, Santha Bhattarcharji has turned the spotlight firmly for the first time onto Margery's much overlooked daughter-in-law, who, following the sudden deaths of Margery's son and his father during their stay in Lynn, stayed on to spend more than a year and a half with Margery between the end of 1431 and April 1433 as a young widow (pp. 390–1).[28] As Bhattarcharji suggests, there is absolutely no reason to discount the likelihood that the daughter-in-law also played a role in helping to script Margery's book. For one thing it would completely explain the hybrid German–English script and linguistic expression that the second scribe found so difficult to decipher. It would also provide a more feasible time-frame for the *Book*'s first writing: given the son's business affairs and his having become mortally ill so quickly after his arrival at Lynn, there was very little time at his disposal to write down an entire book within the month between his arrival and death. The daughter-in-law, on the other hand, had plenty of time to get the first version of the book written during her long encounter with her mother-in-law in Lynn, as Bhattarcharji emphasises. Even if she were not party to the *Book*'s first inscription, the daughter-in-law would have had ample time to recount tales of those holy women who had been prominent in and around Danzig in order to stir Margery's imagination and help her recast her visionary experiences within new and exciting narrative frameworks. As the *Book* announces elsewhere, Margery was happy to talk at great length 'alwey of the lofe and goodnes of owyr Lord, as wel at the tabyl as in other place' (p. 151).

Margery's daughter-in-law, as a resident of Danzig, would certainly have been familiar with Dorothy von Montau (d. 1394), who had been born in the town and whose likely influence upon Margery has been posited by previous commentators.[29] It may even be that Margery's seemingly impulsive decision to accompany her daughter-in-law back to Danzig in 1433 was impelled in part by a wish to visit in person the region within which the type of female spirituality she had been espousing for most of her adult life had also long been thriving. For instance Danzig supported one of the first Brigittine foundations and had provided a stop-off point for Bridget's daughter, Katharina, as she carried her mother's remains back to Sweden.[30] With Mechthild having had a clear influence on aspects of Bridget's writings – the soul as a room to be swept clean by its 'housekeeper' is probably the best-known testimony to this – and with the Danzig foundation still offering indulgences at the time of Margery's three-month stay there, there were doubtless multiple reasons for Margery's visit beyond the mere compulsion endorsed by Christ which she documents (p. 393).[31] Moreover, all of these reasons seem to be female-focused: on her own sense of duty to a sometimes reluctant daughter-in-law; on a wish to meet her unseen German granddaughter; and on a desire to visit a locale within which pockets of female spirituality continued to be subject to cult status. Indeed, it seems likely that Margery's determination to get her book written in its entirety once and for all when she returned to Lynn was also spurred on by her protracted stay in this region and her journey home, most likely via new Helfta, Magdeburg and the important spiritual centre of Erfurt.[32] It is in Erfurt that the most authoritative Latin copy of Mechthild's *Liber* was produced in 1370, claiming, too, to being an accurate copy of the original.[33] In an essay documenting the strong Carthusian predilection for such writings Dennis Martin identifies Erfurt as a pivot for dissemination of the writings of all three Helfta visionaries and other women like them: for example, the former Erfurt, MS J 2 Halle (now Universitätsbibliothek Y c8° 6) begins with the words *Collectorium ex libris devotarum feminarum* and includes works by Birgitta, Mechthild, a 'certain holy Margareta', Catherine of Siena, Gertrude of Helfta and Hildegard of Bingen.[34] Mechthild, then, was patently a particular favourite within wider European Carthusian circles in the fifteenth century; and, as Voaden notes, her work tended to 'travel in convoy' with the works of other holy women through those Carthusian and Brigittine networks with which we know Margery had regular encounters, both at home and abroad.[35]

Margery's Continental sojourn thus offered her the opportuninty for direct contact with communities – both lay and religious – where the spirituality of women had long been nurtured, providing her with evidence of an elite spiritual community of holy women that she could bring to bear upon her life back in Lynn. Indeed this is testified to by the rapidity with which she visited the Brigittine house of Syon Abbey upon her return to England, where, she records, a young man she meets on Lammas Day chooses to refer to her specifically as Mother – a common epithet, of course, for a seasoned holy woman (pp. 418–20). Within three years or so, Margery had found a new amanuensis to transcribe her son's and/or daughter-in-law's seemingly indecipherable first draft, and had him record the events of this important German adventure as a second book appended to the first. Also incorporated into the manuscript at this point were Kempe's own prayers, which, as mentioned, bear traces of German holy women's influence.[36] Although these prayers were likely composed many years before the inception of the *Book*, a precedent for their incorporation had already been established by

Margery's likely intertexts – that is to say, those texts which directly or indirectly influenced her writing – or, in Hope Emily Allen's words: 'the flotsam and jetsam of popular devotion in manuscripts of English origin'.[37]

As mentioned earlier, Margery Kempe not only read – or had read to her – Bridget's revelations but is very likely to have had access to Mechthild's text in one or more of the ways documented, access which appears to have had significant influence upon a number of episodes in the *Book*.[38] Such a possibility has previously been entertained by Allen, who points out that Margery's vision of a celestial dance with the Lord, his mother, and holy virgins in Chapter 22 ('I schal take the be the on hand in hevyn and my modyr be the other hand, and so schalt thu dawnsyn in hevyn wyth other holy maydens and virgynes', p. 138) is based on a remarkably similar visionary episode within Mechthild's book, when, on the feast of All Saints, Mechthild sees 'a wondyrfulle goynge ande ledynge abowte in manere of a karole' (fols 48r–v).[39]

Choreographically, a medieval 'karolynge' was circular and the dancers' revolving movements thus evoked for Mechthild – and clearly for Margery too – the perfect and harmonious circle of beatitude in heaven, as well as the holy woman's role as *sponsa Christi* dancing with her Bridegroom at the celestial marriage feast.[40] We suggest, however, that the direct correlations between both texts go far beyond this initial example. Elsewhere in her text, for example, Margery draws upon the same type of musical hermeneutics that everywhere proliferate in Mechthild's writing.[41] For Mechthild, heaven is not only inseparable from the musical harmony enjoyed by the choir at Helfta – she was, after all, its chantress – but God, himself, *is* divine music. On one occasion, for instance, divine love is envisioned as a 'full feyr mayd syngyng' (fol. 66v); on another, Mechthild's own singing in church brings about both mystical encounter and union with God, so that the breath they take in their singing is drawn from the same divine source (fol. 72v). In Margery's case, we can recall how her first spiritual awakening takes the form of 'a sownde of melodye so swet and delectable, hir thowt, as sche had ben in paradyse' (p. 61). She also relates how, for many years during the Palm Sunday procession, 'sche herd gret sowndys and gret melodiis wyth hir bodiy erys, and than sche thowt it was ful mery in hevyn' (p. 338).

There are also strong areas of comparison when it comes to the treatment of the Trinity in both texts, where it takes up residence in the devotee's heart upon the reception of the Eucharist. Mechthild's *Boke*, for example, again in Part V, describes how Mechthild becomes 'a full restefull and a full deliciouse trone of God for her cler and clene soule' (fol. 100r). When she gives instructions to those who ask for advice, she is filled with God's grace 'as if she had spoken of þe mowth of God, *sittyng in her*' (fol. 100r).[42] This same image reappears in Chapter 86 of Margery's text, where Christ articulates how, in Margery's capacious soul:

> my Fadyr sittyth on the cuschyn of golde ... and ... I the Secunde Persone, thi love and thi joy, sytte on the red cuschyn of velvet ... [and] the Holy Gost sittyth on a white cuschyn. (p. 373)

Most significantly, in this same context, both women also recount detailed first-person instructions from Christ about how they should worship the Trinity, both retellings bearing overtones, too, of the Athanasian Creed, 'Quicumque vult'. Continuing his final monologue, Christ instructs Margery thus:

> [Th]u thynkyst thu maist not worschepyn the Fadyr but thu worschep the Sone, ne thu may not worschep the Sone but thu worschep the Holy Gost ... thu thynkyst that eche of the iii personys in Trinite hath that other hath in her Godhed, and so thu belevyst verily, dowtyr, in thy sowle that ther be iij dyvers personys and oo God in substawnce, and that eche knowyth that other knowyth, and ech may that other may, and eche wil that other wil. And, dowtyr, this is a very feith and a ryght feyth, and this feith hast thu only of my yyfte. (pp. 373–4)

It is through this teaching that Margery ultimately deepens her understanding of the Trinity, mirroring exactly the experiences of Mechthild where she, too, is subjected to a monologue by Christ on exactly the same theme:

> fyrst þou shalt worship and prayse þe myȝt of þe fader which ys allmyghty and with þe which myght he worchith in þe sone, and the holy goost after hys wyll, which myȝt no creatur may fully comprehend in heven ne in erth. Also in þe same maner þou shalt worship þe wysdome of þe sonne which may nouȝt be enserchid be mannys wytte, which wysdome the sone fully comownyth with þe fader and þe holi gost after hys wyll. And þis wysdome may no creatur fully talke. Also after þat þou shalt worship þe benygnyte of þe holy gost, which

benignyte þe holy goost plentevouslye comownyth with þe fader and
þe sone after his wylle, which benignyte he partith nouȝt fully to no
creatur. (fol. 70v)

Christ's exposition on the Trinity here subtly links itself with the
sacrament of the Eucharist again, in both cases evoking the concluding
doxology of the Canon of the Mass that celebrates the glory of God
and envisions the grace of the Trinity uniting the human soul with
God through the Eucharist: 'Through + him, and with + him, and
in + him, all honour and glory are unto thee, God the Father
al+mighty, in the unity of the Holy + Ghost'.[43] No reader familiar
with both texts could miss the similarities between Mechthild's and
Margery's discourses on the Trinity here. Indeed, such similarities
embedded everywhere in Margery's visionary meditation on Christ's
discourse on Holy Communion, suggest to us that Margery – whether
consciously or unconsciously – recasts her meditational or visionary
experience within the context of Mechthildian spirituality. In this
way the startlingly similar and deeply embodied Trinitarian theology
shared by both women demonstrates clearly the type of diachronic
encounter between them that we are arguing for here – and it is an
encounter that is both spiritual *and* textual.

Similarly, compelling resonances emerge in the ways in which both
women toy with the possibility of universal salvation and establish
themselves as direct mediators for the release of souls suffering
in purgatory via their tears, prayers, and intercessions. Margery
recounts, for example, how, on her pilgrimage to Jerusalem begun in
1313, she undertakes a twenty-four-hour vigil in the Church of the
Holy Sepulchre and a tour along the Via Dolorosa, episodes which
sharpen her perception of the living and the ubiquitous presence
of the Passion. During the procession Margery desires to identify
herself with Christ so intensely that, when she comes up on to
Mount Calvary, she experiences her first crying fit, 'wrestyng hir
body on every syde, spredyng hir armys abrode as yyf sche schulde
a deyd' (p. 167). This moment marks a turning-point in Margery's
meditational experience, with all her preceding practice of Passion
meditation seeming to culminate in it, and with these fits of crying
and roaring lasting for many years afterwards (e.g. p. 68).[44] Such
experiences on this pilgrimage create an indelible memory which
Margery is then able to channel into her later meditations. Indeed,

such memories and re-enactments are emblematically submerged in one meditation undertaken during the Good Friday liturgy, when her first response in the Church of the Holy Sepulchre is again violently reanimated:

> [T]he mende of owr Ladiis sorwys, whech sche suffryd whan sche behelde hys precyows body hangyng on the crosse and sithyn beriid befor hir syght, sodeynly ocupiid the hert of this creatur, drawyng hir mende al holy into the Passyon of owr Lord Crist Jhesu, whom sche behelde wyth hir gostly eye in the syght of hir sowle as verily as thei sche had seyn hys precyows body betyn, scorgyd, and crucifyed wyth hir bodily eye, whech syght and gostly beheldyng wrowt be grace so fervently in hir mende, wowndyng hir wyth pite and compassyon, that sche sobbyd ... spredyng hir armys abroad, seyd wyth lowde voys, 'I dey! I dey!' ... hir labowr was so greet. Than wex sche al blew as it had been leed and swet ful sor. (pp. 275–6)

Here Margery's memory of her affective responses seems to replicate her subsequent devotion so intensely that she again spreads her arms and cries out uncontrollably, to the extent that 'wex sche al blew as it had been leed' (p. 276). Whilst scholarly discussions of these bodily responses are many and diverse, what has not been recognised is how closely they follow similar episodes within Mechthild's own devotional practices. For example:

> [W]hanne she sang in þe queer she ȝave so all her entent and besynes to God with all her myȝtes +`as´ if she hadde brenned all hoole in love, in so moch þat she wyst not what she did and shewyd somtyme full mervelouse countenaunce in her poort as in spredyng abrode her + hondes and somtyme she lifte hem up an hiȝe. (fol. 99v)

Similarly, the text describes the sudden change of colour in Mechthild's face brought about by her ecstasies, where 'her face and her handes semyd of colour chaunged in maner of a sodeyne crabbe which chaungith þe colour whanne it is sode or bake' and where 'she was allmoost lifles to syȝt' (fol. 99v). Although the motif of figures throwing up their arms in despair was widely diffused in thirteenth-century art, Mechthild's treatment is not merely borrowed from these types of visual images.[45] Rather, these highly affective responses to the Passion can be contextualised within the culture of holy tears and *imitatio Christi*, testified to by Christ's words to Mechthild elsewhere, 'what man or woman heeldith oute teerys for devocion of my passyon, + y wyll receyve h'e'm as þou3 he had suffryd passion bodely for me' (fol. 29v), and his listing of six ways of achieving the devotion of tears.[46] Elsewhere the text records how Mechthild received a gift of tears at the thought of Christ's passion: 'A wounder affection she hadde in thinkyng, in hering, and in spekyng of Cristes passion in so moch þat full selde she my3t speke þerof withouten teeris' (fol. 99v).

There are countless examples in Margery's book, of course, of her drawing upon the trope of holy women's redemptive tears as a particularly efficacious intervention for the salvation of souls. In Chapter 57, for instance, Margery's weeping for the souls in purgatory, along with the souls of Jews, Saracens, and all false heretics, forms part of a series of charitable intercessory prayers to God that all people, whoever they are and whatever they have done, should be turned to the faith of Holy Church. Indeed, Margery is clearly hard-placed to believe that God would turn away any contrite soul because of its former sinfulness – and to that end she prays to become 'a welle of teerys' (p. 277) to prompt compassion for the suffering and the damned (pp. 274–8). The well of tears is also a recurrent image in Mechthild's work, associated with the purgative properties of Christ's wound and the water flowing from his sacred heart where 'all þo þat desyred gostelye regeneracion' may be washed clean (fol. 39r). Indeed, the link between a woman's tears and purgatory remains important in both texts. In Chapters 59 and 64 and 65 of the *Book*, for example, Margery returns concertedly to the theme of purgatory, first recording the pain she felt when she received visions of the damned, and then her anger with God that he could ever allow anybody to be subject to such damnation. There follows protracted, and sometimes contentious, argumentation, with Christ eventually persuading Margery that he does not wish divine vengeance for anyone, reassuring her that 'ther is no man dampnyd but he that is wel worthy to be dampnyd, and thu schalt holdyn the wel plesyd wyth alle my werkys' (p. 303). He also assures Margery of her own role as successful intercessor by means of weeping, prayer and concerted love for him, telling her: 'Thu wepist so every day for mercy that I must nedys grawnt it the' (p. 302). Similarly, Mechthild's text also records visions of hell and purgatory and a questioning of God about the damnation of sinners such as Samson, Solomon, and Trajan. Here God's response is equally gnomic as he explains his rather vague reasons. In the case of Samson, for example, he tells her: 'y will þat it be unknowe of men what mercy hath do with þe soule of Salomon þat fleisly synnes mowe be þe more eschewyd of men' (fol. 94v). Later, we hear the full extent of how Mechthild's tearful intercessions have released other souls from purgatory: 'Whanne þis holy mayde had seid þis preyer with such entencion, she sey a grete multitude of soules ȝeld thankyng to God with a full grete gladnes for her delyveraunce' (fol. 95). Indeed, elsewhere, these souls are fully enumerated as Christ gives each sister, as a token of friendship, 'a thousand soules which he shulde delyver from all boundys of synne for her prayers and sen hem to þe hye kyngdome of hevyn' (fol. 49r). Such enumeration is echoed in Margery's own account, when he assures her: 'many hundryd thowsand sowlys schal be savyd be thi prayers' (pp. 79–80). While, as Newman has shown, the efficacy of holy women's intercessory prayer for purgatorial relief of suffering souls was a common trope within their writings and *Vitae*, nevertheless, the specific correlations between Mechthild's and Margery's recorded intercessions, all interspersed with direct speech, interrogation, and conversation with Christ, are highly suggestive of more direct influence – sometimes even at the level of replicated image and vocabulary.[47]

This suggestion is strengthened considerably when we consider where the chapters devoted to the purgatorial narratives are placed in Margery's book. Whilst Chapters 57, 59, and 64 concern themselves with Margery's intercessions via prayer, tears, and affective bodily responses on behalf of suffering purgatorial souls, they are interspersed with Chapters 58, 61, and 62 that concern themselves with the reading of named and unnamed devotional works, including the 'swech other' texts mentioned above. What we are positing, therefore, is that there is a direct, albeit unstated, link between the 'swech other' books enumerated in Chapters 58, 61, and 62 and the Mechthildian elements that seem to have been appropriated into Margery's narrative in the intervening chapters: the one sets off use of the other, so to speak, transforming this part of the *Book* into a quasi-devotional compilation of just the sort that the priest was no doubt reading with and to Margery and setting up a whole new set of encounters between Mechthild, Margery, and the latter's internal and external audiences. For Anna Harrison, Mechthild's book, as a collaborative venture between an, at first, reluctant Mechthild and at least two other nuns at Helfta, reflects what she terms 'a protracted tangle of talk' between the women and the sources that went into its production.⁴⁸ Such a 'tangle of talk' – what Laura Grimes has termed a 'conversational theology', and another version, perhaps, of Hope Emily Allen's 'flotsam and jetsam' – probably best reflects the way in which Margery's intertextual materials, including Mechthild's writing, were absorbed into her book.⁴⁹ By far the greatest influence, moreover, appears to have been exerted by Part V of Mechthild's text – in fact, the very same part that had a discernible influence upon the anonymous woman writer of the early fifteenth-century *A Revelation of Purgatory*.⁵⁰ This latter text, written in 1422, also revolves around visions of purgatory and successful intercessory interventions of an enclosed holy woman who, like Margery's priest, seems to have found in Mechthild's work 'on fro fer that schal fulfillyn [her] desyr' (p. 279). Indeed, with Margery having been directly exposed to works like Mechthild's by her priest and confessor from 1413 to 1421, or by her daughter-in-law or some other agent years afterwards in her old age, and with *A Revelation* dating itself as having been written in 1422, it is not beyond the bounds of possibility that Book V of Mechthild's text was circulating independently – and perhaps even anonymously – from the rest of the work and that its special appeal to women like the Winchester visionary and Margery Kempe led to its absorption into aspects of their own writing without direct citation.⁵¹ Nicholas Royle's view on the subtle – and often unruly – dynamics of intertextual appropriation is helpful for understanding the type of process we are arguing for here, within which the source materials become 'textual phantoms which do not necessarily have the solidity or objectivity of a quotation, an intertext or explicit, acknowledged presence and which, in fact, do not come to rest anywhere'. As Royle pointedly adds, 'phantom texts are fleeting, continually moving on, leading us away', a concept that chimes perfectly with Allen's 'flotsam and jetsam' and the 'tangle of talk' that Harrison sees as characterising the productive environment of the Helfta writings, and which no doubt also characterised Margery's encounters with the reading priest and his mother.⁵² By way of conclusion, therefore, we would like to posit a complex process of entangled encounters within which Mechthild's writing, in its variety of forms, left its mark upon both Margery Kempe's spirituality and her writing. Indeed, given the evidence that has long hidden in plain sight within the *Book* and its contexts, this not only speaks to the inconceivability of Mechthild's *Boke*'s having been unknown to Margery and her contemporaries but also to the certainty of Mechthild's having been a central – albeit long overlooked – figure within the devotional canon of fifteenth-century England.[53]

Notes

1. Margery Kempe, *The Book of Margery Kempe*, ed. Barry Windeatt (Cambridge: D. S. Brewer, 2006). All quotations will be taken from this edition, unless otherwise stated, cited by page number in the main text (here at p. 278).
2. On private reading as devotional practice promoting self-reflection see Jennifer Bryan, *Looking Inward: Devotional Reading and the Private Self in Late Medieval England* (Philadelphia: University of Pennsylvania Press, 2008). Bryan discusses Mechthild of Hackeborn's *Boke* on p. 36, pp. 90–3, and Margery Kempe on pp. 12, 19, and 20. See also Mary C. Erler, *Women, Reading and Piety in Late Medieval England* (Cambridge: Cambridge University Press, 2002).
3. Both texts were circulating in Middle English by the early fifteenth century, for which see 'The life of Marie d'Oignies', in Jennifer Brown (ed.), *Three Women of Liège: A Critical Edition of and Commentary on the Middle English Lives of Elizabeth of Spalbeek, Christina Mirabilis and Marie d'Oignies* (Turnhout: Brepols, 2008); and Elizabeth of Hungary, *Two Middle English Translations of the Revelations of St Elizabeth of Hungary*, ed. Sarah McNamer (Heidelberg: Universitätsverlag C. Winter, 1996). McNamer problematises this authorial attribution in her introduction.
4. It is likely that one or other of the medieval scribes expanded '*sp'alis*', the abbreviation of the Latin word *specialis*, to *spiritualis* at some stage in the text's manuscript history. Editions of these two texts include: Mechthild of Hackeborn, *Liber specialis gratiae*, ed. Dom Ludwig Paquelin, in *Revelationes Gertrudianae ac Mechtildianae*, 2 vols (Paris: H. Oudin, 1875–7), vol. II, pp. 1–422, hereafter cited as *Liber*. An edition of the Middle English translation, based on British Library, MS Egerton 2006, is available as *The Booke of Gostlye Grace of Mechtild of Hackeborn*, ed. Theresa A. Halligan (Toronto: Pontifical Institute of Mediaeval Studies, 1979). All citations of the Middle English text, however, will be taken from *The Boke of Gostely Grace, edited from Oxford, MS Bodley 220 with Introduction and Commentary*, ed. Naoë Kukita Yoshikawa and Anne Mouron with assistance of Mark Atherton, Exeter Medieval Texts and Studies (Liverpool: Liverpool University

Press, forthcoming 2022), hereafter cited as *Boke* followed by relevant folio number.
5 Margery Kempe, *The Book of Margery Kempe*, ed. Sanford Brown Meech and Hope Emily Allen, EETS OS 212 (London: Oxford University Press, 1940), here at p. lxvi.
6 *Ibid.* pp. 376–8.
7 *Ibid.*, p. lxvi.
8 On this see Marea Mitchell, *The Book of Margery Kempe: Scholarship, Community, and Criticism* (New York: Peter Lang, 2005).
9 For a brief but detailed account of this process see Ernst Hellgardt, 'Latin and the vernacular: Mechthild of Magdeburg – Mechthild of Hackeborn – Gertrude of Helfta', in Elizabeth Andersen, Henrike Lähnemann, and Anne Simon (eds), *A Companion to Mysticism and Devotion in Northern Germany in the Late Middle Ages* (Leiden and Boston: Brill, 2014), pp. 131–55 (for Mechthild of Hackeborn: pp. 137–41).
10 Oxford, Bodleian Library, MS Trinity College 32; Oxford, Bodleian Library, MS Digby 21; Cambridge, University Library, MS Ff. 1.19.
11 Halligan, ed., *Boke*, pp. 6–7.
12 See Liz Herbert McAvoy, '"O der lady, be my helpe": women's visionary writing and the devotional literary canon', *The Chaucer Review*, 51:1 (2016), 68–87. Some areas of this present chapter are indebted to this article, with thanks to the journal for permission to reproduce here.
13 See Rosalynn Voaden, 'The company she keeps: Mechtild of Hackeborn and late Medieval devotional compilations', in Rosalynn Voaden (ed.), *Prophets Abroad: The Reception of Continental Holy Women in Late-Medieval England* (Cambridge: D. S. Brewer, 1996), pp. 51–69.
14 *The Myroure of oure Ladye*, ed. John Henry Blunt, EETS ES 19 (London: N. Trübner, 1973), pp. 38–9, 276–7. Mechthild's name translates into Middle English variously as: Mawde, Moll, Molte, Molde, Maude, Maute and Matilde, see Voaden, 'Company', p. 54 n. 15 and p. 55.
15 This text is a meditative prose life of Christ, for an edition of which see *A Mirror to Devout People (Speculum devotorum)*, ed. Paul J. Patterson, EETS OS 346 (Oxford: Oxford University Press, 2016), p. 6.
16 *Myrowre*, p. 365.
17 Naoë Kukita Yoshikawa, 'The *Liber specialis gratiae* in a devotional anthology: London, British Library, MS Harley 494', in Marleen Cré, Diana Denissen, and Denis Renevey (eds), *Late Medieval Devotional Compilations in England* (Turnhout: Brepols, 2020), pp. 341–60.
18 *Testamenta Eboracensia: A Selection of Wills from the Registry at York*, vol. 2, ed. James Raine, Surtees Soc., 30 (1855), pp. 65–6; and *Book*, ed. Meech and Allen, p. lxvi.

19 *A Collection of Ordinances and Regulations for the Government of the Royal Household* (London: John Nichols, 1790), pp. 37–9; C. A. J. Armstrong, 'The piety of Cicely, duchess of York: a study in late mediaeval culture', in *England, France and Burgundy in the Fifteenth Century* (London: Hambledon, 1983), pp. 135–56, pp. 140–2.
20 Vincent Gillespie, 'The mole in the vineyard: Wyclif at Syon in the fifteenth century', in Helen Barr and Anne M. Hutchinson (eds), *Text and Controversy from Wyclif to Bale: Essays in Honor of Anne Hudson* (Turnhout: Brepols, 2005), pp. 131–62, p. 137.
21 See Naoë Kukita Yoshikawa, 'Carmelite spirituality and the laity in late medieval England', in Catherine Innes-Parker and Naoë Kukita Yoshikawa (eds), *Anchoritism in the Middle Ages* (Cardiff: University of Wales Press, 2014), pp. 151–62. Some discussions of the following section are indebted to this essay.
22 Allen identifies Alan as one of Margery's principal confessors (*Book*, ed. Meech and Allen, p. 259, n. 6/9). In Chapter 8 below Susan Maddock identifies his probable surname as Warnekyn and speculates that he was much younger than previously thought, having been confused with a considerably older Alan by generations of scholars. For this reason we leave his birth date (c. third quarter of the fourteenth century) undetermined.
23 A. G. Little and E. Stone, 'Corrodies at the Carmelite friary of Lynn', *Journal of Ecclesiastical History*, 9 (1958), 8–29, pp. 9, 15–17.
24 See A. B. Emden (ed.), *A Biographical Register of the University of Cambridge to 1500* (Cambridge: Cambridge University Press, 1963), pp. 381–2, for the list of his works credited by John Bale.
25 Significantly, Alan's grandfather, Stephen Warnekyn, who moved to Lynn from a German-speaking part of the Continent in the second half of the fourteenth century, is very likely to have communicated in German at home and Alan's father, Alan Warnekyn senior, may also have had some German. We speculate that there is a good possibility that Alan of Lynn was brought up in a multilingual and multicultural (English–German) milieu and this facilitated his role as a conduit for transmitting Mechthild's *Liber/Boke* to Margery. For Alan's family see Maddock, Chapter 8 as before.
26 For a more detailed analysis of Margery's trip to Danzig, see McAvoy, '"O der lady"'.
27 Sebastian Sobecki, '"The writyng of this tretys": Margery Kempe's son and the authorship of her book', *Studies in the Age of Chaucer*, 37 (2015), 257–83.
28 Santha Bhattacharji, 'Margery Kempe's daughter-in-law as scribe', unpublished paper delivered at the Leeds Medieval Congress, July 2014.

29 See Allen's comments in Kempe, *Book*, ed. Meech and Allen, p. lix. See also Clarissa M. Atkinson, *Mystic and Pilgrim: The Book and the World of Margery Kempe* (Ithaca: Cornell University Press, 1983), esp. pp. 179–81; David Wallace, *Strong Women: Life, Text and Territory 1347–1645* (Oxford: Oxford University Press, 2012), pp. 1–60.
30 Thomas Andrew Dubois (ed.), *Sanctity in the North: Saints, Lives and Cults in Medieval Scandinavia* (Toronto: University of Toronto Press, 2008), p. 296.
31 See *The Liber Celestis of Bridget of Sweden*, vol. 1, ed. Roger Ellis, EETS 291 (Oxford: Oxford University Press, 1987), II.ii, p. 118.
32 By this date the old Helfta, housing Mechthild and her contemporaries, had been destroyed and was superseded by a new monastery some distance away from the first. For a fuller account of this journey, see again McAvoy, '"O der lady"'.
33 Wolfenbüttel, Herzog August Bibliothek, Guelferbytanus codex 1003 Helmst.
34 Martin, 'Carthusians', p. 135.
35 Voaden, 'Company', p. 66.
36 For a detailed examination of the production of Book II see the essay by Laura Kalas, Chapter 11 below. For an illuminating discussion of Margery's prayers, see Josephine A. Koster, Chapter 3 below.
37 *Book*, ed. Meech and Allen, p. lix.
38 Again see Allen's Prefatory Note in *Book*, ed. Meech, and p. lxvii. Halligan also suggests a possible influence of Mechthild on Margery Kempe in *Booke*, 'Introduction', p. 59.
39 Allen points this out in *Book*, ed. Meech and Allen, n. 52/27, p. 283.
40 Mechthild of Hackeborn, *The Book of Special Grace*, trans. and intro. Barbara Newman (New York: Paulist Press, 2017), 'Introduction', pp. 1–34, pp. 25–6.
41 For more on this see Naoë Kukita Yoshikawa, 'Heavenly vision and psychosomatic healing: medical discourse in Mechtild of Hackeborn's the *Booke of Gostlye Grace*', in Naoë Kukita Yoshikawa (ed.), *Medicine, Religion and Gender in Medieval Culture* (Cambridge: D. S. Brewer, 2015), pp. 67–84.
42 *Boke*, V. 22, fol. 100r.
43 *The Sarum Missal in English*, Part I & II, trans. Frederick E. Warren (London, 1911), I, p. 48. Noticeably, in Mechthild's vision which occurs during Mass, she says to Christ: 'Y seke nouȝt þerof and I wyll noon oþer thing but þat þis day þou be praysyd and worshipped *of þysilf, and in thysilf, and by thysilf*' (Part 2, cap. 2, fol. 58r, our emphasis). As Barbara Newman comments on this passage: 'This Trinitarian formula

echoes the final prayer of the Canon of the Mass', Newman, *Book*, p. 262, n. 4.
44 On the history of such holy weeping and tears of devotion see Kimberley Christine Patton and John Stratton Hawley (eds), *Holy Tears: Weeping in the Religious Imagination* (Princeton: Princeton University Press, 2005). For a more recent treatment of Margery Kempe's tears specifically see Laura Kalas Williams, '"Slayn for Goddys lofe: Margery Kempe's melancholia and the bleeding of tears', *Medieval Feminist Forum: A Journal of Gender and Sexuality*, 52:1 (2016), 84–100.
45 Moshe Barasch, *Gestures of Despair in Medieval and Early Renaissance Art* (New York: New York University Press, 1976).
46 See Patton and Hawley, *Holy Tears*.
47 See Barbara Newman, 'On the threshold of the dead: purgatory, hell, and religious women', in *From Virile Woman to WomanChrist: Studies in Medieval Religion and Literature* (Philadelphia: University of Pennsylvania Press, 1995), pp. 108–36.
48 Anna Harrison, '"Oh! What treasure is in this book?" Writing, reading, and community at the monastery of Helfta', *Viator*, 39:1 (2008), 75–106, p. 94.
49 See Laura M. Grimes, 'Theology as conversation: Gertrud of Helfta and her sisters as readers of Augustine' (PhD dissertation, University of Notre Dame, 2004), p. 49.
50 See McAvoy, '"O der lady"'.
51 Part I of the *Boke*, documenting liturgical visions more relevant to the cloister than the laity, was likely too voluminous to be circulated easily as a single volume. Similarly, Parts VI and VII were cut from most early copies and translations, probably because of their hagiographical tenor. Traces of Part V, however, are found in a number of literary works: Dante's *Purgatorio* and the poems of the *Pearl*-poet, amongst others. An examination of this influence is undertaken by Liz Herbert McAvoy in *The Enclosed Garden and the Medieval Religious Imaginary* (Cambridge: D. S. Brewer, 2021).
52 Nicholas Royle, *The Uncanny* (London: Routledge, 2003), p. 280.
53 A longer version of this essay first appeared as Liz Herbert McAvoy and Naoë Kukita Yoshikawa, 'Mechthild of Hackeborn and Margery Kempe: An Intertextual Conversation', *Spicilegium*, 4 (2021), 1–18. Thanks are due to the Leverhulme Trust for funding the collaboration that produced both essays.

3

The prayers of Margery Kempe: a reassessment

Josephine A. Koster

Unfamiliar with the generic and linguistic conventions of medieval English prayer, modern readers frequently miss, or misidentify, components of Margery Kempe's so-called 'mystical' discourse, or ignore it as slavishly imitative of liturgical texts. A major challenge for the twenty-first-century study of Kempe's style and sources is tuning our ears to the language of Middle English liturgy – to hear the resonances Kempe and her intended audience would have heard and responded to, and to understand the implications of their deployment. A case in point is the critically neglected collection of prayers that follows the conclusion of Book II of *The Book of Margery Kempe*. Anthony Goodman, for example, says that they 'handily distil the essence of her devotion' and pays no further attention to them; Naoë Kukita Yoshikawa remarks on them at the end of her study of Kempe's devotional practices, but not at length.[1] Few relatively recent works treat the prayers at length: Barbara Zimbalist examines them in the light of Kempe's evolving authority to represent the voice of God in her own words; and Nicholas Watson uses them to try to identify the scribal interventions in the second draft of the *Book*.[2] In this chapter I argue that a reconsideration of the palaeographic evidence and the context of the prayers indicates that Kempe and her successive amanuenses modified orthodox prayer traditions to create the impression of an authentic voice with which readers could identify, and that this increases our need to treat them as more than a liminal text.

Little attention has been previously given to scribal presentation. Kempe's prayers are copied as a separate, pendant treatise to *The*

Book of Margery Kempe, now British Library, Additional Manuscript 61823, which was probably copied c. 1440–50 by the scribe Richard Salthows (or 'Salthouse'), and was preserved and annotated at the Charterhouse of Mount Grace in Yorkshire. In his edition Barry Windeatt numbers the lines of the prayer collection as if it were a continuation of Book II of Margery's *Book*; palaeographically, however, it appears that Salthows regarded it as a separate work. The second part of the *Book* ends on fol. 120r with an interfoliated bicolour "A · M · E · N ·" followed by Trinitarian trefoils to indicate the closure of the main text.[3] The prayers begin on a clean verso on fol. 120v, marked by one of Salthows's rare flourished ascenders, giving additional palaeographic formality to the new section. The same Trinitarian trefoils are used at the conclusion of the prayers on fol. 123r, this time appearing half a dozen times between the word 'Amen' and the rubricated abbreviation for 'Amen' and preceding his scribal colophon, further calling attention to the prayer collection as a distinct unit of content.

The layout of the text of the prayers differs in several ways from the text of the *Book*. Salthows copies the fifteen individual prayers as if they were one contiguous document, without any of the rubrication or scribal flourishes used in the main text to indicate chapters, *nomina sacra*, and the like.[4] Usually when scribes inserted prayers or short devotional texts in the flyleaves or empty spaces of a Book of Hours or other manuscript, they copied them as individual texts, often with pen flourishes to indicate the end of each prayer, or, more often, with the abbreviations for the *Pater Noster* and *Ave Maria* that a devout Christian expected to see appended to each individual prayer.[5] By contrast Salthows lays out these texts as a kind of devotional memoir, with no such interruptions, as what Nicholas Watson calls 'the Great Prayer'.[6] The narrator says '[t]hys creatur, of whom is tretyd beforn, usyd many yerys to begynnyn hir preyerys on this maner', establishing the text as narrative evidence of a conforming Christian's long-term pious practices.[7] The Margery of the prayers is portrayed as devout, orthodox, and mainstream: 'sche cam to chirche, knelyng beforn the sacrament in the worschep of the blissyd Trinite (Fadir, Sone, and Holy Gost, oo God and iii Personys), of that gloryows Virgine, Qwen of Mercy, owr Lady Seynt Mary, and of the xii apostelys' (pp. 421–2), modeling the humble behaviour expected of lay folk. In highlighting these orthodox practices, Salthows introduces 'thys creatur' as an ideal member of the community of worshippers, in contrast to the controversial figure she may have been in Lynn owing to her ministry.[8]

The manuscript exemplar (or exemplars) for these prayers has not been identified. But a logical place to encounter them was in the flyleaves of her own prayer book or Book of Hours (sometimes called a primer), where they might have been written down for her by one of the many learned clerks or spiritual directors she consulted, or even by someone she paid to record them. Kempe is described in the *Book* as using her prayer book in church (p. 83), which is not surprising; as Laurel Amtower wryly notes in her discussion of middle-class book ownership, such '[b]ooks ... were chic'.[9] Several fifteenth-century English women are recorded as leaving Books of Hours or similar manuscripts in their testaments.[10] Or Kempe may have bequeathed her book to a religious foundation; John B. Friedman and David N. Bell document the high percentage of bequests of books from lay owners to churches and houses of religious in this period.[11] Whatever Salthows's exemplar was for these texts or whatever Kempe's earlier amanuensis used as a model, the manuscript layout preserves her prayers collectively as a formal witness to her devotional exercises.

Recent scholarship has delved into the question of how and by whom Kempe's work was disseminated. Absent Kempe's own testament, it is impossible to prove but reasonable to conjecture that Robert Spryngolde, her confessor and possible amanuensis, might have inherited the manuscript in which Kempe's prayers were recorded (or even transcribed them for her), and that he provided the exemplars from which Salthows made his surviving copy.[12] Anthony Bale has argued persuasively that 'it was at Norwich Cathedral, within a literate and sophisticated community of Benedictine monks, that Margery Kempe's story was being told and preserved, probably within five to ten years after her death', and that 'Salthouse's making of the *Book* suggests a desire to record Kempe's life and visions for posterity ... parallel to a monastic record or a hagiographic document, building an orthodox and institutional textual edifice of a remarkable devout woman'.[13] The role of the clerical amanuensis in authorising the practices of a female visionary has been well documented; Janette Dillon notes that '[t]he greatest testimony a cleric could offer to a female visionary was of course his decision to document her life or her visions in writing'.[14] In recording the prayers and practices of Margery, as they may have witnessed them, as a recognisable text, the second scribe and Salthows contribute to the image Kempe wished to present of herself: the devout laywoman as a model for others.[15] Given the content of the prayers and their representation of Kempe as mediatrix for other sinners, as I will argue later in this chapter, this clerical validation is even more important.

Whilst some collections of vernacular prayers circulated independently, such as the prayers of St Anselm or the near-contemporary devotional treatise *The Fifteen Oes* associated with Bridget of Sweden, medieval personal prayers are most often found inserted haphazardly in other manuscripts, often on flyleaves or spaces left blank within the contents.[16] In Kempe's manuscript, bounded by palaeographic flourishes, we encounter them as a purposeful assemblage: they are a collective witness to her devotion. But how we see them as connected to the *Book* itself is complicated. The prayers address some of the themes included in the *Book*, but not the major ones, such as devotion to the body of Christ and to his suffering, or the intervention of the Virgin and other saints, which calls into question when or why they were gathered into one unit. Windeatt seems correct in assigning at least some of these prayers to Kempe's 'middle years' [p. 421]; as he notes, the penultimate petition concerning Lazarus notes that 'I have ben in that holy stede ther thi body was qwik and ded and crucifiid for mannys synne' suggesting that it was written after Kempe came home from Jerusalem in 1415. Windeatt also points out that the speaker twice refers to 'my crying', but not to the cessation of those episodes, which would place the composition of at least some of the prayers in the decade between the events of the two books of her main narrative. He more cautiously proposes that the narrator's request that God 'make my gostly fadirs for to dredyn the in me and … lovyn the in me' (p. 423) may 'suggest [Kempe's] own composition of the prayers as a whole' (p. 421). Watson likewise ventures that these prayers 'may have been part of the original draft … or be a product of the period between the two drafts', but provides no evidence for this claim.[17] There is no way, of course, to identify the circumstances in which they were recorded, although, *pace* Sebastian Sobecki, it seems unlikely that Kempe dictated them to her son John as he lay on his sickbed, even though there is one tantalising petition in the bidding prayer for 'alle bedred men and women' (p. 425).[18] The third prayer in the collection, which asks for the quenching of bodily lust, mirrors the concerns she expresses for her son's soul in Chapter 1 of the second part of the *Book*, but that thematic connection alone cannot concretely assist with dating the compilation, or clearly establish the relation of the two texts.

The form and content of the prayer collection, however, support the notion that Kempe and her copyists not only appropriated and reworked examples of contemporary prayers to which she was exposed but also composed prayers for which there are no obvious models to reflect and validate her own devotional practices. The fifteen individual prayers that make up the collection draw on a variety of medieval models – the Office of Our Lady, the liturgy of the Mass, the Psalms, and possibly collections of aphorisms and saints' lives. Medieval English prayers are conventional in both form and language, and are usually presented in the context of Latin doctrinal prayers, especially the *Pater Noster* and *Ave Maria*. R. N. Swanson notes that the ubiquitous combination of these two prayers 'allowed them to become almost a currency of spirituality, to be cashed in by anyone capable of reciting them' and that they are usually 'included in the beginning of any private devotional session, in church or without'.[19] The description of Margery's public devotional practice at the beginning of the prayer collection, however, does not include this very common and orthodox practice, and Salthows tags neither the individual petitions nor the complete sequence with the common *Pater* or *Ave* abbreviations. Instead the text reports that Margery began her prayers by reciting the words of the initial hymn for Tierce in the Hours of Our Lady, *Veni Creator Spiritus*, 'wyth alle the versys' (p. 422). Hope Emily Allen suggests this is an echo of the influence of the legend of Dorothea of Moldau but these texts would have already been familiar to Kempe through observing the daily canonical Hours as well as the hymn's central role in the liturgy of Pentecost.[20] As in the first four prayers of her collection, she is shown requesting divine illumination and grace to resist temptation; if she were following the daily Office for Tierce, this hymn would be followed by Psalm 120, *ad Dominum tribularer*, rendered in Middle English as 'Whanne y was set yn tribulacioun, y criede to þe lord, & [he] herde me'.[21] Given the role weeping plays in Margery's piety, this juxtaposition of sources provides a more immediate source for her idiosyncratic devotions.

Windeatt suggests that the Middle English prayer known as *The Fifteen Oes* also 'may have offered [Kempe] an example to emulate' in constructing the text that follows (p. 421), but there is no convincing linguistic evidence of this in the texts themselves. *The Fifteen Oes*, which probably originated in Yorkshire in the mid- to late fourteenth century and were mistakenly attributed to Bridget of Sweden, centre on the corporal sufferings of the crucified Christ, and encourage the petitioner to use them as a focus for affective meditation on his bodily pain. Unlike the language used in these examples of Kempe's devotions, the language of *The Fifteen Oes* is vividly physical and descriptive, recounting the drops of blood falling from Christ's 'delicious bodi' and describing in great detail how Christ was scourged, tied, and nailed to the cross, and wounded by Pilate's soldiers.[22] Whilst *The Fifteen Oes* may be at the root of some of Kempe's descriptions of Christ's sufferings in her recounted visions in Chapters 28 and 61 of the *Book*, there is no evidence of their specific language in the collection of her prayers. Instead we must look elsewhere for the models for their language and form.

One of the first differences we find between the text of the *Book* itself and the prayers is the voice of the speaker. Kempe's prayers are recorded in first-person singular voice, quite different from the third-person narration Salthows (or his exemplar) uses in the two parts of the *Book* itself. The singular grammatical constructions are important, since, when first person is used in Middle English vernacular prayers, it is often plural, drawing on the Latin rubric *Oremus*, 'Let us pray', that introduced most prayers in the canonical hours and the Mass.[23] Here, readers encounter Kempe's voice instead as individual and personal. Intriguingly, Salthows, normally a most careful and reliable scribe, stumbles once in this regard, on fol. 121v, line 10. The Mount Grace annotations correct Salthows's original 'hym' to 'the', raising the tantalising possibility that his exemplar might have been in third person, and demonstrating how thoroughly he was committed to presenting this text as if it were Kempe's own voice. The choice to represent these prayers in the first person tells us a great deal about whoever chose to put this collection together. It creates the image not of a representative 'evyn-Cristen' (p. 423) but of a very specific person who has a particular, established relationship with the sacred personae being addressed. Yoshikawa argues that the 'whole enterprise of her prayer

[is] one that establishes Margery's position in the community ... as the medium by which God communicates with her fellow Christians'.[24] This self-presentation as an individual whose expressions are worthy of being recorded is part of the building of that 'textual edifice' of validated piety to which Bale referred.[25]

But that is not the only notable stylistic characteristic we encounter in this collection. Rhetorically, absence is as much a feature of these prayers as is the actual content. A number of very typical petitions that *would* resonate strongly with the themes Kempe stresses in the *Book* are missing from these fifteen prayers. Besides the omission of *Pater Nosters* and *Ave Marias*, the prayers show only a few instances of the language that Nicholas Watson drily describes as drawing on 'a mercantile late religious culture imbued with the financial imagery of recompense and satisfaction – numbering masses for the dead and years in purgatory and reciting Aves and Pater Nosters by the hundreds in expiation of sin'.[26] Only one prayer is specifically directed to the Virgin Mary, despite Margery's well-documented devotion to her and the frequency of exemplars for Marian prayer in contemporary Middle English. Likewise, only one prayer is directed collectively to Sts Mary Magdalen, Mary the Egyptian, St Paul, and St Augustine, figures who were venerated for their apostolic and intercessory roles. Typically, as Charity Scott-Stokes among others has shown, Books of Hours and primers also include interpolated prayers to the owner's name saint, or to saints to whom she or he was personally devoted. A woman's prayer book often included prayers to St Margaret and St Katherine; with Margaret being Kempe's name saint and the patroness of her parish church, this omission is particularly glaring.[27] Finally there is very little mention of the Passion or the physical sufferings of Christ, which might have been expected on the basis of the descriptions of Margery at prayer found in the *Book*. Given that '[s]che was so ful of holy thowtys and medytacyons and holy contemplaycyons in the Passyon of owyr Lord Jhesu Crist, and holy dalyawns that owyr Lord Jhesu Crist dalyed to hir sowle, that sche cowde nevyr expressyn hem aftyr, so hy and so holy thei weryn' (p. 169), the absence of prayers invoking these subjects reinforces the notion that these devotions were composed independently of the composition of the *Book* itself. The pages holding these prayers in the manuscript of the *Book* show some of the heaviest wear in the entire manuscript as well, suggesting that at least some of its later readers paid attention to this text independently of the main text.

Initially the content we encounter seems quite traditional, expressions that might be dictated by a confessor or spiritual director to an obedient congregant and recorded by a willing clerk. The first five petitions demonstrate her conformity to the orthodox strictures of the Church; the speaker rejects any 'knowyng and undirstondyng of the prevyteys of God be the tellyng of any devyl of helle' (p. 422), perhaps to prevent repetition of the successful temptations she endured when her visions first began (pp. 52–5). Further, she makes clear the limitations of her knowledge, stating that, with God's help, she does not desire to 'knowyn, heryn, seen, felyn, ne undirstondyn in my sowle in this lyfe mor than is the wil of God' (p. 422), an important assertion for a woman who had been accused of both Lollardy and heresy. Equally conventional and unsurprising is the sole prayer addressed exclusively to the Virgin. Given the important role that the ultimate Christian mediatrix plays in the *Book*, the perfunctory presence of Marian invocation in the prayers again suggests the separation of this work from Kempe's main narrative. Instead, a litany of clichés ('welle of grace, flower and fairest of alle women that evyr God wrowt in erth, the most worthiest in hys syght, the most leef, der, and derworthy unto hym ... benyngne Lady, meke Lady, chariteful Lady') leads into a straightforward request for intercession on behalf of Margery and her 'gostly fadrys' (p. 427). When compared to the effusive and personal language Kempe uses to address Mary in the *Book* itself, this language seems flat and underwhelming. Even the short punning Prayer Five, where she prays that Jesus 'make my wil thi wyl, and thi wil my wil, that I may no wil han but thi wil only' (p. 423), has the feel of a conventional aphorism or pious motto that could easily be memorised and recited as part of a devotional exercise.

However, it does not take long for Margery's idiosyncratic self-importance to become evident, again raising the question of whether she, or her spiritual advisers, composed the language that is preserved in the text. Her prayer about her gift of compunction is one of only a few places where she resorts to the language of mercantile transaction that marks early fifteenth-century English devotional texts, asking God to increase the flow of her tears so that they will 'moryn my meryte in hevyn, <and> helpyn and profityn my evyn-Crysten sowlys, lyvys or dedys' (pp. 422–3).[28] And she pointedly reminds her Creator that 'thu knowist what scornys, what schamys, what despitys, and what reprevys I have had thefor' and 'it is not in my power to wepyn neythyr lowde ne stille'. Her petition that God 'excuse me ageyn al this world to knowyn and to trowyn that it is thi werke and thi yyfte' (p. 423) sounds almost as much chiding as request. The humble, typical penitent has disappeared, replaced with a figure confident of her worth for salvation.

But it is in Prayers Six and Seven where we most clearly encounter Kempe as rhetor, deliberately creating and adapting devotional texts that met her individual pious needs. Prayer Six converts a recognisable form, the bidding prayer, into the most complex text in this devotional collection. This intercessory prayer, the only part of the medieval Mass usually spoken in the vernacular, dates back at least as far as the early eleventh- century, but became common in Middle English after Archbishop Thoresby's prescriptions for lay instruction in 1357.[29] Richard Pfaff points to an English rubric for bidding prayer elements from the mid-1380s that specifies that the priest turn 'ad populum et dicat in lingua materna sic' [to the people and speak in the mother tongue thusly]. Thence follow petitions for the leaders of the church, the specific clergy in charge of the church where the prayers are said, for peace, for the king, 'et cetera more solito' [and the rest as usual]. Then, after more liturgical exchanges in Latin, 'Item conversus ad populum dicat sacerdos in lingua materna oremus pro animabus N. et N more solito' [Item: the priest, turned to the people, says in the mother tongue, 'Let us pray in the usual manner for the souls of N. and N.'].[30] Kempe's complex and personal adaptation of the bidding prayer formula, containing eleven individual petitions, is the earliest one I am aware of that is not preserved in a liturgical milieu – either in the rhythmic translations that circulated in works like *The Lay Folks Mass Book* in churches that followed the Use of York or in the *Quattuor Sermones* for churches that followed the Use of Sarum. The speaker adapts the form and language of this part of the Mass to express her own devotion in characteristically idiosyncratic terms.

From the handful of medieval bidding prayers that survive, none of which exactly duplicates another, it is clear that the contents may vary, but that the arrangement, expression, and voice of those contents were fairly consistent. The rear flyleaf of Wyggeston Hospital, Leicester, Ms. 9 preserves a bidding prayer from a York monastery dating to the very early fifteenth century that likely resembles what Margery heard at Mass in her own parish of St Margaret's and on her various journeys throughout England.[31] It begins with prayers to 'all the holi court of heuene' for the ecclesiastical hierarchy, for the king and queen of England and their children, and various secular authorities. The 'ersbisshop of Yoor' takes precedence over the 'ersbishhop of Cauntuworbiry'; there are prayers for the religious of the houses of St William of York and St Mary of Southwell; and, after a series of petitions for the dead, the ill, and various sinners, it concludes with prayers for the fruits of the earth and for good weather for the crops. The genre's range of subjects from the divine to the mundane clearly appealed to Kempe and her scribes, but, in characteristic manner, she reshapes the orthodox genre to her own purposes.

   The voice in surviving liturgical bidding prayers is always that of the priest who turns around and invites the congregation to join him collectively in prayer, not the voice of the congregants themselves.[32] However, in her adaptation, Kempe appropriates that sacerdotal identity for herself as she offers petitions on her own behalf. Almost every petition begins not with the collective plural 'Let us pray' but with 'I cry the mercy, Lord', as she narrows the focus from the amassed body of Christians to her individual needs. She prays for 'alle the statys that ben in Holy Chirche, for the Pope and alle hys cardinalys, for alle erchebischopys and bischopys', but then personalises the request by asking that God 'make me worthy to be partabyl of her preyerys, and hem of myn, and eche of us of otheris' (pp. 423–4). This is not a generic request but a specific, grammatically singular petition that involves a transaction with the clergy – she wants them to be as worthy of her prayers as she is of theirs. While this is consistent with her constant rebuking of errant clergy in the first part of the *Book*, it is still an extraordinary rhetorical move when proposed by a laywoman. In the construction of the prayer she asserts that her authority to convey grace is as relevant and valid as that of the clergy she prays for. She is no longer just praying *for* them; she uses them as a vehicle to request grace for herself. And Salthows and her other amanuenses, by preserving this text, validate Kempe's authority as mediatrix for her fellow Christians, including those who are supposed to be the channel of grace to the laity instead of vice versa.

Kempe adapts the traditional bidding prayer petitions in other ways as well. She gives short shrift to a prayer for the royal family to skip to a petition for 'alle lordys and ladiis that arn in this world' (p. 424). This is not unprecedented; the unidentified bidding prayers in *The Lay Folks Mass Book* request grace for wealthy people who perform acts of charity and the Wyggeston Hospital prayer offers petitions 'for þe lord of þis toune & for þe leuody' and their children, and also for 'alle þo þat honuren þis kirke wit bok or wit belle or any oþir ournament'.[53] One of the bidding prayers preserved in *The Lay Folks Mass Book* asks that all those who donate or pay their tithes be offered 'meid in þe blise of heuen'.[34] But Kempe instead asks God to 'sett [the rich] in sweche governawnce as thei most plesyn <the> and ben lordys and ladys in hevyn wythowtyn ende' (p. 424). Her concern for social precedence, it seems, extends even to the afterlife.

Her next petition, for the souls of Jews, Saracens, and other heathen peoples, moves even further away from conventional bidding prayer contents and perspectives. Whilst bidding prayers can include petitions for the well-being of spiritual pilgrims, Kempe's may be the only vernacular instance of a bidding prayer for non-Christians. Noting that God has the power to 'drawe' anyone to him (in the medieval sense of attracting, enticing, or leading spiritually), Kempe converts this request on behalf of the souls of many others to one particularised to her own situation.[35] Identifying herself as one of the already converted, Kempe prays that God will exert his power on the unredeemed so that 'al this worlde wer worthy to thankyn the for me' (p. 424). Thus, with characteristic self-importance, she switches the focus of her petition from all the unbaptised to her own particular situation, rhetorically subverting the liturgical purpose of the bidding prayer to petition for the well-being of others. She does go on to pray for other categories of sinners and the sick, the Latin rubric's 'et cetera more solito', but adds a request that they be redeemed more speedily *because* of her intercession. She constantly establishes herself as the unit of measure for salvation. When she asks mercy for 'alle my gostly faderys' she adds the tag 'that thu vochesaf to spredyn as mech grace in her sowlys as I wolde that thu dedist in myn' (p. 425). Even when she prays for the souls in purgatory, she personalises the request: 'Be as gracyows to hem as I wolde that thu wer to myn yf it wer in the same peyne that thei arn in' (p. 425), deploying what Watson calls the 'as-if topos' to include her hearers in her devotions.[36] She prays in the same way for *her* friends and enemies, for those who have given *her* charity, and so on, rhetorically placing herself at the centre of Christianity, the figure most in need of prayer and most worthy of the attention of other Christians. In preserving this prayer Salthows and her amanuenses reinforce the persona Kempe has constructed, that of the devout laywoman so familiar with Christ and his promises that she can assert her individual worth as a vehicle of grace.

When Kempe moves beyond her liturgical models, we see her innovations even more markedly. Prayer Seven, which immediately follows the reworked bidding prayer, is noteworthy for its novelty and (using the word advisedly) originality. Syntactically, the prayer consists of a single sentence, but what a sentence it is. It begins with the kind of alliteration, rhythmic cursus, and rhyme seen in *The Lay Folks Prymer* and similar devotional guides:

> I thank the for al helth and al welth,
> for al riches and al poverte,
> for seeknes and alle scornys,
> for alle spitys and alle wrongys,
>   and for alle divers tribulacyons.
>
> (pp. 425–6, layout mine)

This is one of the few places in the sequence (other than Prayer Five) where the syntactic structure lends itself to memorisation or recitation; however, the number of tangled phrases and clauses that follow makes it sound more like the transcript of actual utterances than a carefully designed pious exercise. Kempe may well have thought that this is how vernacular prayer *should* sound, if she had encountered the metrical paraphrases of the liturgy and Hours that were common in late fourteenth and early fifteenth century Middle English prayer, but, if so, this is a kind of cursus that she does not seem to use often. Instead, her sentence enumerates the reasons the she has to thank Christ, deploying the language of mercantilism that Watson noted but that Kempe so rarely uses.[37] She reels off an inventory of natural gifts:

> Dropys of watyr, fres and salt, chesely[s] of gravel, stonys smale and grete, gresys growyng in al erthe, kyrnellys of corn, fischys, fowelys, bestys and leevys upon treys whan most plente ben, fedir of fowle er her of best, seed that growith in erbe, er in wede, in flowyr, in lond, er in watyr whan most growyn. (p. 426)

The rhythm is that of a *copia* or litany, though the contents refer to the mundane, not the sacred.[38] The speaker argues that it would take all of these manifestations of divine creation *plus* souls as pure and effective as the Virgin's to express her gratitude for being spared the 'schenshep of Sathanas' (p. 426) – and even then, they would not be sufficient. The sentiment of an overwhelming debt of gratitude owed to Christ for his mercies is commonplace in medieval prayer, but this kind of enumerative reflection is utterly Kempe's own. The devotional hyperbole is consistent with the language of the *Book*, but the unconventional syntax and format make it unlikely that this was a prayer dictated to Kempe by one of her many spiritual directors. It would be hard to imagine an audience who would read this prayer and try to imitate it – or even less likely to imagine those readers memorising it for their own private meditation. It has the ring of authentic experience, and its preservation by Salthows or Kempe's previous amanuenses conveys a sense of verisimilitude that encourages her readers to engage personally with her spiritual journey toward redemption.

The final prayer in Kempe's collection is for 'alle tho that feithyn and trustyn, er schul feithyn and trustyn, in my prayerys into the worldys ende' (p. 428); her confidence in her own spiritual standing is so strong that she believes that others will turn to her to intercede with Christ for their sins. Whilst a virgin martyr in a saint's life might adopt such a rhetorical stance, as in the prayers associated with the popular legends of the eleven thousand virgins, it is highly unusual in the voice of a layperson and speaks powerfully to the image of holiness and communion with the divine that Kempe, along with Salthows and her other amanuenses, has preserved.[39] In this prayer Kempe presents herself as a way to salvation for her fellow Christians, appropriating sacerdotal authority, and the preservation of her devotions becomes part of that transformation. The sentiments themselves are (mostly) those of conventional prayer, but the expression of them establishes the speaker as someone who has defined her own spiritual role as being equally as effective in intercession as priests are.

The issues we encounter in this complex collection of prayers go far beyond what can be discussed in the scope of this chapter. Clearly, in both content and purpose, the prayers of Margery Kempe have more importance than simply as a pendant to her *Book*. They show a systematic refashioning of the identity of the first-person speaker as someone who knew and wished to promote her authority as an intercessor with Christ on behalf of her fellow Christians, and as a standard against which the proper behaviour of those fellows, especially the clergy, might be measured. This act of pious preservation suggests that Kempe and her immediate supporters were trying to reinforce her orthodoxy, demonstrating her familiarity with the language of the liturgy and approved means of expressing private religious devotion in the vernacular. As well, their efforts document her singularity as a particular and authentic recipient of divine grace. As both a record of spiritual exercises and an attempt to reproduce the actual language of a woman many of whose contemporaries believed was directly blessed by God, this assemblage of prayers deserves much more than liminal status in our ongoing encounters with the complex *Book of Margery Kempe*.

APPENDIX: Incipits of the individual prayers[40]

1. The Holy Gost I take to witnesse (8351–71)
2. And, Lord, for thi hy mercy, alle the teerys (8372–92)
3. And, as anemst any erdly mannys love (8392–6)
4. Lord, make my gostly fadirs for to dredyn the in me (8398–401)
5. Good Jhesu, make my wil thi wyl (8401–2)
6a. Now, good Lord Crist Jhesu, I crye yow mercy (8403–12)
6b. I cry the mercy, blisful Lord, for the Kyng of Inglond (8413–16)
6c. I cry the mercy, Lord, for the riche men in this worlde (8417–19)
6d. I cry the mercy, Lord, for Jewys, and Sarazinys, and alle hethen pepil (8419–32)

6e. I cry the mercy, Lord, for alle fals heretikys and for alle mysbelevarys (8433–7)
6f. I cry the mercy, Lord, for alle tho that arn temptyd and vexid wyth her gostly enmiis (8438–41)
6g. I cry the mercy, Lord, for alle my gostly faderys (8442–4)
6h. I cry the mercy, Lord, for alle my childeryn, gostly and bodily (8445–8)
6i. I cry the mercy, Lord, for alle my frendys (8449–54)
6j. And thei that han seyd any evyl of me, for thi hy mercy, foryefe it hem (8455–9)
6k. I cry the mercy, Lord, for alle the sowlys (8460–4)
7. Lord Crist Jhesu, I thank the for al helth (8465–71)
8. Here my preyeris, for thow I had as many hertys and sowlys (8472–95)
9. I prey my Lady, whech that is only the modyr of God (8496–505)
10. I blisse my God in my sowle (8506–8)
11. And specyaly I blisse the, Lord, for Mary Mawdelyn (8509–15)
12. Have mend, Lord, of the woman that was takyn in the vowtre (8516–21)
13. Have mend, Lord, of Lazer that lay iiii days ded in hys grave (8522–7)
14. Gramercy, Lord, for alle tho synnys that thu hast kept me fro (8528–32)
15. And for alle tho that feithyn and trustyn (8533–6)

Notes

1 Anthony Goodman, *Margery Kempe and Her World* (London: Pearson Education, 2002), p. 6; Naoë Kukita Yoshikawa, *Margery Kempe's Meditations: The Context of Medieval Devotional Literature, Liturgy, and Iconography* (Cardiff: University of Wales Press, 2007), pp. 132–3.

2 Barbara Zimbalist, 'Christ, creature, and reader: verbal devotion in *The Book of Margery Kempe*', *Journal of Medieval Religious Cultures*, 41:1 (2015), 1–23; Nicholas Watson, 'The making of *The Book of Margery Kempe*', in Linda Olson and Kathryn Kerby-Fulton (eds), *Voices in Dialogue: Reading Women in the Middle Ages* (South Bend: University of Notre Dame Press, 2005), pp. 395–434.

3 References to the manuscript of the *Book* are to the digitised manuscript provided by the British Library at www.bl.uk/manuscripts/Viewer.aspx?ref=add_ms_61823_fs001r [accessed 22 July 2020].
4 As I will argue later in this chapter, the prayers should be read as individual units, not one collective 'Great Prayer'. The Appendix to this chapter contains the incipits of the individual prayers, as I read them; they do not always correspond to the paragraphing in Windeatt's edition.
5 For a concise discussion of the inclusion of these prayers in Books of Hours see R. N. Swanson, 'Prayer and participation in late medieval England', *Studies in Church History*, 42 (2006), pp. 130–9.
6 Watson, 'The making of *The Book of Margery Kempe*', p. 413.
7 *The Book of Margery Kempe*, ed. Barry Windeatt (Cambridge: D. S. Brewer, 2004), p. 421. All subsequent quotations from *The Book* refer to this edition by page number.
8 Watson, 'The making of *The Book of Margery Kempe*', p. 396. Laura Varnam argues in 'The importance of St Margaret's church in *The Book of Margery Kempe*: a sacred place and an exemplary parishioner' that the prayers particularly mark her out as an exemplary parishioner at Pentecost, see *Nottingham Medieval Studies*, 61 (2017), 197–243, p. 222.
9 Laurel Amtower, *Engaging Words: The Culture of Reading in the Later Middle Ages* (New York: Palgrave, 2000), p. 28.
10 John B. Friedman, *Northern English Books, Owners and Makers in the Late Middle Ages* (Syracuse: Syracuse University Press, 1995), pp. 11–22.
11 Ibid., pp. 1–11; David N. Bell, *What Nuns Read: Books and Libraries in Medieval English Nunneries* (Kalamazoo: Cistercian Publications, 1995), pp. 17–22.
12 For further details of the connections between Spryngolde, Salthows, and Norfolk see Anthony Bale, 'Richard Salthouse of Norwich and the scribe of *The Book of Margery Kempe*', *Chaucer Review*, 52:2 (2017), 173–87, and Varnam, 'The importance of St Margaret's church', pp. 209–10, 232–4. The question of whether or not Books of Hours were counted as 'paraphernalia', items typically kept in a woman's chamber and therefore hers to bequeath where she wished, has recently been investigated by Cordelia Beattie, 'Married women's wills: Probate, property, and piety in later medieval England', *Law and History Review*, 37:1 (2019), 29–60.
13 Bale, 'Richard Salthouse of Norwich', pp. 182 and 184. Though it is not immediately germane to my argument, Julie A. Chappell has speculated about the motives of the Carthusian community at Mount Grace in the

first two chapters of *Perilous Passages: The Book of Margery Kempe, 1534–1934* (New York: Palgrave Macmillan, 2013).

14 Janette Dillon, 'Holy women and their confessors or confessors and their holy women?' in Rosalynn Voaden (ed.) *Prophets Abroad: The Reception of Continental Holy Women in Late-Medieval England* (Woodbridge: D. S. Brewer, 1996), pp. 115–40, p. 125.

15 The literature on Kempe's self-fashioning is extensive; see for instance Diane Watt, *Medieval Women's Writing: Works by and for Women, 1100–1500* (Cambridge: Polity, 2007), pp. 116–35; Katherine J. Lewis, 'Margery Kempe and saint making in later medieval England', in John H. Arnold and Katherine J. Lewis (eds), *A Companion to The Book of Margery Kempe* (Cambridge: D. S. Brewer, 2004), pp. 195–215; Rebecca Krug, 'Margery Kempe', in Larry Scanlon (ed.), *The Cambridge Companion to Medieval English Literature, 1100–1500* (Cambridge: Cambridge University Press, 2009), pp. 217–28; Rebecca Krug, 'The idea of sanctity and the uncanonised life of Margery Kempe', in Andrew Galloway (ed.), *The Cambridge Companion to Medieval English Culture* (Cambridge: Cambridge University Press, 2011), pp. 129–46; Laura Varnam, 'The crucifix, the pietà, and the female mystic: devotional objects and performative identity in *The Book of Margery Kempe*', *Journal of Medieval Religious Cultures*, 41:2 (2015), 208–37; Varnam, 'The importance of St Margaret's church'; and Chapter 7 below.

16 Josephine Koster (see also J. K. Tarvers), 'The language of prayer in Middle English, 1200–1400: a rhetorical taxonomy' (PhD dissertation, University of North Carolina at Chapel Hill, 1985).

17 Watson, 'The making of *The Book of Margery Kempe*', p. 429, note 17.

18 Sebastian Sobecki, '"The writing of this tretys": Margery Kempe's son and the authorship of her book', *Chaucer Review*, 37 (2015), pp. 257–83. Liz Herbert McAvoy and Naoë Kukita Yoshikawa suggest that Kempe's daughter-in-law may have been responsible for much of the first writing of the *Book*, in Chapter 2 above.

19 Swanson, 'Prayer and participation', p. 133.

20 *The Book of Margery Kempe*, ed. Sanford. B. Meech and Hope Emily Allen, EETS OS 212 (London: Oxford University Press, 1940), p. 349. On Kempe and Pentecost see Varnam, 'The importance of St Margaret's church', p. 222.

21 H. Littlehales, *The Prymer or Lay Folks Mass Book*, EETS OS 105 (London: Kegan Paul, 1895), p. 20.

22 C. Meier-Ewert, 'A Middle English version of the *Fifteen Oes*', *Modern Philology*, 68 (1971), 355–61. See also *The Fifteen Oes* (Westminster: William Caxton, 1491), Bibliographic identifier 20195. In EEBO,

part of Jisc Historic Books, https://data.historicaltexts.jisc.ac.uk/view?pubId=eebo-99836861e&terms=Caxton%20The%20Fifteen%20Oes [accessed 22 July 2020].
23 See Koster (Tarvers), 'The language of prayer in Middle English', chapter 3.
24 Yoshikawa, *Margery Kempe's Meditations*, p. 132.
25 Bale, 'Richard Salthouse of Norwich', p. 184.
26 Watson, 'The making of *The Book of Margery Kempe*', p. 418.
27 Charity Scott-Stokes, *Women's Books of Hours in Medieval England* (Cambridge: D. S. Brewer, 2006), pp. 12–15. On the significance of St Margaret's church to Kempe's devotional life see Varnam, 'The importance of St Margaret's church'.
28 Watson, 'The making of *The Book of Margery Kempe*', p. 418.
29 Susan Powell, 'The transmission and circulation of *The Lay Folks' Catechism*', in A. J. Minnis (ed.), *Late-Medieval Religious Texts and Their Transmission: Essays in Honour of A. I. Doyle* (Woodbridge: D. S. Brewer, 1994), pp. 67–84, p. 67.
30 Richard W. Pfaff, *The Liturgy in Medieval England: A History* (Cambridge: Cambridge University Press, 2012), p. 419.
31 Now Leicestershire Records Office MS 10 D 34, fol. 84r. I am grateful to the Leicestershire Records Office for permission to quote from this unpublished prayer.
32 Cf. Thomas Frederick Simmons (ed.), *The Lay Folks Mass Book: Or the manner of hearing mass, with rubrics and devotions for the people, in four texts, in English according to the use of York, from manuscripts of the Xth to the XVth century*, EETS OS 71 (London: N. Trübner and Co., 1879), pp. 64–80.
33 *Ibid.*, pp. 74 and 76.
34 *Ibid.*, p. 69.
35 *MED* s.v. 'drauen' (v). 2b, 2c.
36 Watson, 'The making of *The Book of Margery Kempe*', p. 421.
37 *Ibid.*, pp. 418–19.
38 Laura Kalas discusses this passage as an example of Kempe's engagement with the natural world in Chapter 11 below.
39 László Sándor Chardonnens and Clarck Drieshen, 'A Middle English version of Saint Ursula's prayer instruction in Nijmegen, Universiteitsbibliotheek, HS 194', *Studies in Philology*, 110:4 (2013), 714–30.
40 Line numbers refer to Windeatt's edition; the division of items does not always coincide with Windeatt's editorial decisions for the placement of paragraphs.

II

Internal encounters

4

The Book of Margery Kempe: autobiography in the third person

Ruth Evans

Encountering the *Book*

In this chapter I focus on one of the *Book*'s most salient features, namely Margery Kempe's systematic use of the third person (including the phrase 'this creatur') to refer to herself.[1] Kempe's closest contemporary, the English anchorite and author Julian of Norwich, whom Kempe visited in or soon after 1413, also refers to herself as a (not 'the') 'creature', but writes her spiritual memoirs in the first person.[2] Why did Kempe – who presents herself as a 'synful caytyf' (p. 41), compelled to tell how she was moved by grace to love God – transpose her narrative entirely into the third person? Although this feature has been much discussed, it has received very little sustained narratological analysis.[3] I draw on Philippe Lejeune's analysis of third-person narration in modern autobiographies to argue that Kempe's use of the third person is a mode of figuration that both inscribes her divided identity and precludes the reader's encounter with a knowable life.[4]

Religious autobiography in the third person (where the author styles themselves as 'the servant of God') is predominantly a later, male-authored genre.[5] The *vitae* of late medieval holy women, such as St Bridget of Sweden (1303–73) and the beguine Marie of Oignies (d. 1213), works that are among the *Book*'s most important intertexts, are written in the third person because they are biographies, written by the women's confessors.[6] However, the female authors of the sister-books (*Schwesternbücher*), a fourteenth-century genre of life-writings in German, Middle Dutch and Latin by Dominican nuns from south Germany and Switzerland, sometimes refer to themselves in the third person. For example, Elsbet Stagel (d. 1360), a friend of Heinrich Suso, from the convent at Töss, in Winterthur, Switzerland, identifies herself in the third person ('The blessed Sister Elsbet Staglin who wrote all this') within the Töss sister-book.[7] The Oetenbach sister-book's use of the third person plural throughout may not be scribal but intended by the nuns as a figure.[8]

Kempe, who did not know how to write, dictated her experiences to two male scribes in succession, probably consulting others as she worked.[9] We do not know if she approved the final text of the *Book*. Although some critics, such as Barry Windeatt, equivocate about whether the use of the third person reflects Kempe's own usage or if it is 'a scribal conversion' from her dictated, first-person account, I agree with Nicholas Watson that it is Kempe's usage. However, I read the effects of this usage very differently.[10] Watson argues that the use of the third person 'does ... much to conventionalize the narrative into something approximating a saint's life', that is, as if written by an authorising other. It is also, he asserts, a way for Kempe to avoid seeming vainglorious: 'There is great pressure on an account that would refuse vanity at the same time as raising its protagonist to such a height, and it seems likely that third-person narration provided Kempe with a means of easing that pressure'.[11] But Watson does not recognise the narratological distinction between the utterance [*énoncé*] and the enunciation [*énonciation*], which calls in question the subject's conscious intention. I argue that the use of the third person as a figure allows Kempe to articulate her selfhood as a tension between identity and difference, unity and division. It also throws into sharp relief what is implicit in all autobiographical texts, namely, to borrow Johannes Wolf's terms, their status as both writing (*graphē*) and the documentary recording of a life (*bios*).[12]

This tension between identity and difference is seen in a passage where Kempe repudiates her early, post-conversion self *as if* to substantiate the judgement of others that she was presumptuous and to convey the distance between her two selves. She imagines herself *as* others might speak about her, or *as if* she were speaking about someone else.[13] The passage contains a rare example of the first person that is not in reported speech: 'of the whech on of the hardest [of those temptations] I purpos to wrytyn for exampyl of hem that com aftyr, that thei schuld not trostyn on her owyn self, ne have no joy in hemself as this creatur had' (p. 66). The surprise intrusion of the first person and the use of the present tense ('I purpos to wrytyn') allows the narrator to distance her present self from her earlier, vainglorious self. It also highlights one of the *Book*'s rhetorical figures, namely the topos of what Vance Smith calls (in another context) 'the intervals of the self', a reference to what Augustine in the *Confessions* describes as 'inter me ipsum et me ipsum' [between myself and myself]: a doubling of identity, which the switch from third to first person and the sequence of tenses vividly bring out.[14]

Most readers accept that Kempe is talking about herself when she writes in the third person because they understand the *Book*'s narrative mode within the horizon of expectations of what Lejeune calls 'the autobiographical pact': the reader's assumption that the author's name, which in modern printed autobiographies usually appears on the title page, is also that of the protagonist and the narrator, and that what is narrated is to be taken in the literal sense.[15] Though the *Book* is clearly more than a set of propositional statements about its historical subject, it cannot conversely be read as 'a pure narrative'.[16]

All autobiography, whether in the first or (rare) third person, inscribes the duality that every speaker bears within them by virtue of being a speaking subject, namely the distinction between the utterance [*énoncé*] and the enunciation [*énonciation*], the *act* of utterance that presupposes a speaker and an addressee, and which is culturally and socially situated.[17] Utterance and enunciation are not the same. Kempe makes statements about herself (*énoncés*), but those statements are largely in the third person (an aspect of their *énonciation*). They constitute an 'attitude of communication'.[18] In the words of Émile Benveniste, 'It is in and through language that man [*sic*] constitutes himself as *subject*, because language alone establishes the concept of "ego" in reality, in its reality which is that of being'.[19] In autobiography the narrator's identity is always doubled, and this doubling is an effect of the distinction between the subject of the utterance and the subject of the enunciation.

As Benveniste's use of 'ego' indicates, the subject in psychoanalysis also derives its foundations from language, although the relation of psychoanalysis to language exceeds that of linguistics, in that the concept of the unconscious posits that the subject is not the origin of meaning nor completely in control of it. In the words of Paul Verhaeghe and Frédéric Declercq 'the subject is not a decision-making instance, but an ever-failing realization of one's identity'.[20] For Jacques Lacan the subject is always 'caught up in a constituting division'.[21] All speaking subjects are alienated from themselves, divided by the bar between the conscious and the unconscious, which is an effect of the signifier.[22] But the unconscious is also the big Other of language and culture. When the subject speaks, its subjectivity is constituted in and through the symbolic order: what Lacan describes as 'concrete discourse qua field of the subject's transindividual reality', the operations of which 'are those of history, insofar as history constitutes the emergence of truth in reality (réel)'.[23] Since the subject's act of addressing assumes an addressee, the subject also constitutes themself intersubjectively. Kempe's situation in history and her awareness of her interlocutors determine, consciously or unconsciously, her choice of third person and her self-naming as 'this creature'.

I argue that our encounter with the *Book*'s historical author is mediated through the *Book*'s tropological substitution of third for first person, and that this substitution not only reveals the split that makes possible the functioning of the subject but also denies the possibility of totalising accounts of the *Book* as either *bios* or *graphē*.[24] The figure of the third person is an effect of language, and we can analyse its effects without positing unconscious motivations. This linguistic splitting or doubling is not evidence of an underlying mental pathology in Kempe, but rather reveals the *Book*'s 'constituting division' as both a life *and* a writing.

The third person as a play of figures

Kempe's self-styling as 'this creatur' and her choice of third-person narration are often conflated by critics, but they are two distinct figures of speech. Kempe never calls herself 'Margery Kempe' or 'Margery', but rather 'sche' or 'this creatur', or variants of the latter, including 'the (for)sayd creatur' and 'the creatur'. She is identified only once within the text, as 'Mar. Kempe of Lynne' (p. 415), although she is called 'Margery' sixteen times in reported speech.[25] 'Creatur' means 'created thing', as opposed to the Creator, or simply 'person' (the person that is the subject of this text), as in the opening of Chapter 1: 'Whan this creatur was xx yer of age or sumdele mor, sche was maryed to a worschepful burgeys and was wyth chylde wythin schort tyme, as kynde wolde' (p. 52).[26] The deictic 'this' in 'this creatur' introduces a third figure, which is also often overlooked in readings of the *Book*. As far as possible I will deal separately with these figures.

As Lejeune observes, systematic use of the third person is rare in modern autobiographies because the only clues that impose an autobiographical reading are paratextual, and the reader of a long text is apt to forget the genre. Most instances of third person are used in 'a contrastive and local manner', but in the *Book* there is such minimal contrast with the first person that most readers are not conscious of it as a figure.[27] Third person is the *Book*'s default mode. Since there is no genre of autobiographical writing in the fifteenth century, Kempe is not violating its conventions. However, the contrast between her practice and that of other female spiritual writers, such as Julian, is striking, and demands closer attention.

When a writer switches from the first to the third person, provided the reader accepts 'the autobiographical pact', a third-person utterance does not make a simple statement about a character, as in a novel, but functions (Lejeune's words):

> Like a *figure of enunciation* within a text that we continue to read as discourse in the first person. The author talks about [herself] *as if* it were someone else who was talking about [her], or as if [she] were talking about someone else [but this] *as if* concerns enunciation alone: utterance continues to be subjected to the strict and proper rules of the autobiographical contract.[28]

This perception of the erasing of the enunciation is perceived as a fact of enunciation, what Lejeune describes as 'an unnatural ellipse of the enunciation', one that gives 'contrast and tension to the [autobiographical] text'.[29]

The use of the third person as a figure for 'I' is not, Lejeune observes, an 'indirect' manner of talking about the self, but rather 'another way of achieving, in the form of a *splitting*, what the first person achieves in the form of a *confusion*: the inescapable duality of the grammatical "person". Saying "I" is more customary ... than saying ["she"] when one talks about [oneself], but it is not simple.'[30]

'I' is no less a figure than the third person. All autobiography is indirect. The subject of the statement (Kempe qua historical subject) is divided from the subject of the enunciation ('this creatur'), and this would be true whichever grammatical person were used (I or she). This division entails, in the words of Lejeune, that every speaking subject, even when using 'I', 'rests fundamentally on a *split* [or] rather ... functions thanks to this split'.[31] As Paul de Man argues, the interest of autobiography 'is not that it reveals reliable self-knowledge – it does not – but that it demonstrates the impossibility of closure and of totalization ... of all textual systems made up of tropological substitutions'.[32] Although the *Book* does not exactly make a game of the tension between the autobiographical contract and its use of the third person (since autobiography as we know it today does not yet exist as a genre in the early fifteenth century), Kempe's practice, in the enunciation, of vacating the place of the 'I' and occupying the place of the third person, while keeping the 'I' of the statement at the forefront of the reader's mind (through dialogue and other forms of self-reference), foregrounds Kempe's split subjectivity and thus the impossibility of fixing the identity of the *Book*.

I return to the passage I quoted from above to consider this doubling in more detail:

> The fyrst ii yer whan this creatur was thus drawyn to owyr Lord, sche had gret qwiete of spyryt as for ony temptacyons. Sche myght wel dure to fastyn, it greved hir not. Sche hatyd the joys of the world. Sche felt no rebellyon in hyr flesch. Sche was strong, as hir thowt, that sche dred no devylle in helle, for sche dede so gret bodyly penawce. Sche thowt that sche lovyd God mor than he hir. Sche was smet with the dedly wownd of veynglory and felt it not, for sche desyryd many tymes that the crucifix schuld losyn hys handys fro the crosse and halsyn hir in tokyn of lofe. Ower mercyful Lord Crist Jhesu, seyng this creaturys presumpcyon, sent hir, as is wrete befor, iii yer of greet temptacyon, of the whech on of the hardest I purpos to wrytyn for exampyl of hem that com aftyr, that thei schuld not trostyn on her owyn self, ne have no joy in hemself as this creatur had. (p. 66)

This narrative is punctuated by anaphoric statements – 'sche hated', 'sche felt', 'sche was' – that look like reported speech, but are not. Kempe is talking about herself *as if* another were talking about her. These third-person statements are in free indirect style: 'Sche myght wel dure to fastyn, it greved hir not' is something Kempe might have said conversationally about her earlier self. The interpolation 'as hir thowt' implies self-criticism, but when repeated in the sentence that follows – '[s]che thowt that sche lovyd God mor than he hir' – it contradictorily suggests a criticism of God for not loving her enough. The play of figures has the effect of interposing another narrator between Kempe and the reader, not the second scribe translating Kempe's words for the reader, but Kempe ironically dissociating herself from who she was and marking the intervals of the self (*inter me ipsum et me ipsum*).

While Kempe speaks as 'I' in the *Book*'s many passages of dialogue, direct speech paradoxically offers further opportunities for third-person narration as a play of figures, as in the following passage, when Kempe is arrested by Bedford's men on suspicion of being a Lollard and brought before the Archbishop of York, who questions her about what she had said to Lady Westmorland, whose daughter, Lady Greystoke, she had supposedly counselled to leave her husband:

> 'My Lord, ... I saw not my Lady Westmorlond this too yer and mor. Sir, sche sent for me er I went to Jerusalem and ... I wyl gon ageyn to hir for recorde that I mevyd no sweche mater.'
> 'Nay,' seyde thei that stodyn abowtyn, 'late hir be putte in preson, and we schal sendyn a lettyr to the worshepful Lady, and yyf it be trewth that sche seyth, late hir go qwite wythowtyn dawnger.' (p. 266)

Where Kempe uses 'I' in direct speech, her onlookers' response, also in direct speech, of course refers to her in the third person. The effect is to merge Kempe's customary mode of narration with that of hostile outsiders. By continuing the dialogue rather than translating their response into reported speech ('they said that I should be put in prison ...'), Kempe achieves distancing, so that she simultaneously performs as herself in the first person and talks about herself as if she were a spectator of that performance, dramatising the tension – present throughout the *Book* – between identity and difference that makes the speaking subject fugitive. Moreover, in both passages of dialogue and third-person narration an alternative text – in the first person – haunts the narrative, making it bilingual.[33] The *Book* never speaks with a single voice.

Third-person narration allows Kempe to distance herself from others' discourse about her as a form of protection, self-irony and self-authorisation,[34] as in this catalogue of the varied reactions to her bellowing:

> For summe seyd it was a wikkyd spirit vexid hir; sum seyd it was a sekenes; sum seyd sche had dronkyn to mech wyn; sum bannyd hir; sum wisshed sche had ben in the havyn; sum wolde sche had ben in the se in a bottumles boyt; and so ich man as hym thowte. ... Sum gret clerkys seyden owyr Lady cryed nevyr so, ne no seynt in hevyn, but thei knewyn ful lytyl what sche felt, ne thei wolde not belevyn but that sche myth an absteynd hir fro crying yf sche had wold. (p. 165)

Kempe understands very well her fellow Christians' scepticism, which is based in the big Other of the sceptical procedures of canonisation and attitudes to miraculous phenomena.[35] At stake is the issue not of 'belief' in miracles but of discernment of spirits: is the origin of her bellowing natural or supernatural? But third-person narration allows Kempe to assume an authority for her unshakeable trust in 'what sche felt', another of the *Book*'s key tropes. The distancing produced by the sarcastic use of anaphora – 'summe seyd ... sum seyd ... sum seyd' – and by free indirect discourse to mime the voices of those deriding her behaviour further expresses the irresolvable tension between the view of Kempe as a person who consciously sought to deceive others by pretending to bellow so as to achieve an authority that would put her on a par with female saints, and of Kempe as a person whose bellowing is unconsciously produced.

'This creatur': on not being the cause of oneself

A second distinctive feature of the *Book*'s third-person narration is Kempe's systematic reference to herself as 'this creatur'. It's important to recognise that this is her self-appellation, not the scribe's. For Watson 'this creatur' is almost certainly *not* the priest scribe's phrase but Kempe's, a phrase that in his view allows her to achieve a balance between the desire to be recognised as saintly and the desire for humility.[36] 'Creature', meaning 'created thing (as distinct from the Creator); person', is of course common in late medieval English and Continental women's writing. In her book *Das fließende Licht der Gottheit* [*The Flowing Light of the Godhead*], the thirteenth-century

German writer Mechthild of Magdeburg uses 'creature(s)' generally for 'person(s) created by God' and specifically for herself: 'I, sinful, lazy creature', 'I, unworthy creature', not as a third-person locution but in apposition to the first person, although once she imagines the soul of God addressing her as 'the pitiful creature'.[37] The French beguine and mystic Marguerite Porete also uses 'creature(s)' for 'person(s) created by God', though never specifically for herself.[38]

It seems likely, however, that Kempe borrowed 'creatur' from the English anchorite and author Julian of Norwich, whom she visited in or soon after 1413, some three years before Julian died (1416).[39] Although Kempe does not seem to have known Julian's writings, Julian may have conveyed to Kempe the importance that she attached to 'creature'. In *A Vision Showed to a Devout Woman* (c. 1385) Julian refers to herself as 'a sinfulle creature' (*Vis.* 3.17) and as 'the wrechid, sinfulle creature' (*Vis.* 6.4), and she uses 'creature(s)' seventy times in the later *A Revelation of Love* (c. 1393–1415), for herself and for other persons.[40] In the rubric of the *Vision* Julian introduces herself as 'a devoute woman' (*Vis.* Rubric, 1), but in *A Revelation* she changes this to 'a simple creature unletterde' (*Rev.* 2.1). Watson and Jenkins argue that the term 'creature' is for Julian more than 'a gesture of modesty'. It shows her awareness that in visionary writings – *Piers Plowman* is an example – it is those individuals that are 'helpless in their untutored createdness, not the educated, who experience visions', and the switch she makes from 'a devoute woman' to 'a simple creature unletterde' declares that she speaks not as a gendered subject but as a representative of everyone.[41] Kempe's use of 'creatur' is also gender-neutral, as Catherine Akel notes, in accordance with the widespread medieval belief that 'men and women are spiritually equal in God's sight'.[42]

Although Kempe may have borrowed 'creatur' from Julian because of its use in visionary writing and its gender neutrality, their practices are markedly dissimilar.[43] Julian consistently writes in the first person, and never calls herself 'this creature' or 'the creature'. Articles and demonstratives are significant. In their introduction Watson and Jenkins refer to Julian repeatedly as 'the creature' to emphasise that she sees herself as a 'creature' rather than an 'interpreter', but it would be more accurate to say that Julian sees herself as 'a creature'. Despite two uses of 'creatur' in the *Book* to mean 'person', it is notable that Kempe does not refer to any other individual in the narrative as a 'creatur'. It is a phrase she reserves uniquely for herself. Unlike Julian, Kempe does not ever modify 'creatur' with an adjective that would indicate her attitude towards it. We know only that it carries special weight for Kempe in her project of self-creation as poesis.

One of the most striking moments of that project of self-begetting is Kempe's *imitatio Christi* at Calvary, when she simultaneously becomes the suffering Christ and gives birth to him (pp. 162–6). The episode also marks the onset of her bellowing, as if Kempe were giving birth to herself. In the *De Trinitate* (c. 400–17 CE) his meditation on the nature of the Creator, Augustine observes that:

> Those who suppose that God is of such power that he actually begets himself, are if anything even more wrong [than those who claim they know God's nature], since not only is God not like that, but neither is anything in the world of body and spirit. There is absolutely no thing whatsoever that brings itself into existence.[44]

In a comment on this passage Lacan notes that no one can assume their 'own causality', not because 'I am the creature' (that is, I can't assume my causality because God created me), but because not even the Creator can give birth to himself.[45] Ever the provocateur, Lacan reads Augustine as if he were a Lacanian *avant la lettre*, as if he were saying that no one, not even God, can bring themselves into being because we are not in control of our own creation as subjects, divided as we are by the bar between the conscious and the unconscious, which is an effect of language. It is probable that Kempe did not know the *De Trinitate*, but she is part of a religious culture that recognises the limitations of self-poesis. Figuring herself in the third person as 'this creatur' may have provided her with a way of saying '*I* am not the creature', that is, I do not assume my own causality.

'This creatur': deixis

Kempe's third, third-person figure is the deictic 'this' in 'this creatur'. In pragmatics, deictics are words such as *this, that, I, you, now, then, here, today* that do not have a constant meaning but depend for their meaning on the time, place or situation in which a speaker

Autobiography in the third person

is speaking (or writing), and which are to be interpreted from the position of the speaker.[46] Their referent is provided not by semantic conditions but by context: situational positioning. In a statement such as 'I am going there tomorrow', the meanings of 'I', 'there' and 'tomorrow' depend on the listener knowing the context that explains who the 'I' is, where 'there' is and what day of the week it is when the speaker is speaking in order to understand what day 'tomorrow' refers to. Yet the category of deictics (also called indexicals by linguists and philosophers of language) – words whose meaning is context-dependent – is far from straightforward.

The descriptive content of the *Book*'s repeated phrase 'this creatur' is not sufficient to identify Kempe as the referent. The reader has to resolve the semantic deficiency by mapping the context, drawing on the notion of the 'autobiographical pact' and on the idea of the speaker/narrator as *origo*. The demonstrative 'this' often functions as a proximal deictic, indicating closeness to the speaker, as opposed to 'that', a distal deictic, indicating distance from the speaker.[47] But 'this creatur' is never contrasted with 'that creatur', revealing the extent to which the narrative sees events from Kempe's point of view and not that of her scribes or her audience. In the *Book* 'this creatur' is not only a spatial but a temporal deictic, and it is both intra- and extra-diegetic. It refers to Kempe, as author and narrator, and to herself as the subject of her text, either within an immediately preceding portion of discourse (it is backward-pointing), or in the here and now (from her perspective) of the *Book*'s dictation.[48] It means 'the person I was just speaking about, i.e. I/me', as is implied by the occasional use of analogous phrases such as 'The beforn-seyd creatur' (p. 119) or 'the forseyd creatur' (p. 215), or it means 'the person that is the subject of the episode I'm now recounting, i.e. I/me', as in 'this creatur went owt of hir mende' (p. 54).

Although the *Book* prefers the demonstrative 'this' in collocation with 'creatur', the definite article is also used deictically to refer to Kempe: 'the creature was stabelyd in hir wyttys' (p. 56); 'The creatur seyd …' (p. 143); 'the creatur of whom this boke is wretyn' (p. 143); 'whan the creatur was in cherche …' (p. 382). In these examples the whole expression 'the creatur' functions deictically. 'This' is used in the *Book* with other referents beside 'creatur': 'a prest was sor mevyd for to wrytin this tretys' (p. 51); 'The prest whech wrot this boke' (p. 141); 'this holy woman [Kempe's 'specyal frende']'

(p. 140); 'this preste' (p. 186); 'this good man' (p. 187). Although all of these are discourse-specific, none presents any problems of interpretation. 'This' means 'the treatise / book / holy woman / priest / man' that has just been mentioned.

'Creatur' also refers to a set of historical, context-independent meanings, which I discussed above, namely, a person created by God, or that class of devotional writers that are (in Watson and Jenkins's words) 'helpless in their untutored createdness'.[49] At times the indexical meaning of 'this creatur' is folded into its symbolic meaning, that is, the phrase does not only point to Kempe as the subject of the narrative but designates a class of beings, under all of which Kempe might be subsumed: persons created by God, simple and untutored writers of devotional literature, textual subjects. For example, consider the following passage:

> The prest whech wrot this boke, for to prevyn this creaturys felyngys, many tymes and dyvers tymes he askyd hir qwestyons and demawndys of thyngys that wer for to komyn – unsekyr and uncerteyn as that tyme to any creatur what schuld be the ende … (p. 141)

The phrase 'this creaturys felyngys' refers to Kempe's feelings, but the priest's aside – 'unsekyr and uncerteyn as that tyme to any creatur what shuld be the ende' – places Kempe as 'creatur' within a general class of creatures (persons), of which she is nevertheless exceptional, because she can see into the future where others cannot. Although there are times when one could substitute 'Margery Kempe' for 'this creatur', the context-bound, intentional, attentional and subjective aspects of 'this creatur' cannot be reduced to a proposition about Kempe ('Margery Kempe is this creature') without bypassing the psychological reality of this self-naming to Kempe. Similarly, the deictic phrase 'hys creatur whych had forsakyn him' (p. 55) cannot be reduced to a simple proposition: 'his [Christ's] Kempe that had forsaken him'. As Levinson explains, 'Indexical reference … introduces complexities into the relation between semantics and cognition – that is, between, on the one hand, what sentences mean and what we mean when we say them and, on the other hand, the corresponding thoughts they express.'[50] The hybridisation that results from the folding of indexical into symbolic meaning can be understood in terms of the split subject of linguistics (that is, the subject is divided between the subject of the utterance and the subject of the enunciation) and of psychoanalysis (divided by the bar between the conscious and the unconscious, which is an effect of the signifier), and the ultimately undecidable nature of the *Book*, which presents itself as both the documentary recording of a life and a mode of figuration, or play of figures (faces, personae), which I locate in its systematic third-person narration. The gestural use of 'this' in 'this creatur' insists on the autobiographical nature of the narrative (I am pointing at myself, a living person, situated in time and space), whereas the symbolic use of 'this creatur' (the author, persons, untutored persons) insists on the text as writing, that is, the text exceeds its deictic, context-bound, autobiographical reference.

Conclusion

I have argued that the *Book*'s third-person narration is a play of figures that puts on display the mechanisms by which Kempe's self is represented in discourse, and which thwarts attempts to read the *Book* autobiographically. My voice is never uniquely mine. Yet we cannot *not* read the *Book* autobiographically. Lejeune emphasises the indirect character of all autobiography. Kempe's third-person narration draws particular attention to that indirectness. The reader never encounters directly the self that is talking about itself. That encounter is always mediated. The use of third person throughout the *Book* produces an effect of 'unvoicing' and 'stepping back' that foregrounds its mode of figuration and invites our attention to the complexity of effects that are produced through that game of figures: distancing (above all), irony, self-criticism and the miming of the discourse of others as a way either to substantiate or to ward off criticism.[51] However, whilst Kempe's near-ubiquitous use of the third person often locates her as a shrewd observer of herself, it may also suggest that there is no place in her culture – in late medieval, female, devotional culture – from which she can speak as an I. As I have also argued, if the *Book*'s rhetorical practices delineate an impasse between autobiography and writing that is replicated in the polarised critical responses to the *Book*, its failure to move beyond that impasse is nevertheless highly productive in its insistence on the *Book*'s 'constituting division' as both a life and a writing.[52]

Notes

I would like to thank Christina Hildebrandt for conversations about the *Book*, this volume's editors Laura Kalas and Laura Varnam for their support, and Johannes Wolf for his generosity in exchanging ideas as we developed our contributions.

1 *The Book of Margery Kempe*, ed. Barry Windeatt (Cambridge: D. S. Brewer, 2004). References to the *Book* are to page numbers. There are only four instances in the *Book* where the text uses 'I' in direct narration (there are of course many in direct speech): when the first scribe comes to England, 'meved, I trost, thorw the Holy Gost' (p. 47); when Christ sends Kempe great temptations for three years, 'of the whech on of the hardest I purpos to wrytyn …' (p. 66); after the anchorite in Lynn prophesies that Kempe will be helped on her pilgrimage to Jerusalem: 'so it befel as the ankyr had prophecyed in every poynt, and, as I trust, schal be wretyn more pleynly aftyrward' (p. 124); and lastly when the text comments on Kempe's praise of God: 'Wyth swech maner of thowtys, and many mo than I cowde evyr writyn, sche worschepyd and magnifyed owr Lord Jhesu Crist' (p. 377). It is not clear why Kempe uses 'I' at these moments. The first person plural is used once, when, after receiving the command from Christ that she henceforth dress herself in white clothes, Kempe is commanded to visit the bishop of Lincoln, and after he has made her bring her husband John before him to give consent to her taking of the mantle, the ring, and the white clothes, 'the Bysshop dede no mor to us at that day, save he mad us rygth good cher and seyd we wer rygth wolcome' (p. 106). Here Kempe, uncharacteristically, thinks of herself and her husband as a couple.

2 On the date of Kempe's visit to Julian see Nicholas Watson and Jacqueline Jenkins (eds), *The Writings of Julian of Norwich:* A Vision Showed to a Devout Woman *and* A Revelation of Love (University Park: Penn State University Press, 2006), p. 6. Subsequent in-text quotations from Julian's 'Vision' and 'Revelation' refer to this edition by chapter and line number.

3 Felicity Riddy and Ruth Evans use the work of Émile Benveniste and Philippe Lejeune, but do not deal at length with the *Book*'s third-person narration; see Riddy, 'Text and self in *The Book of Margery Kempe*', in Linda Olson and Kathryn Kerby-Fulton (eds), *Voices in Dialogue: Reading Women in the Middle Ages* (Notre Dame: University of Notre Dame Press, 2005), pp. 439–43; 'Afterwords' in Olson and Kerby-Fulton, *Voices in Dialogue*, pp. 456–7; and Evans, '*The Book of Margery Kempe*', in Peter Brown (ed.), *A Companion to Medieval English Literature and Culture, c.1350–c.1500* (Oxford: Blackwell, 2007), pp. 507–21.

4 Philippe Lejeune, 'Autobiography in the third person', in *On Autobiography*, ed. Paul John Eakin, trans. Katherine Leary (Minneapolis: University of Minnesota Press, 1989), pp. 31–51.
5 On the use of third person in religious autobiography as a development of monastic convention see Richard John Lawes, 'Accounts of intense religious experience in autobiographical texts by English Catholics 1430–1645, and in the writings of George Herbert' (DPhil thesis, University of Oxford, 2001), p. 175. Hope Emily Allen speculates that Kempe may have been influenced by German religious autobiographies, such as that by the Dominican friar Henry Suso (1295–1366), who writes his *vita* in the third person and who styles himself the 'Servant [of God]': see 'Prefatory note', *The Book of Margery Kempe*, ed. Sanford Brown Meech and Hope Emily Allen, EETS OS 212 (London: Oxford University Press, 1940), pp. liii–lxviii, pp. liv–lvi. For Suso in England see R. Lovatt, 'Henry Suso and the medieval mystical tradition', in Marion Glasscoe (ed.), *The Medieval Mystical Tradition in England: Papers Read at Dartington Hall, July, 1982* (Exeter: University of Exeter Press, 1982), pp. 47–62.
6 Birgitta of Sweden, *Life and Selected Revelations*, ed. Marguerite Tjader Harris, trans. Albert Ryle Kezel, intro. Tore Nyberg (New York: Paulist Press, 1990); Jacques de Vitry, *The Life of Marie d'Oignies*, trans. Margot H. King (Toronto: Peregrina, 1989).
7 See Gertrud Jaron Lewis, *By Women, for Women, about Women: The Sister-Books of Fourteenth-Century Germany* (Toronto: Pontifical Institute of Mediaeval Studies, 1996), p. 24. There is no evidence that Kempe knew the sister-books, but on her possible knowledge of a Middle Dutch sister-book see the notice on Godelinde Perk's homepage of a forthcoming essay 'From riches to rags: conversion narratives and mnemonic strategies in *The Book of Margery Kempe* and the sisterbook of Diepenveen': www.mod-langs.ox.ac.uk/people/godelinde-gertrude-perk [accessed 21 July 2020].
8 Lewis, *By Women, for Women*, p. 27.
9 On the collaborative nature of the *Book*'s authorship see Anthony Bale, *The Book of Margery Kempe: A New Translation* (Oxford: Oxford University Press, 2015), pp. xvii–xx.
10 Windeatt, *Book*, p. 42. Nicholas Watson, 'The making of *The Book of Margery Kempe*', in Olson and Kerby-Fulton, *Voices in Dialogue*, pp. 395–434, pp. 400–5.
11 Watson, 'The making of *The Book of Margery Kempe*', pp. 402 and 403. Riddy disagrees with the first proposition, see 'Text and self', pp. 435–53, p. 441.
12 Johannes Wolf, Chapter 5 below.

13 Watson draws attention to the *Book*'s frequent reliance on simile, 'on the tags "as" and "as if"', but does not link this topos to the *Book*'s use of third-person narration, see 'The making of *The Book of Margery Kempe*', pp. 419–21.
14 D. Vance Smith, 'Irregular histories: forgetting ourselves', *New Literary History*, 28:2 (1997), 161–84, p. 165. The phrase occurs in Book X of the *Confessions* in which St Augustine discusses how the habits of his past life produce 'deceptive sights' in his sleep that convince him 'to do what the real ones can't' while he's awake, and questions where his real self resides: 'Could I really not be myself at such times …? Yet there's so much difference between the two selves [*inter me ipsum et me ipsum*] from the moment I pass from here into sleep or pass back from there to here.' See Augustine, *Confessions*, trans. Sarah Ruden (London: Penguin, 2018), p. 315.
15 Lejeune, 'The autobiographical pact', p. 12. For critiques of 'the autobiographical pact' see Paul de Man, 'Autobiography as de-facement', *Modern Language Notes*, 94:5 (1979), 919–30, p. 922, and Lejeune, 'The autobiographical pact (bis)', *On autobiography*, pp. 119–37, and 'Le pacte autobiographique, vingt-cinq ans après', *Signes de vie* (Paris: Seuil, 2005), pp. 11–35. In *Margery Kempe's Dissenting Fictions* (University Park: Pennsylvania State University Press, 1994), Lynn Staley challenges the view that there is 'an absolute equation between the *Book*'s author and its subject' (p. 3), but her emphasis on Kempe's self-conscious rhetorical strategies does not fundamentally undo the assumption that a knowable life precedes and informs the writing.
16 Lejeune, 'Autobiography in the third person', pp. 31–51, p. 42.
17 For the terminology see Émile Benveniste, *Problems in General Linguistics*, trans. Mary Elizabeth Meek (Coral Gables: University of Miami Press, 1971), and Sophie Marnette, *Speech and Thought Presentation in French: Concepts and Strategies* (Amsterdam: John Benjamins, 2005), pp. 19–38. Charles Bally makes a similar distinction between '*dictum*' (the propositional content of an utterance) and '*modus*' (the attitude of the speaker towards the *dictum*), see *Linguistique générale et linguistique française* (Berne: Francke, 1932), pp. 35–6.
18 Lejeune, 'Autobiography in the third person', p. 32.
19 Benveniste, *Problems*, p. 224.
20 Paul Verhaeghe and Frédéric Declercq, 'Lacan's analytical goal: "Le Sinthome" or the feminine way', in Luke Thurston (ed.), *Re-Inventing the Symptom: Essays on the Final Lacan* (New York: The Other Press, 2002), pp. 59–83, p. 63.
21 Jacques Lacan, 'Science and truth', in *Écrits*, trans. Bruce Fink (New York: Norton, 2006), pp. 726–45, p. 727.

22 Jacques Lacan, 'The function and field of speech and language in psychoanalysis' (1953), in *Écrits*, pp. 197–268, p. 242.
23 Lacan, 'Function and field', p. 214.
24 See Wolf, 'Margery Kempe as de-facement', Chapter 5 below.
25 See Janet Cowen, 'Naming and shaming in *The Book of Margery Kempe*', in Jane Roberts and Jinty Nelson (eds), *Essays on Anglo-Saxon and Related Themes in Memory of Lynne Grundy* (London: King's College Centre for Late Antique and Medieval Studies, 2000), pp. 157–79, pp. 165 and 171.
26 See *MED* s.v. 'creature' (n.), 1 (a) and 2.
27 Lejeune, 'Autobiography in the third person', p. 42.
28 *Ibid.*, p. 32.
29 *Ibid.*, p. 33.
30 *Ibid.*, p. 33.
31 *Ibid.*, p. 34.
32 De Man, 'Autobiography as de-facement', p. 922.
33 Lejeune, 'Autobiography in the third person', trans. Annette Tomarken and Edward Tomarken, *New Literary History*, 9:1 (1977), 27–50, p. 36. This is an earlier version of the 1989 chapter with the same name.
34 Lejeune, 'Autobiography in the third person', in Eakin (ed.), *On Autobiography*, p. 40.
35 Steven Justice, 'Did the Middle Ages believe in their miracles?', *Representations*, 103:1 (2008), 1–29, p. 6.
36 Watson 'The making of *The Book of Margery Kempe*', pp. 401–5.
37 See Mechthild von Magdeburg, *Das fließende Licht der Gottheit, Nach der Einsiedler Handschrift in kritischem Vergleich mit der gesamten Überlieferung*, 2 vols, ed. Hans Neumann with Gisela Vollmann-Profe (Munich: Artemis, 1990/1993). Translation: Mechthild of Magdeburg, *The Flowing Light of the Godhead*, trans. Frank J. Tobin (New York: Paulist Press, 1998), pp. 77, 166, 245.
38 Marguerite Porete, *Le mirouer des simples ames: Speculum simplicium animarum, Corpus Christianorum: Continuatio Mediaeualis* vol. 69, ed. Romana Guarnieri (Turnhout: Brepols, 1986); Marguerite Porete, *The Mirror of Simple Souls*, trans. E. L. Babinsky (Mahwah: Paulist Press, 1993), e.g., p. 175.
39 I owe this suggestion to Nicholas Watson.
40 Watson and Jenkins (eds), *The Writings of Julian of Norwich*, pp. 69, 73, and 124. In *A Vision* there is a third instance of 'creature' for a person: a reference to Mary as a 'simpille creature' (p. 71). On the dating of Julian's texts see Nicholas Watson, 'The composition of Julian of Norwich's *Revelation of Love*', *Speculum*, 68:3 (1993), 637–83.
41 Watson and Jenkins (eds), *The Writings of Julian of Norwich*, pp. 7–8.

42 Catherine S. Akel, 'Familial structure in the religious relationships and visionary experiences of Margery Kempe', *Studia Mystica*, 16 (1995), 116–32, p. 116. However, I disagree with Akel's argument that Kempe's 'references to herself move from the objectified, gender-neutral, spiritual "creatur" to the subjectified and subordinated reality of "dowtyr," "wyf," and "modyr"', roles that are 'are strictly regulated by male kinship ties' (p. 116).

43 On Julian's use of 'creature' to indicate spiritual modesty, see *Rev.* 6.42–5: 'For oure soule is so presciously loved of him that is highest, that it overpasseth the knowing of alle creatures: that is to say, there is no creature that is made that may wit how mekille and how swetely and how tenderly oure maker loveth us.'

44 Augustine, *De Trinitate*, 1.1: *The Trinity*, in *Works of Saint Augustine: A Translation for the 21st Century*, trans. Edmund Hill, ed. John E. Rotelle, vol. 5, 2nd edition (Hyde Park, NY: New City Press, 1991).

45 Lacan, 'Science and truth', p. 734.

46 Stephen C. Levinson, 'Deixis', in Laurence R. Horn and Gregory Ward (eds), *Handbook of Pragmatics* (Oxford: Blackwell, 2004), pp. 97–121. For Levinson deixis is generally organised 'in an egocentric way', with the 'deictic centre' of an utterance anchored in the speaker as the central person, the time at which the speaker produces the utterance as the central time, the speaker's location at utterance time as the central location, the discourse centre and the social centre, see Stephen C. Levinson, *Pragmatics* (Cambridge: Cambridge University Press, 1983), p. 64.

47 But deixis does not always involve space or proximity (see Levinson).

48 Its use to refer to the subject of the text is common enough in Chaucer, see A. C. Spearing, *Textual Subjectivity: The Encoding of Subjectivity in Medieval Narratives and Lyrics* (Oxford: Oxford University Press, 2005), p. 127.

49 Watson and Jenkins (eds), *The Writings of Julian of Norwich*, p. 7.

50 Levinson, 'Deixis', p. 99.

51 Lejeune, 'Autobiography in the third person', in Eakin (ed.), *On Autobiography*, p. 39.

52 See, for example, Watson, 'The making of *The Book of Margery Kempe*' and Riddy, 'Text and self'.

5

Margery Kempe as de-facement

Johannes Wolf

We are given the new creature before the old.[1]

This *Book* weighs 630 grams.[2] It sits heavily in one hand as I hold it, the plastic cover retaining a welcome coolness in the July weather. Its front cover is striking, dominated by blocks of orange and black. Large black lettering informs me that this is *The Book of Margery Kempe*. Immediately below these words is an image of a medieval woman – colouring and profile indicate this is a reproduction from stained glass. Long orange hair tumbles down over her shoulders and her head is framed by a halo. Her eyes are directed downwards at a carefully measured angle; her right hand extends from crossed arms to form a blessing. Plunging from the top right-hand corner are a series of arrow-like rays signifying divine inspiration accompanied by the dove of the Holy Ghost. She is a holy woman, a visionary, touched by grace. She is not, however, Margery Kempe.

This is not particularly surprising – few representations of Middle English authors produced by their contemporaries have made it down to us. Indeed, the picture has been rather well-chosen; drawn from All Saints, the parish church of the Norfolk village Bale, some thirty miles east of Kempe's hometown of King's (then Bishop's) Lynn, it is fifteenth-century and therefore roughly contemporaneous with Kempe. It also speaks to the particular East Anglian context that produced and enabled her journeys and visions, where booming wool industries and active trade with the continent enriched an ascendant mercantile class whose spiritual ambitions are still visible in the 'wool churches' that dot the countryside of counties rendered destitute in the intervening centuries.³ A fitting decision, certainly; but not one accomplished without some (however unavoidable) slippage, some movement, some translation. An edition printed in the twenty-first century; a fifteenth-century stained glass window in Bale; and, most importantly, a name. What are we to make of this encounter?

Most straightforwardly, we should think harder about articles. This is *a* book of *the* text we call the *Book of Margery Kempe*. There are many others; editions and translations proliferate. Where, amongst all these instances of *a* book, is *the* book? If the *Book* is an identifiable object, it cannot be my *Book*, which notes below not-Kempe that it is a critical edition – already spliced by analysis, discernment, newly put-forth (*edi*). It might be argued that the *Book* is British Library Additional MS 61823, the only extant manuscript witness we have, stored for centuries in a cupboard in Pleasington Old Hall, Lancashire, and identified by Hope Emily Allen in 1934.⁴ Yet this manuscript is already explicitly a copy, and frames the story of its own becoming as one of scribal labour and re-production – already supplementary, prosthetic to an origin. Perhaps the predecessor to Add. MS 61823 has the best claim to originality, but even this version enshrines the complex states of its own construction through copying, interpretation, and translation. The prologue to the *Book* invites us to look back further still, to witness the difficult first attempt at transcription and then to go *even further*. By demonstrating its own genesis in fragmentary and sometimes abortive steps, the *Book* invites us to answer the challenge of its own lost origins. It stirs the detective in all of us.⁵

This stirring suggests that the term 'the *Book*' marks not so much a particular object as a structural pole or the centre of a mechanism; a point of retrievable presence at which our desire for origins can be satiated, at which work can end. Ironically this desire opens the endless task of establishing the interpretative horizons within which one could move from the specific, indeterminate intimacy of the indefinite article (a book) to the closed and authoritative sense produced by the definite (the *Book*). This second, definitive pole – constituted by desire and deferral – pulls ultimately in the direction of Margery Kempe herself, a figure whose particular priorities and inclinations are usually treated as an essential component of any encounter with the *Book*. This pole exists because the *Book* tempts

Margery Kempe as de-facement

us, both in its own terms and in its recent reception history, to read it *autobiographically*.[6] In the process, the goal of the definite article blurs with the goal of recognising Kempe as a living historical entity, a *bios* working itself into *graphē*.[7] It is the history and implications of reading the *Book of Margery Kempe* as an autobiography that this chapter will interrogate. The dynamics of the text are shaped by histories of reading and technologies of subjectivity that repeat and reproduce themselves in the act of reading, offering to readers the contours of a subject and a person. These histories produce the frames and legacies at work when, like prophets or necromancers, we summon the dead and encounter *The Book of Margery Kempe*.

The blurb on *my* book describes the *Book* as 'the earliest surviving autobiography in English', a claim whose history stretches back to the rediscovery of what is now MS 61823. In her 1934 letter to the editor of the *Times*, Hope Emily Allen announces the discovery of '[t]he reminiscences of a medieval old lady' known as Margery Kempe. As she summarises '[t]his remarkable Middle English autobiography', Allen asserts that:

> Margery Kempe brings to life not only famous persons of the early fifteenth century, but also humble ones, at home and abroad. She writes in a charming English, giving familiar details omitted by most medievals, and with telling echoes of direct discourse ... for all her vagaries, she emerges from her story as a woman of great character and force.[8]

This summary touches on many of the central concerns of those readers and writers who have engaged with the *Book* for the last eighty-five years. There is the sense that it is as much historical, *documentary*, as it is literary, a reliable reportage underwritten by unpretentious (or unrefined) and 'charming' prose. There is the awareness that Kempe's work gives us an insight into the domestic and practical spheres of fifteenth-century England. Most importantly, Allen describes the figure behind the *Book*, a person who 'emerges from her story as a woman of great character and force', a historical figure uncoiling from vellum pages in an unmediated encounter with the dead. Here Allen calls the *Book*, for the first time in its history, an '*autobiography*'.

The first edition of the *Book* to reach the reading public was a translation by the manuscript's owner, William Erdeswick Ignatius

Butler-Bowdon, and published in 1936; the scholarly edition prepared for the Early English Text Society would take a further four years to appear, owing in part to a battle over editorial control in which Allen would lose out to Sanford Brown Meech.[9] Guided by an introduction by R. W. Chambers, reviews of the 1936 translation worked to consolidate the impressions originally given by Allen. *The Times* announces in large print 'Margery Kempe's Own Story: The First English Autobiography'; the article runs over the page, where it competes for space with a map illustrating military deployments in the first months of the Spanish Civil War.[10] The *Times Literary Supplement*'s E. H. W. Meyerstein quotes Butler-Bowdon to affirm the *Book*'s status as '"the first extant biography in the English tongue"', before adding a range of genres: 'a spiritual *auto*biography, a travel book and a domestic chronicle all in one'.[11] To Meyerstein, Kempe's prose reflects 'a remarkable nervousness and simplicity' compared to the (male) poets of the age, but is nevertheless commendable as 'vivid and original'. A day later G. G. Coulton describes the *Book* as 'a very precious psychological document' in *The Observer*, adding that it is 'nakedly autobiographical'.[12] Both reviewers settle upon the fundamental accessibility of the *Book*; what it lacks in literary achievement, it makes up for in clarity and simplicity: a naked text through which we gain unprecedented access to 'the heroine of this present autobiography'.[13] Even these two reviews disagree, however, over what exactly constitutes Kempe's *true character* – what should, or should not, appear in a text bearing the generic markers of autobiography; what is, or is not, relevant to Kempe as a *bios*, a lived life. Butler-Bowdon's decision to relegate some of Kempe's more visionary moments to an appendix – an inverted version of de Worde's redaction, some four hundred years earlier – meets divergent responses. For Coulton, the decision is 'wise', and the appendix is given 'no room in this review'; Meyerstein, by contrast, argues that 'the passages are *integral to the autobiography* ... at least as conceived by Margaret of Lynn'.[14] These disagreements suggest that the assignation of the term *autobiography* settles very little; that assumptions about the causal *bios* of the text radically structure interpretative performances. Rather than settling differences, autobiography drafts Kempe herself into textual work; versions of her proliferate at the same rate as readings. Different Margerys for different *Books*.

The effect of the wishes and desires brought by readers to texts has long been a hallmark of autobiographical theory. In his 1975 *On Autobiography* Philippe Lejeune works to make the particular relationship between text and reader represented by autobiography key to a definition of the genre. Coining the term 'autobiographical pact' to describe this phenomenon, Lejeune argues that autobiography is 'a mode of reading as much as it is a type of writing; it is a historically-variable *contractual effect*'.[15] The contract between author and reader guarantees the threefold identity of the *name* of one individual who performs the roles of author, narrator, and protagonist.[16] Autobiography is the name we give to the effects of this legal structure, which offers the promise of a historical subject linking three iterations of the same name. Modern editions of the *Book* perform this threefold association for their readers by supplying Kempe's name on the cover and title page of their editions, a stamp and guarantor of authenticity that demonstrates the 'intention to honour [the] *signature*' of the autobiographical author.[17] Margery Kempe is the proper noun whose signature binds the three necessary functions of the autobiographic subject together, and teaches us to read a certain way.

From this junction – where a textual inscription underwrites the cohesion of a historical subject – it is a small step to invite the disintegration of the project as such. This is effectively what de Man sets out to do in his 1979 'Autobiography as De-facement', beginning with a challenge to the assumptions behind the genre:

> We assume that life *produces* the autobiography as an act produces its consequences, but can we not suggest, with equal justice, that the autobiographical project may itself produce and determine the life and whatever the writer *does* is in fact governed by the technical aspects of self-portraiture and thus determined, in all aspects, by the resources of his [*sic*] medium?[18]

Undoing the causal assumption that life precedes the text demystifies the process of autobiographical production by reminding us of the implications of this text-life – which is never the life of a *bios*. Instead the structure of the life is the result of the 'technical aspects' of reproducing historical life, a medium-dependent act determined by the structures of genre and writing. De Man's suggestions here chime with developments in the history of Kempe scholarship, which have largely shifted from a treatment of the *Book* as an idiosyncratic production to a recognition of the generic frameworks and resources provided by the lives of Continental religious women, especially the *vita* of St Bridget of Sweden.[19] Yet de Man follows the implications of this medium dependency further: if the causal chain is reversed and the *graphē* precedes and produces the *bios*, then we are on the border of an entirely different type of being – or non-being.

For de Man, autobiography is a type of prosopopoeia; it is a type of writing that generates 'a voice or face by means of language'.[20] Margery Kempe is a product of autobiography, a 'voice or face' conjured by, and encountered through, the *Book* – sometimes with a little help from All Saints, Bale. By invoking the structure of prosopopoeia de Man effectively flattens distinctions between autobiography and other forms of representation – which simply work to produce different effects – with autobiography becoming 'one mode of figuration among others'.[21] Having levelled the playing field, de Man goes on to argue – and here Lejeune is clearly in the background – that the prosopoetic mode of signification proper to autobiography is echoed in *any text* inscribed (or signed) by the name of an author. Every authored text performs autobiographical prosopopoeia by virtue of being authored; autobiography is 'a figure of reading or of understanding that occurs, to some degree, in all texts … [it] makes explicit the wider claim to authorship that takes place whenever a text is stated to be *by* someone and assumed to be understandable to the extent that this is the case'.[22] The prosopoetic mode is operative whenever the fact of authorship determines the readerly engagement; whenever, that is, we use the 'voice or face' *produced by* the text to justify or limit the movements of signification in the text itself. The irony of this reversal is that autobiography introduces a problem – how to reach, firmly and clearly, the *bios* behind the *graphē* – that it has itself generated by autobiographical reading practices. In challenging this circular logic, de Man argues:

> What we are deprived of is not life but the shape and sense of a world accessible only in the privative way of understanding. Death is a displaced name for a linguistic predicament, and the restoration of mortality by autobiography (the prosopopoeia of the voice and the name) deprives and disfigures to the precise extent that it restores. Autobiography veils a defacement of the mind of which it is itself the cause.[23]

In this reading there is no prior life. From the perspective of the autobiographical mode, rejecting the assumption of a life prior to the act of the writing 'deprive[s]' us of 'life'; what de Man points out, however, is that this rejection in fact 'deprive[s]' us of a world that can be understood only in terms of a 'privative' model of meaning-generation. This second form of deprivation is, of course, really a form of liberation: the displacement and deferral that mobilise language use are an invitation to enter into the play of *différance*, a haunted space beyond the death/life binary.[24] Reading autobiographically, de Man suggests, is a way of forestalling this recognition, of smuggling the promise of an encounter with *bios* into a medium which would be liberated by its absence. The complaints over authorial control and 'instability' that we see in the Book of Margery Kempe can be read, therefore, as essential products of prosopoetic structures that seek to stabilise writing and deflect attention: 'autobiography veils a de-facement of the mind of which it is itself the cause'. An encounter might, then, be a de-facement – a de-facement whose effects are palpable in both the *Book* and the forms of response it has engendered.

The focus in de Man's article rests squarely on the act of reading. As such, the 'technical aspects of self-portraiture' with which he opens are de-emphasised in favour of the production of a prosopoetic mode of response.[25] Yet his (implicit) engagement with Lejeune reminds us that there is room in the 'technical aspects' of certain forms of writing for a 'contractual effect', a guide which invites and structures a response. *The Book of Margery Kempe* offers exactly this kind of guide in its opening pages.

> Thys boke is not wretyn in ordyr, every thyng aftyr other as it wer don, but lych as the mater cam to the creatur in mend whan it schuld be wretyn, for it was so long er it was wretyn that sche had forgetyn the tyme and the ordyr whan thyngys befellyn. And therfor sche dede no thing wryten but that sche knew rygth wel for very trewth.
> (p. 49)

This straightforward statement, occurring at the close of the 'textual preface' of the *Book*, is responsible for some conceptual heavy lifting. In a move typical of autobiography, it displays a superficial textuality in order to encode a fundamental rejection of the structures of textuality itself. In describing the circumstances of its production

– '[t]hys boke is not wretyn in order ... but lych as the mater cam to the creatur' – the *Book* displays an awareness of the technical process and selective labour that produces a text. Yet it does so only in order to impose a privative model of meaning by allowing in the determinative power of the author by the back door. For if this passage suggests the *Book*'s variability (and it *is* variable), it does so only in order to assert the primacy of the psychological processes of Kempe. It drives against the organisational demands and complexities of literary production, relying instead upon appeals to Kempe's 'mend', prioritising in the process a kind of experiential realism.[26] '[T]he tyme and the ordyr when thyngys befellyn' – that is, the requirements of conventional linear narrative – are subordinated to the order of Kempe's internal reality in a gesture reminiscent of the 'stream of consciousness' narratives of the twentieth century.

This commitment to non-linear storytelling is upheld later in the text, where comments in parentheses refer the reader back to earlier chapters and events – '[r]ede first the xxi chapetre, and than this chapetre aftyr that', we are told at the end of Chapter 16. Simple asides like this reinforce the fundamental elements of the autobiographical mode; they mark an active resistance to any attempts to reconfigure or restructure the *Book* according to a linear progression of historical, narrative time. Instead they contribute to the discursive construction of the *Book*'s own naturalness, suggesting access to a private subjectivity unmediated by restrictive attention to literary style or rhetorical norms.[27] This discursive work is rewarded, as we have seen, by the responses of 'charming English' and 'prose of remarkable ... simplicity' given by Kempe's earliest twentieth-century reviews.[28] These reviewers had indeed been charmed, convinced of the immediacy and clarity of their encounters with the medieval world by historically contingent and isolable structures. These structures work to hide Kempe's own self-fashioning as a textual subject produced through the play of signification everywhere dissimulated. By resisting literary and narrative order, a gesture that may seem to be *textualising* in fact achieves the exact opposite effect: it anchors the experience of textuality in a *bios* that governs the rules of its execution and subordinates its effects to an unreachable life.

Yet the possibility of retrieving the unmediated life remains a haunting possibility, constantly deferred and explored throughout the *Book*. For Kempe this tension is primarily expressed in terms of frustrated communication, especially across languages. As she travels abroad and is systematically abandoned by her fellow English speakers, she finds that she must navigate the complex linguistic terrain of Europe. In Rome she finds herself without a priest and therefore unable to confess – a situation which is briefly alleviated by the miraculous appearance of John the Evangelist, who 'asoyled hir of hir synnes' (p. 183). A more sustained and mundane solution is however, required, and offers itself in the form of a 'Dewcheman, a good clerke, and a wel lernyd man', later named as 'Wenslawe' (p. 198). Wenslawe cannot, however, speak English, and after some time relying upon 'an interpretowr, a man that telde her eythyr what other seyde', Kempe turns to divine assistance. Asking Wenslawe and 'other that lovedyn owir Lord' to pray for the 'grace to undirstondyn hir langage and hir speche', she settles in to wait.

> And aftyr therten days the preste cam ageyn to hir to prevyn the effect of her preyerys, and than he undirstod what sche seyd in Englysch to hym, and sche undirstod what that he seyd. And yet he undirstod not Englisch that other men spokyn; thow thei spokyn the same wordys that sche spak, yet he undirstod hem not, les than sche spak hirselfe. Than was she confessyd to this preste of alle hir synnes, as ner as hir mende wold servyn hir. (p. 185)

Divine intervention underwrites the fantasy of effortless communication; it is only through an act of 'grace' that Kempe is able to confess her sins – something which she then does voluminously. Crucially, however, this miracle does not teach Wenslawe English or Kempe German; both characters appear to keep speaking their own languages, with understanding passing effortlessly between and above their words. Indeed even the exact 'same wordys that sche spak' spoken by another individual fail to register with Wenslawe at all, remaining as unintelligible sound-patterns without clear meaning. This miracle licenses, in other words, a *private language*, a grace-fuelled medium of supra-linguistic perfective communication. We could describe the investments of this gesture as representative of 'ideology' in the specific and technical sense Derrida uses in 'Signature Event Context': a 'philosophical tradition dominated by the self-evidence of the *idea*', a system in which '[c]ommunication ... vehiculates a representation as an ideal content', where language as communication exists to transmit the internal reality of the idea held in the 'mend', and is measured by the degree to which it succeeds or fails in this enterprise.[29] The encounter between Wenslawe and Kempe, then, plays out as a fantasy of super-prosopopoeia: of overcoming the deferral represented by the *graphē* in its entirety in order to reach, fully and totally, the human subject behind it, encountering an author in fully illuminated clarity.[30]

The Wenslawe episode bears a striking resemblance to a similar miracle recorded in the prologue to the *Book*. The first manuscript of the *Book* – the version dictated by Kempe – was, we are told, copied by a scribe from the Low Countries, 'an Englyschman in hys birth' (now usually identified as one of Kempe's sons), whose facility with his mother tongue seems to have waned in the decades since his birth.[31] The result is far from satisfactory, as Kempe's priest discovers: 'The booke was so evel wretyn that he cowd lytyl skyll theron, for it was neithyr good Englysch ne Dewch, ne the lettyr was not schapyn ne formyd as other letters ben. Therfore the prest leved fully ther schuld nevyr man redyn it, but it wer special grace' (pp. 47–8). This is a repeat of the situation in Rome (it even includes a 'Dewcheman'); Kempe's desires to communicate effectively and with clarity are frustrated by their dependence on linguistic and written media. The key identifier of autobiography is again on display here in the self-inflicted tension between the private subject (internal, subjective) and language (external, historical). Once again the *Book* frames this barrier as fundamentally insurmountable by humans without the help of God; without special grace 'ther schuld nevyr man redyn it', rendering Kempe obsolete and forgotten. Divine assistance is, of course, forthcoming. At Kempe's insistence and after her prayers, her priest attempts a second reading of the text, only to discover that 'it was mych more esy, as hym thowt, than it was beforntym. And so he red it ovyr beforn this creatur every word, sche sumtym helpyng where ony difficulte was' (p. 49). The problem of language is once again resolved by Kempe's lucky patrons, and the *Book* can continue to signify to new audiences. Communicative links are restored and enabled through miracle. Suggestively, this passage goes on to describe Kempe's own editorial presence, helping her readers with any 'difficulte[s]' they might encounter along the way. Divine and mundane editorial processes therefore intermingle, as they did in the case of Wenslawe's 'interpretowr'.

There is no room to doubt the relative importance of each; in both cases it is special grace which actually enables the kinds of communication of which the *Book* invites us to dream. It is none the less instructive that the *Book* continues to offer us moments of human work and interpretation as juxtapositions, implications which tend to reach across time and reflect our own labours in search of authentic encounters with (the *Book* of) Margery Kempe.

At the beginning of the *Book* we are told in no uncertain terms that '[a]lle the werkys of ower Saviowr ben for ower exampyl and instruccyon, and what grace that he werkyth in any creatur is ower profyth, *yf lak of charyte be not ower hynderawnce*' (p. 41, emphasis mine). It is tempting to read this final clause as a pre-emptive attack on critics of Kempe, a condemnatory, even slightly comical, dismissal of those who would doubt the validity of the *Book*'s narrative – a doubt rooted in 'lak of charyte'. But it may also be read as an element of a more programmatic function executed across the text – one that seeks not only to assert *control* over meaning but that attempts to do so precisely by *inserting conflict* into the narrative in the first place. The *Book* opens the door to a life, suggests however fleetingly the existence of a *bios* whose reality is inaccessible without both hard human labour and a divine spark. This tension is the fundamentally productive core of autobiography, which feeds off 'the postulated opposites between self and world, literature and history, fact and fiction, subject and object'.[32] Our modern responses are prompted by the text's own invitation to enter to the play of *bios* and text, to sift and distinguish between fact and fiction.

The *Book* is patterned by instances of suspicion and interrogation, effectively modelling for future readers the dynamics of autobiographical interpretation. Wherever Kempe goes, she is hounded by attempts to interpret or reframe her behaviour. Her private conversations with the Virgin Mary, St Peter, St Paul, St Katherine, 'er what seynt in hevyn sche had devocyon to' prompt rumours that 'sum evyl spyryt vexid hir in hir body, or ellys that sche had sum bodyly sekenesse' (pp. 115–16); at the Church of John Lateran in Rome the locals are so disturbed by her devotions that they repeat the same suspicions almost verbatim, believing Kempe 'vexyd with sum evyl spiryt, er a sodeyn sekenes, not levyng it was the werk of God, but rathar sum evyl spiryt, er a sodeyn sekenes' (p. 186). *Sickness* is a constant preoccupation amongst Kempe's detractors precisely because the responses it engenders continue to systematise the process of de-facement identified by de Man. The structure of diagnosis parallels the process of prosopoetic reading: the examiner (reader) searches on the surface of the self (text; *graphē*) for traces of a hidden truth (the individual; the life; the *bios*). As the *Book* represents a series of responses to a mysterious exterior, it replays exactly the tension of autobiography – whose fictions ask us to discover and isolate a single historical cause behind the play of writing and re-enact a fundamental act of de-facement.

The investments of the diagnostic response are particularly clear in an episode that occurs towards the end of the first part of the *Book*. By this point in her career Kempe has managed to shift the perceptions of her Norfolk contemporaries in her favour. When a Franciscan friar called William Melton arrives in town to preach, however, troubles begin anew. Despite the warnings of the parish priest, Melton is unable to forgive the disruptions to his sermons produced by Kempe's 'boystows wepyng'. When her friends intercede on her behalf, Melton comes clean, declaring 'he wolde not levyn that it was a yyft of God', casting suspicions on the source of her behaviour. He adds that the irrepressible nature of Kempe's behaviour suggests a physiological or psychological disorder – a 'cardiakyl, er sum other sekenesse' (p. 290). The Franciscan turns to the language of diagnosis, of pathological interpretation, in order to make sense of Kempe's actions. He offers an isolable and identifiable *bios* as the source for a performance he cannot reconcile with his beliefs. Melton goes on to offer Kempe a kind of pathological plea deal; provided she 'wolde be so aknowyn' – provided, that is, she accept Melton's diagnosis and mark herself as a physiologically dis-ordered subject – he will allow her to re-enter the congregation (p. 290).[33] Kempe's reintegration into her community rests here upon her capacity to become a legible life; she can be integrated only as a *face*, as the function of a prosopoetic mode. Melton is not here interested in statements of belief – whether or not Kempe actually has visions – so much as statements that produce a recognisable life, an isolable and understandable actor. What is needed is Kempe's *own acknowledgement of illness*, an identification with 'kendly sekness'. Melton offers Kempe a way to inscribe a recognisable self through the discourses of medical language; to still the operations of displacement and interpretation and settle them around diagnosis. It is important to note that whilst the *Book*'s narrative rejects this form of analysis it continues to invite and produce exactly these kinds of responses. Kempe's appeal to supra-linguistic religious experience is another form of prosopopoeia, of affirming the existence of a determining *bios*; two outputs of the same discursive structure. To their examiners and readers, saints and madwomen speak a language of de-facement empowered by the formal demands of autobiography.

Nearly six hundred years later, Kempe is still under medical examination. Indeed, Kempe's interactions with Melton effectively predict a strain of Kempe criticism popular in the twentieth century. The deployment of clinical and psychiatric knowledge to elucidate Kempe has been an uncomfortable – and recurrent – tendency in Kempe scholarship. In 1990 Claridge, Pryor, and Watkins suggested that '[i]t is more than likely that she was a schizophrenic, for whom the religious beliefs of her day provided a means of escape from the daily life with which her inadequate personality could not cope'.[34] A decade later Richard Lawes would draw explicitly on the definitional terms provided by the infamous Diagnostic and Statistic Manual of Mental Disorders published by the American Psychiatric Association to diagnose both Kempe and Julian of Norwich; Kempe ends up with a diagnosis of temporal lobe epilepsy and a post-partum psychotic episode. Lawes argues that the 'disruption of identity' and 'ongoing puzzling experiences' of the psychotic breaks he reads in the *Book* 'might be expected to produce self-questioning' and generate a propensity towards self-reflection and autobiographical work.[35] Yet de Man's reading of autobiography as prosopoetic reveals a circularity to Lawes's argument; if autobiography produces the subject, complete with psychoses, then these psychoses cannot be assigned a causal factor. Read this way, Lawes appears to be caught in the tautologous claim that the generic markers of autobiography are the product of a particular self – a self that can be identified only through the generic markers of autobiography. Diagnostic readings that aim to *overcome* the language barriers offered by the *Book* in order to discover illness find themselves outflanked, contained, within the logic of the text.

A language of opposition – and complicity – governs one of the most instructive examples of the pathological strand of the Kempe tradition. Written in 1999 by Mary Hardiman Farley, a registered psychiatric nurse in a Los Angeles hospital, 'Her Own Creature' takes especial aim at those critics who attempt analyses of the *Book* without the necessary clinical experience to do so.[36] Farley cites examples of patients under her care, arguing that 'critical exegesis' should 'resist the temptation to explicate' the fact that Kempe is restrained following her difficult pregnancy – because such readings arise from uninformed, lay responses to medical procedure.[37] Farley takes issue, for instance, with David Aers's treatment of the *Book* in his *Community, Gender, and Individual Identity*.[38] Aers's argument that the *Book* 'resists [the] conventional sublimations' through which gendered identity is produced is, for Farley, tantamount to malpractice: his reading of Kempe 'valorises her delusional system', rather than engaging in the 'reality testing' which we are told is 'important in the clinical management of twentieth-century Western psychotics'.[39] From Farley's perspective Aers has failed to 'manage' Kempe properly; indeed he appears to have failed his duty of care towards her. The condemnatory ethical charge of such asides is revealing and demonstrates explicitly the investments of the autobiographical mode. Farley has made Kempe into a *bios* here; a full life, a full person, resurrected long before the Last Judgement. Kempe would no doubt be unimpressed (although not unsurprised) to find herself 'closyd in an hows of ston' as one of Farley's patients (p. 93). The ambiguous possessive pronoun of 'Her Own Creature' thus comes into sharp focus and turns on its author; this Kempe is *Farley*'s, a product of medicalised de-facement. A far cry from the ranging, challenging figure of fifteenth-century England, this Kempe is a twentieth-century patient, sedated and sequestered away in a Los Angeles psychiatric ward.

If there is a Margery Kempe under clinical watch in California, then there is a version of the *Book* which exists as patient case notes, filed in a psychiatrist's office. What kinds of relation, if any, can be drawn between *this Book* and the *Book* that lies on my desk to my right: folded open, creased, annotated? And where between these two *Books* should the other *Books* that have appeared in the course of this chapter – the text copied by Kempe's son; the manuscript updated and authorised by Kempe; MS Additional 61823; the version translated by Butler-Bowdon; the troubled edition created by Hope Emily Allen and Stanford Brown Meech; etc. – be placed? An exact constellation of these various acts of reading is beyond this chapter, but the question of structure (and therefore of investment) is not.

Books of Margery Kempe have proliferated in both the medieval period and ours, but the full scope of these gestures in their local and colourful specificities have been somewhat occluded by appeals to the autobiographical mode. These appeals have ranged in application and effect but, in allowing a prosopoetic textual ontology to dominate, have disguised the processes and ideologies shared by the *Book* and its modern critics. To read the *Book* autobiographically is to risk forgetting that the *Book* is also reading us, that the persons conjured by this interaction are the result of a cross-fertilising traversal of text and self. This forgetfulness is a de-facement; of our critical capacities, of Kempe, and of the multifarious potentialities of the *Book*. By refusing the conclusions of autobiographical reading, we can trouble interpretative ruts and break open dead-end conclusions: if *Books* have proliferated, then so too can Margery Kempes. Fresh readings and responses can multiply without autobiographical hierarchy, spreading laterally in new encounters that are rhizomatic, *radical*, and already immanent. They can be found in a *Book* 'shot through with streams of song': sobs that stick in the throat, roars that frustrate sermonising, and tears that run through our fingers.[40]

Notes

Parts of this chapter were read in 2018 at the 'Margery Kempe Studies in the 21st Century' conference; the supportive and stimulating environment produced by organisers, speakers, and audience members has helped a great deal to make the present piece possible. My thinking on this topic has been challenged and deepened by stimulating exchanges with Ruth Evans, the support of editors Laura Varnam and Laura Kalas, and most of all the constant intellectual energy and firm guidance of Nicolette Zeeman.

1. E. H. W. Meyerstein, 'Among the English classics: the autobiography of Margery Kempe', *Times Literary Supplement* (10 October 1936).
2. This description is of *The Book of Margery Kempe*, ed. Barry Windeatt (Cambridge: D. S. Brewer, 2004). Following references to the *Book* will be drawn from this edition with page numbers cited in parentheses.
3. For an overview of the area in the Middle Ages see Christopher Harper-Bill (ed.), *Medieval East Anglia* (Woodbridge and Rochester, NY: Boydell Press, 2005).

4 'Margery Kempe's own story: the first English autobiography', *The Times* (30 September, 1936); Hilton Kelliher, 'The rediscovery of Margery Kempe: a footnote', *Electronic British Library Journal* (1997), available online at: www.bl.uk/eblj/1997articles/article19.html [last accessed 5 July 2019].

5 This invitation to investigation has been taken up by Julie A. Chappell in *Perilous Passages: The Book of Margery Kempe, 1534–1934* (Basingstoke: Palgrave Macmillan, 2013).

6 As a generic sub-category, medieval autobiography has received varying treatment over the years. For critiques that distance medieval life-writing from autobiography see Paul Zumthor, 'Autobiography in the middle ages?', trans Simon Sherry, *Genre*, 6 (1973), 29–48, and A. C. Spearing, *Medieval Autographies* (Notre Dame: University of Notre Dame Press, 2012). For cautiously optimistic responses to the term see Eugene Vance, 'Augustine's *Confessions* and the grammar of selfhood', *Genre*, 6 (1973), 1–28, and John V. Fleming, 'Medieval European autobiography', in Maria DiBattista and Emily O. Wittman (eds), *The Cambridge Companion to Autobiography* (Cambridge: Cambridge University Press, 2014), pp. 35–48.

7 The English word 'biography' is borrowed from post-classical Latin *biographia*, which is adapted from Ancient Greek *bio-* ('life') and *-graphia* ('writing; representation; description'). See the *Oxford English Dictionary*, 'biography' (n.), sense 1. The question of how a historical life (*bios*) relates to a collective semiotic structure (writing; *graphia* – the noun form is *graphē*) is key to theories of autobiography, as will be discussed below.

8 Hope Emily Allen, 'A medieval work: Margery Kempe of Lynn', Letter to the Editor, *The Times* (27 December 1934).

9 W. Butler-Bowdon (trans.), *The Book of Margery Kempe 1436* (London: Cape, 1936); for discussion of the scholarly edition and Allen's forceful sidelining from the project see John Hirsh, *Hope Emily Allen, Medieval Scholarship, and Feminism* (Norman: Pilgrim Books, 1988), Deanne Williams, 'Hope Emily Allen speaks with the dead', *Leeds Studies in English*, 35 (2004), 137-60, and Kathryn Maude, 'Citation and marginalisation: the ethics of feminism in medieval studies', *Journal of Gender Studies*, 23:3 (2014), 247–61.

10 'Margery Kempe's own story'. Marea Mitchell examines the identification and response to the *Book* in *The Book of Margery Kempe: Scholarship, Community, and Criticism* (New York: Peter Lang, 2005); chapter 4 (pp. 55–72) discusses the early media reaction. David Wallace also develops an account of the political and social context of the *Book*'s discovery and the responses of its early readers in *Strong Women: Life, Text,*

and Territory, 1347–1645 (Oxford: Oxford University Press, 2011), pp. 61–132.
11 Meyerstein, 'Among the English classics' (emphasis mine).
12 G. G. Coulton, 'The woman in white: Margery Kempe of Lynn', Observer (11 October 1936).
13 Ibid.
14 Meyerstein, 'Among the English classics'; Coulton, 'The woman in white' (emphasis mine).
15 Philippe Lejeune, On Autobiography, trans. Katherine Leary (Minneapolis: University of Minneapolis Press, 1989), p. 30.
16 Ibid., p. 11.
17 Ibid., p. 14.
18 Paul de Man, 'Autobiography as de-facement', Modern Language Notes, 94:5 (1979), 919–30, p. 920.
19 On Kempe's use of Bridget of Sweden see Gunnel Cleve, 'Margery Kempe: a Scandinavian influence in medieval England?', in Marion Glasscoe (ed.), The Medieval Mystical Tradition in England: Exeter Symposium V: Papers Read at the Devon Centre, Dartington Hall, July 1992 (Woodbridge: D. S. Brewer, 1992), pp. 162–78, and Julia Bolton Holloway, 'Bride, Margery, Julian and Alice: Bridget of Sweden's textual community in medieval England', in Sandra J. McEntire (ed.), Margery Kempe: A Book of Essays (New York and London: Garland, 1992), pp. 203–21.
20 De Man, 'Autobiography as de-facement', p. 930.
21 Ibid.
22 Ibid., pp. 921–2.
23 Ibid., p. 930.
24 Différance is the term Jacques Derrida uses to describe effects of the space between signs and their referents. For Derrida, this space cannot ever be overcome and the referent can never be reached as it is always a new sign with a new referent – an endless trace. Différance is the energetic and endless play of meaning in this space, where distinctions between presence and absence and life and death are suspended. See Derrida, 'Différance', trans. A. Bass, Margins of Philosophy (Brighton: Harvester Press, 1982), pp. 1–27.
25 De Man, 'De-facement', p. 920.
26 This statement foregrounds the associative disorder of the Book in a manner that could be read as reflective of the '*écriture feminine*' popularised by Hélène Cixous, for whom women's writing is the oppositional antidote to 'self-admiring, self-stimulating, self-congratulatory phallocentrism'; see 'The laugh of the Medusa', trans. Keith and Paula Cohen, in Robyn Warhol-Down and Diane Price Herndl (eds), Feminisms

Redux: An Anthology of Literary Theory and Criticism (New Brunswick: Rutgers University Press, 2009), pp. 416–31, p. 419. A convincing feminist tradition has read the *Book* as to varying degrees representative of a positive articulation of gendered speech in the face of medieval patriarchy - see, for instance, Liz Herbert McAvoy, *Authority and the Female Body in the Writings of Julian of Norwich and Margery Kempe* (Cambridge: D. S. Brewer, 2004), esp. pp. 170–204; Williams, 'Hope Emily Allen'; and Sarah Beckwith, 'Problems of authority in late medieval English mysticism: language, agency, and authority in *The Book of Margery Kempe*', *Exemplaria*, 4 (1992), 171–99. Yet the logic of this particular moment, placed at the end of a male clerical prologue, aims instead to control the proliferation of meaning through reference to a single, localised, historicised *bios*. Through this gesture Kempe is (in the words of Cixous) 'called in by the cops of signifier, fingerprinted, remonstrated, and brought into the line of order', a subject constituted through the extremely specific order of disorder: 'Beware, my friend, of the signifier that would take you back to the authority of a signified!' ('Medusa', p. 429).

27 Katherine J. Lewis also explores the rhetorical structures of the *Book* in Chapter 6 below, approaching the text as a codified copy of an oral history told and retold through confession.

28 Meyerstein, 'Among the English classics'; Allen, 'A medieval work'.

29 Jacques Derrida, 'Signature event context', *Margins of Philosophy*, pp. 307–30, p. 314.

30 For a different perspective on multilingualism in the *Book* see Jonathan Hsy, *Trading Tongues: Merchants, Multilingualism, and Medieval Literature* (Columbus: Ohio State University Press, 2013), pp. 131–56. Hsy argues that the *Book* is 'a textual participant in a translingual network of creation that … troubles stable linguistic orientations' (p. 133).

31 On the identity of the scribe see Sebastian Sobecki, '"The writyng of this tretys": Margery Kempe's son and the authorship of her book', *Studies in the Age of Chaucer*, 37:1 (2015), 257–83. Recent studies have also suggested an expanded role for Margery Kempe's daughter-in-law; on this, see Naoë Kukita Yoshikawa and Liz Herbert McAvoy, Chapter 2 above.

32 R. B. Bosse, 'Margery Kempe's tarnished reputation: a reassessment', *14th Century English Mystics Newsletter*, 5:1 (1979), 9–19, p. 13; Laura Marcus, *Auto/biographical Discourses: Theory, Criticism, Practice* (Manchester: Manchester University Press, 1994), p. 7.

33 Laura Kalas describes this episode as a 'medical false confession' in *Margery Kempe's Spiritual Medicine: Suffering, Transformation and the Life-Course* (Cambridge: D. S. Brewer, 2020), p. 42.

34 Gordon Claridge, Ruth Pyor and Gwen Watkins, *Sounds from the Bell Jar: Ten Psychotic Authors* (Basingstoke: Macmillan Press, 1990), p. 61.
35 Richard Lawes, 'Psychological disorder and the autobiographical impulse in Julian of Norwich, Margery Kempe, and Thomas Hoccleve', in Denis Renevey and Christiania Whitehead (eds), *Writing Religious Women: Female Spiritual and Textual Practices in Late Medieval England* (Cardiff: University of Wales Press, 2000), pp. 217–45, p. 232.
36 Mary Hardiman Farley, 'Her own creature: religion, feminist criticism, and the functional eccentricity of Margery Kempe', *Exemplaria*, 11:1 (1999), 1–21.
37 *Ibid.*, p. 4.
38 David Aers, *Community, Gender, and Individual Identity: English Writing 1360–1430* (New York: Routledge, 1988), pp. 73–116.
39 *Ibid.*, p. 74; Farley, 'Her own creature', p. 4.
40 Cixous, 'Medusa', p. 421.

6

Margery Kempe, oral history, and the value of intersubjectivity

Katherine J. Lewis

The Book of Margery Kempe begins with Margery's failed attempt to tell the story of her life. Following a difficult childbirth and fearing that she will die, Margery sends for her confessor, wishing 'to be schrevyn of alle hir lyfetym, as ner as sche cowde', and especially of a particular 'thing whech sche had so long conselyd'.[1] But this attempt is thwarted by the confessor's impatient lack of empathy. He cuts her off before she gets to the long-hidden 'thing' and begins sharply to rebuke her, thus 'sche wold no mor seyn, for nowt he mygth do' (p. 53). Margery's mental breakdown and her first visions are instigated by a combination of being pitilessly reproached and the fear that she would be damned because her confession is left incomplete and her sins unabsolved. Despite this distressing false start, the *Book* testifies to Margery's ultimate success not just in telling the story of her life but in having it recorded. Although Margery's story is now a text, which is why we know about it, long before her story was written down it existed in oral form. The confessor's reaction is unpromising, but subsequently Margery finds other clerics willing to listen to her. Having originally been silenced, the *Book* tells us that she had many opportunities to articulate her life-story, culminating in the narrations which were written down to form the *Book*. The *Book* can thus be identified as a form of oral history, and this chapter treats it as such, applying current methodologies of oral history to an analysis of its internal operations. This approach may seem incongruous, given that, ordinarily, the practice of oral history entails an exchange between an interviewer and interviewee, and I cannot interview Margery

Kempe myself, sadly. But I can engage in a dialogue with her nonetheless, via her *Book,* and thereby reflect from a new perspective on some well-trodden areas of debate revolving around the genesis of the text and Margery's role within this.[2]

My analysis employs the notion of intersubjectivity alongside post-positivist approaches to memory in order to revisit the manner in which the *Book* was created. These are used to argue for Margery Kempe's decisive role in determining both the content and the form of the *Book.* Forging an encounter between Margery Kempe and the methodologies of oral history allows for fresh reflection on the status of the *Book* as a historical narrative. My approach thus aligns itself with existing scholarship which contends that the *Book* offers access to vital truths about the experiences of an individual medieval woman regardless of the precise accuracy of events described within it. By focusing on the function of confession as a vehicle for Margery's repeated rehearsal of her life-story, this chapter sheds new light on the decades-long process of refinement by which she encountered and re-encountered her self, and constructed the identity finally preserved in the *Book.*

The *Book* has often been discussed as a form of autobiography or life writing.[3] But to date only Robert C. Ross has analysed the *Book* in relation to oral history scholarship. He made the important observation 'that to treat Margery's text as a form of oral life-history is perhaps the best method of approach to its compositional integrity'.[4] Ross drew on Luisa Passerini's influential study of Fascism and working-class people in Turin, based on her interviews with men and women who had worked at the Fiat factory in Turin from 1917 to 1944.[5] Noting points of similarity between the structure and content of the *Book* and Passerini's interviews, and the tactics for self-representation which they disclose, Ross discussed what this reveals about the nature of memory, both as a process and as evidence for lived experience. Ross also fruitfully paralleled Passerini's interviews with passages from the *Book* to accentuate the collaborative relationship between Margery and her scribes.[6] Debate continues to revolve around how much control over the *Book*'s shape and substance should be assigned to Margery herself, rather than those scribes, especially the priest scribe. Scholars have drawn differing conclusions about whose agency determined the arrangement of the material and the unfolding narrative it presents of Margery's experiences and spiritual progress.[7] Moreover, the manuscript which survives today is not the one created by Margery and her priest scribe, which is lost, but is a copy created by Richard Salthouse.[8] Ross judged that 'Margery's text is essentially raw data that have been partially edited by a priest who "interviewed" Margery, while reworking an original document no longer recoverable'.[9] This process of interview is implied in the Proem. Once the priest was finally able to read the original version of the *Book*: 'he red it ovyr beforn this creatur every word, sche sumtym helpyng where ony difficulte was' (p. 49).[10] However, the content of the *Book* itself challenges the notion of 'Margery's text' being, prior to its writing down, 'essentially raw data' which needed to be put into comprehensible order by the priest scribe. Because, as noted above, she had already told and retold her life-story regularly in the twenty-plus years between the inception of her visions and the time at which it was finally written down.[11] Approaching the relationship between Margery and her priest scribe in the light of the methodologies of oral history highlights that the *Book* constituted a collaborative encounter within which Margery's agency was crucial.[12]

Scholarly debates about oral history have moved on since Ross wrote in the early 1990s, especially with regard to perceptions of the relationship between interviewer and interviewee, and of the subjective nature of memory.[13] Those doing oral history in the 1970s self-consciously adopted an approach of scientific objectivity.[14] Interviews were treated as sources producing information which could then be subjected to conventional empiricist forms of evaluation. There was unease about the influence historians may have on interviewees, as oral history recordings and the written transcripts based upon these are inevitably shaped by the interests of the historian to some degree. But starting in the late 1970s and early 1980s there was a marked conceptual shift which saw historians move from trying to position themselves outside the process by which oral history sources were created (as purportedly detached observers) to emphasising the collaborative nature of that process.[15] This is termed intersubjectivity.[16] Ross does not discuss this methodological development, although Passerini was one of its foremost theorists.[17] The work of Valerie Yow has also been very influential, in her call for historians to be explicit about their own agendas, while ensuring that they focus on what is important to the interviewee.[18] Her guidelines on how best to conduct interviews have become benchmarks of good practice and the necessity for empathy on the part of the historian is stressed by her and others.[19] Indeed, discussing the ways in which a historian's emotions are 'enlisted' by the process of research, Michael Roper argues that conscious empathy and affectivity should form part of historians' methodologies.[20] In common with other modern readers of the *Book*, I experienced a strong reaction to Margery the first time I read it.[21] Rather than putting aside that reaction, in what follows I have taken my cue from Yow and Roper and incorporated it within my analysis of the *Book*, in order to be able to draw more productive conclusions about its form and content. Unlike the testy confessor I have listened to Margery's words empathetically.

Another key development within oral history has been the shift in focus away from the life history, the term used by Ross, which tended to emphasise chronology and linear progression between life stages. Historians instead draw on the concept of the life-story, described by Lynn Abrams as 'a creative narrative device used by an individual to make sense of their past'.[22] She further states: 'The interview thus becomes one of the very means by which the self is constructed and reconstructed through the active process of telling memory stories.'[23] The notion of memory as an active process, and of memory as the subject of oral history, not just its source, has been articulated influentially by Alessandro Portelli.[24] From an empiricist perspective, memory, perceived as inherently unreliable, and history, understood as an objective and factually substantiated account of the past, have sometimes been viewed as inherently antithetical.[25] But Portelli contends that trying to winnow oral history sources for 'fact' by comparing them to more conventional and thus 'reliable' documentary evidence is highly problematic and denudes them of their distinctive value as individual testimonies of experience and perception. Portelli asserts: 'Subjectivity is as much the business of history as the more visible "facts". What the informant believes is indeed a historical *fact* (that is, the *fact* that he or she believes it) just as much as what really happened.'[26] Thus, he affirms, 'there are no "false" oral sources'; indeed, their value lies in the very subjectivity which makes those who champion more strictly empiricist approaches so uneasy.[27] The Proem to the *Book* is explicit about its subjective nature, stating: 'Thys boke is not wretyn in ordyr, every thyng aftyr other as it wer don, but lych as the mater cam to the creatur in mend whan it schuld be wretyn, for it was so long er it was wretyn that sche had forgetyn the tyme and the ordyr whan thyngys befellyn. And therfor sche dede no thing wryten but that sche knew rygth wel for very trewth' (p. 49). Rather than seeing it as a drawback that we have to take Margery's word for it when she tells us that her account is true, Portelli's approach valorises the evidential value of her statement as a form of historical truth in itself.

Indeed oral history explicitly challenges hierarchies of 'truth' and 'reliability' conventionally applied to different types of historical evidence.[28] In discussing these issues oral historians acknowledge the vital role which other disciplines have played in helping them to develop their approaches: sociology, anthropology, ethnography, psychoanalysis, and folklore studies among others.[29] Ross stated in a footnote that he intended to write an article showing that 'feminist criticism has created more problems than it has solved while it has fashioned a Margery that quite certainly did not and does not exist in text or in fact'.[30] But ironically there has been an intrinsic link between feminism and oral history since the late 1960s. Indeed some historians claim oral history as an inherently feminist praxis because of the challenge it presents to established master narratives of history, founded on allegedly objective scientific methods which are in fact profoundly androcentric.[31] Indeed it is a way of doing history that can be applied to any variety of historical inquiry.[32] Oral history's status as a form of 'history from below' and its emphasis on foregrounding the history of ordinary people via recording interviews is central to its ethos as well as being its chief methodology. It can be a vehicle for combating oppression and injustice suffered by those whose voices and experiences had previously been marginalised or silenced altogether.[33] It is especially valued as a means of bringing subjective experience and emotion into discussions of past events and their impact.[34] In this regard oral history can be said to do history not only from below but from the inside out.[35] Thus oral history methodologies give us tools to challenge the intellectual and academic hierarchies that have often produced dismissive assessments both of the *Book* and of Margery Kempe.

A highly regarded example of oral history which focuses on an individual woman's recalled experiences is Daniel James's *Doña María's Story: Life, History, Memory, and Political Identity*.[36] Like Margery Kempe, Doña María Roldán (1905–89) was an ordinary, yet extraordinary woman. She lived and worked in the Argentinian meatpacking community of Berisso, becoming the first female shop steward at her plant and playing a key role in the development of the union there. She was also an ardent supporter of Juan Domingo and Eva Perón (Evita). In characterising Doña María's retelling of her life-story James notes that she did not follow a consistent diachronic structure but zig-zags backwards and forwards, and the narrative is not always internally consistent.[37] Following Portelli, James sees this as valuable, rather than problematic: 'Oral testimony is more messy, more paradoxical, more contradiction-laden [than autobiography], and perhaps, because of this, more faithful to the complexity of working-class lives and working-class memory.'[38] He also highlights the extent to which this 'messy' narrative is, nontheless, highly emplotted in terms of what Doña María chose to tell and how she told it. In addition, she drew on a range of different modes, both formal and informal, to tell her story. For example, James analyses how Peronist discourses about women are echoed in her account and to what ends.[39]

As mentioned in my introduction, it is, obviously, impossible for modern historians working on the Middle Ages to interview medieval people. We cannot sit face to face with them, or ask them direct questions about their experiences and record these. But historians who draw on oral history sources for their study of the recent past do not always create the interviews upon which they base their analyses. It is commonplace for them to consult archived interviews and transcripts, often asking new questions of material created by others. Sometimes the precise circumstances in which an interview (or interviews) was conducted are not known, and this can be the case even if a recording survives. Moreover, published transcripts of non-extant recordings do not always include the original questions.[40] These issues are paralleled in modern approaches to the *Book*, of whose creation we know something, but not everything. A wealth of fascinating scholarship has demonstrated the plausibility of the events and encounters which the *Book* tells us that Margery experienced, via nuanced readings which draw expertly on a wide range of contextual evidence.[41] We can triangulate Margery's existence in the past, and ongoing research is revealing ever more information about members of her family and their social, professional, and religious networks. It is generally assumed that she was the Margery

Kempe recorded as paying dues to the guild of the Holy Trinity in Lynn in 1437–38.[42] But there is currently no direct external evidence for Margery Kempe or her personal experiences and encounters as described in the *Book*. As a result the *Book*'s status as history is, for some, highly equivocal, because it is impossible to gauge for sure how much of its contents is true (i.e. actually happened), and how much is exaggeration, embellishment, or invention. However, it is important to note that historians' approaches to other forms of medieval historical narrative, especially chronicles, have moved away from the traditional view of them as repositories of 'facts' from which the 'fictional' rhetorical casing needs to be pared away in order to reconstruct a 'true' version of events. As Matthew Kempshall asserts, rather than attempting to excise these components it is essential to understand their function within medieval historical methodologies and their status as 'narrative strategies' for creatively and engagingly reconstructing the past in a plausible fashion.[43] This was a crucial means of enhancing chronicles' closely interwoven objectives of providing both information and moral instruction for readers in the present and the future. Marcus Bull highlights the value of applying narratological theories (which oral historians have long been applying to their sources) to the analysis of eyewitness crusade chronicles, stating that this tactic 'can deepen our understanding of both the past as lived experience and the means by which we are granted access to that experience'.[44] Moreover, in discussing approaches to evaluating the truth and accuracy of oral history sources, James makes the following provocative statement: 'It is clearly important to try and verify the factual accuracy of historical material found in oral interviews from other sources. Yet I think that very often this ... is largely an exercise in professional glorification on the part of the academic historian.'[45] Indeed he reveals that he had jeopardised his relationship with Doña María on several occasions by interrupting her to ask her to assign precise dates or other forms of category to her narrative.[46] Outlining his methodology James acknowledges his debt to anthropology, and especially the work of Gelya Frank, quoting her crucial observation that life-story research 'emphasises the truth of the telling versus telling the truth'.[47] Frank's formula further legitimises the Proem's claim that the *Book* contains nothing but 'very trewth' (p. 46). Thus approaching the *Book* from the perspective of oral history and treating it as a form of life-story provides firm conceptual ground from which to determine its unambiguous authority as a historical narrative.

Both the *Book* and oral history interviews share a common concern of detailing the process by which the life-story, originally an oral narrative, came to be recorded in writing. The *Book*'s Proem takes us through the saga of the three men who were involved with Margery in its composition (pp. 47-50). This culminates in the partnership between Margery and the priest scribe, who between them produced the final version of the *Book*. James's transcript of Doña María's life-story begins thus:

> In 1930 Doña María and her husband arrived in the community whose past and present identity is inscribed in the Centro Cívico [cf Berisso]. She raised her family, worked in the plants, engaged in political activism, and worshiped her God during the following six decades, all within the confines of the social and cultural space called Berisso. This book is devoted in large measure to transmitting her life-story. Although it is one woman's story, it is not a story that stands on its own. Her narrative must be read as one thread within the web of narratives that form Berisso's story.[48] Her unique voice carries within it tones and lyrics imbued with the sharp outlines and the fading traces of the cultural, ideological, and moral context that Berisso bequeathed to her.
>
> The translation of Doña María's testimony is mine. The testimony was recorded between January and September 1987 and in June 1988. I have edited the transcript, shortening, condensing, and at times reconfiguring the order of parts of her testimony. I have also omitted from Part 2 most of the extended translations of testimony that appear in Part 3, chapters 1-4.[49]

James here follows good practice, including some direction to the reader as to how the narrative should be approached, as well as an account of his handling of Doña María's testimony. Similarly to James's characterisation of Doña María's life-story as 'messy', the Proem comments on the apparently haphazard structure of the *Book*'s contents, which were, as we have seen, 'not wretyn in ordyr ... but lych as the mater cam to the creatur in mend' (p. 49). In both cases we are shown the workings in order to establish that what follows really does constitute the words of the speaker Margery Kempe or Doña María, albeit these have not simply been recorded, but also edited by the scribe or historian. Both texts are presented as authentic records of the women's memories and of their reflections upon these, revealing the meanings which they gave to their experiences.

As a result of its seemingly disorganised format the *Book* has been characterised variously as 'honest', 'unashamed', 'earthy', 'charming', as if the contents spontaneously erupted out of her.[50] But the order of the narrative is far from uncontrived; there is a discernible coherence to its ordering as an account of the development of Margery's vocation, enabled by her intimacy with Christ, and of the places and encounters to which this calling led.[51] Besides, as already noted, by the time Margery's life-story was written down she had been telling it for over twenty years. After her first failed attempt in Chapter 1 'to be schrevyn of alle hir lyfetym, as ner as sche cowde', very similar wording is used when, later, Margery speaks to Richard Caister, to whom Margery tells 'al hyr maner of levyng fro hyr chyldhod as ny as it wolde come to hir mende' (p. 114). To the English friar in Rome Margery 'schewyd hym hire lyfe fro the begynnyng unto that owyr as ny as sche mygth in confessyon' (p. 154). Once she and the German priest in Rome can understand each other 'sche confessyd to this preste of alle hir synnes, as ner as hir mende wold servyn hir, fro hir childhode unto that owre' (p. 185). To a priest of St Margaret's in Lynn 'sche schewyd al hir lyfe, as ner as sche cowde, fro hir yong age, bothe hir synnes, hyr labowrys, hir vexacyons, hir contemplacyons, and also hir revelacyons and swech grace as God wrowt in hir thorw hys mercy, and so that preyste trustyd ryth wel that God wrowt ryth gret grace in hir' (p. 316). Thus the *Book* not only relates her life-story with respect to the events and experiences which shaped her, it explains the confessional process by which she turned those events and experiences into a narrative. Throughout the *Book* we see Margery actively creating herself by articulating her memories over and over again.[52] The summary of what she tells Richard Caister about her manner of living, her conversations with Christ and other holy figures, her emotional reaction to these, and those who slander her as a result, is perhaps intended to be representative of the substance of what she told clerics on such occasions (pp. 114–17). Although we are told several times that Margery habitually narrated her life from her childhood, the events of her childhood are excluded from the *Book*, which begins instead with what was the epiphanic moment in her life-story: the pivotal occasion on which she first saw Christ (pp. 52–6).⁵³

Moreover, what is important is not only Margery's frequent retelling of her life-story but the identity of the men to whom she tells it. Richard Caister was regarded as a saint by the time the *Book* was written down; the English friar in Rome is 'a maystyr of divinite and the Popys legat' (p. 154); the German priest is 'a wel lernyd man, hily belovyd, wel cherschyd, and myche trostyd in Rome, and had on of the grettest office of any preste in Rome' (p. 185). The first high-ranking cleric whom Margery encounters, Philip Repingdon, Bishop of Lincoln, is described as 'cownselyng hir sadly that hir felyngys schuld be wretyn' (p. 105). Moreover, the archbishop of Canterbury, Thomas Arundel, 'aprevyd hir maner of levyng' (p. 111). Starting in the Proem, and throughout the *Book*, it is emphasised that those who endorse her way of life and her revelations are well-educated and often in positions of authority (e.g. pp. 46, 90, 123, 394). The account of the friar (possibly William Melton) who will not put up with Margery's weeping and crying out in his sermons is very revealing in this respect. When Margery's two key supporters, Alan of Lynn and Robert Spryngolde, try to convince the friar that her crying 'was a yyft of God', they are described not by name but as 'a worshepful doctowr of divinite ... and elde doctowr, and a wel aprevyd' and 'a bacheler of lawe, a wel growndyd man in scriptur and long exercisyd' (p. 289). It has often been noted that the emphasis on the status and qualifications of Margery's supporters is a tactic for endorsing what she tells them and thus the contents of the *Book*.⁵⁴ However, these men, especially those to whom Margery confesses, did not passively receive what she told them, they were also fundamentally involved in assisting her own shaping of that telling. Because, significantly, confession was (indeed, is) a dialogue; an interview whose form derives from questions posed and answers given.⁵⁵ For this reason Alexander Freund, drawing on Foucault, has argued that confession is a direct antecedent of the oral history interview.⁵⁶ Just like the oral historian, the confessor is not detached and disinterested, he has a clearly defined role and objective; he is required to evaluate and draw conclusions from the confessee's responses to his questions. Considering how the *Book* begins it seems highly likely that a key question asked of Margery was 'so, when did you first have these visions of Christ?'⁵⁷

Quantification of the length of time and frequency with which she had experienced a range of 'gostly comfortys and bodily comfortys' such as sounds, smells, and a sensation of burning love alongside her visions of Christ and saints likely also derives from questions (pp. 192–4).

Whenever Margery confesses, her clerical interlocutor is thus actively helping her to give meaning to her experiences and memories. We see intersubjectivity in action: between them they create a version of her life-story for that moment. It would never have been exactly the same twice.[58] What survives to us as the *Book* is the product of the time at which Margery's life-story was eventually written down, and possibly adapted further when the surviving manuscript was produced. Sebastian Sobecki states, 'Margery Kempe *had* the book in her before anyone wrote it down'.[59] To take his point further: the book owed its existence in Margery to her frequent practice of confession. The *Book* is thereby the product of collaboration, not just with the priest scribe but with the many others to whom Margery had previously relayed her life-story.[60] Indeed if the priest scribe was Robert Spryngolde, Margery's confessor for forty years, this claim for the fundamental role of confession in the shaping of the *Book* is strengthened further.[61] Within the *Book* emphasis is placed on the sheer number of times that Margery tells and retells her life-story to many different men. Whilst those men played an important part in its formation, this emphasis leads me to believe that Margery's narrative choices were decisive in creating what was to become the *Book*'s structure.[62] It is significant that Margery secures permission from the archbishop of Canterbury to have her confession heard as often as she wishes (p. 274). There are penitential motives at work here, given Margery's palpable perception of her status as a 'synful caytyf' (p. 41) who required absolution. Although technically, having once confessed 'alle hir synnes, as ner as hir mende wold servyn hir, fro hir childhode unto that owre' (p. 185), and completed her penance, she did not need to keep relating her sins from childhood as she tells us she does. Moreover, at an early stage in the *Book* Christ tells Margery, 'I ... foryefe the thi synnes to the utterest poynt', promising her that she when she dies she will go straight to heaven, avoiding both hell and purgatory (p. 71). Perhaps Margery continued to confess, regardless of this reassurance, just to be on the safe side.⁶³ But another reason why Margery sought the privilege of frequent confession was surely the opportunity this offered to retell her life-story frequently and thus collaboratively to refine it in conversation with well-educated and well-regarded men. Given her predilection for the dramatic, and her familiarity with homiletic discourse, she was doubtless a very good judge of pace and tone too. The embodied nature of oral history and the inherently performative character of the interview are subjects for study in their own right. Analysis of an interviewee's body language and gesture is as important as analysis of what they say.⁶⁴ There is a trace of performativity in Chapter 1's account of Margery's wish to kill herself during her breakdown, 'into wytnesse therof sche bot hir owen hand so vyolently that it was seen al hir lyfe aftyr' (p. 55). When telling this part of her life-story to confessors Margery could show them her scar; the text certainly implies this by stating that it was 'wytnesse' to the horrifying physical effects of the demonic visions she had experienced.

However, given the nature of the patriarchal power dynamic between Margery and the men to whom she spoke, some may question the claim that she exerted primary narrative control over the form and content of the *Book*. The fact that she was a woman and thus, according to contemporary gender ideology, morally and intellectually inferior, provides another explanation for Margery's frequent confession.⁶⁵ She seeks male clerical verification of the spiritual authenticity and thus legitimacy of her visions.⁶⁶ The relative authority of interviewer and interviewee and the implications of this concern oral historians today.⁶⁷ Often the relationship between the two is inherently unequal and this is one of the reasons why empathy is deemed so vital to the interview process. The interviewer's privilege should not result in them telling interviewees what their lives mean, or in using interviewees to ventriloquise their own preconceptions and priorities. James discusses this with respect to his relationship with Doña María and describes a 'redemptive urge' among oral historians which can give rise to such problems during the process of creating oral history.⁶⁸ However, he also contends that to presuppose that the interviewee is inevitably victimised and exploited by the experience seriously underplays the interviewee's capacity to negotiate the terms of communication within an interview.⁶⁹ He gives as an example this exchange from an early stage in his interviews with Doña María:

> DJ: How did the strike of ninety-six days come about?
>
> DM: Because this woman, this one, that one all said to themselves ... Me, for instance, who taught me? The book of life, not the university, pardon me, professor, the university is the best that humanity has because there you learn and the shadows of the mind disappear and wisdom emerges but you know that the university of life is beautiful.[70]

She repeated this equalising claim many times during the months of their encounters; it evidently functioned as a riposte to James's attempts to impose categories of chronology and form on her narrative, mentioned above. Moreover, Doña María's assertion of the value of her different sort of education is borne out by her life-story which relays a number of instances in which she demonstrates eloquence and poise during exchanges with male authority figures. In particular, when she meets Perón she argues so skilfully and compellingly in favour of women having the vote that he asks whether she's a *doctora*, only to be told by a male colleague of Doña María's, amidst laughter, that 'she's a meatpacker'.[71] There are clear parallels here in the way that many of Margery's face-offs with high-ranking ecclesiastics are presented. We are told that people in Lincoln 'merveyled of hir cunning', lawyers telling her 'we han gon to scole many yerys, and yet arn we not sufficient to answeryn as thu dost. Of whom hast thu this cunnyng? And sche seyd: "Of the Holy Gost"' (p. 269). The *Book* continually reiterates her privileged understanding, Christ telling her himself 'ther is no clerk in al this world that can, dowtyr, leryn the bettyr than I can do' (p. 301). On the basis of this spiritual authority Margery challenges both the conduct and the assumptions of the men whom she encounters, which suggests that she would be equally forthright in ensuring what she believed to be the proper, truthful recording of her life-story. It was vitally important to ensure that the recorded story was convincing, in order to support the claims it made about her spiritual privilege. If part of the reason why the *Book* was written was to counter criticism of Margery's way of life, highlighting the truth of her experiences and their endorsement by a panoply of elite and well-qualified clerics was a crucial means of explaining and justifying her conduct and ministry.[72] The status of the *Book* as 'a schort tretys and a comfortabyl for synful wrecchys' and Christ's statement that 'be this boke many a man schal be turnyd to me and belevyn therin' is also crucial (p. 41, p. 379). Margery's account needs to be authentic and believable because her voice carries Christ's voice; thus the historical truth of the text is the prerequisite for its theological truth. Having her life-story written down would also testify to the veracity of her experiences and to her holiness after her death, when she would no longer be there to relate it in person.

To conclude, a confession of my own: I have never been able to be objective about Margery Kempe and her *Book*. While writing this chapter I realised that there is no other medieval text which I have revisited and reconsidered so frequently in the nearly thirty years since I first read it. Margery matters to me. For this reason I find the attitudes to subjectivity espoused by those working on oral history both valuable and inspiring, especially Yow's call for historians not to 'pretend there is nothing going on inside of us that is influencing the research and interpretation' but instead to employ inner feelings as part of our methodological toolkits.[73] My encounters with Margery over the years feel like a form of intersubjectivity because they have impacted not only my understanding of the medieval past but also my development as a historian; my evolving conception of what history is and how best to do it. When I first read the *Book* I became preoccupied with whether or not it constituted 'telling the truth', wanting very much, somehow, to be able to prove that what Margery said happened, really had happened, with reference to external documentary corroboration. But I find now that I am far more interested in the truth of Margery's *telling*. I was particularly struck by this assertion, with which James concludes his account of reading Doña María's life-story for gender:

> I think that we must pay Doña María the respect of assuming that her recounting of her life faithfully reflects – mediated as her telling is by existing narratives and dominant ideologies – the way in which a working-class woman experienced gender and class relations in a particular historical era.[74]

With a little necessary tweaking of the wording, I would say exactly the same of Margery Kempe. The *Book* presents itself as Margery's own true story about her life, scrupulously recorded in a collaborative process which enhances, rather than diminishes her ownership of that narrative, and the claims it makes about her uniqueness. Bringing the *Book* into dialogue with oral history and its methodologies, in concert with the insights enabled by my personal encounter with Margery, has therefore brought me to the conclusion that what makes *The Book of Margery Kempe* history is its form as much as its content.

Notes

This chapter was inspired by my encounter with the research of Lindsey Dodd to whom I am extremely grateful for invaluable guidance about the practice and scholarship of oral history. I would also like to thank the editors for their extremely helpful comments on a draft of this chapter.

1 *The Book of Margery Kempe*, ed. Barry Windeatt (Cambridge: D. S. Brewer, 2006), pp. 52–3. All subsequent page references are given parenthetically in the text.
2 Oral history methodologies have rarely been brought to bear on medieval sources but for important exceptions see Lori Ann Garner, '"Stories which I know to be true": oral tradition, oral history, and voices from the past', *The Oral History Review*, 43 (2016), 263–91, and Bronach C. Kane, *Popular Memory and Gender in Medieval England: Men, Women and Testimony in the Church Courts, c. 1200–1500* (Woodbridge: Boydell Press, 2019), esp. pp. 4–9.
3 E.g. Ellen M. Ross, 'Spiritual experience and women's autobiography: the rhetoric of selfhood in *The Book of Margery Kempe*', *Journal of the American Academy of Religion*, 59 (1991), 527–46; Karen A. Winstead, *The Oxford History of Life-Writing, Volume 1: The Middle Ages* (Oxford: Oxford University Press, 2018), pp. 69–79.
4 Robert C. Ross, 'Oral life, written text: the genesis of *The Book of Margery Kempe*', *The Yearbook of English Studies*, 22 (1992), 226–37, p. 226.
5 Luisa Passerini, *Fascism in Popular Memory: The Cultural Experience of the Turin Working Class*, trans. Robert Lumley and Jude Bloomfield (Cambridge: Cambridge University Press, 1987).
6 Ross, 'Oral life, written text', pp. 228 and 236.
7 Useful summaries of differing viewpoints on the issue are provided by Sebastian Sobecki, '"The writyng of this tretys": Margery Kempe's son and the authorship of her book', *Studies in the Age of Chaucer*, 37 (2015), 257–83, pp. 266–7, and Anthony Bale, 'Richard Salthouse of

Norwich and the scribe of *The Book of Margery Kempe*', *The Chaucer Review*, 52 (2017), 173–87, pp. 175–6.

8   Bale highlights the necessity of considering Salthouse as a further editor of the *Book*, 'Richard Salthouse', pp. 176–7.

9   Ross, 'Oral life, written text', p. 236; cf. John Hirsh's suggestion that the scribe put Margery's 'random thoughts into a larger context' by asking her questions about her experiences, 'Author and scribe in *The Book of Margery Kempe*', *Medium Aevum*, 44 (1975), 145–50, p. 149.

10 The point that Margery helped him make sense of the text is reiterated at the very end of Book I (p. 384). The recording of Book II was different, the scribe tells us that this time he himself directly wrote down Margery's account of subsequent experiences 'aftyr hyr owyn tunge' (p. 385).

11 I would like to thank Felicity Riddy for first drawing my attention to Margery's propensity for repeatedly retelling her life-story during an MA seminar on the *Book* in 1992; see Felicity Riddy, 'Text and self in *The Book of Margery Kempe*', in Linda Olson and Kathryn Kerby-Fulton (eds), *Voices in Dialogue: Reading Women in the Middle Ages* (Notre Dame: University of Notre Dame Press, 2005), pp. 435–53, p. 445.

12 Similarly, Diane Watt, in highlighting the collaborative nature of this relationship, states that Margery was '*intimately* involved in the composition of her own text' (emphasis in original) and strongly counters interpretations which deny Margery's compositional agency, see Watt, *Medieval Women's Writing: Works by and for Women in England, 1100–1500* (Cambridge and Malden: Polity, 2007), pp. 119 and 131.

13 See Paul Thompson with Joanna Bornat, *The Voice of the Past: Oral History*, fourth edition (Oxford: Oxford University Press, 2017), pp. 23–70, and Robert Perks and Alistair Thomson (eds), *The Oral History Reader*, third edition (London and New York: Routledge, 2016), pp. 1–21, for more detailed discussion of what follows.

14 Oral history is generally regarded as a technique rather than a type of history, hence it is conventional for its practitioners to talk about 'doing' oral history, e.g. Donald A. Ritchie, *Doing Oral History: A Practical Guide*, third edition (Oxford: Oxford University Press, 2014).

15 Perks and Thomson, *Oral History Reader*, pp. 135–46.

16 Kathryn Anderson and Dana C. Jack, 'Learning to listen: interview techniques and analyses', in Perks and Thomson, *Oral History Reader*, pp. 179–92, present instructive reflections on the innate intersubjectivity of the interview.

17 Luisa Passerini, 'Work ideology and consensus under Italian fascism', *History Workshop Journal*, 8 (1979), 82–118.

18 Valerie Yow, '"Do I like them too much?": effects of the oral history interview on the interviewer and vice-versa', *The Oral History Review*, 24 (1997), 55–79. The relationship between historian and interviewee is further discussed below.
19 Valerie Raleigh Yow, *Recording Oral History: A Guide for the Humanities and Social Sciences*, third edition (Lanham: Rowman & Littlefield, 2015); practical guidance is also provided by Thompson and Bornat, *Voice of the Past*, pp. 266–402.
20 Michael Roper, 'The unconscious work of history', *Cultural and Social History*, 11 (2014), 169–93, p. 171; see also Yow, '"Do I like them too much?"', pp. 69–70. Donald Bloxham has recently argued that it is both valid and advantageous for historians to make considered value judgements about the past, *History and Morality* (Oxford: Oxford University Press, 2020).
21 Alicia Spencer-Hall's paralleling of Margery Kempe and Kim Kardashian West offers a perspicacious analysis of modern responses to Margery, see *Medieval Saints and Modern Screens: Divine Visions as Cinematic Experience* (Amsterdam: Amsterdam University Press, 2018), pp. 147–92.
22 Lynn Abrams, 'Transforming oral history through theory', in Thompson and Bornat, *Voice of the Past*, pp. 132–9, p. 135.
23 *Ibid.*, p. 135; see also Lynn Abrams, 'Liberating the female self: epiphanies, conflict and coherence in the life stories of post-war British women', *Social History*, 39:1 (2014), 14–35.
24 Alessandro Portelli, 'The peculiarities of oral history', *History Workshop*, 12 (1981), 96–107.
25 For more detailed discussion of approaches to memory see Thompson and Bornat, *Voice of the Past*, pp. 238–65; Perks and Thomson, *Oral History Reader*, pp. 297–310.
26 Portelli, 'The peculiarities of oral history', p. 100 (emphasis in the original).
27 *Ibid.*, p. 100.
28 Thompson and Bornat, *Voice of the Past*, pp. 188–237.
29 Abrams, 'Transforming oral history', pp. 132–9. Although in this chapter I refer to historians throughout it should be noted that it is not only historians who do oral history.
30 Ross, 'Oral life, written text', p. 236, n. 30. His planned article was apparently never published.
31 Yow, '"Do I like them too much?"', pp. 66–8; Sherna Berger Gluck and Daphne Patai (eds), *Women's Words: The Feminist Practice of Oral History* (New York and London: Routledge, 1991).
32 Thompson and Bornat, *Voice of the Past*, pp. 140–87.

33 Perks and Thomson, *Oral History Reader*, pp. 569–80.
34 This is highlighted by Lindsey Dodd, *French Children under the Allied Bombs, 1940–45: An Oral History* (Manchester: Manchester University Press, 2016).
35 Susan J. Matt, 'Current emotion research in history: or, doing history from the inside out', *Emotion Review*, 3 (2011), 117–24.
36 Daniel James, *Doña María's Story: Life, History, Memory, and Political Identity* (Durham, NC, and London: Duke University Press, 2000). I owe to Lindsey Dodd the idea of paralleling Doña María with Margery Kempe.
37 James, *Doña María's Story*, pp. 158–9.
38 Ibid., p. 242.
39 Ibid., pp. 213–43.
40 Lindsey Dodd makes use of archived interviews in '"It's not what I saw, it's not what I thought": challenges "from below" to dominant versions of the French wartime past', forthcoming in a special issue of *Conserveries mémorielles: revue transdisciplinaire*, no. 25, 2021. The issue of drawing on interviews which she did not create will be further discussed in her forthcoming book *Feeling Memory: Remembering Wartime Childhoods in France*.
41 E.g. Anthony Goodman, *Margery Kempe and Her World* (London: Pearson Education, 2002); Kate Parker, 'Lynn and the making of a mystic', in John H. Arnold and Katherine J. Lewis (eds), *A Companion to Margery Kempe* (Cambridge: D. S. Brewer, 2004), pp. 55–74; Sobecki, 'Margery Kempe's son'. See also the excellent explanatory notes to *The Book of Margery Kempe*, trans. Anthony Bale (Oxford: Oxford University Press, 2015).
42 On the guild entries see Laura Kalas, Chapter 11 below.
43 Matthew Kempshall, *Rhetoric and the Writing of History, 400–1500* (Manchester and New York: Manchester University Press, 2011), p. 3.
44 Marcus Bull, *Eyewitness and Crusade Narrative: Perception and Narration in Accounts of the Second, Third and Fourth Crusades* (Woodbridge: Boydell Press, 2018), p. 3.
45 James, *Doña María's Story*, p. 135.
46 Ibid., p. 135.
47 Ibid., p. 137.
48 Similarly, Margery Kempe's narrative can be read as one thread within Lynn's story see Laura Varnam, 'The importance of St Margaret's church in *The Book of Margery Kempe*: a sacred place and an exemplary parishioner', *Nottingham Medieval Studies*, 61 (2017), 197–243.
49 James, *Doña María's Story*, p. 31.

50 These representative descriptors taken from www.bl.uk/collection-items/the-book-of-margery-kempe and www.bl.uk/people/margery-kempe [accessed 8 June 2020].
51 As discussed, for example, by Nicholas Watson, 'The making of *The Book of Margery Kempe*', in Olson and Kerby-Fulton, *Voices in Dialogue*, pp. 295–434, pp. 406–7.
52 Cf. Abrams, 'Transforming oral history', p. 135. Margery's frequent relation of her life-story throughout the *Book* calls into question the Proem's statement that she had forgotten the timing and ordering of events by the time they were written down.
53 The epiphanic moment within women's life-stories is defined by Abrams as the event or experience which 'offers her a way of explaining to herself who she is now in order to explain to the audience (and herself) who she was then', Abrams, 'Liberating the female self', 23.
54 E.g. Goodman, *Margery Kempe*, p. 89.
55 With thanks to Damian Riddle for useful discussion of the experience of confession.
56 Alexander Freund, '"Confessing animals": toward a *longue durée* history of the oral history interview', *The Oral History Review*, 41 (2014), 1–26.
57 For the likelihood of questions determining aspects of the *Book*'s narrative see my discussion above.
58 This was influenced by Joanne Bornat, 'Remembering and reworking emotions: the reanalysis of emotion in an interview', in Perks and Thomson, *Oral History*, pp. 434–44 (p. 436).
59 Sobecki, 'Margery Kempe's son', p. 281 (emphasis in the original).
60 Riddy, 'Text and self', p. 438, and Sobecki, 'Margery Kempe's son', p. 280, also underline the collaborative nature of the *Book*. One of the interviewees, Rachel, whom Dodd discusses in '"It's not what I saw"', had retold her story of wartime experiences many times with a didactic purpose before it was finally recorded.
61 For the strong possibility that Spryngolde was the scribe see Sobecki, 'Margery Kempe's son', pp. 271–8.
62 Watson similarly argues 'that Kempe herself, not her scribe, was primarily responsible for the *Book*'s structure, arguments and most of its language', 'Making of the *Book*', p. 397.
63 Margery's compulsive need to confess is established early in the *Book*, pp. 63–4.
64 James, *Doña María's Story*, pp. 183–5.
65 For discussion of medieval misogynistic traditions see Alcuin Blamires, *Woman Defamed and Woman Defended* (Oxford: Clarendon Press, 1992).

66 Rosalynn Voaden, *God's Words, Women's Voices: The Discernment of Spirits in the Writing of Late-Medieval Women Visionaries* (Woodbridge and Rochester, NY: York Medieval Press, 1999).
67 See works cited above in notes 18 and 19.
68 James, *Doña María's Story*, p. 138.
69 Ibid., pp. 139–40. Bornat admits that she originally considered one of her interviewees, Mrs Lockwood, as 'some kind of resource that would switch on in response to my questions. The idea that she might be an active agent in the interview, not simply an "empty vessel" without ideas and perspectives of her own had not occurred to me', 'Remembering and reworking emotions', p. 439. Sometimes interviewees contest historians' analysis of their life stories, e.g. Katherine Borland, '"That's not what I said": interpretive conflict in oral narrative research', in Perks and Thomson, *Oral History Reader*, pp. 412–23.
70 James, *Doña María's Story*, pp. 140–1.
71 Ibid., pp. 174–5, for Doña María's account of the meeting, pp. 182–3 for James's discussion of this and other comparable incidents.
72 Goodman, *Margery Kempe*, p. 92, states that the *Book* may have been intended to assuage 'clerical controversy about her'; Riddy, 'Text and self', pp. 436–7, contends that the *Book* was being written at the same time Margery was looking after her husband, following his fall and incapacity, after which we are told she was heavily criticised for having prioritised her spiritual pursuits and not looked after him properly, pp. 329–32; Watson, 'Making of the *Book*', p. 395, points out that the *Book* testifies to Margery having garnered a national reputation by 1417.
73 Yow, '"Do I like them too much?"', p. 70.
74 James, *Doña María's Story*, pp. 242–3.

7

'A booke of hyr felyngys': exemplarity and Margery Kempe's encounters of the heart

Laura Varnam

In Chapter 53 of *The Book of Margery Kempe*, Margery has been imprisoned in a house in Beverley, Yorkshire, belonging to 'on of the mennys wifys that had arestyd hir'.[1] But she does not allow this confinement to prevent her from continuing to address the communities that gather around her with 'comownycacyon and good wordys', just as she justified her speech in the previous chapter when a clerk tried to silence her by citing St Paul's prohibition against women preachers (p. 253). Margery defies her jailers and persists in her encounter with the people of Beverley by standing 'lokyng owt at a wyndown, tellyng many good talys to hem that wolde heryn hir, in-so-meche that women wept sor and seyde wyth gret hevynes of her hertys: "Alas, woman, why schalt thu be brent?"' (p. 260). Margery's good tales from the window establish a community of supportive women who demonstrate their empathy by weeping and lamenting her possible fate 'wyth gret hevynes of her hertys'. Furthermore, when Margery tells the good wife of the house that she is thirsty 'and the good wife seyde hir husband had born awey the key, wherfor she myth not comyn to hir, ne yevyn hir drynke' (p. 260), Margery's female allies collude to subvert the husband's power. 'The women tokyn a leddyr and set up to the wyndown, and yovyn hir a pynte of wyn in a potte, and toke hir a pece, besechyng hir to settyn awey the potte prevyly and the pece, that whan the good man come, he myth not aspye it' (p. 260). The window becomes a permeable threshold for nourishment and exchange, sustained by female bonding and resistance. Men may try to lock doors against Margery in her *Book*, but women find a way to open a window and let their sister speak.

This empowering encounter between Margery Kempe and the women of Beverley – in which her voice is heard and their hearts are affected – is a springboard for my argument in this chapter that the *Book* represents Margery as an exemplary laywoman whose interaction with her internal audience and external readers is predicated on an emotional exchange that takes place in the heart. In *Margery Kempe and the Lonely Reader*, Rebecca Krug argues that Margery produced her *Book* in order to 'find, sustain, and interact with fellow believers who were also looking to live lives of intense spiritual engagement'.[2] This interaction with her fellow believers, especially women, depends upon the cultivation and 'stirring' of a heart-felt devotion that draws the reader towards Margery and, through Margery, towards Christ. It is critically accepted that as readers we can learn from Margery Kempe's *Book*, as recent work on her exemplarity has demonstrated, but precisely *how* we are to do this, through what mechanisms that learning takes place, repays further investigation.[3] The Proem describes Margery's text as a 'booke of hyr felyngys and hir revelacyons' (p. 46) and in the first part of this chapter I will show how those feelings create affective bonds with her internal audiences and her external readers that enable us to put her good example into practice and, furthermore, to examine how a life such as Margery's becomes exemplary in the first place.

In my discussion of the 'stirring' of emotions in Margery's *Book*, I am indebted to A. S. Lazikani, whose book *Cultivating the Heart* 'avoids the terminology of texts "producing" or "creating" feeling, referring instead to language stimulating, nurturing or shaping' affective experience:

> Texts may introduce new modes of feeling, awaken feeling that is latent, enable expression of affective pain when it is otherwise inexpressible, and intensify sensation. But they cannot 'produce' feeling in a vacuum.[4]

This is crucial to my argument in the second part of this chapter that *The Book of Margery Kempe* draws upon pre-existing methods of 'stirring' the emotions by using, and repeating, an inset Middle English lyric, the imagery and rhyme of which would have been familiar to a lay audience: 'Lord, for alle thi wowndys smert, drawe al the lofe of myn hert into thyn hert' (p. 305).[5] As I will demonstrate, the heart is specifically activated in the *Book* as the locus for a stirring of compassion and empathy through the appeal to Christ's painful wounds and this enables Margery to bond both with her supporters and with her readers. The imagery of the heart at the centre of an emotional exchange between Christ and the devotee is a well-established trope in Middle English lyrics and it forms part of a long tradition of the heart as a source of devotion and emotion, crystallised in the cult of the Sacred Heart at Helfta in the thirteenth century, as Rosalyn Voaden and Naoë Kukita Yoshikawa have shown, and burgeoning in the fifteenth century.[6] The heart is a central image in Mechthild of Hackeborn's *Booke of Gostlye Grace*, which Liz McAvoy and Naoë Kukita Yoshikawa's Chapter 2 above argues was influential for Margery's *Book*, and I will show how the imagery of the heart in *The Book of Margery Kempe* relates to Mechthild's 'cardiocentric spirituality' as well as to the Middle English lyric tradition.[7] Yoshikawa argues that 'the trope of the physical and metaphorical hearts serves to generate devotional aspiration' and I will show how the use of the embedded heart lyric in the *Book* functions as a shorthand for how Margery's readers might put her aspirational example into practice.[8]

Margery Kempe's 'unruly' exemplarity and supportive female networks

Margery Kempe's appearance at the window in Chapter 53 frames her as a visible exemplar. The women of Beverley, both literally and metaphorically, look up to her and the episode exploits the rich symbolic potential of this location to establish her authority. Her elevated position, although no pulpit, commands her audience's attention and her desire for a drink recalls Christ's thirst on the cross (John 19.28-9). Margaret Hostetler has persuasively argued that this episode 'manipulates the images of spatial discourse specific to anchoresses' in order to draw on and critique the ways in which enclosure produces holy women's subjectivity.[9] 'The opening of the window and the exchange of food as corrupting factors are commonplace in anchoritic texts', Hostetler notes, drawing on Aelred of Rievaulx's portrayal of the gossiping anchoress, but here the encounter is spiritually edifying and emotionally stirring for the audience of women.[10] Kempe's *Book* thus 'alert[s] the reader to how enclosure … can unite or connect women', who in this case band together to rebel against the good woman's husband as a result of their compassion for Margery's plight.[11]

The framing of this episode at the close of Chapter 53 is significant because earlier in the chapter Margery's relationship with local women appears to be less than supportive.[12] When she is accused of Lollardy in Hessle, 'women cam rennyng owt of her howsys wyth her rokkys [distaffs], crying to the pepil: "Brennyth this fals heretyk!"' (p. 258) and when she is brought into Beverley, her disruption of gender norms is foregrounded when 'men of the cuntre' tell her to 'forsake this lyfe that thu hast, and go spynne and carde as other women don' (p. 258). Windeatt notes the appropriately anti-Lollard stance of this imagery, quoting Bodley MS 649: 'tak the to thi distaff, coveyt not to be a prest ne prechour, schal never cloc henne be wel crowing cok'.[13] And yet, at the end of the chapter, Margery persists in telling 'good talys'. The women violently brandishing their distaffs and calling for Margery to be burned are diametrically opposed to the women beneath the window who experience 'gret hevynes of her hertys'. The *Book* deliberately offers us these two images of female community to choose from – one threatening, one nourishing – and 'yf lak of charyte be not ower hynderawnce' as the Proem to the *Book* carefully notes (p. 41), we will imitate the latter group (and the extended description of the window episode would support the text's investment in this second response).[14] Chapter 53 demonstrates that Margery's exemplarity is not uncontested in the *Book*'s internal timeline, and indeed Diane Watt has argued for the importance of a feminist reading of the text which accommodates 'discord and disagreement' in its recuperation of 'the marginalized female presences within the *Book*'.[15] It is striking, then, that both responses unite women in subversive, communal action, whether breaking out of the houses in which, ironically, they should be spinning, or attempting to break in to the house that serves as Margery's prison.

Margery Kempe is, as Anthony Bale puts it, an 'unruly figure' and her unruliness is, I argue, a crucial part of the way her exemplarity works in the *Book*.[16] Kempe is neither a straightforwardly positive or negative exemplum in her text and it is in her encounters with others in the *Book* that potential exemplary responses to her are tested and negotiated. Margery's exemplarity is always in process because it is being created anew in each moment of encounter, and this is in large part because Margery is a laywoman whose holy identity, as I have argued elsewhere, depends upon repeated performances of piety for its authority, authenticity, and shape.[17] Margery is creating a new model for intense lay piety which, naturally, is open to critique within the *Book* and in our encounter with it as readers. Individual episodes must be contextualised, therefore, in order to examine the discourses within which they are operating; Chapter 53, as we have seen, engages with enclosure and women's speech in public space, for example. But what many of these encounters have in common is that they model an emotional response which the reader can imitate in order to put Margery's example into practice in their own engagement with her text, and in this chapter I will focus specifically on those emotional responses which are located in the heart.

The *Book* invites us to think more flexibly about how we understand interactions between medieval exemplary texts and their readers, and precisely how and where those interactions take place. Here my work extends Jessica Rosenfeld's recent article on 'Envy and exemplarity in *The Book of Margery Kempe*' in which she offers a definition of exemplarity as 'a space where imitation and identification are both invited and contested'.[18] In the *Book* 'one witnesses a narrative of someone *choosing* exemplarity for herself, openly negotiating her relationship to other holy women and thinking about the possibilities of others worshipping and imitating her'.[19] And it is not only her relationship with *holy* women that is negotiated, as I will show. Rosenfeld concludes that 'as exemplary figure, Margery begets desire, but does not predetermine the transformation of that desire into particular actions or experiences' and, whilst I concur with Rosenfeld overall, there is one particular 'script for the performance of feeling', to use Sarah McNamer's helpful phrase, that is very clearly offered by the *Book* for imitative action and that is the aforementioned lyric about the heart, a key image in Margery's text and one that also reflects the *Book*'s encounter with the work of Mechthild of Hackeborn as I will discuss below.[20] This lyric directly enables the reader to transform desire into efficacious devotional experiences.

Before I examine this notion in further detail, however, it is important to contextualise Margery's encounters with supportive women in the *Book*. Whilst my analysis of Chapter 53 demonstrates the need for a nuanced picture – the need for which Diane Watt rightly called – critical discussion has often been quick to dismiss Margery's female relationships out of hand. Colleen Donnelly, for example, declares that Margery Kempe 'lacked female friends and was generally at odds with the women around her', remaining 'aloof and estranged from female community'.[21] She contends that the 'salient lack of female friendship and affection found in Margery's text ... suggests that Margery apparently failed to make ties, or severed the ones she had, with female family members, neighbours, and matrons of the community'.[22] But these claims are not fully borne out by the *Book* itself or indeed by recent work on Margery's female friendships and their significance (including important new research by Anthony Bale and Daniela Giosuè in Chapter 9 below). In fact, Margery established a wealth of supportive social and spiritual relationships with a variety of women in England and abroad, from meetings with high-status individuals such as Margaret Florentyne and Julian of Norwich (discussed by Bale and Giosuè (Chapter 9, this volume), and Tara Williams (Chapter 13, this volume) respectively) to informal encounters with unnamed women or groups of women, such as the Beverley community discussed above. As Karma Lochrie argues, 'it is important to see in Kempe's book that she inhabits and is fostered by a female community that the narrative itself credits' and, as I will show, these encounters are often grounded in mutually supportive affective exchange.[23] Indeed, such is Margery's 'charismatic appeal' to women that the Mayor of Leicester fears that she has 'comyn hedyr to han awey owr wyvys fro us and ledyn hem wyth the' (p. 236).[24] Here Margery appears like a Pied Piper of Hamelin figure, stealing women away from their husbands; it is no wonder 'men of the cuntre' wish she would 'spynne and carde as other women dor' (p. 258). The Mayor also hints at a fear of autonomous groups of women; led by Margery in her eye-catching white clothes, what havoc might such women cause? I have written elsewhere about the empowering possibilities of female support networks as a way of authorising Margery's identity as a holy laywoman and, moreover, creating a space for a female devotional independence that sidesteps clerical control.[25] The priest who criticises Margery's emotional response to the pietà in Chapter 60, for example, is corrected by a good lady who becomes 'hir avoket [advocate]' and declares Margery to be a 'good exampyl to me, and to other men also, the grace that God werkyth in hir sowle' (p. 286). This chance encounter in a Norwich church contributes to Margery's exemplarity as an emotional role model, inspired by the Virgin Mary's compassion, and depicts a devotional practice that is mutually enriching for women.

Both Kathy Lavezzo and Jonathan Hsy have explored the queer potential of Margery's emotional and physical encounters with women in her *Book*. Lavezzo has analysed 'the homoerotics of compassion' that arise from the 'sobs and sighs' exchanged between women, arguing that 'Margery's affective mourning exerts a unifying effect that is twofold, binding together both the *Book* itself and, at times, the women represented in it'.[26] Building on Lavezzo's work, Jonathan Hsy examines the ways in which Margery's encounter with female lepers in Chapter 74 opens up the possibility for 'illicit desires *between* women' in the *Book*.[27] Hsy concludes his essay by suggesting that we need to 'go farther in acknowledging how this woman's non-normative or socially unorthodox desires disperse and inflame unexpected desires in others – including readers of the *Book* itself' and that the full impact of the 'affective "touch" on readers' requires further investigation.[28] The use of 'touch' here invokes Carolyn Dinshaw's concept of the 'touch across time', and this chapter takes up Hsy's call by showing that for the reader that touch can take place in an emotional encounter in the heart.[29]

A number of Margery's interactions with women combine physical and emotional touch and create a safe and nurturing space for Margery's body when overcome by devotional feelings. When she is on her way to Rome she encounters a woman who has a Christ-child doll and she observes other women playing with this doll in their devotions, they 'puttyn schirtys therupon and kyssyn it as thei it had ben God hymselfe' (p. 177). The women's 'worshep' and 'reverens' moves Margery deeply and her intense emotional response has a reciprocal effect on the women:

> Whan thes good women seyn this creatur wepyn, sobbyn, and cryen so wondirfully and mythtyly that sche was nerhand ovyrcomyn therwyth, than thei ordeyned a good soft bed and leyd hir therupon, and comfortyd hir as mech as thei myth for owyr Lordys lofe, blyssed mot he ben! (p. 178)[30]

The maternal affection that the women practised on the Christ-child doll is now lavished on Margery as they comfort her on a good soft bed. Lavezzo argues that 'Margery not only turns from spectator into spectacle, but also shifts from her position as an imagined recipient of feminine attention to its outright object'.[31] The women are bound together by emotional imitation, and, in another episode in Rome, compassion is shown to transcend differences of language and geographical background when Margery is overcome by the Passion of Christ:

> The good women, havyng compassyon of hir sorwe and gretly mervelyng of hir wepyng and of hir crying, meche the mor thei lovyd hir. And therfor thei, desiryng to make hir solas and comfort aftyr hir gostly labowr – be sygnys and tokenys, for sche undirstod not her speche – preyid hir, and in a maner compellyd hir, to comyn hom to hem, willyng that sche schulde not gon fro hem. (p. 209)

The women's imitative compassion increases their love for Margery and they cannot bear to part from her. The women's behaviour towards Margery is exemplary and this is reinforced by the passage's use of vocabulary that echoes the *Book*'s statement of purpose in the Proem. They desire to 'make hir solas and comfort' just as the *Book* is described as 'a schort tretys and a comfortabyl for synful wrecchys, wherin thei may have gret *solas and comfort* to hem' (p. 41). The reader of *The Book of Margery Kempe* can achieve 'solas and comfort' for themselves by imitating the 'solas and comfort' which is offered to Margery in such encounters with supportive women. But the *Book* goes further than merely providing us with individual episodes of positive emotional imitation. By way of a repeated lyric that draws on popular devotional language and imagery, the text shows us precisely how we can take Margery's book of feelings to heart in our own performative reading practice.

Stirring the heart towards God

Larry Scanlon argues that a person becomes 'exemplary precisely by transforming his or her actions into a moral narrative' and this is what happens to Margery's life in her *Book*.[32] As the Proem declares, 'alle the werkys of ower Saviowr ben for ower exampyl and instruccyon, and what grace that he werkyth in any creatur is ower profyth, yf lak of charyte be not ower hynderawnce' (p. 41). But if Margery Kempe is to function as an 'exampyl', a 'model to be imitated', precisely how is that imitation meant to occur?[33] The Proem hints that the reader's attitude will be crucial to this process as a lack of charity will hinder our ability to learn from the text and, as we have already seen, a positive emotional outcome is envisaged because by reading this treatise sinful wretches 'may have gret solas and comfort', in addition to being able to understand 'the hy and unspecabyl mercy of ower sovereyn Savyowr Cryst Jhesu' (p. 41). A significant part of Christ's mercy is the way in which he encourages Margery to love and follow him:

> This lytyl tretys schal tretyn sumdeel in parcel of hys wonderful werkys, how mercyfully, how benyngly, and how charytefully he *meved and stered* a synfyl caytyf unto hys love, whech synful caytyf many yerys was in wyl and in purpose, thorw *steryng* of the Holy Gost, to *folwyn* oure Savyowr ... This creatur, whych many yerys had gon wyl and evyr ben unstable, was parfythly *drawen* and *steryd* to entren the wey of hy perfeccyon, whech parfyth wey Cryst ower Savyowr in hys propyr persoone *examplyd*. Sadly he trad it and dewly he went beforn. (pp. 41–2)

Christ is the ultimate example and the *Book* establishes exemplary imitation as a spatial and emotional forward movement in the metaphor of following the path that Christ has walked before and in verbs such as 'meved', 'stered', and 'drawen'. As in modern English, to be 'moved' can be both literal and emotional, and to be 'drawen' can mean pulled, attracted, and directed (both emotionally and spiritually).[34] The *Book*'s use of 'steryd' is especially fertile here. From the verb 'steren' it means to guide or lead but given its collocation with the verb 'meven', I would suggest that 'steryd' and 'steryng' also drawn on the meaning of 'stiren'.[35] This verb means 'to set in motion' but also 'to affect emotionally; to stir up (someone's feelings), of emotions or feelings: be aroused'.[36] The association of stirring with the emotions and the generation of a virtuous state can also be found elsewhere in the *Book*. In Chapter 16 Margery's 'communycacion was so mech in the lofe of God that the herars wer oftyntyme steryd therthorw to wepyn ryt sadly' (p. 112) and in Chapter 74, when Margery kisses and speaks to the female lepers, the *Book* tells us that she 'steryd hem to mekenes and pacyens' (p. 327). The potential for enlivening spiritual qualities is also evident when Margery marvels at the miraculous 'steryng and mevyng of the blyssed sacrament', which 'schok and flekeryd to and fro as a dowe flekeryth wyth her wengys' (p. 129). The association of the term with the Holy Spirit in the form of a dove here takes us back to the Proem's description of the 'steryng of the Holy Gost' which enables the 'synfyl caytyf' Margery to follow Christ's example.

The *Book*'s use of the word 'stirring' to refer to the stimulation of devotional feeling chimes with A. S. Lazikani's argument, discussed above, that texts do not '"produce" feeling in a vacuum', rather they 'awaken feeling that is latent' and 'enable expression of affective pain when it is otherwise inexpressible'. In *The Book of Margery Kempe* this stirring of emotion is specifically activated by the use and repetition of the inset Middle English lyric of the heart, which first appears in Chapter 65: 'Lord, for alle thi wowndys smert, drawe al the lofe of myn hert into thyn hert' (p. 305). The heart is specifically activated in the *Book* as the locus for a stirring of compassion and empathy and it enables Margery to bond both with her supporters and with her readers. The heart had a crucial role in medical and spiritual understandings of the body in this period. As Victoria Blud has shown, whilst 'the modern view takes the brain as the organ of inspiration, the mediaeval view held that the mysteries and miracles of humanity were all proper to the heart'.[37] Furthermore, while 'the capacity for reason might be consulted in the mind, emotion and holy thoughts are granted to the heart'.[38] The heart is one of the most ubiquitous images in *The Book of Margery Kempe* and it is invoked as a space of emotional experience, authenticity, and devotional connection. Christ tells Margery to 'lofe thow me wyth al thin hert, for I love the wyth al myn hert' (p. 97; cf. p. 134) and the phrase 'al myn hert' is frequently invoked as a guarantee of strong and authentic feelings. Margery prays 'wyth al hir hert' (p. 153; cf. 183) and thanks God with all her heart (p. 161; cf. 287) and the importance of the heart in this respect is highlighted when the mayor of Leicester fears that Margery 'menyth not wyth hir hert as sche seyth with hir mowthe' (p. 235). The fire of love is kindled and burns in her heart (p. 228; p. 285) and, like the women of Beverley, Margery feels 'sorwe and hevynes ocupying hir hert' (p. 208; cf. 352). The heart is thus conceived as a site of containment, full of occupying emotion, but the strength of Margery's feelings can threaten its stability. She feels that 'hir hert schulde a brostyn asundyr' when she receives the gift of holy tears at Calvary (p. 163) and when God speaks sweetly to her soul she weeps 'as hir hert schuld a brostyn' (p. 134), this fear of rupture paradoxically reinforcing the importance of protecting the heart as a secure habitation for devotional feelings.

The heart is also a space for divine encounter as God tells Margery that he sits in her heart (p. 336) and that she has 'gret cawse to lovyn me ryth wel and to yevyn me al holy thin hert, that I may fully restyn therin' (p. 374), and I will return to the heart as a space of rest later in this chapter. There is a reciprocity of encounter with God's heart, however, as in Chapter 85 God declares that he is 'ryth besy bothe fornone and aftyrnone to drawe thin hert into myn hert, for thu schuldist kepyn thi mende altogedyr on me' (p. 368). This echoes the drawing together of Christ and Margery's hearts in the embedded lyric which I argue functions as a shorthand for how the reader might put Margery's example into practice.

The first appearance of the lyric in Chapter 65 is when Christ tells her to say to him 'Jhesus est amor meus' and he explains:

> Dowtyr, I have drawe the lofe of thin hert fro alle mennys hertys into myn hert. Sumtyme, dowtyr, thu thowtyst it had ben in a maner unpossybyl for to ben so, and that tyme suffrydyst thu ful gret peyne in thin hert wyth fleschly affeccyons. And than cowdyst thu wel cryen to me, seying, 'Lord, for alle thi wowndys smert, drawe al the lofe of myn hert into thyn hert.' (p. 305)

The lyric repeats Christ's vocabulary of 'drawing' the heart, and the Red Ink Annotator of the *Book* has drawn a heart in the margins of the manuscript next to the lyric to highlight the imagery.[39] But Christ has not only drawn Margery's love from men's hearts to his own, he has given her a devotional tool, 'a script for the performance of feeling', which she can employ when she is overcome by 'fleschly affeccyons'.[40] And the *Book* repeats the lyric on two further occasions, with small variations, as evidence for its usefulness and efficacy for Margery. The first repetition is in Chapter 88 when Margery is spending time in her chamber with her scribe working on her text, rather than attending church. God speaks to Margery about Robert Spryngolde's sharpness towards her and the remedy that God gave her:

> For thow he hath be scharp to the sumtyme, it hath ben gretly to thy profyte, for thu woldist ellys an had to gret affeccyon to hys persone.

And whan he was scharp to the, than thu ronne wyth al thy mynde to me, seying, 'Lord, ther is no trost but in the alone!' And than thu crydist to me wyth a thin hert, 'Lord, for thi wowndys smert drawe alle my lofe into thyn hert.' And, dowtyr, so have I do. (p. 380)

The Red Ink Annotator once again draws attention to the lyric by bracketing the lines in the margin. The lyric appears to be recalled from memory here because, whilst the content and function of the prayer are the same, there are slight variations in phrasing ('thi wowndys' rather than 'alle thi wowndys'; 'alle my lofe' rather than 'the lofe of myn hert'). This second version of the lyric focuses on Margery's use of the prayer and her manner of feeling when she performed it. Margery has stirred within herself the appropriate devotional feeling (she 'crydist to me wyth al thin hert') and Christ does precisely as she requests in the prayer ('so have I do'). This successful performance of the lyric primes the reader to be similarly optimistic about its effects when it appears again, for the third time, in Margery's prayers at the end of her *Book*:

And I prey the, Sovereyn Lord Crist Jhesu, that as many men mote be turnyd be my crying and my wepyng as me han scornyd therfor, er schal scornyn into the werdys ende, and many mo yf it be yowr wille. And, as anemst any erdly mannys love, as wistly as I wolde no love han but God, to lovyn above al thinge and alle other creaturs lovyn for God and in God, al so wistly qwenche in me al fleschly lust, and in alle tho that I have beholdyn thi blisful body in. And yeve us thin holy drede in owr hertys for thi wowndys smert. (p. 423)

By this stage of the *Book* the lyric has been internalised and become part of Margery's devotional practice. In the lyric's first appearance it was offered to Margery by God as a remedy for 'fleschly affecyons' and here Margery's desire for God to 'qwenche in me al fleschly lust' triggers that association. But, rather than merely quoting the lyric, Margery adapts it for this particular context: 'yeve *us* thin holy drede in *owr* hertys for thi wowndys smert.' The shift to plural pronouns co-opts the reader into the process of exchange and rather than drawing our love into Christ's heart, as in the original formulation of the lyric, Margery prays for the opposite movement and for a different emotion altogether: for Christ's 'holy drede' to enter our hearts. The appearance of 'holy drede' – awe or reverence for God – might seem surprising here; God regularly reassures Margery to 'drede the not' in the *Book*.⁴¹ Rebecca Krug argues that Margery lived in a state of perpetual fear in the world but here the reverent dread of God is an emotion to be desired.⁴² In Chapter 77 of the *Book*, Christ explains to Margery that dread is the first stage of the process through which believers come to love God:

> Sumtyme, dowtyr, I make erde-denys [earthquakes] for to feryn the pepil, that thei schulde dredyn me. And so, dowtyr, gostly have I don wyth the and wyth other chosyn sowlys that schal ben savyd, for I turne the erthe of her hertys up-so-down and make hem sore afeerd, that thei dredyn veniawnce schulde fallyn on hem for her synnys. And so dedist thu, dowtyr, whan thu turnedist fyrst to me, and it is nedful that yong begynnarys do so, but now, dowtyr, thu hast gret cawse to lovyn me wel, for the parfyte charite that I yyf the puttyth away al drede fro the. (p. 334)

For Margery, whose example the reader is to follow, dread has been banished by charity and replaced by love. This emotional earthquake is located in the heart and is a crucial part of the process of 'turning' the soul towards Christ. When Margery adapts the lyric in her prayers at the end of her *Book*, it appears in a passage that begins with her desire that 'as many men mote be *turnyd* be my crying and my wepyng as me han scornyd therfor' (p. 423). Before our hearts can be drawn into Christ's heart, they must be prepared by experiencing holy dread, and the *Book* facilitates this by including an adapted version of the lyric in the prayers, a part of the text that is specifically designed for performance.

This imagery of the heart at the centre of an emotional exchange between Christ and the devotee is a well-established trope in Middle English lyrics. Margery's confessor Richard Caister, the holy vicar of St Stephen's, Norwich, makes a similar appeal in his 'Hymn': 'Ihū, for þi woundys smerte, / on fote and handys too, / make me meke and lowe in hert, / and þe to loue as I schulde doo.'⁴³ In the Carthusian miscellany British Library MS Additional 37049, folio 20r features a drawing of the wounded Christ who gestures to his side wound and says in a speech scroll: 'þeis woundes smert bere in þi hert & luf god aye / if þow do þis þu sal haf blys with owten delay.'⁴⁴ On the left-hand side of the page is a lyric entitled 'Querela Divina' in which Christ asks mankind to have his passion in mind, particularly the piercing of his heart which is depicted visually in the centre of the page: 'O man vnkynde / hafe in mynde / my paynes smert. / Beholde & see / þat is for þe / percyd my hert.' Mankind is shown as a layman kneeling at Christ's feet and he replies, 'O lord right dere / þi wordes I here / with hert ful sore.'[45] The hert/smert rhyme, the invocation of the wounds, and the goal of loving Christ functions similarly to the lyric in Margery's *Book* and, just as there the lyric is repeated with variation, the 'Querela divina' also recurs just a few pages later in Additional 37049 on folio 24r.[46] Jessica Brantley has shown that the opening of the 'Querela Divina' was 'widespread, and almost always occurs with some kind of image of Christ's pains' such as a depiction of the wounds or heart.[47] In Margery's *Book* the first appearance of her lyric is accompanied by a heart in the margins of the manuscript. Brantley argues that the lyrics with their 'dialogic interaction between the divine and human' can be understood as 'performative meditations' and I argue that the lyric in Margery's *Book* operates in precisely the same way in Margery's deliberate use of the lyric within her prayers.

In devotional culture Christ's wounded heart is frequently depicted as a space of refuge and sanctuary that is especially available to women. In Julian of Norwich's *Revelations*, Christ invites her into his body through the wound in his side and similarly in Mechthild of Hackeborn's *Booke of Gostlye Grace* the Lord 'schewede her þe wound of his herte and seyde: "Goo in here þat þou maye haffe reste."'[48] The heart is a crucial and repeated image in Mechthild's work, operating as a locus of exchange with Christ, a dwelling-place of comfort, and a source of friendship and connection, both with the godhead and with other women.[49] When Mechthild sees the wound in Christ's heart, the Lord tells her that their love is joined together there: 'In this wounde of luffe sette alle togedders þi luffe to my luffe of þe godhead, for þis wounde es of so grete wydenes þat hitt drawes togeddere heuene ande erthe ande alle þat bene in þame' (p. 175). The heart is imagined as a treasury of divine gifts shared between friends when Mechthild has a vision in which she hears the pulse of the divine heart beating and welcoming the soul: 'com forthe, my freende, þat þou maye reseyue alle gyftes whiche oo freende may gyffe to anothere frende' (p. 326). Symbolic connections are frequently drawn between Mechthild, Christ, and her sisters, when she sees visions in which cords or sunbeams are emitted from Christ's heart and enter their hearts.[50] This connection is especially associated with women in *The Booke of Gostlye Grace* when Christ's heart appears in the likeness of a house in which Mechthild sees four virgins – Meekness, Patience, Softness, and Charity – and he tells her 'ȝiffe þowe desyre to haffe þe vse of my presens and dwelle with me in this howse, stodye to conforme þe to the frendeschippes ande to the homelynes of þees virgyns' (p. 372). 'Conforme' here means to model oneself upon and the communal affection and familiarity of the female virtues here is akin to what we have seen in Margery's *Book*, where women take Margery into their beds or make their homes hospitable to her.[51] When Mechthild wishes to give Christ a present of her heart, he explains:

> 'þowe maye nevere gyffe me a derere ne a more delectable presente þan ȝiff þowe make to me a lytelle howse of þyne herte, in the which I maye delyte and abyde þareyn. Þis howse schalle have botte a wyndowe þorowe whiche y maye speke to menne and departe forth my gyftes.' Offe þis sche hadde vnderstondynge þat here mowth schulde be þat oone wyndowe, with þe whiche mowth sche schulde mynystre Goddes worde be doctrine ande comforth to hem þat come to here. (pp. 388–9)

Mechthild's heart has a window through which she is instructed to preach and comfort humankind, just as Margery offers good tales at the window of the Beverley house to her heavy-hearted female audience. For both women the heart enables devotional exchange and connection with both God and their audiences, and empowers them in their own devotional lives.

Conclusion: heart-felt exemplarity

In Chapter 78 of Margery's *Book*, Christ reinforces Margery's exemplarity by declaring that 'I have ordeyned the to be a merowr amongys hem, for to han gret sorwe, that thei schulde takyn exampil by the for to have sum litel sorwe in her hertys for her synnys, that thei myth therthorw be savyd' (pp. 338–9). By reading Margery Kempe's book of feelings and mirroring her sorrow with their sorrow, humankind can be saved. Margery's exemplarity works by stirring readers' emotions, in their response to individual encounters between Margery and her communities and by way of the embedded lyric that operates as a specific and efficacious emotional script that they can imitate. Margery's female supporters in particular see themselves reflected in her mirror and put that model into practice in their own lives, feeling sorrow for themselves and gathering around Margery when she needs it most. Rebecca Krug argues that:

> As the *Book* unfolds, it invites its readers to see themselves, too, as participants in this spiritual community, to imagine themselves as companions on a spiritual quest, and to read themselves into the pages of the *Book* itself as active agents participating in the same process of reflection, revision, and self-creation in which Kempe, as both author and reader, engages.[52]

That active agency is grounded in emotional imitation so that like 'this creatur' the reader too might be 'parfythly drawen and steryd to entre the wey of hy perfeccyon, whech parfyth wey Cryst ower Savyowr in his propyr persoone examplyd' (p. 42). Feeling for and alongside Margery Kempe also builds communities which are mutually supportive and especially empowering for women's devotional identities, and this might offer a springboard for further feminist engagement with the *Book*. In an article entitled 'Heart feminism', Anne Pollock analyses modern biological, medical, and popular understandings of the heart as an organ in order to suggest that 'thinking with the heart has value for feminist theory':

> Heart feminism's mode ... resonates with Hillary Rose's early eighties argument that feminists should ground our epistemology in 'hand, brain, and heart': which is to say not only in the 'abstraction of male and bourgeois thought,' but also in activism and caring labour.[53]

One of the characteristics of the heart-as-organ that Pollock identifies is its receptivity as a hydraulic system: 'the heart sends blood out by contracting, and because the system is in a loop it need not suck blood back in. It just sends it away, no need of beckoning it to return. By opening again, the blood flows on back. The hospitality of this opening, making space for blood to return, should be understood as agential.'[54] This circularity also characterises the flow of emotions between the hearts of Margery, Christ, and her readers and it leads to a welcoming hospitality when Christ's heart becomes a refuge and a source of friendship and community, as we saw in Mechthild's visions. Margery's emotional exchanges with women in her *Book* generate an 'activism and caring labor' that we as modern scholars, teachers, and students would do well to follow when we encounter *The Book of Margery Kempe* in the twenty-first century.

This chapter is dedicated to the memory of Rebecca Henderson, a brilliant medieval scholar whose courage, persistence, energy, and above all kind-heartedness are an example to us all.

Notes

1. *The Book of Margery Kempe*, ed. Barry Windeatt (Cambridge: D. S. Brewer, 2004), p. 259. All subsequent quotations refer to this edition by page number.
2. Rebecca Krug, *Margery Kempe and the Lonely Reader* (Ithaca: Cornell University Press, 2017), p. 20.
3. See Jessica Rosenfeld, 'Envy and exemplarity in *The Book of Margery Kempe*', *Exemplaria*, 26:1 (2014), 105–21, and Laura Varnam, 'The importance of St Margaret's church in *The Book of Margery Kempe*: a sacred place and an exemplary parishioner', *Nottingham Medieval Studies*, 61 (2017), 197–243.
4. A. S. Lazikani, *Cultivating the Heart: Feeling and Emotion in Twelfth- and Thirteenth-Century Religious Texts* (Cardiff: University of Wales Press, 2015), p. 4.
5. This rhyming couplet appears, with small but significant variation, three times in the *Book* (pp. 305, 380, and, in Margery's prayers, on p. 423). I will show in detail below how it draws upon the 'smert/hert' rhyme which is typical of such devotional lyrics and their operations.
6. Rosalynn Voaden, 'All girls together: community, gender and vision at Helfta', in Diane Watt (ed.), *Medieval Women in Their Communities* (Toronto: University of Toronto Press, 1997), pp. 72–91, and Naoë Kukita Yoshikawa, 'Mechtild of Hackeborn and Cecily Neville's devotional reading: images of the heart in fifteenth-century England', in Anita Auer, Denis Renevey, Camille Marshall, and Tino Oudesluijs (eds), *Revising the Medieval North of England: Interdisciplinary Approaches* (Cardiff: University of Wales Press, 2019), pp. 25–38.
7. Yoshikawa, 'Mechtild of Hackeborn and Cecily Neville's devotional reading', p. 33. On Mechtild's influence on Kempe's *Book* see McAvoy and Yoshikawa, Chapter 2 above, and Liz Herbert McAvoy, '"O der lady, be my help": women's visionary writing and the devotional literary canon', *Chaucer Review*, 51:1 (2016), 68–87.

8 Yoshikawa, 'Mechtild of Hackeborn and Cecily Neville's devotional reading', p. 28.
9 Margaret Hostetler, '"I wold thu wer closyd in an hows of ston": re-imagining religious enclosure in the *Book of Margery Kempe*', *Parergon*, 20:2 (2003), 71–94, p. 78.
10 Ibid., p. 78.
11 Ibid., p. 79.
12 Diane Watt has discussed Margery's 'troubled' relationships with women, in particular her daughter-in-law and maidservant, in her chapter 'Margery Kempe' in Liz Herbert McAvoy and Diane Watt (eds), *The History of British Women's Writing, 700–1500* (London: Palgrave Macmillan, 2011), pp. 232–40.
13 Windeatt, p. 258, n. 4325 and cf. n. 4430.
14 Here I follow Nicholas Watson's suggestion that the *Book* 'invites us to struggle with it in order to be edified by it', in particular by the way that it 'continually tempts us into refusing' her example, see Nicholas Watson, 'The making of *The Book of Margery Kempe*', in Linda Olson and Kathryn Kerby-Fulton (eds), *Voices in Dialogue: Reading Women in the Middle Ages* (Notre Dame: University of Notre Dame Press, 2005), pp. 395–434, p. 424. I discuss the *Book*'s exemplarity in more detail in Varnam, 'The importance of St Margaret's church', pp. 202–5.
15 Watt, 'Margery Kempe', p. 239.
16 Anthony Bale, trans., *The Book of Margery Kempe* (Oxford: Oxford World's Classics, 2015), p. x.
17 Laura Varnam, 'The crucifix, the pietà, and the female mystic: devotional objects and performative identity in *The Book of Margery Kempe*', *The Journal of Medieval Religious Cultures*, 41:2 (2015), 208–37.
18 Rosenfeld, 'Envy and exemplarity', p. 106.
19 Ibid., p. 110.
20 Ibid., p. 117. Sarah McNamer, 'Feeling', in Paul Strohm (ed.), *Middle English* (Oxford: Oxford University Press, 2007), pp. 241–57, p. 246.
21 Colleen Donnelly, 'Menopausal life as imitation of art: Margery Kempe and the lack of sorority', *Women's Writing*, 12:3 (2005), 419–43, pp. 419 and 422.
22 Ibid., p. 420.
23 Karma Lochrie, 'Between women', in Carolyn Dinshaw and David Wallace (eds), *The Cambridge Companion to Medieval Women's Writing* (Cambridge: Cambridge University Press, 2003), pp. 70–88, p. 76.
24 Ibid., p. 75.
25 Varnam, 'The crucifix, the pietà, and the female mystic'.
26 Kathy Lavezzo, 'Sobs and sighs between women: the homoerotics of compassion in *The Book of Margery Kempe*', in Louise Fradenburg

and Carla Freccero (eds), *Premodern Sexualities* (London: Routledge, 1996), pp. 175–98, p. 180.
27 Jonathan Hsy, '"Be more strange and bold": kissing lepers and female same-sex desire in *The Book of Margery Kempe*', *Early Modern Women*, 5 (2010), 189–99, p. 192.
28 *Ibid.*, p. 194. The queer potential of *The Book* has also been put into practice in Robert Glück's modern novel *Margery Kempe* (London: High Risk Books, 1994).
29 Carolyn Dinshaw, *Getting Medieval: Sexualities and Communities, Pre- and Postmodern* (Durham, NC: Duke University Press, 1999), p. 21.
30 Margery also meets good wives who 'leyden hir in her owyn beddys for Goddys lofe' in Chapter 27 (p. 157).
31 Lavezzo, 'Sobs and sighs', p. 187.
32 Larry Scanlon, *Narrative, Authority, and Power: The Medieval Exemplum and the Chaucer Tradition* (Cambridge: Cambridge University Press, 1994), p. 34.
33 *MED* s.v. 'exaumple' (n.) 4a).
34 *MED* s.v. 'meven' (v.), 1 and 5; 'drauen' 1a), 2b) and c).
35 *MED* s.v. 'steren' (v.1), 1. This association is also made in the use of 'hyr mevynggys and hyr steringgys' later in the Proem (p. 46).
36 *MED* s.v. 'stiren' (v.) 1 and 9a). In her edition of *The Book* Lynn Staley makes a similar association, arguing that 'steryngys' comes from the verb 'stirren' [*sic*], 'a term frequently used by Richard Rolle ... to describe the physical symptoms of his passionate spiritual ecstasy. It became a "key word" for those writing about or talking about devotion and/or subjectivity' and she concludes that 'Kempe's uses of it should be seen as one more instance of her self-conscious use of language'. See Lynn Staley, ed., *The Book of Margery Kempe*, TEAMS Middle English Text Series https://d.lib.rochester.edu/teams/publication/staley-the-book-of-margery-kempe [accessed 22 July 2020], note to Book I, line 160.
37 Victoria Blud, 'Emotional bodies: cognitive neuroscience and mediaeval studies', *Literature Compass*, 13:6 (2016), 457–66, p. 461. See also Heather Webb, *The Medieval Heart* (London: Yale University Press, 2010), pp. 1–9.
38 Blud, 'Emotional bodies', p. 461,
39 Fol. 78.v.
40 McNamer, 'Feeling', p. 246.
41 *MED* s.v. 'drede' (n.) 3. For the biblical phrase 'drede the not' as a sign of God's protection of Margery see for example: Chapter 5, 'drede the nowt, dowytyr, for thow schalt have the vyctory of al thin enmys' (p. 72); Chapter 14, 'thow al the worlde be ayens the, drede the not'

(p. 99); Chapter 42, 'drede the not, dowtyr, for thu and alle that ben in thy cumpany schal gon as safe as yyf thei wer in Seynt Petrys Cherch' (p. 211).
42 Krug, *Margery Kempe and the Lonely Reader*, chapter 4 'Fear', pp. 135–72.
43 'Richard de Caistre's Hymn', in Carleton Brown (ed.), *Religious Lyrics of the XVth Century* (Oxford: Clarendon Press, 1939), pp. 98–100, p. 99.
44 Jessica Brantley, *Reading in the Wilderness: Private Devotion and Public Performance in Late Medieval England* (Chicago: University of Chicago Press, 2007), pp. 215–16 and plate 7.
45 *Ibid.*, p. 215.
46 *Ibid.*, figure 6.2.
47 *Ibid.*, p. 216.
48 *The Booke of Gostlye Grace of Mechtild of Hackeborn*, ed. Theresa A. Halligan (Toronto: Pontifical Institute of Mediaeval Studies, 1979), p. 382. All subsequent quotations refer to this edition by page number. Julian of Norwich, *A Revelation of Love*, ed. Marion Glasscoe (Exeter: Exeter University Press, 1976; revised edition 1993), p. 35.
49 For further discussion of the importance of the Sacred Heart to Mechthild and her fellow Helfta visionaries see Voaden, 'All girls together'.
50 See for example p. 228 and pp. 273–4.
51 *MED* s.v. 'conformen' (v.) 1.
52 Krug, *Margery Kempe and the Lonely Reader*, p. 3.
53 Anne Pollock, 'Heart feminism', *Catalyst: Feminism, Theory, Technoscience*, 1:1 (2015), 1–30, p. 3.
54 Pollock, 'Heart feminism', p. 10.

III

Encountering the world

8

Margery Kempe's home town and worthy kin

Susan Maddock

It is a testament to the thoroughness of Sanford Brown Meech's trawl of records in King's Lynn for people mentioned in the *Book* that so little more was uncovered during the following three-quarters of a century.[1] A fresh encounter with the archival evidence was long overdue, not only to include manuscripts which were inaccessible to Meech[2] but also to provide a fuller context to the extracts published in 1940. The scope of research also required expansion socially, beyond the small number of burgesses who left the biggest imprint on Lynn's archival record, and geographically, to explore the connections and interests of Lynn families outside the town. As a result of this wider approach, a clearer picture is beginning to emerge of Margery Kempe's birth and marital families, her relationships with different status groups in her home town, and her encounters with other notable individuals such as Alan of Lynn.

John de Brunham's background and career

The Brunham name, combined with evidence that the family still owned land in the Burnham parishes of north Norfolk in the early fifteenth century, allows us to be confident that Margery Kempe's ancestors came from there, rather than one of several other Burnhams in England.[3] The first Brunham at Lynn who can be definitively linked with Margery is her grandfather, Ralph. A burgess of Lynn before 1333 and probably by 1324, when he entered the merchant guild, he had several properties in the town, and was resident in

Chequer ward by 1328.⁴ Records of borough administration are patchy for his lifetime, but Ralph's name appears in two lists of the borough's governing group of jurats, made in 1342 and 1349.⁵ He must have survived the Black Death, which swept through Lynn in summer 1349,⁶ because he was amerced for failing to attend the borough's leet court on 28 October that year, but does not appear in a tax assessment, 1357, suggesting he had died before then.⁷

Ralph's son, John (Margery Kempe's father), was probably born in the early 1330s. A merchant, like his father, he was admitted as a burgess of Lynn in 1353.⁸ A burgess, or freeman, was an inhabitant of the borough who had full civic rights: he – men only – could apply for admission by right of birth, by purchase, or after completing an apprenticeship to an existing burgess of Lynn, provided that burgess was a merchant. In the late fourteenth century, there were around 150 burgesses – fewer than 10 per cent of adult men in the town – and only around a quarter of them, all merchants, played a substantial part in running the town's affairs.

John de Brunham moved rapidly up the borough hierarchy: he was one of the four chamberlains – the borough's financial officers – in 1355–56, and twice more in the 1360s. Between 1365 and 1384 he represented Lynn in Parliament six times, and in 1370–1 he served the first of five annual terms as mayor (the others were in 1377–78, 1378–79, 1385–86 and 1391–92). Finally, from 1393 to at least 1402, he held the uniquely influential role, combining elements of governmental, religious, and financial authority, of alderman of the Holy Trinity merchant guild.⁹ As alderman he was not only the head of a spectacularly wealthy association of merchants and the town's premier religious guild; he was also second only to the mayor in the borough's governing elite. He died between 24 December 1412 and 16 October 1413: probably closer to the latter date, as 'John Brunham of Lynne' was named in a court of common pleas suit in June 1413.¹⁰

Margery's father also had a national profile which outranked his Lynn contemporaries. He was appointed to several commissions of array from 1377 (a year in which his own ship, the *James*, was on naval service) to 1399; and he was the only Lynn burgess in his lifetime to be appointed a justice of the peace for Norfolk, as well as for Lynn, bringing him into close contact with the county's aristocracy and gentry.¹¹ In 1383, wearied by the extent of work

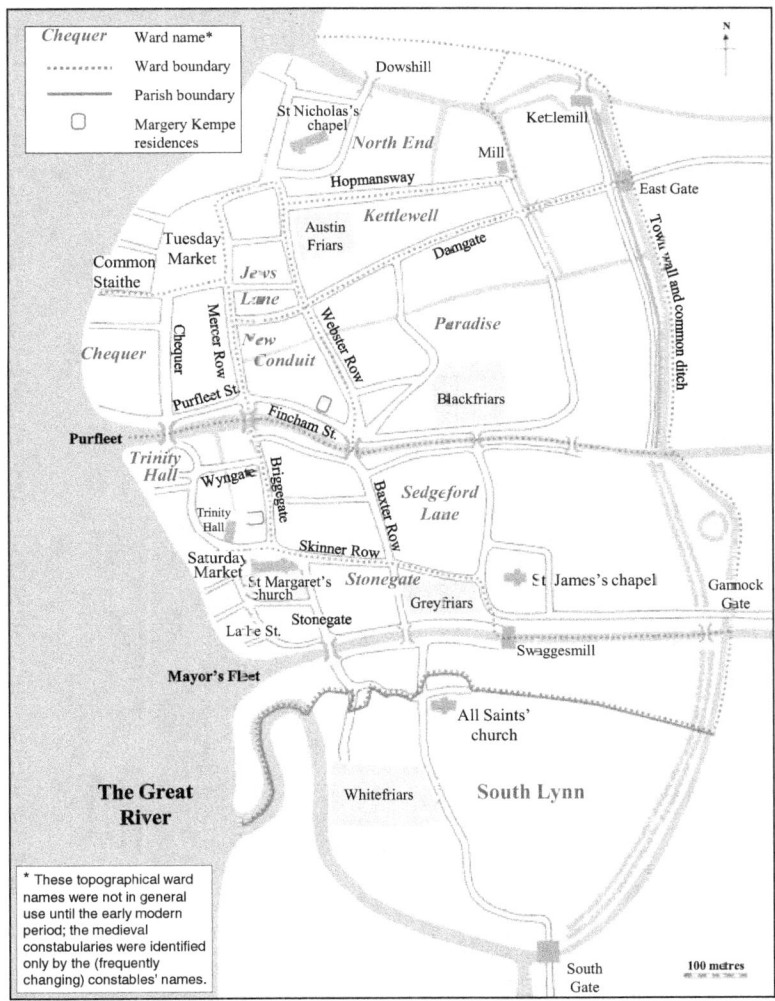

Figure 8.1 Late medieval Lynn.

he was asked to do for the Crown, he obtained an exemption from being compelled to serve 'at the supplication of the king's sister, the duchess of Brittany': Joan Holland, Richard II's half-sister, and second wife of the fourth John, duke of Brittany.[12] The king had let the duke have the Castle Rising estate, 8 kilometres from Lynn, and

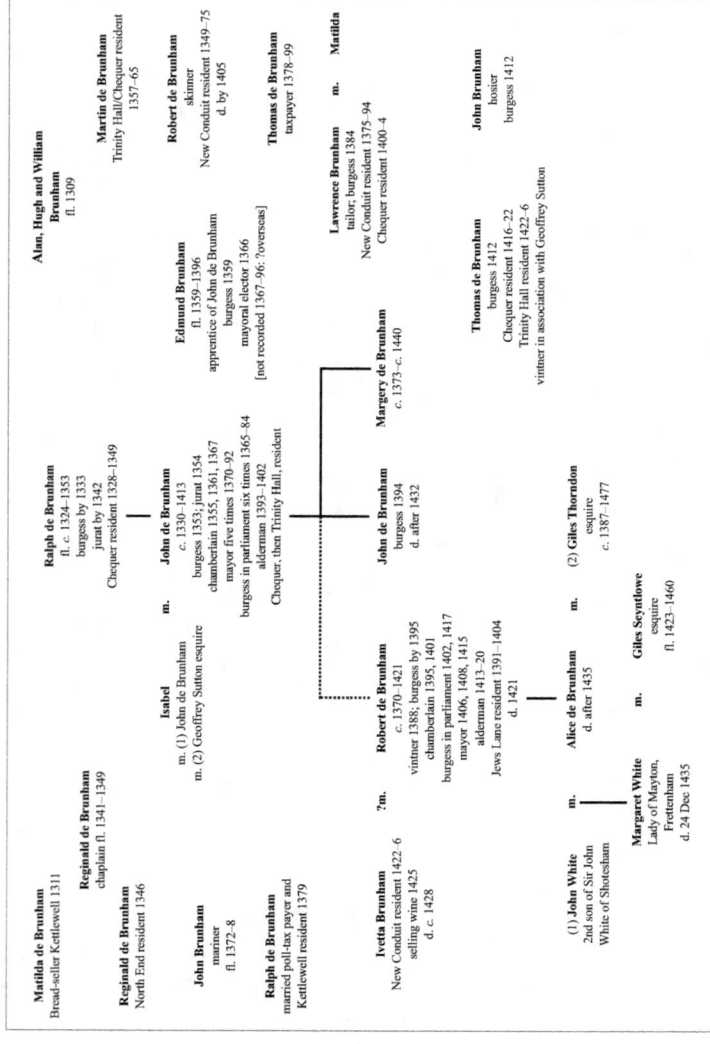

Figure 8.2 People named Brunham recorded as living or working in Lynn between 1300 and 1440.

the duke and duchess first stayed at the castle in 1378, during John de Brunham's second mayoralty.[13] The borough always sent gifts on such occasions: in 1378, six cartloads of wine, wax, sturgeon, oats, and herring (some supplied by Brunham himself) were sent up the road to Castle Rising.[14] As mayor John would have met the duchess in 1378, and doubtless on other occasions, too.

The last year or two of John de Brunham's life must have been blighted by the 'contentions, rumours, disagreements, disputes, dissensions and controversies' which dominated the borough's political life in the early fifteenth century, especially between 1411 and 1416.[15] In company with the mayors who served from 1399 to 1406 – Edmund Belleyeter (John de Brunham's former apprentice), John Wentworth, Robert Botekesham, and Thomas Waterden – he was accused of excessive and unauthorised expenditure: in particular, on a costly legal campaign against Henry Despenser, bishop of Norwich and the town's lord, in the years before Despenser's death in 1406. This centred on the bishop's alleged failure to maintain his quay at the mouth of the Purfleet, rendering the port unsafe for ships and the town vulnerable to flooding, but also cited maladministration by the bishop's officers, and questioned the legal basis of the bishop's secular jurisdiction in Lynn.[16] Brunham was described in the context of the disputed expenses as a former mayor, but in reality it must have been his role as alderman which was under scrutiny. The five were also accused more generally of 'wrongs, oppressions, injustices, exactions, extortions, evils, and vexations'.[17]

We do not have John de Brunham's testament, although we know he made one, and only one of his executors has been identified: fellow-burgess, William Herford.[18] The names of men who acted as his widow's feoffees, although not necessarily the same as his executors, provide clues as to what kind of men they might have been. Named in a deed of 1419, they were Sir John Ingoldisthorpe, Edmund Oldhall, Laurence Trussebut, Stephen Gybon (a substantial landowner at North Lynn), three Lynn burgesses – Edmund Belleyeter, Richard Denby, and William Herford – and Thomas Wymondham.[19] Sir John Ingoldisthorpe and Edmund Oldhall, esquire, were prominent East Anglians and royal servants. Both served overseas under the earl of Arundel in 1388; both acted as justices in Cambridgeshire, and Oldhall in Norfolk, too; Sir John followed Oldhall as sheriff of Norfolk in 1402, and Oldhall was sheriff again in 1413. Oldhall was also receiver of duchy of Lancaster estates in Norfolk, Suffolk, and Cambridgeshire from 1399 until his death in 1417.[20] Laurence Trussebut of Shouldham had never been a soldier, but he was much in demand in administrative roles from the mid-1390s onwards, and he served alongside Oldhall as a Norfolk justice of the peace from 1401. He was also a Lynn justice, 1395–1415, and by 1414 held the key post of bishop's steward at Lynn. He had died by Easter 1418.[21] Whereas Ingoldisthorpe and Oldhall may have headed the list of Brunham feoffees mainly to lend gravitas, Trussebut had interests in Lynn, in addition to extensive rural landholdings, and was an experienced estate manager. His advice had also been valued by the borough, which paid him an annual retainer in the 1390s.[22] The Brunham feoffees represent a combination of landowning, administrative, and mercantile experience and status which outshines other lists of executors or feoffees named in surviving records from early fifteenth-century Lynn, testifying that John de Brunham's connections went well beyond his home community.

The Brunhams and the Loks

Margery's devotion to her parish church might suggest that she grew up close to St Margaret's, and the Brunham family home does indeed appear to have been just 60 metres north of the church, on a site (115–16 High Street) occupied since the 1960s by part of a block of shops with flats above. Although the house has long gone, a report of a site visit in 1416 by a panel of burgesses shows that it was timber-framed and had a projecting first-floor jetty. The panel of jurors had been summoned to inspect a stone wall which the adjoining owners on the south side (executors acting on behalf of the Lok family) were erecting along what they believed to be their boundary. Towards the street frontage they had encountered a problem: the new wall 'was obstructed by projecting points and did not have the space it should because the timber tenement sometime John Brunham's encroaches, damages and overhangs the stone wall'.[23] The jurors decided the wall was in the wrong place, and must be rebuilt.[24]

John de Brunham's wife at the time of his death was Isabel, first named in 1410 as a beneficiary in the will of the Brunhams' next-door neighbour in Briggegate, Margery Lok. Like the Brunhams the Loks were a wealthy merchant-burgess family, owning property inside and outside the town, but they seem not to have had the Brunhams' political ambitions: they did their civic duty (taking their turns as chamberlains, for example), but never became mayors. John Lok, John de Brunham's contemporary, died in 1393, leaving his widow, Margery, and a son, William, who died in 1408.[25] William's testament names his wife, Margaret, and his son, Thomas, who was left in the care of his grandmother, Margery. Two years later, in 1410, Margery Lok herself died, leaving a detailed testament and last will which show she was a Trussebut from Shouldham, 13 kilometres south of Lynn, where the Lok family was also long established.[26] Laurence Trussebut, who may have been Margery Lok's brother, was named as an executor by both William and Margery Lok, and Margery made bequests to Laurence's wife and children. Another link between the two families was the apprenticeship to John Lok of a Thomas Trussebut who became a burgess of Lynn in 1385 and went on to enjoy a successful career as a merchant.[27]

Margery Lok's personal bequests included coral rosary beads, plus forty shillings, to Isabel de Brunham and twenty shillings to 'Margery my god-daughter'. Margery was a popular name, so Margery Lok's god-daughter was not necessarily Margery Kempe, but it is a strong possibility, and Margery de Brunham may even have been named after Margery Lok. In addition Margery and William Lok each bequeathed twenty shillings to Alice White, Robert de Brunham's daughter and Margery Kempe's niece.[28] That the Trussebut/Lok and Brunham families' friendship was long-standing is suggested by John de Brunham's acting as a feoffee, with several Trussebuts (including Laurence), of additions to the Trussebut estates in Shouldham in 1386.[29] In 1416, following the adjudication on the boundary wall between the Loks' house and the former Brunham family home, Isabel, with the consent of her late husband's executors, offered the Lok executors a gift of twenty shillings towards the cost of rebuilding.[30]

William Lok's widow, Margaret, lived in another Lok family house, six doors north of the Brunhams', in which she had a life interest under her late husband's will. She may have been in poor health, as a nurse called Agnes is mentioned by both William and Margery Lok, which may be a reason for custody of young Thomas being given to his grandmother. Unusually, Margaret Lok seems not to have remarried; much more unusually – uniquely, in fact – she is twice referred to in leet records as 'Dame' (*domina*).[31] Might Dame Margaret Lok have been the 'worschipful woman whech had takyn the mentyl and the ryng', and her house the venue for the reunion dinner with Master Alan which was such a joyful occasion for Margery Kempe?[32] That the Loks were long-standing friends of the Brunhams would explain why Margery was made welcome as a last-minute guest.

Isabel de Brunham was still alive in 1428, when she and her second husband, Geoffrey Sutton esquire, levied a final concord on three houses and a quay in Lynn.[33] Isabel's new husband was probably the Geoffrey Sutton who served overseas as a man-at-arms under Robert, Lord Willoughby of Eresby, between 1417 and 1426.[34] Willoughby was a prominent figure in Lincolnshire, but also had Norfolk interests: he and his wife were occasional visitors to Lynn; he became a Norfolk justice in 1414, alongside Laurence Trussebut and Edmund Oldhall; and Willoughby's sister, Margaret, married Oldhall's son, William.[35] A Geoffrey Sutton, esquire, is also recorded in commercial contexts in London in 1429 and in Wisbech in 1433.[36] A man who had done military service under a noble commander and had mercantile interests might well seek in marriage a wealthy widow in a well-connected merchant family. Isabel's status as John de Brunham's widow remained stronger in the public consciousness than her new one as an esquire's wife, however, as appears from her continued identification in records at Lynn as 'Isabel Brunham', rather than as Isabel Sutton.[37]

Isabel was not the only member of the Brunham family to marry a man with military experience and the status of esquire. Robert de Brunham's daughter, Alice, married first John White, a knight's second son and lord of the manor of Mayton Hall at Frettenham, 10 kilometres north of Norwich, and secondly Giles Thorndon, an esquire in the service of John Wodehouse (Thorndon remarried after Alice's death and his later career, in Ireland, is well known), while Alice's daughter, Margaret, married Giles Seyntlowe, esquire. However, memorials in Frettenham church to Alice and Margaret show Alice's continuing pride in being the 'daughter and heir of Robert Brunham of Lynn'.[38] We may see a parallel between the continued identification of Isabel and Alice as Brunhams of Lynn and Margery's being addressed by the bishop of Worcester as 'John of Burnamys dowtyr of Lynne', rather than as John Kempe's wife (p. 225).

The Kempes of Lynn

It has been suggested that Margery's assertion that John Kempe seemed an unlikely match for her because 'sche was comyn of worthy kenred' (p. 57) was ill-founded, as well as unkind.[39] He was a merchant-burgess of Lynn, as was Margery's father, and at that stage of his career could not expect to hold any higher office than that of chamberlain. But the Kempes did not have the same high-level social clout as John de Brunham, whose daughter might have been expected to marry into the county gentry, had she not fallen for John Kempe.

The Kempes of Lynn were a branch of a family at Barton Bendish and, later, at Shouldham Thorpe, both parishes adjacent to Shouldham. The names John and Simon run through the Kempe family from at least 1317, and two John Kempes, father and son, were still living at Shouldham Thorpe in the 1490s.[40] The Kempes were never lords of manors, however, and their land holdings were modest: a Margaret Kempe, for example, had a house and a few acres of land in Barton Bendish when she died in 1429.[41] By contrast Laurence Trussebut owned more than 330 acres of arable and meadow land in Shouldham, Thorpe, and Fincham, in addition to the Trussebut manor at Shouldham.[42]

Margery's father-in-law, John Kempe senior, was a merchant engaged in the Baltic trade: a very successful one, judging by the size of his claim for goods detained in Prussia in 1385.[43] He purchased his burgess-ship in 1351, and married by 1352, when he and his wife, Margaret, levied a final concord on two houses in Lynn.[44] By 1379 he was living in New Conduit ward, almost certainly in the house in Fincham Street which later became his eponymous son's home.[45] Cloth exports were still being made in his name in 1392, months before he died, although by then his two sons must have been working with him.[46] Merchants were not permitted to trade on their own account before their admission as burgesses, which explains the promptness with which Simon Kempe and his brother John purchased their burgess-ships after their father's death, being

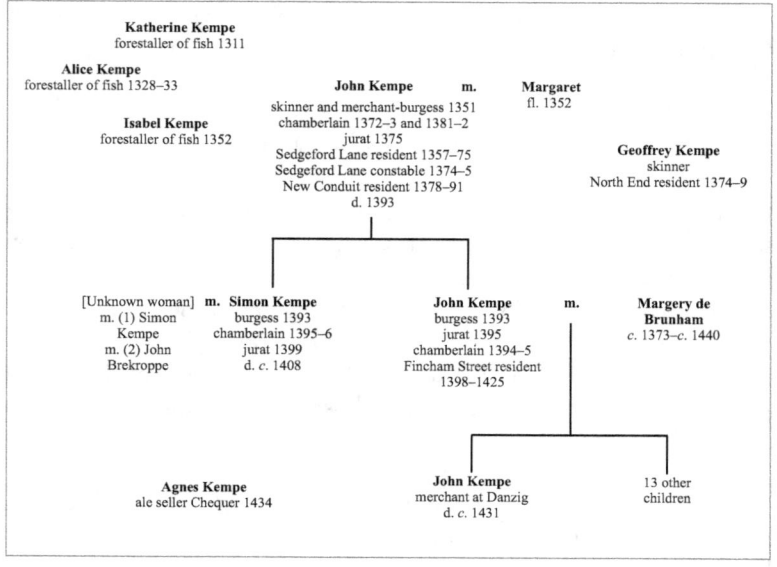

Figure 8.3 People named Kempe recorded as living or working in Lynn between 1300 and 1440.

admitted on the same day, 28 May 1393.[47] Both made a promising start in civic life, each serving a year as chamberlain and entering the borough's ruling group, but whereas Simon remained a jurat until his death, between 1405 and 1410, John Kempe's name disappears from records of guildhall meetings within three or four years of his election as a jurat in 1395.[48] This lack of ambition fits well with Margery's description of him as being 'content wyth the goodys that God had sent' (p. 58).

Margery Kempe's friends and supporters in a time of conflict

The *Book* contains no hint of the internal conflicts which beset Lynn's governing community in the early fifteenth century, taking a stand on just one public issue: opposing the grant of independent parochial status to St Nicholas, a daughter chapel to St Margaret's church.[49] The campaign for St Nicholas had two main phases, in

1378–81 and 1426–32, before and after the chapel was rebuilt, on a spectacular scale and without any contribution from the borough.[50] The North End ward, centred on St Nicholas, was the wealthiest in Lynn, thanks to its prime location and the number of wealthy merchants who lived there.[51] Margery was speaking the simple truth in describing those who pursued the cause of St Nicholas, and whose wealth had made it so much 'the grettar and the fayrare', as 'ryche men, worshepful marchawntys, [who] haddyn gold anow, whech may spede in every nede' (pp. 147–8). They were a small group loyal to their local chapel and having the funds to champion it, and there is no reason to suppose that partisan feelings on that issue fed into conflicts over the borough's governance.[52]

Historical studies of late medieval Lynn by Stephen Alsford, Kate Parker, and Anthony Goodman have made progress in elucidating the discords of the early fifteenth century, but their focus remained, understandably, on the minority of players – all merchant-burgesses – who are best documented.[53] The involvement of artisans in the conflicts has been noticed, but underestimated. Goodman judged four artisans involved in a riot in 1415 to be 'scapegoats, small fry with large mouths' and such men were also dismissed by some of their contemporaries, notably by one rich merchant as 'cobblers, tailors, etc.; unfit people, twenty of them not worth a penny'.[54] The role of artificers in what Alsford recognised as 'the most mercantile of our towns' deserves reassessment.[55]

As we have already seen, Margery's father was one of five leading burgesses accused of maladministration in the last years of Henry Despenser's bishopric. He was also among 106 burgesses who, with sixty-six non-burgesses, bound themselves in December 1411 to abide by a settlement to be formulated by eighteen named arbitrators. By this time he was an old man, and had ceased to be active among the twenty-four jurats: his name was still included among the twenty-four in a draft of this submission, but an official copy, written in the royal chancery in 1413, places him, like an afterthought, at the end of a list of eighty-four 'middling', or ordinary, burgesses.[56] Robert Brunham, however, appears among the 'powerful' twenty-four and he was also a member of the arbitration panel, together with six other *potenciores*, five *mediocres*, and six *inferiores* (non-burgesses). A new constitution devised by a quorum of ten arbitrators, none of them *potenciores*, survived a legal challenge by the old elite, and was endorsed by Archbishop Arundel as chancellor on 17 November 1412.[57] Written out on two large parchment sheets, 'sealed with the great seal of England in green wax', the document was presented to a congregation of four hundred in the guildhall at Lynn on 12 December 1412.[58] This must have been a tense occasion, and the reformist mayor, Roger Galyon (whose re-election in 1412, for a second year running, had been secured by the simple expedient of admitting as burgesses 112 non-burgesses *en bloc* two days before the election), was supported on the bench by several authority figures, most of them from outside the borough. Among them were Edmund Oldhall, in his capacity as receiver to the duchy of Lancaster and Henry de Nottingham, bailiff of the duchy's liberty in Norfolk; two Norfolk justices, Simon Baret of Heacham and Laurence Trussebut; and two other Norfolk landowners, both well-known to Trussebut: Thomas Lovell of Barton Bendish and Walter Godard of Terrington. There were also two religious figures: Prior Thomas Heveningham, and Alan Warnekyn, doctor of theology, of the order or convent of the Carmelite friars in South Lynn: the man known to Margery as Master Aleyn.

The Carmelite friar, Alan of Lynn, was described by the first editors of the *Book* as 'the most illustrious of Margery's friends at Lynn'.[59] His being relatively well known has not prevented his being confused with another, much older, Carmelite friar, Alan of Gaywood. An assumption that the two were the same was first made in the eighteenth century by Francis Blomefield, the Norfolk historian, and has since been followed by others. Anthony Goodman recognised that Alan of Gaywood was a different man, but followed previous scholars in accepting a birth date (1347–48) for Alan of Lynn deduced solely from testimony given by Alan of Gaywood.[60] Alan of Lynn's single recorded appearance in the guildhall, however, gives us his family name of Warnekyn: one all but unknown in late medieval England, except at Lynn.

Stephen Warnekyn, a tailor, was almost certainly one of the foreign craftsmen who moved to Lynn from German-speaking parts of the Continent in the second half of the fourteenth century.[61] He is recorded in leet rolls as resident in Jews Lane ward, 1374–79, and died before 1388.[62] An Alan Warnekyn who was assessed for poll tax in 1379 as a married artificer with two servants is likely to have been Stephen's son: he lived in Trinity Hall ward from at least 1375 to 1394 and was admitted as a burgess of Lynn in 1385.[63] If the Carmelite friar were a son of Alan Warnekyn the burgess, he was not an old man when Margery met him: he may have been much the same age as Margery herself. That fits well with the lively figure he cuts in the *Book*: examining and weighing the stone which had fallen on Margery's back (p. 84), for example, and leaving his house to dine in town (p. 317), or to take the ferry across the river (p. 270). Nor is there any hint that the sickness he suffered was a disease of old age (p. 316). The *Book* does describe him as an 'elde doctowr' (p. 289) in the early 1420s but may be reflecting the maturity of his scholarship as much as age in years. His being invited as one of only two religious authorities to be present at so crucial a public event in the guildhall is a testament to the high regard in which he was held.

Also present on 12 December 1412 was John Wyreham, the only lay inhabitant of Lynn, other than Margery's father and husband, named in the *Book*. Described by Margery as a 'good man' (p. 83), he was in St Margaret's church when she was struck by falling masonry and timber. A mercer, he had been the first-named of the sixty-six non-burgesses obligated to submit to arbitration in 1411.[64] These non-burgesses were all artificers (weavers, cordwainers, tailors, mercers, bakers, butchers, etc.): men who contributed to the borough economy but had no political voice. Forty-six of them, Wyreham included, were among the 112 who became burgesses on 27 August 1412 without any fee (although some money was extracted from many of them over the next year or two) or finding the usual pledges (two burgesses for each new entrant), and most of the rest were admitted within the next two or three years.[65]

The new constitution proved cumbersome in practice: discord and violence continued, and the reforms were annulled in 1416: a decision endorsed, like the 1412 ordinances, by royal letters patent under the great seal.[66] Ultimately, however, the better-off artificers were winners in this series of struggles, helped by two important changes over the next few years. The first was the creation in 1418 of an annually elected common council of twenty-seven burgesses, three from each ward; the second was a new form of admission of artificers' apprentices, introduced in January 1425, following representations made to the mayor, John Permonter, by seventy-three burgess-artificers.[67] Henceforward, apprentices of artificer-burgesses would be entitled to burgess admission without paying a fee, just like merchants' apprentices, effectively giving the artificers equality with their merchant counterparts.

Two good friends to Margery, and to Robert de Brunham, appear to have been sympathetic to the artificers' cause: Robert Spryngolde, parish priest of St Margaret's, and the unnamed 'worshipful burgeys, the which in fewe yerys after was Meyr of Lenne' (p. 290), both of whom interceded with the charismatic, but intolerant, 'good frere' (p. 291) on Margery Kempe's behalf. This 'worshipful burgess' was, almost certainly, John Permonter, the mayor who resolved the conflict between the merchants and artificers in 1425. At the end of his second mayoralty in 1425 he was accorded a uniquely lengthy and heartfelt eulogy, describing him as a respected and energetic man who, in a friendly, humane, and understanding manner, established peace and tranquillity between different status groups in the town.[68] He was a merchant engaged in the wine trade, like Robert de Brunham, and had worked in partnership with him,[69] so it is unsurprising that he appears, with another merchant, John Wesynham, and Robert Spryngolde, as an executor of Robert de Brunham's testament, following Robert's death in 1421. Sebastian Sobecki has already noted that Spryngolde was one of Robert de Brunham's executors, citing a court of common pleas record, 1430.[70] The executors are also named in the town's hall book, 1424, and in two earlier plea roll entries, 1425: in those three instances Spryngolde is named third, suggesting that his role was mainly to lend dignity and status to the more active secular executors.[71] That Permonter was the leading executor is implied by the seizure of his own goods by a man who claimed to be one of Brunham's creditors.[72] There may also have been a family connection between Spryngolde and Permonter: one of the latter's apprentices was Thomas Springold, who became a burgess in 1432.[73]

Spryngolde was chosen as an executor by at least one other Lynn mayor, William Palmer, who died early in 1437, part-way through his mayoralty. Palmer, unlike Brunham, was an artificer – a commercial brewer – and the first non-merchant to become mayor. He had been a leading participant in the artificers' campaign for equality with the merchants, acting as one of their nine representatives in the negotiations initiated by Permonter as mayor in 1425. Palmer's other executors were his wife, Emma, and three artificer-burgesses,

Amory Trewe, John Robynissone, and Geoffrey Gatelee. Probate was granted to Robynissone, who presumably took the lead in administering Palmer's estates, as Permonter had for Robert de Brunham.[74] None the less, it is telling that Spryngolde was willing to lend his authority to prominent burgesses from both sides of what had been a divided community before Permonter's skilfully managed resolution.

Like Permonter, Robert Spryngolde appears to have been greatly respected in Lynn. A letter sent by the mayor and community to the bishop of Norwich, probably in 1410, describes him as upright and wise, an excellent teacher, and one who provides 'great and fruitful refreshment to our souls'.[75] Spryngolde had been the subject of some serious accusation made to the bishop. The letter gives no hint of its nature, other than its relating to his standing in the community, but descriptions of his behaviour in the *Book* (pp. 380–1 and 421) show that Spryngolde could speak sharply on occasion. He seems unlikely to be a flatterer or to have courted popularity, and his forthrightness might have provoked resentment at a time of political tensions in Lynn.

New relationships in later life

The only extant archival records naming Margery Kempe log the two final instalments of her admission fee to the Holy Trinity guild in 1438 and 1439. By this time it was routine for women to be allowed to pay the substantial entrance fee (£5) to enjoy the spiritual benefits of the guild, but it appears to have gone unnoticed previously that Lynn's Trinity guild, unlike most English religious guilds, admitted only men until the 1390s, during the time when Margery's father was the guild alderman.[76] The possible implications of Margery's membership of this prestigious body are considered more fully by Laura Kalas in Chapter 12 below: here our concern is with the social – and possibly familial – relationships suggested by these mundane financial records.

Margery's two documented payments, each twenty shillings, were handed over on her behalf by a guild member named John Ashenden. Together with his friend and business partner, Edward Mayn, Ashenden owned the biggest brewery in Lynn. Like William Palmer, this pair exemplified the successful class of artificer-burgesses. Both had been among the 112 admitted in 1412 and benefited from the reforms introduced in 1418 and 1425. Ashenden was elected to the common council in 1419 and a chamberlain the year after. He joined the twenty-four jurats in 1435 and in 1440 was the second non-merchant to be elected mayor of Lynn. Mayn was never mayor, but did hold office in the Trinity guild: he was one of its four financial officers by 1437.[77] John Ashenden's wife, Isabel, also joined the guild in the 1430s, together with Edward Mayn's wife, Joan: they appear to have paid by instalments of twenty-five shillings, handing over their penultimate payments in 1438. If, as seems likely, they and Margery Kempe had all elected to pay by equal annual instalments, Margery would have arranged to join the guild and made her first payment in 1435, with Isabel and Joan following suit one year later, in 1436: all three should have paid in full by Trinity 1439, and they are not mentioned in a list of debts dated 1441.[78]

One other person is named in connection with Margery Kempe's payment in Lent 1438: Bartholomew Colles, her 'pledge'. Most of the records of debts for guild entry fines in 1437–38 include the names of one or two pledges, or guarantors: John Ashenden and Edward Mayn acted in this role for their wives, and some other pledges, including a few women, bear the same family name as the new entrant. Bartholomew Colles must have known Margery Kempe personally, at the very least. A merchant-burgess, he lived, like the Ashendens and Mayns, in Trinity Hall ward, and in 1445 his widow, Joan, is recorded as a debtor for her £5 admission to the guild.[79] Of Margery Kempe's fourteen children only one – the John Kempe who settled in Danzig – has as yet been identified. Other surviving sons may also have left Lynn, from which the Kempe name disappears after 1439, but one or more surviving daughters may have remained under new names, as married women. The fiduciary relationships between Margery, John Ashenden, and Bartholomew Colles, in combination with the synchronicity of Margery's guild entrance with those of Isabel Ashenden and Joan Mayn, might suggest that one or more of these three wives – Isabel, Joan Mayn, or even Joan Colles – was Margery's daughter.

Whether Margery was still alive in 1440 is unknown, but, at least two men she knew well are documented as meeting in Lynn that year to construct an end-of-life plan for one of the Trussebut family of Shouldham and Lynn. Robert Trusbut, rector of the Suffolk parish of Worlington, was at the priory on 17 May 1440 in anticipation of his death (which occurred within the next few days) to arrange for his burial in St Margaret's church and to make his testament. His sole executor was another of Lynn's 'new men', Simon Baxter: like Ashenden, Baxter was a successful brewer admitted burgess in 1412, a common councillor in 1419, and a negotiator on behalf of the artificers in 1425. The two witnesses to Trusbut's testament were the prior, John Fornesete, and William Melton, Margery's 'good friar'.[80]

Conclusion

That Margery Kempe was a reliable witness to events she describes is no longer in doubt, whilst proof that William Melton was a returning visitor to Lynn boosts the credibility of the annotator of the *Book*'s sole manuscript, who added the name 'Melton' against a reference (p. 298) to the friar who banned Margery from attending his electrifying sermons. Reliability does not equate to impartiality, and Margery Kempe was someone of forceful views, so it is important to understand the familial, social, and political contexts which helped to shape her attitudes. An assumption that she found political and social changes in early fifteenth-century Lynn unpalatable, even distressing, and that her radical change of life was, in part, a quest for an alternative identity, has been a common theme in studies of her life.[81] Her well-connected father's status was, in fact, higher than has previously been appreciated, explaining her being, as Goodman put it, 'at ease with practically the highest in the land',[82] and Margery's assessment of her husband as of lower social worth well founded. Their marriage was, it seems, a love-match, springing from her 'inordinat lovys to hys persone' (p. 332), rather than a dynastic alliance of the kind arranged for her niece, Alice. Despite her youthful pride in her family background, the mature Margery embraced, rather than resented, the changing social order in her home town; one in which merchant-burgesses in her father's mould had begun to share power with successful artisans and commercial brewers. Some of her closest friends and supporters were peacemakers in the long-running conflict over the borough's governance, and also between Margery and those who reacted adversely to her. Acquiring membership of the rich and powerful guild which had embodied the dominance of the old-style merchant-burgesses, but which now included newly empowered artificer-burgesses and their wives, was, perhaps, an endorsement of Permonter's resolution of conflict in the urban community as well as a personal reconciliation with townsfolk who had been so much against her in the past.

Notes

1. Sanford Brown Meech and Hope Emily Allen (eds), *The Book of Margery Kempe*, EETS OS 212 (London: Oxford University Press, 1940), pp. 358–74.
2. Principal among these is William Asshebourne's book, c. 1408–24 (King's Lynn Borough Archives, King's Lynn (hereafter KLBA), KL/C 10/2.
3. Norfolk Record Office, Norwich (hereafter NRO), NRS 7451. 'Burnham' was almost universally spelled 'Brunham', in Norfolk and elsewhere. In this chapter the most common contemporary forms are used for family names, but place names have been modernised.
4. The National Archives, Kew (hereafter TNA), C 241/104/111; KLBA, KL/C 5/2, KL/C 50/50 and KL/C 17/2; Holcombe Ingleby (ed.), *The Red Register of King's Lynn* (King's Lynn: Thew and Son, 1919–22), vol. 1, pp. 137, 143, 159, 174–5.
5. Ingleby, *Red Register*, vol. 1, p. 6; vol. 2, p. 204.
6. Antonia Gransden, 'A fourteenth-century chronicle from the Grey Friars at Lynn', *English Historical Review*, 72:283 (1957), 274; Ingleby, *Red Register*, vol. 1, pp. 87–101 (wills proved in Lynn, May to September 1349).
7. The Duke of Norfolk's archives at Arundel Castle, MD 1475 (leet roll, 1349); KLBA, KL/C 37/7. For a description of the leet court records, analysis of which underpins much of the information in this chapter, see Susan Maddock, 'Society, status and the leet court in Margery Kempe's Lynn', in Richard Goddard and Teresa Phipps (eds), *Town Courts and Urban Society in Late Medieval England, 1250–1500* (Woodbridge: Boydell Press, 2019), pp. 200–19.
8. Ingleby, *Red Register*, vol. 2, p. 173.
9. Stephen Alsford, 'Lynn: mayors and chamberlains': http://users.trytel.com/tristan/towns/mapp1_2c.html [accessed 24 June 2019]; Hamon le Strange,

Norfolk Official Lists (Norwich: Agas G. Goose, 1890), pp. 206–7; KLBA, KL/C 50/30 and 428.
10 KLBA, KL/C 6/3, m. 7v. and KL/C 50/392, both cited in Meech and Allen, *The Book of Margery Kempe*, p. 361 (their date of 19 December is erroneous); TNA, CP 40/610.
11 Andrew Ayton, 'Shipping, mariners and port communities in fourteenth-century England' database: http://reshare.ukdataservice.ac.uk/850665/ [accessed 19 February 2015], citing TNA, E 101/34/25 m. 3; *Calendar of Patent Rolls* (hereafter CPR), 1370-74, pp. 106, 305; *CPR*, 1374–77, p. 500; *CPR*, 1377–81, pp. 126, 474, 515; *CPR*, 1381–85, p. 598; *CPR*, 1385–89, pp. 181, 254–5, 259; *CPR*, 1391–96, p. 587; *CPR*, 1399–1401, p. 214.
12 *CPR*, 1381–85, p. 291.
13 Anthony Goodman, *Margery Kempe and Her World* (London: Pearson Education, 2002), p. 31.
14 KLBA, KL/C 39/37.
15 KLBA, KL/C 2/27; Goodman, *Margery Kempe and Her World*, pp. 35–48.
16 *CPR*, 1401–5, pp. 67, 274; *Calendar of Close Rolls* (hereafter CCR), 1402–5, p. 166; TNA, JUST 1/611.
17 KLBA, KL/C 2/27.
18 KLBA, KL/C 50/392; Meech and Allen, *The Book of Margery Kempe*, p. 361.
19 Devon Heritage Centre, Exeter, 1038 M/T/12/1.
20 TNA, C 76/72, m. 7–8, from the AHRC-funded 'The soldier in later medieval England online database': www.medievalsoldier.org [accessed 29 April 2018]; J. S. Roskell, Linda Clark, and Carole Rawcliffe (eds), *The History of Parliament: The House of Commons 1386–1421* (Stroud: Alan Sutton, 1992), vol. 3, pp. 475–7, 870–2.
21 *CPR*, 1391—96, p. 587; *CPR*, 1391–96, p. 95; *CPR*, 1396–99, p. 229; *CPR*, 1399–1401, pp. 561–2; *CPR*, 1405–8, p. 494; *CPR*, 1408–13, p. 483; *CPR*, 1413–16, p. 421; KLBA, KL/C 10/2. fo. 53r; TNA, CP 40/629, m. 345.
22 Ingleby, *Red Register*, vol. 2, p. 7; KLBA, KL/C 39/42.
23 KLBA, KL/C 10/2, fo. 99.
24 A fuller account is in Susan Maddock, 'Mapping Margery Kempe's Lynn', *The Annual: The Bulletin of the Norfolk Archaeological and Historical Research Group*, 26 (2017), 3–11.
25 Ingleby, *Red Register*, vol. 2, pp. 7–8; KLBA, KL/C 58/1.
26 NRO, BL/O/O7.
27 Ingleby, *Red Register*, vol. 2, p. 23.
28 Maddock, 'Mapping Margery Kempe's Lynn', 13.

29 NRO, HARE 2683–4.
30 KLBA, KL/C 10/2, fol. 99v.
31 KLBA, KL/C 17/13 and 19.
32 *The Book of Margery Kempe*, ed. Barry Windeatt (Cambridge: D. S. Brewer, 2004), p. 317. All subsequent quotations refer to this edition by page number.
33 TNA, CP 25/1/169/186.
34 'The soldier in later medieval England'.
35 *Oxford Dictionary of National Biography*: https:doi.org/10.1093/ref:odnb/50229 [accessed 25 Jun 2019]; KLBA, KL/C 39/47; *CPR*, 1413–16, p. 421.
36 TNA, CP 40/672, m. 247v; *CCR*, 1419–35, p. 258.
37 KLBA, KL/C 7/2, p. 119; KL/C 17/19.
38 Maddock, 'Mapping Margery Kempe's Lynn', 13.
39 Michael D. Myers, 'A fictional-true self: Margery Kempe and the social reality of the merchant elite of King's Lynn', *Albion: A Quarterly Journal Concerned with British Studies*, 31:3 (1999), 377–94, pp. 379–80.
40 NRO, HARE 1199; NRO, NCC will register Norman 57.
41 NRO, NRS 5786.
42 NRO, HARE 2493.
43 Dorothy M. Owen, *The Making of King's Lynn* (Oxford: Oxford University Press, 1984), p. 332.
44 Ingleby, *Red Register*, vol. 2, p. 171; TNA, CP 25/1/166.
45 KLBA, KL/C 17/8.
46 N. S. B. Gras, *The Early English Customs System* (Cambridge, MA: Harvard University Press, 1918), pp. 544–6.
47 Ingleby, *Red Register*, vol. 2, p. 5.
48 KLBA, KL/6/2; Ingleby, *Red Register*, vol. 2, p. 15.
49 Diane Watt, 'Political prophecy in *The Book of Margery Kempe*', in John H. Arnold and Katherine J. Lewis (eds), *A Companion to The Book of Margery Kempe* (Cambridge: D. S. Brewer, 2004), pp. 248–50.
50 Edward Milligen Beloe, *Our Borough, Our Churches* (Cambridge: Macmillan and Bowes, 1899), pp. 141–8.
51 Maddock, 'Society, status and the leet court', p. 207.
52 An overwhelming majority of burgesses – around 130 – resisted the grant of new privileges to St Nicholas in 1378–81 (Ingleby, *Red Register*, vol. 2, pp. 145–50).
53 Stephen Alsford, 'The men behind the masque: office-holding in East Anglian boroughs, 1272–1460': http://users.trytel.com/~tristan/towns/mc7_pt6.html [accessed 23 December 2020]; Goodman, *Margery Kempe and Her World*, pp. 35–48; Kate Parker, 'A little local difficulty: Lynn and

the Lancastrian usurpation', in Christopher Harper-Bill (ed.), *Medieval East Anglia* (Woodbridge: Boydell Press, 2005), pp. 115–29.
54 KLBA, KL/C 6/3 m. 2.
55 Alsford, 'The men behind the masque': http://users.trytel.com/~tristan/towns/mc2_pt2.html [accessed 23 December 2020].
56 KLBA, KL/C 10/2, fo. 48v. and KL/C 2/27.
57 Goodman, *Margery Kempe and Her World*, p. 29.
58 KLBA, KL/C 6/3, m 6.
59 Meech and Allen, *The Book of Margery Kempe*, p. 268.
60 Goodman, *Margery Kempe and Her World*, p. 88.
61 Maddock, 'Society, status and the leet court', 208–9.
62 KLBA, KL/C 17/8-9 and KL/C 12/1.
63 Carolyn C. Fenwick, *The Poll Taxes of 1377, 1379 and 1381: Part 2, Lincolnshire–Westmorland* (Oxford: Oxford University Press, 2001), p. 182; KLBA, KL/C 17/8-12; Ingleby, *Red Register*, vol. 2, p. 18.
64 KLBA, KL/C 2/27.
65 KLBA, KL/C 39/48, 49, 91.
66 KLBA, KL/C 2/29.
67 KLBA, KL/C 6/4 and KL/C 7/2, pp. 30–2.
68 KLBA, KL/C 7/2, p. 53.
69 Roskell, Clark, and Rawcliffe (eds), *The History of Parliament 1386–1421*, vol. 4, pp. 19–20.
70 Sebastian Sobecki, '"The writing of this tretys": Margery Kempe's son and the authorship of her book', *Studies in the Age of Chaucer*, 37 (2015), 273.
71 KLBA, KL/C 7/2, p. 90; TNA, CP 40/656.
72 KLBA, KL/C 7/2, p. 90.
73 KLBA, KL/C 7/3, fol. 19v.
74 TNA, PROB 11/3/371.
75 Goodman, *Margery Kempe and Her World*, p. 90; KLBA, KL/C 10/2, fol. 49v. (This entry, dated 20 April, but not ascribed a year, is followed by one of 16 April relating to a commission of the peace issued 28 April 1410.)
76 Charles Gross, *The Gild Merchant* (Oxford: Clarendon Press, 1890), vol. 1, p. 30, and vol. 2, pp. 157–70 (guild ordinances, 1389, in which 'brethren' only are mentioned); KLBA, KL/C 33/6 (entrance of Peter Mafey's wife, 1396–97).
77 Maddock, 'Society, status and the leet court', pp. 212–13; KLBA, KL/C 38/16.
78 KLBA, KL/C 38/16–18.
79 KLBA, KL/C 17/18–22 and KL/C 38/19.

80 *Hijs testibus: Magistro Johanne Forneset priore ecclesie sancte margarete lenne antedicte ac magistro Willelmo meltun doctoribus sacre theologie* (NRO, NCC will register Doke 121). Probate was granted at Norwich on 26 May 1440.
81 Myers, 'A fictional-true self', pp. 377–9, 394; Kate Parker, 'Lynn and the making of a mystic', in Arnold and Lewis (eds), *A Companion to The Book of Margery Kempe*, p. 72; Goodman, *Margery Kempe and Her World*, pp. 51–2, 208.
82 *Ibid.*, p. 54.

9

A women's network in fifteenth-century Rome: Margery Kempe encounters 'Margaret Florentyne'

Anthony Bale and Daniela Giosuè

Friends of Margery

Margery Kempe is well-known for infuriating people. By her own account she was accused of heresy, hypocrisy, insincerity, and deceit. Her 1413–15 pilgrimage from England to the Holy Land and Rome is marked as much by godliness as by repeated quarrelling with her group of fellow-pilgrims. However, in terms of friendships, alliances, and fortuitous encounters *The Book of Margery Kempe* shows us Kempe's significant band of followers and supporters. These include a bishop, a rector, a vicar, a priest, and several confessors, notably Robert Spryngolde (p. 80), Alan of Lynn (p. 84), William Sleighth olme (d. 1420) (p. 251), and Wenzel of Rome (p. 185).[1] Kempe gained companions during her travels too: Richard 'of Ireland', whom she met in Italy (pp. 176–7); a 'Friar Minor, an Englishman' at Assisi (p. 180); William Weaver of Devon, who accompanied Kempe to Bologna (p. 156); the two German pilgrims who helped her near Jerusalem (p. 161); the handsome 'Sarazyn' who assisted her on Mt Quarantine (p. 173); her followers Thomas Marshall (pp. 223–4, 228, 232, 238–41) and Patrick (pp. 238–41), who accompanied her during her ordeals in Leicester; Marcello who gave her food in Rome (p. 201); the ship's captain who looked after her, as if she were his own mother, between Norway and Gdansk (p. 398); and the English monk who accompanied her from Aachen back to England (p. 407). *The Book of Margery Kempe* foregrounds the role of men, particularly religious men, as Kempe's allies. When describing Kempe's male supporters and companions, the *Book* tends to supply individuating details, like names and defining characteristics, making them a significant presence in the narrative. In Rome 'owr Lord sent [Kempe] grace to han gret lofe and gret favowr of many personys in Rome, bothyn of religyows men and other' (p. 210), suggesting the narrative's particular focus on male, clerical support.

However, Kempe had a number of 'other', female supporters. These include the mystic Julian of Norwich (pp. 119–20), and a York anchoress who 'had lovyd [Kempe] wel' (p. 241) but later spurned her. Kempe was also supported by Joan Beaufort, Lady Westmorland (d. 1440) of Raby (Durham), the daughter of John of Gaunt; Kempe was accused of advising Beaufort's daughter, Elizabeth, to leave her husband (a signal of one of the perceived dangers of female community, mentioned in the *Book*, pp. 265–6). Less exalted women who ally with Kempe include the 'jaylerys wyfe' (p. 231) at Leicester; the Norfolk nuns who 'desiryd to have knowlach of the creatur' (p. 361) in order to be the more stirred to devotion; the 'good woman' near Calais who washed her and gave her a 'newe smok' (p. 413); the German women who pity the elderly Kempe making her way to Wilsnack (p. 403); and the 'good wife' of the hostelry near Aachen who 'assygnyd tweyn maydenys' to stay the night with Kempe to protect her from sexual assault (p. 406). We might recall too the Italian lady Kempe encounters with a holy doll ('a chyst and an ymage therin mad aftyr our Lord', p. 177) and the women who, on seeing Kempe's crying, 'ordeyned a good soft bed and leyd hir therupon, and comfortyd hir as mech as thei myth for owyr Lordys lofe' (p. 178), recording her ability to gain charity from a group of strangers. Likewise Kempe describes how she attracted a community of women who appreciated her devotions in Rome: 'The good women, havyng compassyon of hir sorwe and gretly mervelyng of hir wepyng and of hir crying, meche the mor thei lovyd hir' (p. 209).

Kempe's many moments of female friendship, women's community, and practical sorority have routinely been downplayed. This is hardly surprising because the *Book*, as it is written, barely develops the roles or characters of female allies. Colleen Donnelly attributes this to Kempe's 'desire to participate in a world where only men were empowered', as if reflecting the *Book*'s own search for masculine *auctoritas* through the clergy.[2] However, Kempe's female allies may not be as developed as characters on account of the clerical amanuenses and scribes who wrote down Kempe's book, who may have wished to signal Kempe's embrace by male clergy rather than the more controversial suggestion that Kempe was preaching with or to other women, a charge that carried with it the hint of an allegation of the Lollard heresy.

This chapter concerns one of Kempe's key female interlocutors, referred to as 'Margaret Florentyne' or 'Dame Margarete Florentyn', whom Kempe first encountered in the Italian city of Assisi. In this chapter we posit the identity of Margaret Florentine, who has not previously been identified. It is clear from the *Book* that Margaret Florentine had a house in Rome, although her name suggests that she was of Florence: 'Margherita Fiorentina', Margaret of Florence. Whilst the details given by Kempe are scant, we propose that 'Margaret Florentyne' was Margherita degli Alberti (d. after 1417), a member of the wealthy Alberti banking family. This enables us to place Kempe in the context of Renaissance Rome, leading to a new understanding of her devotional and cultural milieux.

'Hir name was Margaret Florentyne'

Kempe first mentions Margaret Florentine during her visit, on returning from Jerusalem, to Assisi, an important pilgrimage destination. Kempe writes:

> And ther was a lady was comyn fro Rome to purchasyn hir pardon. Hir name was Margaret Florentyne. And sche had wyth hir many Knygtys of Roodys, many gentylwomen, and mekyl good caryage. Than Richard, the broke-bakkyd man, went to hir, preyng hir that this creatur mygth gon wyth hir to Rome, and hymself also, for to be kept fro perel of thevys. And than that worshepful lady receyved hem into hir cumpanye and let hem gon wyth hir to Rome, as God wolde. Whan the forseyd creatur was comyn into Rome, and thei that weryn hir felaws beforntyme and put hir owt of her cumpany weryn in Rome also and herd tellyn of swech a woman was come thedyr, thei had gret wondir how sche cam ther in safte. (p. 181)

We know when this meeting took place, for Kempe was in Assisi in August 1414 (she later indicates that she was there on Lammas Day, i.e. 1 August), a chronology which will become significant. Margaret Florentine here appears as a key ally of Kempe's, as she allows her to trump her fellow pilgrims in getting to Rome more quickly than they. She is clearly presented as a wealthy, grand lady, surrounded by Knights Hospitaller ('Knygtys of Roodys') and 'many gentylwomen'. Margaret Florentine acts in the capacity of a patron, which is empowering within Kempe's narrative as a further example of her ability to attract influential – and in this case wealthy – supporters, akin to the kinds of prestigious networks Kempe enjoyed in England (as described by Susan Maddock in Chapter 8, this volume).

Not long afterwards, Margaret Florentine makes a second, and surprising, appearance in Kempe's account of her journey:

> And in schort tyme ... sche met wyth a worshepful lady, Dame Margarete Florentyn, the same lady that browt hir fro Assyse into Rome. And neithyr of hem cowd wel undirstand other but be syngnys er tokenys and in fewe comown wordys. And than the lady seyd onto hir: 'Margerya in poverte?' Sche, undirstondyng what the lady ment, seyd ayen: 'Ya, grawnt poverte, Madam.' Than the lady comawndyd hir to etyn wyth hir every Sonday and set hir at hir owen tabil abovyn hirself, and leyd hir mete wyth hir owyn handys. Than thys creatur sat and wept ful sor, thankyng owr Lord that sche was so cheryd and cherisched, for hys lofe, of hem that cowd not undirstond hir langage. Whan thei had etyn, the good lady used to takyn hir an hamper wyth other stuffe, that sche myght makyn hir potage therwyth, as meche as wolde servyn hir for a too days mete, and filled hir botel wyth good wyn. And sumtyme sche yaf hir an viii bolendinys therto. (pp. 200–1)

This 'schort tyme aftyr' is probably autumn–winter 1414 and Margaret Florentine is marked again here by her wealth and generosity; she is 'a worshepful lady', an honourable or estimable figure, who provides food, wine, and cash to the destitute Kempe (who had, we are told shortly before this encounter, 'yovyn awey hir good, and had neythyr peny ne halfpeny to helpyn hirself wyth' (p. 199). This vignette of patronage, charity, and friendship has received little attention from modern critics, even though it is part of a transformational moment for Kempe, for in Rome Kempe establishes her piety through her marriage to the Godhead and through other kinds of emulation of one of her key authorities and role models, St Bridget of Sweden (d. 1373).[3]

From Kempe's brief description, we are told that Margaret of Florence is wealthy, connected to Hospitallers, and living in Rome:

all features that tally with the wealthy Florentine widow, Margherita degli Alberti. She was the daughter of Messer Niccolaio di Jacopo degli Alberti (d. 1377) and Isabetta (d. before 1364), and was the oldest of eleven siblings and half-siblings: her brothers Jacopo (d. 1372), Diamante (d. 1408), and Antonio (1356–1415); her sister Giovanna (who married the nobleman and poet Niccolò degli Albizzi/ Alessandri); and her half-siblings, Vitalta, Calcedonio (d. 1414), Altobianco (d. 1417), Niccolò (also known as Cristallo; 1376–1420), Ginevra, and Angelica (d. 1457).[4] Their father Niccolaio was one of the wealthiest men in Europe and one of the leading members of the Alberti family of international bankers and merchants. The extended Alberti family had become a pre-eminent financial business across Europe, with multiple companies (*società*) in Florence and *filiali* in Barcelona, Bologna, Bruges, Genoa, London, Montpellier, Palermo, Paris, Pisa, and Valencia, as well as on the Hospitaller island of Rhodes. The wealth and the public magnificence of the family are encapsulated in Niccolaio's 1377 funeral, which cost more than 3,000 florins.[5] The ostentatiousness of this funeral, and the family's contribution in 1384 to celebrations over the purchase of Arezzo, were, in Susannah Baxendale's words, 'purposeful sumptuary displays at their very best'.[6] For a long time, well into the late fifteenth century, the Alberti family made great displays of generosity, civic charity, and its reputation for fairness.[7] The family patronised the Franciscans of Santa Croce, they built churches on their country estates, and commissioned devotional art (for example the frescos by Spinello Aretino of the life of St Catherine, commissioned by Benedetto di Nerozzo degli Alberti, at the family's country oratory at Santa Caterina dell'Antella).[8]

More importantly, in the context of Margery Kempe and her spirituality, Messer Niccolaio and the Florentine branch of his family had a tradition of patronage of women's devotional communities and especially of devotion to St Bridget of Sweden. In 1372 Niccolaio had founded the Ospedale di Orbatello, initially a complex of small houses for poor women and those who might turn to prostitution; the Orbatello soon became the main women's hospital in Florence.[9] In 1394 Margherita's brother Messer Antonio established a Brigittine house, Santa Maria del Paradiso, at Pian di Ripoli in Florence's south-eastern suburbs;[10] this was the first Brigittine house in Italy and only the third founded outside Sweden. This monastery housed both male and female religious and was adjacent to one of Niccolaio and Antonio degli Alberti's family estates. The monastery was decorated with Brigittine frescos (painted in 1395) by Niccolò di Pietro Gerini and Mariotto di Nardo. These frescos, designed both for meditation and to glorify the Alberti family and their adjacent villa, indicate the Alberti family's immersion in Brigittine iconography and theophany, in a decorative schemata that commemorates Margherita's father, Niccolaio, and draws explicitly on imagery found in St Bridget's *Revelations*.[11] Frederick Antal suggests that the foundation of the Paradiso monastery may have come about through Antonio degli Alberti's encounter with St Bridget herself during her travels in Italy (Bridget visited Florence in 1370 and spent time with various influential Florentine families).[12] Francesca Goggioli has argued that the founding of the Paradiso monastery turned the Alberti villa (also called Paradiso) from a *locus amoenus* into a spiritualised environment that demonstrated the manifestation of divinity as described by St Bridget.[13] Indeed Antonio degli Alberti called his eldest daughter Brigida, and in 1420 she herself gave a significant amount of property to Santa Maria del Paradiso to extend the monastery.[14] The family's devotion to St Bridget of Sweden is also indicated by the fact that Cammilla degli Alberti, illegitimate daughter of Margherita's brother Diamante, herself became a Brigittine sister (named Sister Lucy) at Santa Maria del Paradiso in 1415, just after or around the time that Margery Kempe was in Assisi and Rome.[15] The founding of the Paradiso was one of Antonio degli Alberti's great civic works, but the institution quickly became fraught with Florentine politicking and in the 1400s and 1410s was one of the ways in which the Alberti family strove to maintain its connection with Florence.

During this period the monks and nuns of the Paradiso were reading and writing a number of texts resonant with Kempe's spirituality, including manuscripts of St Bridget's *Revelations*; the *Dialogues* of St Catherine of Siena; festival books of Bridget and Catherine; and vernacular poems celebrating Christ's incarnation, including erotic and spousal love lyrics to Christ (for example 'O Iesu mio tanto dolce', 'Di Christo spose belle', 'Iesu Christo nostro amore', 'O Brigida da Christo eletta sposa', 'O sposa di Giesu Christo', 'Sposa dilecta', and 'Sposa novella del re del Paradiso').[16]

We may recall Margery Kempe's great devotion to Bridget, invoked many times in the *Book* as a role model; during her 1414–15 trip, Kempe spent time at St Bridget's house in Rome, adjacent to the English pilgrims' hospice of St Thomas of Canterbury, and made the acquaintance of the saint's Swedish maid (who described Bridget's 'lawhyng cher', her smiling face) and another man who 'telde hir that he knew [Bridget] hys owyn selfe' (p. 204). Kempe's time in Italy was a crucial moment of emulation of the Swedish saint: Kempe visited the church of St John Lateran, where Bridget had been witnessed levitating (pp. 184–5); Kempe voluntarily put herself into poverty, as Bridget had done (p. 199); Kempe made a mystical marriage with the Godhead, along very similar lines to Bridget's own wedding to the Godhead (p. 190). In Rome Kempe deepened her relationship with St Bridget's legacy, and the Alberti family's commitment to St Bridget provides a plausible context for her development of her devotion to the saint.

By 1414 Margherita degli Alberti was a wealthy widow. Her husband, Alberto di Luigi degli Alberti, was an Alberti kinsman who died in or around 1383, and together they had several children (Adovardo, Caterina, Luigi, Aliso). Margherita was also a strong, capable, and independent woman, who managed her and her family's financial and political affairs; these have been charted by Susannah Baxendale, who evokes Margherita degli Alberti thus:

> Notably, some Alberti women represented their absent menfolk's affairs as well as their own. Margherita di Messer Niccolaio degli Alberti ... stands out particularly in this regard; as procuratrix for her half-brothers, she appointed agents to settle their problems in and out of court; on at least one occasion, she herself appeared before the judges of the Mercanzia on her brothers' behalf. Over the years Margherita also submitted petitions to the Signoria concerning the financial affairs of her sons and daughters.[17]

As Baxendale shows, Margherita degli Alberti was an indomitable and fiercely independent woman; it is easy to see a figure like her as a mentor to the strong, independent, and assertive Margery Kempe. However, this relationship may best be thought of not as one of mentoring but rather as one of civic piety, in which the destitute Kempe was the recipient of the Alberti family's wealth and patronage.

For Kempe this was profoundly authorising but, for Margherita degli Alberti, Kempe may well have been just one of many people who were part of her programme of public charity.

Our understanding of this context is enriched by the following episode, described in *The Book of Margery Kempe* shortly after Kempe encounters Margaret Florentine:

> Than was ther a gret jentylwoman in Rome preyng thys creatur to be godmodyr of hir childe and namyd it aftyr Seynt Brigypt, for thei haddyn knowlach of hir in hir lyve-tyme. And so sche dede. Sithyn God yaf hir grace to have gret lofe in Rome, bothyn of men and of women, and gret favowr among the pepyl. (p. 202)

The Roman 'jentylwoman' naming her child after St Bridget places Kempe and her friends very precisely within the cultural environment of Brigittine–Dominican patronage in Florence and Rome at this time, as traced by Nirit Ben-Aryeh Debby, Maria Oen, and others.[18] The fact that this woman in Rome had known Bridget in her lifetime may further suggest a proximity to the Alberti family. Within the scope of the research for this chapter it has not yet been possible securely to identify an infant named Brigida connected to the Alberti family who was born in or around Rome or Florence in 1414; after the canonisation of Bridget in Rome in 1391, the forename Brigida became fashionable in Italy. We know that Brigida was a popular name in the Alberti family and its circle (e.g. Brigida di Francesco di Giannozzo degli Alberti; Brigida di Antonio degli Alberti; and Brigida, daughter of Filippo Guidetti of Florence).[19]

It is fair to say that the period around 1414–15, when Kempe met Margaret Florentine, was a high point of the Alberti family's international power and wealth. Margherita degli Alberti's brothers, all younger than her, went into the Alberti merchant banking business with great success. Her brother Antonio, a noted poet, had run the Bruges, Bologna, and Venice arms of the Alberti company and was closely linked to the court of Henry Bolingbroke, later Henry IV of England, and exchanged £1,333 6s 8d for 8,888 ducats to fund Henry's 1393 pilgrimage to Jerusalem.[20] As mentioned above, Antonio was also an important patron of the Brigittines in Tuscany, a devotion he shared with Henry IV (who in 1415 founded the Brigittine house at Syon (Middlesex), later visited by Kempe). However, from 1387 – when the Alberti family was banned from civic office-holding in

Florence – into the late 1420s, the family was largely exiled from Florence as a consequence of its rivalry with other leading families and its perceived overreaching power.[21] Eventually all male members of the family were forbidden from living within two hundred miles of the city. More specifically, Margherita degli Alberti was herself banished from Florence from 1411–12 to 1415, following a highly unusual sanction specifically against the Alberti women by Florence's *balìa* (the city's ruling patrician committee).[22] This is then a plausible context for Margaret Florentine's residence in Rome and pilgrimage to Assisi when Kempe encountered her. Rome was by far the most popular place of refuge for political exiles in Quattrocento Italy; it was full of visitors and pilgrims, and its status as an 'open' city was vaunted by the papacy.[23]

Moreover, the Alberti family was closely connected both to key institutions in Rome and to the Hospitallers. From 1376 to 1390 the Florentine banking families were under a papal interdict, and the close relationship between the two was interrupted.[24] However, from the 1390s the Alberti family put great energy into banking for the papacy and, along with the Bardi, Cambi, Medici, Ricci, and Spini companies, the Alberti were the most important bankers to the papacy in the first half of the fifteenth century. Kurt Weissen has demonstrated the importance of the Alberti family in papal banking, and the period of Urban VI's return to Rome, from 1388 to 1413, saw the Florentine merchant banking community re-establishing its links with the papacy with great vigour; Arnold Esch estimates that 211 Florentine bankers were at the papal court at this time.[25] Margherita degli Alberti's nephew, Francesco d'Altobianco degli Alberti, held the position of *depositarius urbis* (a key trustee of the papal finances) in 1427.[26] In short it is clear that the Alberti banking family had deep, significant, and sustained interests in Rome in the first decades of the fifteenth century.

Likewise, from the conquest of Rhodes by the Hospitallers in 1309, Florentine merchant-banking companies had supported the financing of the Hospitallers, via the papal *curia*. Around 1400 the Florentine companies began to show an aggressive interest in Levantine trade, to which the Hospitallers, in control of Rhodes, were key.[27] The Alberti were one of the several Florentine banking companies on Rhodes in this period, but from 1370 until the 1420s the Alberti were the Hospitallers' principal bankers at Rhodes.

Furthermore Margherita's kinsman Cipriano (1335–1415) had been banished in 1393 to Rhodes, where he appears to have developed the Alberti company's close connections with the Hospitallers.[28] As Elisa Soldani and Daniel Duran i Duelt have commented in their study of Florentine business interests in fifteenth-century Rhodes, 'for [the] large merchant-banking companies, the key to accessing the Order [of the Hospitallers], and thus Rhodes, was the Papal Curia'; it makes perfect sense that Margaret Florentine/Margherita degli Alberti would have a large number of 'Knygtys of Roodys' with her, as noticed by Kempe.[29] The Alberti banked for the papacy in both Rome and Avignon.[30] In sum it is abundantly clear that the Alberti family was heavily involved in business in Rome and with the Hospitaller order.

The Alberti family's great wealth, and their pan-European network, was not simply a matter of finance but encompassed public piety. Nirit Ben-Aryeh Debby has charted 'a circle of Dominican Observants and lay supporters working together to promote the cult of Saint Birgitta and secure the well-being of the Paradiso institution in Florence'.[31] This network included the Alberti family, led by the preacher and Observant leader Giovanni Dominici. Dominici was also at the same time working with the Dominican prioress Chiara Gambacorta to establish Bridget's cult in Pisa. As Ben-Aryeh Debby describes it, '[c]ompleting this circle was Bartolomea degli Alberti, the wife of Antonio degli Alberti [i.e. Margherita's brother]. She was the spiritual daughter of Dominici, who in fact dedicated three of his spiritual treatises to her. Giovanni Dominici was directly involved with the Paradiso; he was active in the institutional organisation of the convent, working together with Francesco Datini to establish its reputation.'[32]

Thus the Alberti family, from the 1390s to the 1410s, was crucial to the spread and deepening of St Bridget's cult in Italy; the special devotion to Bridget by the members of this circle, a devotion which grew out of Antonio degli Alberti's founding of the monastery of Paradiso, can help us better understand the significant impact Kempe's encounter with the cult of St Bridget had on her. As Ben-Aryeh Debby shows, one of this group's key concerns was the potential of art in deepening personal devotions; Dominici wrote the *Regola del governo di cura familiare* (a regimen of family management) for Bartolomea degli Alberti (Margherita's sister-in-law) in 1401, in which Dominici suggested that a mother should keep biblical pictures and sculptures in her house to educate her children, recommending especially the Virgin, the baby Jesus at play, and John the Baptist as suitable subjects. Dominici also suggested using pictures of female saints to teach girls about chastity and charity. Ben-Aryeh Debby observes that these suggestions 'show a familiarity with the iconography of his period and a recognition of the utility of art as a teaching tool; children would identify with the painted figures and consequently be instructed along religious lines'.[33]

The similarities here with Margery Kempe's own devotional poses are striking, not only in her emulation of St Bridget but also in the litany of female saints and in the maternally inflected devotion to Jesus as a child; it is in Rome that Kempe visits the house of a destitute single mother and is moved by the sight of the 'lytel manchylde sowkyng on hir brest' to having a vision of Christ's Passion, 'as thei sche had seyn owr Lady and hir sone in tyme of hys Passyon' (p. 202). We are thus presented with an environment in which the Alberti family may have been a significant influence on Kempe's religiosity. Indeed the Brigittine vision of the Virgin dressed in a white gown, which featured in the fresco by Pietro di Miniato at Santa Maria Novella in Florence and may have been commissioned by the Alberti circle, could be seen as intertext of Kempe's controversial white clothing, which she resumed wearing during her Italian trip.

Further information about the Alberti family's devotional priorities and sense of charity can be gained from Margherita degli Alberti's will, which offers a window on to her personal circumstances just three years after Margery Kempe was in Rome.[34] The will, housed in the archive of the Florentine community in Rome, was made at the Camaldolese church of Santa Maria degli Angeli in Florence on 10 July 1417, and states that Margherita was in good health and in full possession of her mental faculties; in 1417 there was an outbreak of the plague in Florence, and the will may have been written as a precaution. At this time Margherita was at least sixty-two years old, and had been pardoned and allowed to return to Florence in 1415. Margherita asks to be buried in the Franciscan basilica of Santa Croce, adjacent to the family's palaces, in her family tomb.[35] Amongst her legacies Margherita gave 25 florins to the Stinche prison; 20 gold florins to the Camaldolese monastery of Santa Maria degli Angeli (the family had long patronised the Olivetan and Camaldolese orders, and the witnesses to the will were drawn from this monastery); 3 florins towards building the walls of Florence; and money to provide for a lamp to be lit, for ten years, at the statue of St Catherine in the Vallombrosian Church of San Jacopo tra i Fossi.[36] Margherita also made careful provision for a dowry for her grand-daughter Costanza, the daughter of her son Adovardo (whose banishment from Florence is referred to at several points in the will). A large part of the will concerns Margherita's legacy to her widowed grand-daughter Aura (the daughter of Margherita's son Aliso); Aura was to receive a large sum of money (800 florins), various linens and woollens, and the right to live in Margherita's *palazzo*, along with the adjoining houses and tower, beside Santa Croce (corresponding with the Alberti properties that survive today on the Via de' Benci).[37] Margherita's great wealth, and the extent of her own financial transactions, is evident in her release of her son Adovardo from a debt of 1,200 florins and the gift to him of 890 florins owed to her by Nerio degli Ardinghelli, a scion of another Florentine banking company. In her will the family is repeatedly referred to as *Albertis de Florentia*, which might explain how Kempe reached the name 'Margaret Florentyne', as the family continued to define itself by its connection to its city.

The will mentions Margherita's palace in Florence and her houses elsewhere, but the information on these properties is illegible due to damage to the document. However, we know that the Florentine Alberti family base in Rome was a house and *fondaco* (trading post and warehouse) in the central Roman *rione* (neighbourhood) of Ponte, in the parish of Sant'Orsola della Pietà; this is precisely the area in which members of affluent Florentine families established themselves and still bears evidence of their presence in many toponyms.[38] This area is not far (about 850 metres) from the English pilgrims' hospice of St Thomas of Canterbury (pp. 181–2, 202–3) and the Casa di Santa Brigida (St Bridget's former home) (p. 204), both sites visited and described by Kempe. The area is dominated by the sixteenth-century church of San Giovanni Battista dei Fiorentini (St John the Baptist of the Florentines), attached to the Florentine expatriate archive in which Margherita degli Alberti's will is now housed. Unusually for Roman archives, the archive of the Archconfraternity holds abundant material produced before the Sack of

Rome in 1527. Among the oldest are documents concerning the Alberti family, including Margherita degli Alberti's 1370 dowry, and her will.

The presence of the will in the Archconfraternity's Rome archive, as well as the presence of various documents relating to other members of Margherita's family, suggests that, at some point, assets of the Alberti family were transferred or bequeathed to the Confraternity, pointing to deep connections between the family and Roman institutions. Following our identification of Margherita degli Alberti's will, and her notary Iohannes de Montaione, future archival work in Florence and Rome is likely to reveal a more developed picture of Margherita degli Alberti's financial, cultural, and devotional affairs in the 1410s, when Margery Kempe met 'Margaret Florentyne'.

Margery Kempe, Renaissance woman

Towards the end of her extended sequence of bidding prayers, which follow Book II at the close of *The Book of Margery Kempe*, Kempe includes a prayer that seems to remember patrons and donors like Margaret Florentine:

> I cry the mercy, Lord, for the riche men in this worlde that han thi goodys in weldyng; yeve hem grace for to spendyn hem to thi plesyng. (p. 424)

Invoking the responsibility of rich people ('riche men') to spend their riches to God's pleasure, Kempe nods towards urgent debates taking place in early fifteenth-century Italy about the nature of wealth and the proper way of spending money with due devotional care. The devotional style taken up by Kempe in Rome – of poverty, mendicancy, mystical vision, itinerant confession, and caring for 'an hold woman that was a poure creatur in Rome' (p. 189) – did not make a saint of her, but it did of a woman who was in Rome at precisely the same time and would almost certainly have been known to the Alberti family: St Francesca Romana / Francesca of Rome (1384–1440). Francesca was of a similar social class to Kempe, and in the early fifteenth century she dedicated herself to relieving Rome's poor and sick and begging for charity whilst also receiving a number of divine revelations, some of which show a marked influence of the spirituality of Catherine of Siena. She made herself voluntarily poor, rejected fine clothing, refused family banquets, insisted on speaking to servants as her equals, and fiercely attacked anyone who swore oaths on God. Later, in 1433, Francesca founded a convent, the Tor de' Specchi. As Guy Boanas and Lyndal Roper have noted, 'Francesca's most distinctive characteristic was that, like Margery Kempe, Catherine of Siena and Bridget of Sweden, she was a married woman, offering a model of holy life to those non-virgins who had taken the spiritually lesser path of matrimony'.[39] Francesca received mystical stigmatic wounds from contemplating the Passion and, like Kempe, experienced floods of mystical tears. As has previously been suggested by P. H. Cullum, there is certainly a shared devotional sensibility between the two women, based on charity, ascetic poverty, mystical communication, and a performative civic piety.[40]

Kempe's time in Rome was clearly a transformative encounter with civic piety at the heart of western Christendom. In the absence of another wealthy woman named Margherita, connected to Florence but resident in Rome around 1414, we propose that Margery Kempe's wealthy benefactress, 'Margaret Florentyne', was Margherita degli Alberti. This identification is based on circumstantial but compelling evidence:

- her name
- her wealth ('mekyl good caryage', 'that worshepful lady')
- her and her family's connection to the Hospitallers ('Knygtys of Roodys')
- her and her family's specific circumstances in exile from Florence in 1412–15
- her family's especial commitment to the cult of St Bridget of Sweden which chimes with that of Margery Kempe
- her circle's interest in public acts of pious charity in the devotional context of fifteenth-century Florence and Rome.

This is not just a way of expanding a footnote to *The Book of Margery Kempe*. This identification will be crucial in helping us to understand women's networks in fifteenth-century Italy, the Brigittine context in which Kempe prospered in Rome, and the prehistory of Kempe's ability to attract, as well as to repel, those around her.

Moreover, by exploring Kempe's encounter with Rome more closely one can place her far from her native Lynn and find her proximal to the Italian Renaissance. Margherita's cousin Lorenzo degli Alberti managed the family's business in Padua and Venice, and his illegitimate son, Leon Battista Alberti (1414–72), became the archetypal 'Renaissance man'. Indeed, Leon Battista Alberti wrote at length about Margherita's family in *Della famiglia*, written when the author was a young secretary in Rome at the Papal *curia*.[41] *Della famiglia* evokes Margherita's brothers and cousins, and although Margherita is not named in its pages one can discern an attitude to public charity that mirrors Margaret Florentine's patronage of Margery Kempe. The fourth book of *Della famiglia* portrays Margherita's son, Adovardo, as a model humanist and urbane proponent of ethical friendship; he argues that 'only friendship based on virtue is strong and enduring'.[42]

In a remarkably influential essay that is now over forty years old, Joan Kelly-Gadol, herself a scholar of Leon Battista Alberti and the Alberti family, argued that women did not have a Renaissance, at least not on the terms proposed by dominant, masculinist historiography. She opened her pathbreaking essay 'Did women have a Renaissance?' with the asseveration that '[o]ne of the tasks of women's history is to call into question accepted schemas of periodization', and took the Renaissance in Italy, from c. 1350 to 1530, as her case in point. Kelly-Gadol argued that in Renaissance Italy society was reorganised 'along modern lines', which led to the social and cultural expression for which the age is known. But, she argued, precisely these developments affected women adversely, so much so that there was no 'renaissance' for women, at least not during the Renaissance:

> The state, early capitalism, and the social relations formed by them impinged on the lives of Renaissance women in different ways according to their different positions in society ... [W]omen as a group, especially among the classes that dominated Italian urban elite, experienced a contraction of social and personal options that the men of their classes did not experience as markedly.[43]

In Kelly-Gadol's account the very things that made the Renaissance a startling period of expansive change were those aspects that excluded women, whose options, according to this reading, contracted as those of the men around them widened. Kelly-Gadol's thesis significantly expanded our understanding of women's opportunities in fifteenth-century Europe and remains useful, although a subsequent generation of scholarship has modulated and qualified it.[44] In particular, wealthy widows (like Margherita degli Alberti) and spiritually ambitious laywomen (like Margery Kempe) could also develop new kinds of empowering relationships in the expansive opportunities offered by a city like Rome at this time. Kelly-Gadol's other scholarly expertise was in the career of Margherita's close relative Leon Battista Alberti, and one cannot help wishing that she had considered his formidable kinswoman Margherita, and the recipient of her charity, Margery Kempe. Whilst neither Margherita degli Alberti nor Margery Kempe is a representative figure, their stories shed light on the ways in which women could encounter each other through bonds of piety and patronage. Kempe's devotional identity was authorised and emboldened during her time in Rome and her unique life story therefore emerges in a wealthy, influential, and spiritually dynamic European, Renaissance context, supported by Margherita degli Alberti, another distinctive and determined woman.

Notes

The authors would like to thank Ivana Ait, Susannah F. Baxendale, Isabelle Chabot, Romina De Vizio, Elizabeth McKnight, Maria Oen, Päivi Salmesvuori, Patrizia Urbani, and Julia Vicioso for their generous assistance.

1. All references to *The Book of Margery Kempe* are given parenthetically and refer to *The Book of Margery Kempe*, ed. Barry Windeatt (Cambridge: D. S. Brewer, 2004).
2. Colleen Donnelly, 'Menopausal life as imitation of art: Margery Kempe and the lack of sorority', *Women's Writing*, 12:3 (2005), 419–32.
3. See Naoë Kukita Yoshikawa, 'Margery Kempe's mystical marriage and Roman sojourn: influence of St Bridget of Sweden', *Reading Medieval Studies*, 28 (2002), 39–58.
4. Details of the family tree are largely taken from Luigi Passerini, *Gli Alberti di Firenze* (Florence: Cellini, 1869), 2 vols, vol. 1, 26–40, and 1, 80–7, tavola I, which is corrected by Pellegrini in Leon Battista

Alberti, *I primi tre libri della famiglia*, ed. F. C. Pellegrini (Florence: Sansoni, 1911), pp. lxx–lxxii.

5   Niccolaio's will is reproduced in Passerini, *Gli Alberti*, 1, 76–7. Margherita and her sisters received dowries of the huge sum of 1,200 florins. See also Isabelle Chabot, 'Messer Niccolò degli Alberti, "pater pauperum". Lettura del testamento', in Christina de Benedictis and Carla Milloschi (eds), *L'ospedale di Orbatello. Carità e arte a Firenze* (Florence: Edizioni Polistampa, 2015), pp. 73–81; Maddalena Modesti, 'Il testamento del *nobilis miles dominus* Niccolò del fu Iacopo degli Alberti. Edizione critica', in De Benedictis and Milloschi (eds), *L'ospedale di Orbatello*, pp. 45–71.

6   Susannah F. Baxendale, 'Exile in practice: the Alberti family in and out of Florence 1401–1428', *Renaissance Quarterly*, 44:4 (1991), 720–56, p. 725.

7   See Gene A. Brucker, *The Civic World of Early Renaissance Florence* (Princeton: Princeton University Press, 1977), p. 325.

8   See David Wright, 'Family ties: Alberti and the architectural patronage and designs of his Florentine forebears', in Arturo Calzona, Joseph Connors, Francesco Paolo Fiore, and Cesare Vasoli (eds), *Leon Battista Alberti: Architettura e Committenti* (Florence: Olschki, 2009), 2 vols, 1, 35–47, p. 37; Isabelle Chabot and Paolo Pirillo, '"Onore e fama" della famiglia: gli Alberti e l'oratorio di Santa Caterina a Rimezzano', in Angelo Tartuferi (ed.), *L'oratorio di Santa Caterina all'Antella e i suoi pittori* (Florence: Mandragora, 2009), pp. 19–43.

9   See Richard C. Trexler, 'A widows' asylum of the Renaissance: the Orbatello of Florence', in Richard C. Trexler, *Power and Dependence in Renaissance Florence* 2 (Binghamton: SUNY Press, 1993), pp. 66–93; also, De Benedictis and Milloschi (eds), *L'ospedale di Orbatello*.

10 Nirit Ben-Aryeh Debby, 'The images of Saint Birgitta of Sweden in Santa Maria Novella in Florence', *Renaissance Studies*, 18:4 (2004), 509–26, pp. 516–17: the monastery was founded in 1392 by Antonio degli Alberti but approved only in 1397; within a few years the monastery lost its premises because of Alberti's exile but was refounded in 1401, and expanded quickly in the early fifteenth century. Bridget was canonised in 1391 and reaffirmed in 1419. The Paradiso's manuscripts have been thoroughly catalogued by Rosanna Miriello, *I manoscritti del monastero del Paradiso di Firenze* (Florence: SISMEL, 2007).

11 Renato Piattoli, 'Il monastero del Paradiso presso Firenze nella storia dell'arte del primo Quattrocento', *Rivista d'Arte*, 18 (1936), 287–309, p. 287.

12 Frederick Antal, *Florentine Painting and Its Social Background: The Bourgeois Republic before Cosimo de' Medici's Advent to Power: XIV*

and Early XV Centuries (London: Kegan Paul, 1948), p. 198; Miriello, I manoscritti, pp. 4–5.
13 Francesca Goggioli, 'Il paradiso ritrovato. Novità sul ciclo pittorico del monastero di Santa Maria e Brigida a Pian di Ripoli', Arte Cristiana, 102 (2014), 201–17.
14 Passerini, Gli Alberti, tavola I (infra 1, 48–9).
15 Another Alberti kinswoman, Nera di Francesco degli Alberti (b. 1425), also became a sister (Sister Caterina) at Paradiso (Passerini, Gli Alberti, tavola II).
16 See further Miriello, I manoscritti.
17 Baxendale, 'Exile in practice', pp. 744–5.
18 See especially Nirit Ben-Aryeh Debby, 'Reshaping Birgitta of Sweden in Tuscan art and sermons', in Maria H. Oen (ed.), A Companion to Birgitta of Sweden and Her Legacy in the Later Middle Ages (Leiden: Brill, 2019), pp. 223–46; Maria H. Oen, 'The iconography of Liber Celestis revelacionum', in Oen (ed.), A Companion to Birgitta, pp. 186–222.
19 The possibility that this 'childe' was the mystic Brigida Baldinotti (born c. 1412–14) is an attractive and intriguing one. Baldinotti was most likely born in Pistoia, north of Florence; see Lisa Kaborycha, 'Brigida Baldinotti and her two epistles in Quattrocento Florentine manuscripts', Speculum, 87:3 (2012), 793–826.
20 Lucy Toulmin Smith (ed.), Expeditions to Prussia and the Holy Land Made by Henry Earl of Derby, Camden Society, New Series, 52 (London, 1894), p. lv. Antonio degli Alberti's writings appear in a large number of manuscripts; see further Giovanni Borriero, 'La tradizione delle rime di Antonio degli Alberti (I–III)', Medioevo letterario d'Italia [in three parts], 1 (2004), 141–70; 3 (2006), 89–135; 5 (2008), 45–100.
21 See Passerini, Gli Alberti, 2, 236, for the 1387 decree of expulsion from Florence.
22 Baxendale, 'Exile in practice', p. 730; Brucker, Civic World, pp. 326–7. Following a conspiracy hatched by Florentine exiles in Bologna, Bindaccio degli Alberti was executed and Alberti women were forbidden to live in the family's houses without permission of the Florentine Signoria.
23 See further Christine Shaw, 'Rome as a centre for Italian political exiles in the later Quattrocento', in Sergio Gensini (ed.), Roma Capitale (1447–1527) (Pisa: Pacini, 1994), pp. 274–88; Ivana Ait, 'Mercanti lombardi e toscani a Roma: testimonianze dalle fonti del XV e XVI secolo', in Sara Cabibbo and Alessandro Serra (eds), Venire a Roma, restare a Roma. Forestieri e stranieri fra Quattro e Settecento (Roma: RomaTrePress, 2017), pp. 119–35.
24 Michele Cassandro, 'I banchieri pontifici nel XV secolo', in Gensini (ed.), Roma Capitale, pp. 207–34.

25 Kurt Weissen, *Florentiner Bankiers und Deutschland (1275 bis 1475), Kontinuität und Diskontinuität wirtschaftlicher Strukturen*, Habilitationsschrift (Basel: University of Basel, 2001), p. 30; Arnold Esch, 'Florentiner in Rom um 1400', *Quellen und Forschungen aus italienischen Archiven und Bibliotheken*, 52 (1972), 476–525, pp. 477–8.
26 Weissen, *Florentiner Bankiers und Deutschland*, p. 32.
27 See Richard A. Goldthwaite, *The Economy of Renaissance Florence* (Baltimore: Johns Hopkins University Press, 2009), pp. 182–202.
28 Passerini, *Gli Alberti*, 2, 160–4; Anthony Luttrell, 'Interessi fiorentini nell'economia e nella politica dei Cavalieri Ospedalieri di Rodi nel Trecento', *Annali della Scuola Normale Superiore di Pisa. Lettere, Storia e Filosofia*, series II, 28:3/4 (1959), 317–26.
29 Elisa Soldani and Daniel Duran i Duelt, 'Religion, warfare, and business in fifteenth-century Rhodes', in Francesco Ammannati (ed.), *Religion and Religious Institutions in the European Economy, 1000–1800* (Florence: Firenze University Press, 2012), pp. 257–70, p. 264.
30 Luttrell, 'Interessi fiorentini', pp. 322–6.
31 Ben-Aryeh Debby, 'The images of Saint Birgitta of Sweden', p. 517.
32 *Ibid.*, p. 518.
33 *Ibid.*, p. 520.
34 Margherita's will is now Rome, Archconfraternity of San Giovanni dei Fiorentini, vol. 732, pergamena 21.
35 Brenda Preyer, '"Da chasa gli Alberti": the 'territory' and housing of the family', in Calzona, Connors, Fiore, and Vasoli (eds), *Leon Battista Alberti*, 1, 3–34. During the 1370s and 1380s, Margherita's father and brothers bought up all the property on Via de' Benci up to piazza Santa Croce.
36 See Wright, 'Family ties', pp. 40–2, on the family's connections to the Camaldolese. Wright shows how the Camaldolese house of Santa Maria degli Angeli received significant and controversial Alberti family patronage in the period 1411–14, as the banished Alberti family members sought to continue to exercise influence and devotion in Florence.
37 On Margherita's special provisions for her grand-daughter Aura see Carlo Carnesecchi, 'Madonna Caterina degli Alberti Corsini: notizie inedite', *Archivio Storico Italiano*, 10:187 (1892), 116–22, p. 118.
38 Esch, 'Florentiner in Rom um 1400', p. 497, on the Alberti residence in the *rione* Ponte; also Egmont Lee, 'Gli abitanti del rione Ponte', in Gensini (ed.), *Roma Capitale*, pp. 317–44.
39 Guy Boanas and Lyndal Roper, 'Feminine piety in fifteenth-century Rome: Santa Francesca of Rome', in Jim Obelkevich, Lyndal Roper, and Raphael Samuel (eds), *Disciplines of Faith: Studies in Religion,*

Politics, Patriarchy (New York: Routledge, 1987), pp. 177–93, p. 180; Catherine of Siena refused to marry.

40 P. H. Cullum, '"Yf lak of charyte be not ower hynderawnce": Margery Kempe, Lynn, and the practice of the spiritual and bodily works of mercy', in John H. Arnold and Katherine J. Lewis (eds), *A Companion to The Book of Margery Kempe* (Cambridge: D. S. Brewer, 2004), pp. 177–94, pp. 186–9.

41 On the background of *Della famiglia* see Leon Battista Alberti, *The Family in Renaissance Florence*, ed. and trans. Renee Neu Watkins (Columbia: University of South Carolina Press, 1969), pp. 2–4.

42 *Ibid.*, p. 266.

43 Joan Kelly-Gadol, 'Did women have a Renaissance?', in Renate Bridenthal, Claudia Koonz, and Susan Mosher Stuard (eds), *Becoming Visible: Women in European History* (Boston: Houghton Mifflin, 1977), pp. 174–201, at p. 175.

44 Especially Sharon T. Strocchia, *Nuns and Nunneries in Renaissance Florence* (Baltimore: Johns Hopkins University Press, 2009); Christiane Klapisch-Zuber, *Women, Family, and Ritual in Renaissance Italy* (Chicago: University of Chicago Press, 1985); Christiane Klapisch-Zuber and David Herlihy, *Tuscans and Their Families: A Study of the Florentine Catasto of 1427* (New Haven: Yale University Press, 1985); Anne Winston-Allen, 'Did nuns have a Renaissance? Libraries and literary activities', in Anne Winston-Allen, *Convent Chronicles: Women Writing About Women and Reform in the Late Middle Ages* (University Park: Pennsylvania State University Press, 2004), pp. 169–204.

10

Margery Kempe, racialised soundscapes, sonic wars, and cosmopolitan Jerusalem

Dorothy Kim

What 'foreign' soundscape does Margery Kempe import back to England? Sarah Salih comes closest to seeing Margery Kempe as a foreigner after her pilgrimage to the cosmopolitan capitals of Rome and Jerusalem, astutely observing that 'on Margery's return, England had become a foreign land'.[1] If one contextualises her particular devotional practices within the heterogeneous Christian, multiracial, multireligious, and cosmopolitan soundscape of Jerusalem, her notorious tears become a sign of orthodox Western Christianity amongst the racialised noise of Eastern Christians, Muslims, and Jews. But in England this orthodox Christian soundscape evokes the racialised, 'foreign' sound of a multiracial Eastern city and thus she crosses the medieval 'sonic color line'.[2] Margery Kempe's post-pilgrimage soundscape reveals how sonic racialisation can happen depending on geographical, historical, and on-the-ground contexts at different ends of the medieval European Continent and how the medieval devotional *sensorium* is used in constructing medieval racialisation.

How do Margery Kempe's loud, and what she describes as overwhelming, tears fit into Jerusalem's complex fifteenth-century soundscape? This chapter contextualises her soundscape in relation to the orthodox devotional frames of the multireligious or multiracial, cosmopolitan, and contested spaces of Jerusalem. I explain how a racialised devotional *sensorium* functions in relation to the Holy Sepulchre and its own sonic wars. Within this particular context, Margery Kempe's tears are ordinary, but as soon as she returns to England those same tears mark her as illegible and 'foreign'.

In addition, this chapter will address an area of feminist Digital Humanities as it rethinks the theoretical frames of immersive Digital Humanities in the process of piecing together a premodern soundscape from current contemporary cues. This latter practice, and digital media experiment, become a way to think about feminist digital multimedia theory.

Medieval urban soundscapes and the 'sonic color line'

There has been a recent upsurge in discussing medieval soundscapes, especially with regards to medieval Western European urban spaces.[3] According to Emily Thompson, 'like a landscape, a soundscape is simultaneously a physical environment and a way of perceiving that environment; it is both a world and a culture constructed to make sense of that world'.[4] She further elaborates that the study of soundscapes should include 'scientific and aesthetic ways of listening, a listener's relationship to their environment, and the social circumstances that dictate who gets to hear what'.[5] However, within medieval studies, much of this work has focused on urban Christian devotional sound, even in cities like Paris with a Jewish religious or racialised minority population. Likewise, in a city like Jerusalem, there is not one Christian sound, but a multitude of Christian soundscapes that often compete with and/or complement each other.

But how is an urban medieval soundscape racialised? In her study of sonic racialisation in twentieth-century America, Jennifer Stoever introduces two key theoretical definitions – the 'sonic color line' and the 'listening ear' – that can both be seen, though with different factors, geographies, contexts, and racialisations, in the premodern past. She writes:

> The sonic color line describes the process of racializing sound – how and why certain bodies are expected to produce, desire, and live amongst particular sounds – and its product, the hierarchical division sounded between 'whiteness' and 'blackness.' The listening ear drives the sonic color line; it is a figure for how dominant listening practices accrue – and change – over time, as well as a descriptor for how the dominant culture exerts pressure on individual listening practices to conform to the sonic color line's norms. Through the listening ear's surveillance, discipline, and interpretation, certain associations between race and sound come to seem normal, natural, and 'right'.[6]

These theoretical frames can be used to reconsider how different pilgrim accounts read Jerusalem's soundscapes and also how Margery Kempe's soundscapes are read in Jerusalem and then back in England. Stoever's work explains how sonic racialisation works: it involves a power dynamic, a specific hegemonic 'listening ear' that can change depending on time period and also local conditions. Both the 'listening ear' and the 'sonic color line' will depend on specific hegemonic ideas of 'normal, natural'. In Margery Kempe's case amongst the other Jerusalem pilgrims, I will contextualise her sound experiences and who sounds like the 'right' Christian.

Geraldine Heng discusses how race as specific religious difference in opposition to Western Christianity is sensorial in her chapter on "State/Nation" in *The Invention of Race in the European Middle Ages*. She explains that the English state's programme of Jewish racialisation relied heavily on the senses:

> The obsessions articulated in the exercise of church and state biopower point to a broad preoccupation with the sensory character of race in the medieval period. Medieval race is *sensual*: the 'continuous cater-wauling' of Jews in prayer in their synagogues, Jewish bodies that waft a fetid stench (*foetor judaicus*), or the distorted hypervisibility of the Jewish face (*facies judaica*), so vividly caricatured in medieval manuscript doodles.[7]

Margery Kempe's tears in Jerusalem participate in white Western Christian racial group identity and formation in a multireligious or multiracial, cosmopolitan Jerusalem. However, although her tears have primarily been read as a mark of gender – and often explained away with virulent antifeminism – they have not been analysed in relation to race, religious contexts, the conditions of specific locations. Her tears have usually been examined only in relation to a framework of English, Christian, gendered devotion.

This chapter will examine Margery Kempe's tears in two different locations and how they are heard in different geographic soundscapes. I will consider the contexts of loud noise, 'de clamore', in late medieval England. The category of 'noise' has a racialised genealogy and aural context in medieval England. It has a long history of being linked to one sensorial marker of Jewish difference and, I would argue, racialisation. This has been discussed in relation to medieval musicological work in Ruth HaCohen's *The Music Libel Against the Jews*, particularly connected to the Jewish boy murder story seen both in the late medieval English version in Chaucer's *Prioress's Tale* and the Vernon Manuscript's miracle of the virgin, 'The Christian Child Slain by Jews' (Oxford, Bodleian Library MS Poet Engl. a. 1).[8] What happens when the 'listening ear' shifts to decide that the same sound either can support Western Christian orthodox identity or is seen as a 'foreign' and racialised soundscape through another set of 'listening ears' who have chosen to construct a different sonic colour line? What occurs upon Margery Kempe's return to England with her loud crying? How does her identity as a white, middle-class merchant woman inform the power dynamics at play in her ostensibly white woman's tears? If premodern categories of race are in flux and contingent on histories, factors on the ground, and geographic and cultural contexts, what do we say about Margery Kempe's white woman's tears in England?

The religious or racial soundscapes on pilgrimage in Jerusalem

The description of fifteenth-century Jerusalem in *The Book of Margery Kempe* is a brief interlude that explains Margery Kempe's wondrous astonishment – to the point that she almost falls off her ass (the animal) and her two German pilgrim companions help her. She asks that they 'beth nowt displesyd thow I wepe sore in this holy place wher owyr Lord Jhesu Crist was qwyk and ded'.[9] Her explanation that 'I wepe sore in this holy place' in memory of Christ's death begins her lachrymose devotional pilgrimage. Several scholars have pointed to the lachrymal mysticisms of Marie d'Oignies and Walter Hilton.[10] Others have contextualised her tears within fifteenth-century affective devotion and its gendered valences connected to affective authority.[11] Terence Bowers emphasises where her tears began, characterising them as 'equivalent of the badge returning pilgrims wore to proclaim that they had visited the holy sites'.[12] Rebecca Krug calls them 'a sign of her devotion, the exceptional grace shown to her, and her extraordinary spirituality'.[13] They are, therefore, central to her self-fashioning devotional identity, and link her to 'the symbolic coordinates of the Holy Land'.[14] Salih explicitly describes her tears and the Jerusalem pilgrimage as 'a crucial stage in the development of her mature style of piety; her journeys enabled self-transformation'.[15]

Margery Kempe's particular form of *imitatio Christi* manifests as uncontrollable weeping, and both Salih and Santha Bhattacharji suggest that her tears, as well as her white clothing, marked her out as foreign upon her return to England.[16] Salih argues that Margery Kempe 'was the blank sheet which was imprinted by her experiences at the pilgrimage sites, so that ever after she was liable to function as an image of a woman witnessing and mourning the Passion'.[17]

Margery Kempe knows she will shed tears in Jerusalem because it is part of the standard practice exemplified in the *Stations of Jerusalem*. This devotional poem appears in MS Ashmole 61, a merchant-class miscellany compiled for a family similar to Margery Kempe's, and likely intended to be read out loud to accommodate those who were not *'literata'*. In the *Stations of Jerusalem* (item 34 in Ashmole 61), the text makes clear that pilgrims in Jerusalem are expected to shed tears, especially during the Stations of the Cross:

> To the temple we werte oure wey.
> ...
> And after this a Zarysen com,
> And callyd us in be a treyn.
> When he hade don, he went hys weye,
> And lokyd the dore with a keye.
> ...
> The warden reysed a crosse full hye,
> And clerkys song the letany.
> And lewd men than ther eyghen wepe,
> That teres fell under ther fete,
> And thankyd God with all ther myght.
>   (lines 100–15)[18]

This description reveals both the geography of the Stations of the Cross and the presence of the Church of the Holy Sepulchre's Muslim keepers ('Zarysen'). It also includes the line of Christian pilgrims following the warden holding up a large cross while the clerics sing the litany. The lay pilgrims are then expected to cry until their tears roll down to the floor and to thank the Lord 'with all ther myght'. Thus the soundscape inside the Church of the Holy Sepulchre includes Latin hymns, extensive crying, and thanks to the Lord (which I expect was done vocally and loudly), as well as the sound of a crowd following the warden with the cross.

This scene painted in the *Stations of Jerusalem*, and its accompanying Christian soundscape on the Via Dolorosa, is echoed in *The Book of Margery Kempe*, culminating in her initial outburst of tears:

> Than went thei to the Tempyl in Jerusalem, and ther wer latyn in on the to day at evynsong-tyme and abydyn therin til the next day at evynsong-tyme. Than the frerys lyftyd up a cros and led the pylgrimys abowte fro [on] place to another wher owyr Lord had sufferyd hys [peynys] and hys passyons, every man and woman beryng a wax candel in her hand. And the frerys alwey, as thei went abowte, teld hem what owyr Lord sufferyd in every place. And the forseyd creatur wept and sobbyd so plentyvowsly as thow sche had seyn owyr Lord wyth hir bodyly ey sufferyng hys Passyon at that tyme ... And whan thei cam up on to the Mownt of Calvarye, sche fel down that sche mygth not stondyn ne knelyn, but walwyd and wrestyd wyth hir body, spredyng hir armys abrode, and cryed wyth a lowde voys as thow hir hert schulde a brostyn asundyr, for in the cite of hir sowle sche saw veryly and freschly how owyr Lord was crucifyed ...
>
> And sche had so gret compassyon and so gret peyn to se owyr Lordys peyn that sche myt not kepe hirself fro krying and roryng, thow sche schuld a be ded therfor. And this was the fyrst cry that evyr sche cryed in any contemplacyon. (pp. 161–3)

Like the *Stations of Jerusalem*, Margery Kempe describes how the 'frerys lyftyd up a cros' and led the pilgrims through the streets of Christ's Passion, and, not unlike modern tour guides, 'teld hem what owyr Lord sufferyd in every place'. Along with the smell and sight of pilgrims holding candles, we also have the accounts of the Passion as told by Franciscan friars. Her description explains exactly how well, extensively, and loudly, the directions in the *Stations of Jerusalem* ask for laymen to 'thank[yd] God with all ther myght'. She does this at every station where she 'cryed wyth a lowed voys as thow hir hert schulde a brostyn asundyr'. This Friday afternoon itinerary with the Franciscan Friars for the Stations of the Cross shows that she is following orthodox practice walking through the Via Dolorosa, and she 'with all ther myght' thanks God at each station for his suffering with loud crying to the point that her heart feels like bursting.

Margery Kempe also describes the intensity and loudness of her tears throughout her time in Jerusalem. The *Book* describes her crying with the Franciscan-led procession. At the Holy Sepulchre, 'the grave wher owyr Lord was beriid', she reacts 'wyth gret weyping and sobbying, as thow sche had seyn owyr Lord beriid even befor hir' (p. 168). Wherever the friars led to whatever holy location, 'sche alwey wept and sobbyd wondyrfully, and specialy whan sche cam ther owyr Lord was nayled on the cros. Ther cryed sche and wept wythowtyn mesur, that sche myth not restreyn hirself' (p. 169). On Mount Calvary 'sche wept, sche sobbyd, sche cryed so lowde that it [was] wondyr to heryn it' (p. 169). This is all related to her contemplative Passion visions and her own holy meditations. Unlike the hostility she encounters back in England, there is not a whiff of disapproval in the passages that describe her tears. Nor does she note any reaction from the Franciscan friars who are leading groups of pilgrims around Jerusalem.

The *Stations of Jerusalem* in Ashmole 61 also point to the Passion's contemplative devotion and its goal of imagining it happening in these locations as well as the approved reaction of tears:

> And at the mydnyght, more and les,
> Our prestys disposyd them to messe,
> ...
> And at the sepulcour many one song
> And housyld pepull ever among.
> ... Som to the Mounte of Calverye,
> And som to other placys therbye,
>
> (lines 387–402)
>
> When we had don, we toke the wey
> To the veyle of Josphey.
> Than passyd we be a cornere
> Ther Jhesu met hys modere dere,
> And thei fell in a swonyng also,
> ...
> And the women of Jerusalem
> Wepyd on Cryst when that he com,
> And he ansuerd on this degre:
> 'Wepe onne your selve and not for me.'
>
> (lines 411–24)

The *Stations of Jerusalem* imagines the Christian noise of song within the Holy Sepulchre and the expected tears, though here linked with imagining the tears of Jerusalem's women at the Passion and specifically at this station, and Christ's direction to 'wepe onne your selve and not for me'. The last exhortation appears to tell 'the women of Jerusalem' to cry for themselves, and undoubtedly the world's sinfulness, rather than for Christ.

Both Margery Kempe and the *Stations of Jerusalem* reflect the Franciscans' emphasis on 'embodied experience ... as an implicit affirmation of the vital presence of the redemptive power of Christ's body inhering in the sanctuaries of the Holy Land'.[19] This relies on the repeated use of 'eyewitness description, as a way of spatializing and pictorializing the journey in the mind's eye of the reader', thereby allowing the pilgrim to interact with their surroundings both as they are and within the framework of affective piety.[20] She is following orthodox Franciscan devotional structures; the Franciscans led the Western Catholic pilgrimage industry in the eastern Mediterranean. Her loud crying then makes her a welcome participant in affective devotion that transforms the Holy Land's geography and architecture. Her copious tears and noisy weeping (and calisthenics) are quotidian in this geographical space. In fact, I would argue that, amidst the other soundscapes in Jerusalem and the Holy Sepulchre, the louder and more Christian noise she performed in her devotion, the better for the Franciscan faction in Jerusalem. They were but one among many Christian, Jewish, and Islamic groups living and worshipping in the city – indeed, the Holy Sepulchre itself was guarded by Mamluks – and all of these groups shared, and competed within, the same larger soundscape.

The heterogeneous soundscape at the Holy Sepulchre and in Jerusalem

Whilst this would have been a commonplace soundscape – every Friday afternoon during the Stations of the Cross with the Franciscans up and into the Church of the Holy Sepulchre – it is not the only soundscape Margery Kempe would encounter during her sonically orthodox devotions. Her walk following the Via Dolorosa reveals that her tears were but one part of a larger range of Christian sound within a city filled with the sounds of religious (and often racialised) worship and everyday life from the Jewish, Muslim, Armenian, and heterogeneous Christian quarters.

The *Stations of Jerusalem* acknowledges the heterogeneity and multiracial makeup of the Christians assembling in this holy location:

> The fyrste prestys are of Inde,
> ...
> And thei synge nother more ne lesse
> Bot the Pater Noster at ther Messe.
> ... In the north syde of that mynster
> They worschype God onne this maner.
>
> (lines 189–204)

> The cyté of Grekys duelle fast by,
> That synngys in the Mounte of Calvery.
> Bot what thei synge or what thei seye,
> Oure prestys wote not what thei praye.
> And when thei reyse the oste onne hye,
> The Grekys kastys up a loud crye.
> ...
> And in that place with drery mode
> They wepe for hym that dyghed onne rode,
>
> (lines 205–24)

> The thyrd cyté are prestys of owre,
> That syngys messe at the sepulcour;
> On the same grave that Our Lord in leye,
> Prestys syng in Latyn every deye.
> Of oure maner is ther songe,
>
> (lines 227–31)

According to the poem, the Indian Christians sing and congregate on the Holy Sepulchre's North Side but without much discord with the Western Roman Catholics. The Greek Orthodox (likely including Syrian and Coptic worshippers), who pray near Mount Calvary, however, are another story. Along with their sonic illegibility ('what thei synge or what thei seye, / oure prestys wote not'), they also make 'loud crye'. Although the *Stations of Jerusalem* reveals that all the different groups sing, how they sing and their location within the Holy Sepulchre and Jerusalem at large are distinct.

A second fifteenth-century account of a Jerusalem pilgrimage echoes the *Stations of Jerusalem* and offers expansive descriptions of how the soundscapes affected the pilgrims. Felix Fabri was a fifteenth-century Dominican monk from Ulm (now Germany) who wrote extensive accounts of his two pilgrimages to Jerusalem, including detailed descriptions of the soundscapes around the Holy Sepulchre.[21] When part of the procession, he describes 'sweet tears of joy and lively songs' ('dulces laetitiae lacrymas cum alacri cantu') during Easter in the Holy Sepulchre, but he later comments on the 'pushing and disorder, and disturbance, and singing, and weeping' ('magna compressio, et tumultus et inquietudo, et cantus et planctus') near Mount Calvary and contrasts this chaotic soundscape to the quiet contemplation he seems to prefer.[22] His complaints sound like any disgruntled tourist remarking on crowds, and the terms 'tumultus et inquietudo' make clear that the noisiness of the Holy Sepulchre was regular and constant.

In fact, in the Stations of Jerusalem, the first morning imagines the pilgrim going to the Church of the Holy Sepulchre where the Muslim caretaker locks them in. Margery Kempe describes being locked in the church for twenty-four hours and released to then go through the city with the Franciscans for the Stations of the Cross, but she provides no details about what she hears within the Holy Sepulchre. Fabri's accounts contextualises the soundscape of what happens inside the church after being locked. He describes the Holy Sepulchre as 'crowded with men and women from all the countries of the world, and there is a great deal of pushing and disorder by reason of the multitude of people. Then one hears spoken there all the languages of the world, and at those times a market of precious rarities is held within the church' [(repletum viris et foeminis, de omnibus mundi regionibus, et est tumultus magnus et compressio prae multitudine. Et ibi tunc audiuntur omnia idiomata mundi, et forum pretiosissimarum rerum et cararum fit tunc in ecclesia').[23] But he also singles out the 'the yells and strange outcries of the Eastern Christians, who fill the church all night long with their discordant clamour' ('propter ululatum et clamores mirabiles orientalium Christianorum, qui tota nocte ecclesiam clamoribus male sonantibus implent').[24]

The soundscape is filled not only with the discordant and loud sounds of the Eastern Christians, whom Fabri sees as part of the problem, but also the market's and indoor traders' loud noise ('propter mercatorum negotiationes'), inside the Holy Sepulchre that was run by Jerusalem's Muslims.[25] In Fabri's 'listening ear', it is not just the Jewish and Islamic soundscapes that are seen as racialised and part of his understanding of the sonic colour line; the soundscape of

Eastern Orthodox Christianity is also seen as 'clamores' to his Western Christian 'listening ear'. Roland Bettancourt describes two striking examples in the Byzantine archives that show how European Western Christianity racialised the Byzantine Empire and Eastern Orthodox Christianity. He explains two such incidents through the eyes of Venetians in the thirteenth-century chronicle of Niketa Choniates and in the tenth-century account of Liutprand of Cremona who described his travels to Constantinople. Both incidents reveal explicit racialisation through Western European eyes. As Bettancourt explains: 'for Westerners, the racial othering of the Byzantines was a repeated trope in both texts and actions, and one thing is clear: some of the Byzantines were not white in Westerners' eyes, even in the highest ranks and echelons of society'.[26] In a multiracial, multireligious, cosmopolitan Jerusalem with soundscapes as a main avenue of religious identity formation and also a way to gain sonic hegemony in the city, racialisation was sensorial. In this case, racialisation happened through the ears as well as the eyes.

Whilst Margery Kempe barely describes any of this noise in her text, what we can discern from both the *Stations of Jerusalem* and Fabri's accounts is that this was the regular, unending, continuous, multivalent soundscape that she encountered on her journey.[27] Her descriptions focus instead on her personal contemplative interaction with the space, and include her 'crying and lamenting' soundscape. However, multiple Jerusalem pilgrimage guides and accounts describe this context to the historical, geographical, and experiential scene.

Medieval Jerusalem's multireligious and multiracial qualities expressed themselves topographically in various quarters throughout the city.[28] Barbara Drake Boehm and Melanie Holcomb remark upon Jerusalem's 'insistent heterogeneity', pointing out that 'locals, both longtime residents and recent immigrants, claimed a heritage of extraordinary diversity, while visitors, whether pilgrim or merchant, soldier or diplomat, traveled there from every part of the known world'.[29] Whilst they characterise the various inhabited groups in Jerusalem as 'ethnically' different, in fact some of them would have been to Margery Kempe racialised groups.[30] Thus, to discuss the various religious or racialised soundscapes of fifteenth-century Jerusalem is to consider how the racialised devotional *sensorium* functions. In the case of Jerusalem, it would depend specifically on whose 'listening ear' would create the sonic colour line. By comparing the two accounts, we can discern something striking. Margery Kempe's account is focused on her experience in relation to orthodox Christian devotional practices. The contexts of both the Ashmole 61 *Stations of Jerusalem* and Felix Fabri's accounts explain the soundscapes, power relations, and how the Western Christian 'listening ear' sorts, organises, and hierarchises this cosmopolitan, multiracial, and multireligious soundscape. Margery Kempe's crying contributes to the Western Christian sound identity machine in fifteenth-century Jerusalem. For Fabri's and other Western Christian pilgrims, she aligns with white, Western Christian sound. She adds to its white noise.

The Franciscans in the Holy Land

The Franciscan *Custodia Terra Sanctae* began with the permission from the Mamluk sultan al-Nasir Muhammad in 1272 'to settle permanently in the Cenacle (*Coenaculum*) on Mount Sion, identified as the site of the Last Supper' and 'to officiate on Mount Calvary in the Church of the Holy Sepulcher and in the Tomb of the Virgin'.[31] They proceeded to obtain land around the Cenacle and founded a monastery and the church of Mount Sion; since then, their order has been intimately connected with the visitation of pilgrims to Jerusalem, and they became official custodians of the Holy Land in 1342.[32] Over time, the Via Dolorosa's route for the Stations of the Cross shifted, and the current route dates from the sixteenth century.[33] However, a Franciscan pilgrimage writer, Fra Niccolò da Poggibonsi, in his work *Libro d'oltramare* (written about his travels from 1346 to 1350), offers a detailed description of the earlier procession route based on his travels between 1346 and 1350.[34] According to Kathryn Blair Moore,

> Fra Niccolò refers to it [the Via Dolorosa] as the 'street of the Temple,' and – unlike previous pilgrim-authors – provides a full account of the spatial and architectural articulation of the route. The pilgrim enters the street of the Temple through the Gate of St. Stephen and follows a road for thirty paces, we are told, to the Church of St. Anne, where the Virgin Mary was born, although we cannot enter, since it has been made a mosque. To the west one then goes underground to the place where Christ healed the paralytic, that is, the

Pool of Bethesda. Proceeding farther one encounters the houses of Annas (at the mosque of the Mujahidin opposite the *Bab el'Atem*), 'where Christ was first led, after being dragged' from Gethsemane before being led to Pilate.[35]

The current route that the Franciscans take on Friday afternoons beginning at 3 pm is not the exact fifteenth-century route, although they began and ended in the same locations and traversed large sections of the Muslim and Christian quarters of Mamluk-controlled Jerusalem. The route begins near the Temple on the Mount/Al Aqsa mosque. Depending on the time of day, Christian pilgrims would have encountered not only the *adhan* (the Muslim call to prayer on Friday which would happen five times per day) but also the streams of the Islamic devout walking to the Al Aqsa mosque for prayer.

My earlier discussion of Felix Fabri illustrated his disapproval of the Holy Sepulchre's soundscape, particularly the loud devotional practice of Eastern Christians that do not give him the quietude to pray silently. He uses similar wording (specifically 'clamoribus') to describe an incident involving the Mamluk guards driving pilgrims out of the Holy Sepulchre, 'making a great noise with the doors' ('faicentes magnum strepitum ad valvas').[36] He makes clear his unease about the clash of different racialised religious soundscapes, as well as his deep disapproval, per his orthodox Christian 'listening ear', of the Islamic sounds within this sacred space.

What Fabri's copious comments about Jerusalem's soundscapes demonstrate is how his 'listening ear' sorts the context of multireligious and multi-Christian groups in conflict over the same sacred spaces. Whilst his side, the Western Catholic contingent, can sing and create Christian noise that is never imagined as 'clamor', Fabri utilises his listening ear to categorise which noise is the enemy of the white Western Christian hegemony even when he's in a location where this faction does not have ascendancy. This is particularly evident in his description of a mosque and Islamic school built opposite the Holy Sepulchre, he claims, 'out of disrespect for the Crucified One, and as an offence to the Christians' ('in despectum Crucifixi, et in praejudicium Christianorum').[37] According to him, the boys at the school 'shout all day long, making a surprising noise' ('toto die mirabili ejulatu clamant').[38] More generally, he notes that

Figure 10.1 *Evagatorium: In Terrae Sanctae, Arabiae et Egypti peregrinationen*, vol. 1, 322.

'[i]n this tower they shout and howl day and night according to the ordinances of their accursed creed' ('Et in hac turre clamant et ululant die ac nocte secundum maledictae suae sectae institutiones').[39] Upon further investigation Fabri likens their embodied prayer and educational practice in sound and ritual as akin to what he has seen of Jewish embodied prayer and sound. He even goes as far as to write down the soundscape and the words and transliterate them into Latin musical notation and text.[40]

His use of 'clamor, clamoris' to describe this racially and religiously hostile soundscape offers a prime example of Felix Fabri using his 'listening ear' to explain the Holy Land's racialised 'sonic color line'. Joy becomes noise, and prayer devolves into shouting for any group not explicitly part of Western Christendom.

Immersive feminist Digital Humanities, sonic war, and the soundscape of Jerusalem

Having contextualised Margery Kempe's sonic valences in Jerusalem during her pilgrimage by way of other pilgrimage accounts, discussions of the city's geography, and its probable soundscapes and practices, I turn to the work of feminist Digital Humanities to re-create, with some multimedia help, Margery Kempe's experience. I went to Jerusalem in March 2018 to record 360-degree video with a Nikon KeyMission 360 of the Friday Stations of the Cross, to post on a YouTube channel. YouTube itself is open access and can be made globally accessible. I chose a 360-degree set-up rather than VR (virtual reality) or more complicated immersive DH models as part of a specific feminist praxis. Several feminist new media and game studies critics, such as danah boyd, have explained that VR makes women consistently motion-sick, which renders the platform media system inaccessible to about half of its potential playing or viewing population.[41] Further scientific research appears to argue that this gendered reaction is related to biological issues around motion and the gendered body's posture. In effect, the issues around centre of gravity explain this phenomenon, but, in reality, what we are discussing is how digital VR design cannot think through a multitude of bodies beyond an able, white, male one of a certain height.[42]

I also did not choose a more complicated and expensive immersive DH set-up that is often used in large-scale museum exhibitions. Along with substantially increased equipment costs, it would have been difficult to stabilise the moving shot. The work most often cited for this spectacular form of immersive DH – often presented in installations at museums and libraries – is Sarah Kenderdine's long list of curated exhibits or installations.[43] As she herself has written about immersive DH as a convergence of 'embodiment, entanglement, and immersion', the theoretical frame she uses is genealogically indebted to the history of the museum, the history of the world's fair, and thus this history of the Victorian diorama, empire, and deeply racialised visions of world heritage sites.[44] Troublingly, however, her theoretical discussions of embodiment and immersion do not address issues around race, gender, and disability.

In fact, in discussing one project, *Pure Land AR*, Kenderdine observes that 'for perceptual sensation to constitute experience – that is, for it to have genuine representational content – the perceiver must possess and make use of his or her sensorimotor knowledge'.[45] Her audience (whom she calls 'user-agents') is meant to interact with her immersive DH projects in ways that reflect their 'inherent physical capabilities', specifically 'dexterous manipulation ... strong arms ... strong neck .. strong knees and legs'.[45] In short, she imagines the 'user-agents' who experience her projects to have one kind of raced, gendered (as she also uses VR), and abled body. Even though multimedia is a way in which different sensory engagement can happen for different abilities, her projects imagine an immersive DH world that is only for this body type.

At a 2013 Austin College DH conference, she explained that she achieved her immersive DH stability in movable DH installations by using a wheelchair for motion and stability, but she never discussed the role of Disability DH theory in her critical praxis. Her kind of immersive DH also requires an interactive set-up that is itself about monumental spectacle. It often involves multiple screens if not an entire room that doubles as an immersive cave, which then necessitates an entry fee and the wherewithal to handle further digital equipment like a tablet or headset to explore the exhibition.

I chose a Nikon 360-degree camera set-up as a form of the feminist digital humanities praxis MEALS: 'material, embodied, affective, labor-intensive, and situated character of engagements with computation can operate experientially for users in shared spaces'.[47] In terms of materiality, the camera's portability along with the fact that I could film using just the camera and a long selfie-stick fit into situating my material, raced, and gendered body in this 360-degree video experience. Since the organisation of perspective has significant power over how a work of art (or, indeed, a text) is viewed, the Margery Kempe digital project allows viewers to see me as I experience the Via Dolorosa.[48] And as a form of intersectional autoethnographic research praxis, as an Asian woman, the 360-degree camera allows you to tip down and see my actual material body as we move along the Via Dolorosa.

The 360-degree camera is not a replication of some imagined, default, omniscient point of view, as is the case in Kenderdine's work. This project is based on an intersectional feminist DH praxis that is specific about the materiality of the digital interfaces; the situatedness of my race, gender, and digital equipment; the affective wall of sight and sound that I experienced; and the ability to view my own reactions to the Via Dolorosa and its visual and sonic experience. Finally, you can watch my own feminist, racialised labour happen. The selfie stick stabilised my camera and allowed me to be read, as I often am in the Mediterranean (North Africa, eastern Mediterranean) as an Asian tourist. Thus, my body and extensions of my body (the selfie stick) are specifically raced and gendered in this project and in its digital film labour.

I chose this format and platform also because it meant I could upload 360-degree video onto YouTube without requiring a VR headset to view it. The 360-degree video allows for portability since it can be viewed with a media device – iPhone, iPad – in very much the ways that I imagine portable media devices in the premodern past (i.e. medieval books and maps) told the story of Jerusalem pilgrimages to readers and consumers. More so than the spectacle of awe-inspiring interactive museum displays or the fully ableist and sexist experience of a VR interface, the 360-degree camera means that this can be private and portable.

The Margery Kempe Channel has multiple slices of immersive video that show my walk with the pilgrims on a late Friday afternoon as we traverse through the meandering parts of the Old City to the Holy Sepulchre.[49] If you watch the clips on a phone or tablet, you can move your device in 360 degrees and see the Via Dolorosa from any angle. The clips clearly demonstrate how Margery Kempe's crying and noise are just a small sonic node in a much more complicated multireligious and competing soundscape. Along with Friday including the Muslim call to prayer, depending on the time, it would also be the beginning of the Jewish Shabbat, which includes a specific set of songs and ritualised prayer for the evening. In my clip, the Franciscans have decided to use a microphone, but in previous trips, I have also seen them use a megaphone. They are, and clearly have been, interested in making as much Christian sound or noise as possible as they traverse the Old City. If you watch further in my clip, you can see the pilgrims traversing parts of the Muslim quarter. The city itself is filled with a multireligious and multiracial soundscape that is still observable today.

But what happens when Margery Kempe comes to the Holy Sepulchre, particularly in the height of her observance of the Passion of Christ? She arrives to a site with a contested history of conflict in which multiple Christian religious groups fought and carved space for themselves within its grounds. Jaroslov Folda describes this mix of Christians in the Holy Sepulchre at the time of the First Crusade as one that 'included the Greek Orthodox, who had rebuilt the church and whose liturgical language was Greek; the Armenian Orthodox, who had their own patriarch and retained their ancient Armenian language; the Syrian Orthodox, or Syrian Jacobites, whose official tongue was Syriac; the Copts, whose altar was in a chapel at the western side of the aedicule and who worshipped in Coptic; and finally the Ethiopians, who had resided there since early Christian times and prayed in Geez'.[50] These are not just a heterogeneous Christian group but also a multiracial and international Christian group with different devotional worship, liturgical traditions, and languages. Who gets primacy, who gets territory, who gets to literally carve space at this site, and who gets to control this space's soundscape is an ongoing tension worked out both with occasional bouts of violence as well as through other means.

In the YouTube era, it is fitting that the tension within the Holy Sepulchre amongst these various factions has also been captured in the multiple videos of broom wars between the Holy Sepulchre's Orthodox, Armenian, and Franciscan factions.[51] These tensions are long-standing: the pilgrimage accounts, like Felix Fabri's, that I have used to contextualise Margery Kempe's journey attest to their use of soundscapes and geography in carving out Holy Land territory.

On my first Jerusalem trip, I, too, encountered the Holy Sepulchre's multiple warring soundscapes. Unfortunately, I wasn't quite able to capture the possibilities of that tension on my last visit in March 2018. This relies on how these tensions can or could erupt depending on local circumstances and conditions. This time around the various main factions – Franciscans, Greek Orthodox, and Armenians – were respectful of each other because of recent political issues that had bonded them together against taxation by the Israeli government.[52] On my previous journey, I had walked with the pilgrims into the Holy Sepulchre with the Franciscans using the megaphone to sing, while the Armenians began a marching and singing procession around the Holy Sepulchre, while the Greek Orthodox began liturgical singing practice.[53] Along with constantly trying to carve up territory in the Holy Sepulchre, the various factions have – through fighting to say liturgies, their own liturgical singing, and devotional practices – attempted to fill the Holy Sepulchre soundscape with their denomination's religious noise. It is thus a holy sonic war and, from descriptions from other fifteenth-century pilgrimage accounts to the city and religious site, it has been ongoing for a long time.

In fact, the fifteenth-century soundscape's specificities asked for Christian noise rather than Christian sonic harmony. Thus, Margery Kempe's loud crying, her Christian noise, would have been orthodox in its practice and sound – as she was following what other Christians were told to do in fifteenth-century pilgrimage guides and adhering to the directions discussed in Felix Fabri's account. She would have also been contributing to the Western Roman Christian sonic machine to carve more sound space and territory in this teeming, multitudinous, often dissonant, and quite overwhelming holy city and holy religious site. Her tears would have helped the Franciscans in their ongoing sonic war against other religious sounds within Jerusalem's streets and within the sanctuary of this sensorially overwhelming Christian site. Her tears and noise would have been orthodox, sanctioned, and rather ordinary.

From the thirteenth century on, England translated architecture from the Holy Land, particularly the Holy Sepulchre's round shape into the English landscape.[54] I would argue that Margery Kempe's tears become a problem only when she leaves Jerusalem's intersectional, multireligious, multiracial, multilingual, and international affective and sonic textures for a homogeneous, English landscape. As Salih has remarked, Margery Kempe came back to England, now a 'foreign land'.[55] Like other pilgrims before her who imported the Holy Land's landscape to England, Margery Kempe also imports something from Jerusalem: its soundscape. She is a legible participant in Jerusalem's international, cosmopolitan, multireligious, and multiracial scene. But without this context, she is illegible and her crying and noise are read in the more homogeneous and parochial England as alarming and dangerous. In fact, her crying is what triggers her visions of Jesus Christ abroad, and it appears also at home:

> Fyrst whan sche had hir cryingys at Jerusalem, sche had hem oftyn-tymes, and in Rome also. And whan sche come hom into Inglonde, fyrst at hir comyng hom it comyn but seldom, as it wer onys in a moneth, sythen onys in the weke, aftyrward cotidianly, and onys sche had xiiii on o day, and another day sche had vii, and so as God wolde visiten hir, sumtyme in the cherch, sumtyme in the strete, sumtym in the chawmbre, sumtyme in the felde whan God wold sendyn hem, for sche knew nevyr tyme ne owyr whan thei scaulde come. (pp. 164–5)

When Margery Kempe returns home, the English read or hear her imported Jerusalem soundscape as alarming and, I would argue, racialised. In fact, her manuscript's rubricators, the Carthusian monks at Mount Grace Priory, write a 'nota de clamore' in the margins to note when she first began to cry.[56] The use of the 'clamor, clamoris' term links back to Felix Fabri's organisation of Jerusalem racialised or religious sounds in which he deems all the non-Western Christian sound to be 'clamor, clamoris'. As I have written earlier, there is a genealogy of the English white Christian 'listening ear' seeing 'noise' and other kinds of 'clamor' as racialised sound well into the late fourteenth and fifteenth centuries. Additionally, there is a long conversation among the Carthusians about what makes a Christian soundscape in the fifteenth century – what sounds 'natural, right'. Both Denis the Carthusian (1402–71) and Johannes Gallicus (1415–73) advocated for a moderate approach to Christian religious soundscapes such that 'polyphony was tolerated, at times cautiously endorsed, provided that it respected the dignity and gravity of plainchant and avoided excesses of rhythmic intricacy.'[57] Margery Kempe's tears do not contribute to Christian 'sonority'. Wegman discusses the musical crisis around polyphony that came to a point in the 1470s and explains: 'what concerned them was not rhythm but sonority. Whether counterpoint was simple or elaborate, it added nothing to plainchant but sound, which in turn was nothing but empty noise.'[58] Wegman suggests that Johannes Gallicus would approve of simple plainchant and 'simple, unmeasured counterpoint' but would advocate that 'their [singing] voices' should not be thrown 'into disorder by any dissonance'.[59] Thus, the Carthusian monks reading Margery Kempe's manuscript – who are the witnesses to her English homecoming, in the context of a longer history of English medieval texts racialising 'loud noise and clamor' and within the fifteenth-century Carthusian discourse of the 'right' and 'natural' Christian soundscape – the Mount Grace Priory Carthusians use a racialised 'listening ear' to deem her, in this instance, to be racialised, to be, as Salih discusses, 'foreign'.

In addition, Margery Kempe's many arrests in reaction to her importing this Jerusalem soundscape into England are similar to Stoever's discussion of how racial soundscapes operate and what the consequences are for those who are deemed to be on the wrong side of the 'sonic color line'.[60] For Margery Kempe, she was arrested for heresy. When she returns from Jerusalem back to East Anglia she is sick and recovering when it is made clear how her East Anglian neighbours react to her racialised Jerusalem soundscape (her tears). As the narrative explains:

> For sche had hir first cry at Jerusalem, as is wretyn beforn.
> And many seyd ther was nevyr seynt in hevyn that cryed so as sche dede, wherfor thei woldyn concludyn that sche had a devyl wythinne hir, whech cawsyd that crying. And so thei seyden pleynly, and meche mor evyl ...
> Sum seyde that sche had the fallyng evyl, for sche, with the crying, wrestyd hir body, turnyng fro the o syde into the other, and wex al blew and al blo, as it had ben colowr of leed. And than folke spitted at hir for horrowr of the sekenes, and sum scornyd hir and seyd that sche howlyd as it [had] ben a dogge, and bannyd hir, and cursyd hir, and seyd that sche dede meche harm among the pepyl. (pp. 219–20)

The text reminds readers again that Jerusalem, not England, is the location of her current devotional soundscape. To the 'listening ear' of her white Christian neighbours in East Anglia, she falls within the realm of devils, dogs, and evil incarnate, epithets often used to isolate racially marked Jews and heathens in medieval hagiography.[61] They diagnose her devotional practices as a form of racialised disability: 'the falling evil'. They pile verbal and physical abuse upon her because of her racialised sound.

Her racialised soundscape, her 'de clamore', also temporarily overrides her privileged status as a white Christian woman when she is arrested after her return from Santiago de Compostela. While contemplating the crucifixion in a church in Leicester, 'sche gan meltyn and al-to-relentyn be terys of pyte and compassyown. Than the fyer of lofe kyndelyd so yern in hir hert that sche myth not kepyn it prevy, for whedyr sche wolde er not, it cawsyd hir to brekyn owte wyth a lowde voys and cryen merveylowslyche, and wepyn and sobbyn ful hedowslyche' (p. 228). When Margery Kempe leaves the church, she is stopped by a man who 'toke hir be the sleve and seyd: "Damsel, why wepist thu so sor?"' (p. 228). He grabs her and wants an explanation for her weeping and noise. Her noise – her racialised and imported Jerusalem soundscape – more than the visual marker of her white clothing appears to be the primary cause for her imprisonment in Leicester and the subsequent accusations that she is a Lollard and 'fals strumpet' (p. 229). Margery Kempe in England, performing exactly what she began in Jerusalem, has crossed the 'sonic color line' and her body and person are, at least for a time, treated accordingly by white English Christian hegemony as racialised, alarming, and eventually criminal.

Margery Kempe and white women tears

Stoever's discussion of the 'sonic color line' makes clear that race-making is not just visual. It involves the other senses and centres on affect or 'race-feeling'. She writes:

> While vision remains a powerfully defining element of race, scholars have yet to account for how other senses experience racialization and enact race feeling, both alone and in concert with sight ... To understand the entanglements of sound, race, and technology and the far-reaching

material consequences of their collusion, *The Sonic Color Line* presents a cultural and political history detailing when, why, and how listening became a racialized body discipline and how it both informed and was informed by emergent sound technologies.[62]

In the case of premodern Europe, the emergent sound technologies include the invention of Western European Christian polyphony in the twelfth century at the cathedral of Notre Dame and Western European notation, as demonstrated by Fabri's ability to write down and translate the sound of a Jerusalem mosque in his travel account. These 'emergent sound technologies' inform the white Western Christian 'listening ear' and its construction of white Western Christian religious identity in relation to a specific soundscape. Added to this is the contextual and in-progress quality of premodern critical race as it is dependent on local geographies, temporalities, and conditions. The white Western Christian 'listening ear' is not a monolith. Rather, it is contextual and contingent as we can see in the case of Margery Kempe in Jerusalem and Margery Kempe returning on her pilgrimage to England. Local genealogies, histories, conditions, geographies, political, and social contexts inform how the white Western Christian 'listening ear' demarcates the biopolitics of race: who is seen as fully human and who is not. Premodern critical race, as I hope to have demonstrated here, is both biopolitical and socio-cultural. It relies on the embodied senses and race feeling, while its power dynamics and structure are contextual by location, geography, social, political, temporal, and cultural factors.

Yet, within this chapter, we must still address the white elephant in the room: Margery Kempe's 'white women tears'. Stoever introduces her definition and theorisation of the 'listening ear' and the 'sonic color line' with an epigraph from the *Guardian* coverage of Jordan Davis's Black racist murder in November 2012 in Jacksonville, Florida: 'Michael Dunn "denied calling the rap 'thug music' but admitted he thought it was 'rap-crap' and that it was 'ridiculously loud'"'.[63] Jordan Davis's heinous murder is an example of how race is also a technology of Black necropolitics that uses the 'sonic color line' to demarcate who is fully human and who gets to live or die.

In Margery Kempe's case, her imported Jerusalem soundscape is racialised temporarily and leads to her arrest. But in the end her whiteness and even her white tears become a vehicle for her white, gendered affective devotion that will lead her to be seen as a religious mystic. The effect of the 'sonic color line' is temporary for Margery Kempe in England as her whiteness and her white woman privilege resurface as the structural node in her life. In the context of a new reassessment of a multiracial late medieval England that, at least in its urban spaces, now can see upwards of twenty per cent of its population as Black men and women, and thus racially marked, how do Margery Kempe's 'white women tears' function in this historical and geographic context?[64] How do 'white women's tears' work in a reassessment of race and affective devotion?

Mamta Motwani Accapadi, who has written one of the first pieces on white women tears, explains that 'the challenge and responsibility of any person who has a "one up/one down" identity, with one identity that is privilege and another that is oppressed, is to recognize when their privileged identity is the operating norm'.[65] The discussion of 'white women tears' as a concept in intersectional analysis has recently been further theorised in Ruby Hamad's book *White Tears / Brown Scars: How White Feminism Betrays Women of Color*, based on her viral *Guardian* article 'How white women use strategic tears to silence women of colour'.[66] Hamad explains that 'white women can oscillate between their gender and their race, between being the oppressed and the oppressor'.[67] She writes: 'white women's racial privilege is predicated on their acceptance of their role of virtue and goodness, which is, ultimately, powerlessness. It is this powerlessness – or, I would argue, this appearance of powerlessness – that governs the nature of White Womanhood.'[68] Hamad discusses how 'this weaponization of white women's distress' is a parallel to white toxic masculinity, a white 'toxic femininity'.[69] What undergirds the discussion of 'white women's tears' as a strategy, a power move, is that 'it is power pretending to be powerless'.[70] In the longer critical history of discussing gendered affective devotion, there has been a lack in discussing intersectionality and the ways in which intersecting identities work in relation to structural oppression and often violence. There has been a lack in discussing race and how intersectionality requires a multi-axis framework in which identities cannot be divorced from the other identities within one situated body. In the case of Margery Kempe, we cannot decouple her race (i.e. her whiteness), her gender, and her disability. Likewise, in discussing a longer history of affective devotion, what has happened to the analysis of race, particularly through a critical whiteness studies lens, as we analyse the function of gender and sexuality? We cannot discuss Margery Kempe's tears and noise without discussing her whiteness because, as she functions from this privileged norm, we can see how race, whiteness, gender, and sound function differently in different geographies and contexts.

Margery Kempe, soundscapes, race, and the Global Middle Ages

Margery Kempe has always been international, embodying a version of the Global Middle Ages before it was a field. If one reads Margery Kempe as a Global Margery Kempe participating specifically in the construction of racialised or religious heterogeneous soundscapes of an international cosmopolitan global city, she is allowed to cry, scream, wail, and enact her devotion in whatever way she sees fit. She is, in this sense, finally given licence to be herself in an environment that accepts her orthodox, visionary Christianity. But when Margery Kempe imports the Christian soundscape of Jerusalem to England, she, for a period, is seen and heard by the white Christian English hegemony as both visually foreign and sonically racialised. She is an example then of how different bodies vis-à-vis the devotional *sensorium* can move in and out of racialisation depending on specific contexts, factors, geographies, and conditions. But she is also an example of how critical whiteness works in different geographic, temporal, social, and political contexts. Margery Kempe's 'white women tears' is a case study in how the 'sonic color line' can work in the premodern archive.

Notes

1. Sarah Salih, 'Two travellers' tales', in Christopher Harper-Bill (ed.), *Medieval East Anglia* (Woodbridge and Rochester, NY: Boydell Press, 2005), pp. 318–31, p. 329.
2. See Jennifer Lynn Stoever, *The Sonic Color Line: Race and the Cultural Politics of Listening* (New York: New York University Press, 2016).
3. For example, Christopher Roman and I edited an entire series on Medieval Sound for the digital journal *Sounding Out!* Dorothy Kim

Margery Kempe, racialised soundscapes, sonic wars 229

and Christopher Roman, 'Introduction: medieval sound', *Sounding Out!*, 4 April 2016, https://soundstudiesblog.com/2016/04/04/17060/ [accessed 21 August 2020]. See Emma Dillon, *The Sense of Sound: Musical Meaning in France 1260–1330* (Oxford: Oxford University Press, 2012) on the soundscape of Paris.

4 Emily Thompson, *The Soundscape of Modernity. Architectural Acoustics and the Culture of Listening in America, 1900–1930* (Cambridge, MA: MIT Press, 2002), p. 1.

5 *Ibid.*, pp. 1–2.

6 Stoever, *The Sonic Color Line*, pp. 7–8.

7 Geraldine Heng, *The Invention of Race in the European Middle Ages* (Cambridge: Cambridge University Press, 2013), p. 80.

8 Ruth HaCohen, *The Music Libel Against the Jews* (New Haven: Yale University Press, 2013). See especially her introduction and chapter 1. Heng, *Invention of Race*, pp. 81–96. She discusses the miracle of the virgin 'The Christian child slain by Jews' extensively.

9 *The Book of Margery Kempe*, ed. Barry Windeatt (Cambridge: D. S. Brewer, 2004), p. 161. All subsequent quotations refer to this edition by page number.

10 See Corinne Saunders, 'Writing revelation: *The Book of Margery Kempe*', in Tamara Atkin and Jaclyn Rajsic (eds), *Manuscript and Print in Late Medieval and Early Modern Britain: Essays in Honour of Professor Julia Boffey* (Cambridge: D. S. Brewer, 2019), pp. 147–66.

11 See Santha Bhattacharji, 'Tears and screaming: weeping in the spirituality of Margery Kempe', in Kimberley Christine Patton and John Stratton Hawley (eds), *Holy Tears: Weeping in the Religious Imagination* (Princeton: Princeton University Press, 2005), pp. 229–41.

12 Terence N. Bowers, 'Margery Kempe as traveller', *Studies in Philology*, 97:1 (2000), 1–28, pp. 25–6.

13 Rebecca Krug, *Margery Kempe and the Lonely Reader* (Ithaca: Cornell University Press, 2017), p. 142.

14 Bowers, 'Margery Kempe as traveler', p. 26.

15 Salih, 'Two travellers' tales', p. 329.

16 See Salih, 'Two travellers' tales', p. 329, and Bhattacharji, 'Tears and screaming', pp. 232–3. Also Einat Klafter, 'The feminine mystic: Margery Kempe's pilgrimage to Rome as an imitatio Birgittae', in Einat Klafter, Victoria Blud, and Diane Heath (eds), *Gender in Medieval Places, Spaces and Thresholds* (London: School of Advanced Study, University of London, 2019), pp. 123–36.

17 Salih, 'Two travellers' tales', p. 330.

18 All quotations from Ashmole 61 refer to George Shuffelton, ed., *Codex Ashmole 61: A Compilation of Popular Middle English Verse*, TEAMS

Middle English Text Series (Kalamazoo: Western Michigan University Medieval Institute Publications, 2008) by line number.
19 Kathryn Blair Moore, *The Architecture of the Christian Holy Land: Reception from Late Antiquity through the Renaissance* (Cambridge: Cambridge University Press, 2017), p. 118.
20 *Ibid.*, p. 118.
21 See Kathryn Beebe, *Pilgrim and Preacher: The Audiences and Observant Spirituality of Friar Felix Fabri (1437/8-1502)* (Oxford: Oxford University Press, 2014).
22 Felix Fabri, *Evagatorium in Terrae Sanctae, Arabiae et Egypti peregrinationem*, ed. Konrad Dietrich Hassler, 3 vols (Stuttgart: Sumtibus Societatis Literariæ Stuttgardiensis, 1843-1849), vol. 1, pp. 309–11; available online at https://archive.org/details/bub_gb_vIPGn7GmROIC/mode/2up [accessed 21 August 2020]. Translation: Aubrey Stewart, trans., *Felix Fabri (ca. A.D. 1480–1483)*, 2 vols (London: Palestine Pilgrims' Text Society, 1893–96), vol. 1, part 2, pp. 378–82; available online at https://archive.org/details/libraryofpalesti08paleuoft/page/n4/mode/2up [accessed 27 August 2020].
23 Fabri, *Evagatorium*, ed. Hassler, vol. 1, p. 346. Translation: Stewart, trans., *Felix Fabri*, vol. 1, part 2, pp. 429–30.
24 Fabri, *Evagatorium*, ed. Hassler, vol. 1, p. 346. Translation: Stewart, trans., *Felix Fabri*, vol. 1, part 2, pp. 429–30.
25 Fabri, *Evagatorium*, ed. Hassler, vol. 1, p. 346. Translation: Stewart, trans., *Felix Fabri*, vol. 1, part 2, p. 430.
26 Roland Bettancourt, *Byzantine Intersectionality: Sexuality, Gender and Race in the Middle Ages* (Princeton: Princeton University Press, 2020), pp. 173–6, esp. p. 176.
27 To sample the sound of a recreated medieval Muslim city see 'Soundscape of a medieval city in the Abbasid Caliphate', *Ambient-Mixer*, https://city.ambient-mixer.com/medieval-middle-eastern-city [accessed 28 October 2019]. As the site explains, this was originally organised and mixed to replicate the sounds of a city during the Abbasid caliphate: 'Developed for a university level course on daily life in the Islamic Middle Ages, this soundscape is meant to go with a slide show and discussion of urban life to give the sense of what it would sound like to walk through a city like Baghdad, Cairo, or Damascus around 1000 AD – including a market, animal noises, horse/donkeys passing by, public fountains, and the adhan (Islamic call to prayer) issuing from multiple mosques at the same time.'
28 A digitised image of a twelfth-century map of the city in The Hague, Koninklijke Bibliotheek, 76, fol. 5, is available through Wikimedia Commons: https://commons.wikimedia.org/wiki/File:Plan_of_Jerusalem,_12th_Century._ca._1200.jpg [accessed 28 October 2019].

29 Barbara Drake Boehm and Melanie Holcomb, 'Pluralism in the holy city', in Boehm and Holcomb (eds), *Jerusalem, 1000–1400: Every People under Heaven* (New York: Metropolitan Museum of Art, 2016), pp. 65–75, esp. p. 65.
30 My own article 'Critical race and the middle ages' explains the issue with the term 'ethnicity' when what we are discussing is race; see *Literature Compass*, 16.9–10 (2019): https://doi.org/10.1111/lic3.12549 [accessed 23 August 2020].
31 Moore, *The Architecture of the Christian Holy Land*, p. 122.
32 *Ibid.*, p. 122.
33 *Ibid.*, pp. 117–18. See also: 'Origins of the Via Dolorosa', *Terra Sancta Museum*, www.terrasanctamuseum.org/en/discover-more/origins-of-the-via-dolorosa/ [accessed 28 October 2019].
34 Moore, *The Architecture of the Christian Holy Land*, p. 132.
35 *Ibid.*, p. 137.
36 Fabri, *Evagatorium*, ed. Hassler, vol. 1, p. 315. Translation: Stewart, trans., *Felix Fabri*, vol. 1, part 2, p. 386.
37 Fabri, *Evagatorium*, ed. Hassler, vol. 1, p. 322. Translation: Stewart, trans., *Felix Fabri*, vol. 1, part 2, p. 396.
38 Fabri, *Evagatorium*, ed. Hassler, vol. 1, p. 322. Translation: Stewart, trans., *Felix Fabri*, vol. 1, part 2, p. 396.
39 Fabri, *Evagatorium*, ed. Hassler, vol. 1, p. 322. Translation: Stewart, trans., *Felix Fabri*, vol. 1, part 2, pp. 395–6.
40 Fabri, *Evagatorium*, ed. Hassler, vol. 1, p. 322.
41 danah boyd, 'Is the Oculus Rift sexist?' *Quartz* (28 March 2014) https://qz.com/192874/is-the-oculus-rift-designed-to-be-sexist/ [accessed 21 August 2020]. For further discussion of this gender bias in VR see Daniel Harvey, 'Is virtual reality sexist?', *Fast Company*, 25 February 2016 www.fastcompany.com/3057012/is-virtual-reality-sexist [accessed 21 August 2020]; Andrew Ross, 'New research suggests head-mounted VR sets are unintentionally sexist', *Massively Overpowered* (12 December 2016) https://massivelyop.com/2016/12/12/new-research-suggests-head-mounted-vr-sets-are-unintentionally-sexist/ [accessed 21 August 2020]; and Justin Munafo, Meg Diedrick, and Thomas A. Stoffregen, 'The virtual reality head-mounted display Oculus Rift induces motion sickness and is sexist in its effects', *Experimental Brain Research*, 235:3 (2017), 889–901, available online: https://link.springer.com/article/10.1007/s00221-016-4846-7 [accessed 21 August 2020].
42 Frank Koslucher, Eric Haaland, and Thomas A. Stoffregen, 'Sex differences in visual performance and postural sway precede sex differences in visually induced motion sickness', *Experimental Brain Research*, 234:1 (2016), 313–22.

43 See Kenderdine's website: https://sarahkenderdine.info [accessed 28 October 2019].
44 See Jeremy Hsu, 'How scientific racism at Chicago's World's Fair shaped "Bioshock Infinite"', *Vice* (19 April 2013) www.vice.com/en_us/article/wnn93x/how-scientific-racism-at-the-chicagos-worlds-fair-shaped-bioshock-infinite [accessed 21 August 2020]; Paul Friswold, 'The forgotten history of racism at the 1904 World's Fair in St. Louis', *Riverfront Times* (2 May 2018), www.riverfronttimes.com/artsblog/2018/05/02/the-forgotten-history-of-racism-at-the-1904-worlds-fair-in-st-louis [accessed 21 August 2020]; and Sara Kenderdine, 'Embodiment, entanglement, and immersion in digital cultural heritage', in Susan Schreibman, Ray Siemens, and John Unsworth (eds), *A New Companion to Digital Humanities*, 2nd edition (Malden: Wiley Blackwell, 2016), pp. 22–41.
45 Kenderdine, 'Embodiment', p. 29.
46 *Ibid.*, p. 33.
47 Jacqueline Wernimont and Elizabeth Losh, 'Introduction', in Wernimont and Losh (eds), *Bodies of Information: Intersectional Feminism and the Digital Humanities* (Minneapolis: University of Minnesota Press, 2018), pp. xiii–xx, p. xiii. See also Jacqueline Wernimont and Elizabeth Losh, 'Wear and care: feminisms at a long maker table', in Jentery Sayers (ed.), *The Routledge Companion to Media Studies and Digital Humanities* (New York: Routledge, 2018), pp. 97–107, p. 98.
48 See John Berger, *Ways of Seeing* (London: Penguin Books, 1977).
49 Dorothy Kim [Margery Kempe], 'Margery Kempe: Jerusalem pilgrimage', 10 parts, 21 October 2019, www.youtube.com/channel/UCx5MHU6qbvfadJrzlnqWH2Q [accessed 21 August 2020]. You can watch this with your tablet or phone and move your device around to see any part of the 360-degree view.
50 Jaroslav Folda, 'Sharing the church of the Holy Sepulchre during the Crusader period', in Boehm and Holcomb, *Jerusalem, 1000–1400*, pp. 131–3, p. 131.
51 You can see this in multiple YouTube videos shot about these battles, for example 'Church of the Holy Sepulcher, monk's fight', 12 November 2008 www.youtube.com/watch?v=ryA_RPiSPRw) [accessed 21 August 2020].
52 Oliver Holmes, 'Jerusalem's Holy Sepulchre church closes in tax protest', *Guardian* (25 February 2018), www.theguardian.com/world/2018/feb/25/jerusalem-holy-sepulchre-church-closes-tax-protest-israel [accessed 21 August 2020].
53 My thanks to Louisa Burnham whose iPad allowed us to read Margery Kempe at the Holy Sepulchre during this Via Dolorosa experience.

54 Nigel Pennick, *Holy Sepulchre: The Round Churches of Britain* (Trumpington, Cambridge: Megalithic Visions, 1974).
55 Salih, 'Two traveller's tales', p. 330.
56 Bhattacharji, 'Tears and screaming', p. 232.
57 Robert C. Wegman, *The Crisis of Music in Early Modern Europe* (New York: Routledge, 2005) pp. 17–19.
58 *Ibid.*, p. 19.
59 *Ibid.*, p. 30.
60 Stoever discusses this in her introduction to *The Sonic Color Line* regarding Jordan Davis and his playing of 'loud music' that justified his murder. See Stoever, *The Sonic Color Line*, pp. 1–2.
61 For instance, see St Katherine in the Katherine Group.
62 Stoever, *The Sonic Color Line*, p. 4.
63 *Ibid.*, p. 1.
64 Rebecca Redfern and Joe Hefner, 'Officially absent but actually present: bioarchaeological evidence for population diversity in London during the Black Death, AD 1348–50', in Madeleine L. Mant and Alyson Jaagumägi Holland (eds), *Bioarchaeology of Marginalized People* (London: Academic Press, 2019), pp. 69–114, esp. p. 106.
65 Mamta Motwani Accapadi, 'When white women cry; how white women's tears oppress women of color', *College Student Affairs Journal*, 26:2 (2007), 208–15, p. 210.
66 Ruby Hamad, *White Tears / Brown Scars: How White Feminism Betrays Women of Color* (London: Trapeze, 2020); Ruby Hamad, 'How white women use strategic tears to silence women of colour', *Guardian* (7 April 2018), www.theguardian.com/commentisfree/2018/may/08/how-white-women-use-strategic-tears-to-avoid-accountability [accessed 13 February 2021]
67 Hamad, *White Tears / Brown Scars*, p. 14.
68 *Ibid.*, p. 108.
69 *Ibid.*, p. 123.
70 *Ibid.*, p. 132.

11

The materialisation of Book II: elements of Margery Kempe's world

Laura Kalas

Sympoiesis is a simple word; it means 'making-with'. Nothing makes itself; nothing is really autopoietic or self-organizing ... *Sympoiesis* is a word proper to complex, dynamic, responsive, situated, historical systems. It is a word for worlding-with, in company. Sympoiesis enfolds autopoisesis and generatively unfurls and extends it.

Donna Haraway[1]

Here my preyeris, for thow I had as many hertys and sowlys closyd in my sowle as God knew wythow[tyn] begynnyng how many schulde dwellyn in hevyn wythow[tyn] ende, and as ther arn dropys of watyr, fres and salt, chesely[s] of gravel, stonys smale and grete, gresys growing in al erthe, kyrnellys of corn, fischys, fowelys, bestys and leevys upon treys whan most plente ben, fedir of fowle er her of best, seed that growith in erbe, er in wede, in flowyr, in lond, er in watyr whan most growyn, and as many creaturys as in erth han ben, and arn, er schal ben and myth ben be thi myth, and as ther arn sterrys and awngelys in thi syght, er other kynnes good that growyth upon erthe ... alle thes hertys ne sowlys cowyd nevyr thankyn God ne ful preysyn hym ...

Margery Kempe[2]

'Nothing makes itself', writes Donna Haraway. In response to the troubling times of the early twenty-first century she calls for the earth's inhabitants to 'make kin in lines of inventive connection' as part of a 'timeplace' of the now, of past remembrances, of the what-might-yet-be, and for us to undergo a sympoietic 'worlding-with' all beings that will create new narratives for earthly flourishing.[3] These narratives, made possible through the dynamic co-operation of the human and nonhuman in 'moving relations of attunement' born from listening and understanding our co-inhabitants, are, according to Haraway, stories made, 'but not made up', encapsulated in an '"ongoingness" … that enables our living and dying well with each other'.[4] Inspired by the Greek 'timeplace' of the *Chthulucene*, in which a diachronic entanglement of all earthly existents operate in ways that are non-ideological and non-hierarcnal, and within which the human and the non-human live and die with each other as deeply connected 'mixed assemblages', Haraway urges a reconciliation and reuniting of the ancient, current, and future beings of the earth, and proposes a harmonious making-of-kin. Yet, written nearly six hundred years prior, the accounts of travel in Book II and the final prayers at the end of *The Book of Margery Kempe* illustrate Kempe's own sympoietic desire.[5] Wishing to enfold the whole of creation within her soul, from grains of sand to creatures past, present, and yet-to-be, a similar asynchronous act of kinship, encounter, and *making-with* unfurls. Her self-identification as an omniferous disciple replete with 'as many hertys and sowlys *closyd in my sowle* as God knew wythow[tyn] begynnyng how many schulde dwellyn in hevyn wythow[tyn] ende' figures her as a divinely appointed vessel for all created beings from the beginning to the end of time. Indeed, by listing every particle of the earth, air, and waters inside her soul, Kempe imparts how her spiritual understanding is predicated on a totalised imbrication of the *ordo creationis*. Such an apotheosis is, in fact, anticipated in the second scribe's introductory Proem, in which he compares Kempe to a 'reedspyr whech boweth wyth every wynd and nevyr is stable les than no wynd bloweth' (p. 42). Wavering back and forth in temptation like a growing plant and subject to the whims of the elements, the natural world is established early on as a metonymy for Kempe as the 'creatur' of the *Book*: a textualised embodiment of God's creation and a spiritual work-in-progress. This *ongoingness* with 'nature', expressed through the 'tunge' and the cognisance of a sixty-five-year-old holy woman, not only chimes with Haraway's call for a revised and co-operative existential narrative but curiously reveals the synchronicity of two seemingly disparate aspects of the *Book*: the authority and genesis of Book II, and Kempe's maturing encounters, *in* Book II, with the natural world. These two distinct phenomena, this chapter argues, concurrently materialise.

In employing the term 'nature' I deliberately invoke its myriad denotations and Middle English etymology – as Creation/creation and the universe; as natural law and immutable force; as moral or political principle; as innate constitution of body or substance, or a supposed type of 'original' state.[6] And though scholarship has persistently acknowledged the different textures of Books I and II, brought about by their variant modes of production, there has been a surprising lack of extended analysis of the specific 'nature' of Book II as a distinct project.[7] One of the most important significations of the *Book*'s structural division is the fact that it is marked by a double bereavement: the death of Kempe's husband, John, and her son (who was probably the first scribe) in c. 1432.[8] Not only does the brutal loss provoked by these sudden life events signal a textual turning point – the terminus of the writing of Book I, and the later priest-scribe's revision of Book I in 1436 and commencement of Book II in 1438 – but it is also a socio-spiritual one: an account of an elderly, grieving woman embarking on an end-of-life pilgrimage born from practical necessity, in accompanying her daughter-in-law home to Danzig, and her own spiritual maturation, as she accepts God's challenge to traverse the landscapes of northern Europe.[9] As Liz Herbert McAvoy and Naoë Kukita Yoshikawa argue in Chapter 2, the influence of the daughter-in-law who remains with Kempe for eighteen months has been significantly overlooked in relation to Kempe's wider literary, emulative, and anecdotal encounters; and even in the *Book*'s production.[10] Her profound grief, however, is an important catalyst, too, for her self-inflicted exile to the Continent in an act of therapeutic remaking. As opposed to the notational travelogue epithet that is often attached to Book II, therefore, I suggest that the loss–recovery hermeneutic reflected in the expedition effects the materialisation of a differently inflected *liber*, and one which presents readers of the *Book* with a much more raw and symbiotic relationship with the elements of the natural world than those which we encounter in Book I. Kempe recounts extensive and quite remarkable travel in Book I to the pilgrimage destinations of Rome, Assisi, Middelburg, the Holy Land, and Santiago de Compostela, but these trips are largely punctuated with references to the urban geography: the places, buildings, sites of religious interest, and their potential for spiritual succour. But in Book II the elements and landscapes become more overtly entangled in Kempe's spiritual self. As Diane Watt has noted in relation to the northern European pilgrimage, 'the environment intrudes much further into Kempe's consciousness'.[11] Whilst Haraway points to the ecological imperative to *create* narratives of human–world co-operation and not just tell them, Margery Kempe negotiates a wilderness of elemental and human hostility in a time whose dominant worldview was predicated on paradigms of universal connectedness. The ancient philosopher Empedocles (c. 495–435 BCE) held that the four elements of the universe – earth, air, fire, and water – existed in perpetual motion: being bound, through love, or separated, through strife. Medical writings from Galenic sources described further environmental systems of cold, hot, wet, and dry, and the four humours of the human body, which connected humankind to its macrocosmic context.[12] Kempe's negotiation with the elements thus speaks to Jeffrey Cohen and Lowell Ducket's urge that we must overthrow reactions to the elements as 'hostile' and instead understand the way they surround us in an expanse of 'storied matter'; to notice the narrative power of matter to interact with human life.[13] Within her encounters of peril and dereliction, a new narrative is indeed created that is contingent upon the convergence of her old age and narration of her encounters in the 'wild'. In the jeopardy and the sanctuary of the northern European peregrinations – the rough waters, raging tempests of the air, the terrain of the earth – where losses are transformed and the world encountered anew – the *timeplace* of Book II unfolds. In reconciling with the elements, Kempe is made more acutely prescient of her own inextricable place in the universe and bestowed with a greater assurance that all will be well.

This chapter explores two convergent aspects of the *Book*'s operations. The first section considers the distinct texture and *making* of Book II as an end-of-life activity, memorialising Kempe's new eschatological understanding as an elderly holy woman recently returned from overseas travel and fully entered into the Holy Trinity Guild as reflective of the zenith of her authority.[14] The second section illustrates how the peculiarity of Book II plays out through an increased emphasis on Kempe's relationship with the natural world and the matter of creation, largely through her pilgrimage to northern Europe where the immediacy of her encounters with microcosmic beings and the macrocosmic cold night sky reflect a richer understanding of the universe and her own intrinsic place

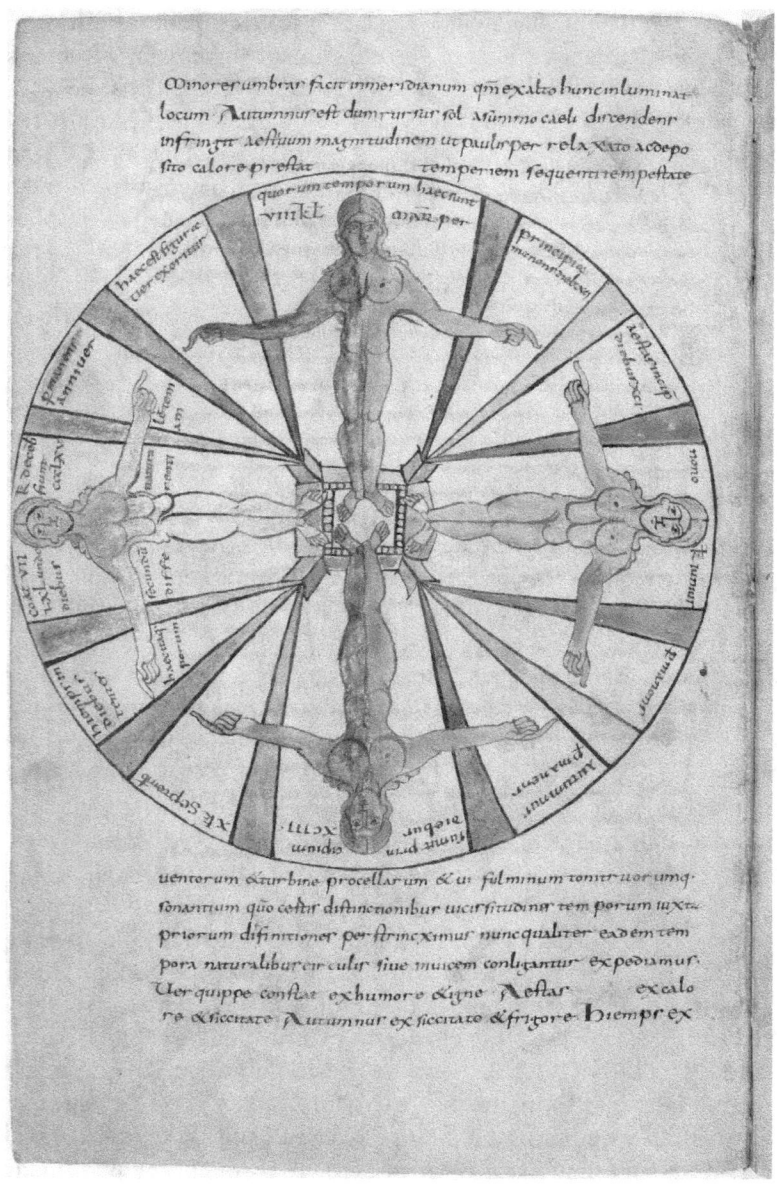

Figure 11.1 Wheel of the Four Seasons with connected elements and human characteristics. Isidore of Seville, *De natura rerum*. Ville de Laon Bibliothèque municipal, ms 422, fol. 6v.

within it. What, then, is at stake when we consider the inextricability of Book II and Kempe's visceral connectedness to the natural world? How does uncovering Kempe's sympoiesis with nature and writing in this later 'timeplace' re*make* our own encounter with the *Book*?

Making-with Book II

The dictation of Book I probably began in c. 1431, some twenty years after Kempe's spiritual conversion – and was copied in 1436 – whilst Book II was written in 1438, when Kempe was approximately sixty-five years old.[15] Importantly, the priest-scribe begins the *Secundus liber* by emphasising Kempe's own authority as author – that it is written in her '*owyn tunge*' (p. 385) evidences an increased insistence upon her voice as more legitimised and immediate than perhaps Book I's production-history had allowed, as scholars such as Diana Uhlman and Nicholas Watson have commented. Indeed, Watson notes that Book II 'read[s] like a close transcription of an oral narration'.[16] Furthermore, the explicit temporal specificity of Book II's content, in describing the grace wrought in Kempe during the 'yerys that sche levyd aftyr' (p. 385), reveals that this section of the *Book* is less reliant on memory and mythology than Book I which, even when recorded, was distanced by 'xx yer and mor' from the first revelations (p. 46), and more focused upon her recent physical and spiritual interactions with the world during a specific life-moment, and with a particularly linear trajectory.[17] Book II also begins with Kempe's defiance of church hegemony since she has not been granted permission to travel overseas by her confessor, indicative of a mature holy woman assured of her own validation as God's authorised disciple and also in the throes of a bereavement shared only with God, and her daughter-in-law. Such grief might be revealed by her being 'hevy in cher and in cuntenawnce' at the prospect of seafaring with her daughter-in-law to Germany (p. 394); anxious at her past 'perell' on the water (p. 391), she is driven by divine locution that she should nevertheless embark and resolutely takes 'hir leve' on an exigent and salvific journey (p. 395) – a journey which Sebastian Sobecki regards to be following the trope of *perigrenatio pro amore Dei*.[18] The sense of more deliberate fashioning in the *Secundus liber* is initially voiced by the priest-scribe, who establishes its narrative raison d'être by bearing witness not only to its authentic testimony in Kempe's 'owyn tunge' but also to its edifying substance: it is written in order to 'honowr … the blisful Trinite that hys holy werkys shulde be notifyid and declaryd to the pepil', and, crucially, to impart the 'grace' that was wrought in Kempe during the rest of her life (p. 385). Moreover, a significant spiritual symbolism hitherto unexplored surrounds the notification that Book II is first written on 28 April 1438, 'in the fest of Seynt Vital Martyr' (p. 385), whose hagiography and legacy Kempe would have inevitably encountered during her Italian travels between 1413 and 1415.[19] There are churches dedicated to St Vitalis in Rome (most notably the Basilica di San Vitale), and the *Book* notes how Kempe visited the Stations of Rome: '[she] wolde a gon the Stacyownys' (p. 205), and also departed Rome *after* Easter or Passover, suggesting a plausibility that she was still in Rome on Vitalis's feast day.[20] Many Italian cities housed churches of St Vitalis, including in Venice (the eleventh-century Chiesa di San Vitale) and Bologna (the Chiesa di Santi Vitale e Agricola); both cities that Kempe is known to have visited.[21] St Vitalis, a knight, consul, and early Christian martyr, was born in Milan in the first or second century CE, and, revealed as a Christian, was sentenced to death. According to Jacobus de Voragine's thirteenth-century *Legenda aurea*, which circulated vastly in the later Middle Ages, Vitalis was executed by order of the judge, Paulin, by half-drowning and burial under the seabed in a curious conflagration of water, earth, air, and fire:

> Then said Paulin: Bring him [Vitalis] for to do sacrifice, and if he do it not, make a deep pit unto the water and put his head thereunder. And so they did, and there buried him quick, in the year of our Lord fiftyseven. And the priest of the idols that had given this counsel was anon taken of the devil, and cried seven days continually and said: S. Vital thou burnest me, and the seventh day the devil threw him in the river and there died shamefully.[22]

A Middle English version of the saint's life similarly emphasises the combination of water, earth, and fire for the completion of the tale:

> [Paulis] chargid hem [his ministers] to maken a depe pitt til thei come to the water and therin to biryen hym quycle and casten upon hym erthe and stoones. And so they diden aboute the yere of grace seven and fifty vndir then Nero. Which doon anoon the preste of the temple

the which yafe counceil of this maner of deth of Vital was arrept and takyn of a devil and wex wode in the same place six daies crying thus, 'thou brennystine seynt vital thou brennyst me', and on the seventh day the devyl threw hym in a flode and so myserably and wretchidly he deid.²³

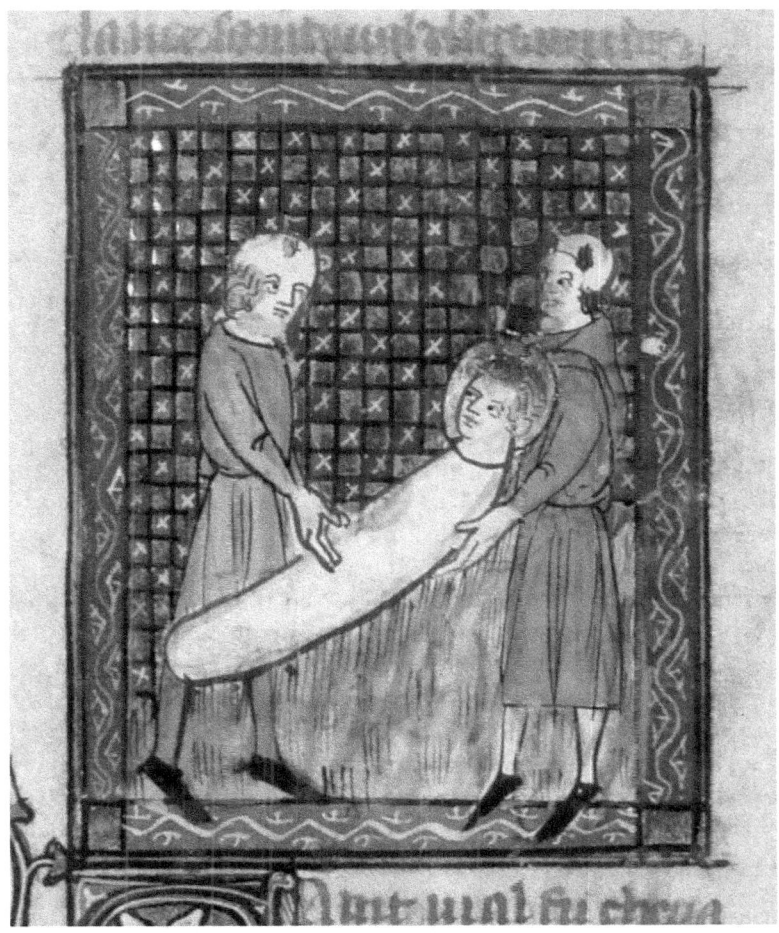

Figure 11.2 The Martyrdom of St Vitalis, *Vies de saints*, Richard of Montbaston and collaborators. Bibliothèque nationale de France, Français 185, fol. 230.

Put to death by the waters and the earth itself, and deprived of life-giving air, Vitalis's restoration to the universal elements is confirmed by his posthumous, retributive harnessing of the flames in which his executor burns. But such a martyrdom by being buried alive would also have had resonances with the 'death to the world' of the medieval anchorite, 'buried' in her cell – not least Kempe's own adviser, Julian of Norwich. The anchoress is even advised in the *Ancrene Wisse* to dig her own grave with her fingernails: 'ha schulden schrapien euche dei þe eorðe up of hare put þet ha schulen rotien in' [they should scrape up the earth every day from the grave in which they will rot].[24] The elemental human relationship with the earth to be found in these spiritual and allegorical semioses is inscribed implicitly in Book II. Indeed, in the Second Revelation of the Long Text, Julian envisions herself to be led to an underwater land:

> One time my understanding was led downe into the sea-grounde, and ther saw I hilles and dales grene, seming as it were mosse begrowen, with wrake and gravel. Then I understood thus: that if a man or woman wher there, under the brode water, and he might have sight of God – so as God is with a man continually – he should be safe in soule and body, and take no harme.[25]

Julian's 'sea-grounde', in which she envisions the natural matter of plants, stones, and a verdant, underwater and undulating landscape is, despite its awesome depths, imbued fully with God's love and protection; where one can *see* God with clarity. It reveals Julian's mystical understanding of the spiritual safety of an underwater burial place such as that in which St Vitalis is deposited, and resonates with Kempe's own cognition of and engagement with the symbolic value of Vitalis's feast day as she situates Book II, along with the penitential potentialities of the natural world, in the *Secundus liber*. This also gestures towards further evidence of the real-life contemplative encounter between the two women, which might have involved Julian sharing with Kempe her revelations about God's presence in the natural world. It is a connection that is strengthened when compared with Julian's parable of the Lord, whose servant falls into a 'slade' in an unforgiving terrain which was 'lang, harde, and grevous' but which teaches Julian how God's devoted servants are loved more 'hyely and blissefully' if they fall, and suffer: a sentiment that is repeatedly implied by Kempe in Book II.[26] The ascetic value to be gained from an uncomfortable relationship with nature, and especially the sea, has been explored by Amy Appleford, who describes the sea ground as 'an imaginative voyage to an environment in which humans normally cannot survive', where 'the "visitacioun" of God can do the impossible, even allow humans who have "sight" of God to survive under water, beyond the natural capacity of the human body'.[27] She adds that 'ascetic piety used the sea as a medium of mortification, as an environment essentially hostile to air-breathing human beings, especially through bodily immersion'.[28] Such an aqueous theology, which harnesses the salvific opportunities of water for asceticism, or rebirth through the oppositional act of baptism, reveals the multiple hermeneutics of the elemental power of water, intrinsic to Kempe's own desire for immersion in a 'welle of teerys' (p. 277). She thus assimilates the feast day of Vitalis, his seabed martyrdom, and the influence of Julian's spiritual perspicacity surrounding God's omnipresence in the natural world within the subtext of the *Secundus liber*. Whilst the use of feast days was a conventional means of documentational dating in the Middle Ages, the particular concomitance of St Vitalis's hagiography with the genesis of Book II seems to intimate how Kempe and her scribe gesture towards her own sanctified life and position in the divinely created world, deliberately harnessing a particular, salvific meta-narrative. Vitalis's water–earth burial in the *Legenda aurea* is redolent of Kempe's visceral connection with the natural world in Book II, and its very production, as end-of-life phenomena on trajectory towards her own indelible legacy.

A further encounter between the writing of Book II and Kempe's end-of-life activities is witnessed by her entry into the Holy Trinity Guild in Lynn. Kempe begins the dictation of Book II on 28 April 1438, the feast day of St Vitalis. Just before, during Lent, her penultimate payment to the Holy Trinity Guild was made, as recorded in the 1437–38 guild account roll:

Pl[egius] Bertholomeus Colles D[e] Margeria Kempexx s.
    Recept' in quadragesima per Iohannem Asheden xx s.

[Pledge Bartholomew Colles From Margery Kempe   20s.
    Received in Lent via John Asheden 20s.]

Kempe makes her full [plenam], or final, payment in Lent 1439, as recorded by the scabin on 22 May 1439: 'len' die veneris in septimana

Pentecostis Anno r[egni] r[egis] Henrici Sexti post conquestum Septimodecimo' [on Friday in the the week of Pentecost in the seventeenth year of the reign of King Henry the sixth after the conquest (22 May 1439)]. The accounts state:

> Et D[e] Iohanne Assheden pro Int[ro]itu Margerie Kempe i[n] plena[m] soluc[i]o[n]em xx s.
>
> [And from John Assheden for the entry of Margery Kempe in full payment 20s.][29]

As I have suggested elsewhere, it is likely that Kempe first entered the guild earlier than 1438 since the standard admission fee was 100 shillings. If she made five equal payments of 20 shillings, she may well have made her first payment, and joined the guild, in 1435 and not 1438; considerably earlier than first thought.[30] But the synchronicity of Kempe's membership in the Holy Trinity Guild (noted to be 'as masterful and wealthy as any in England')[31] and her commencement of Book II cannot be overlooked. They are significant as coalescent end-of-life activities which signify her authority and sagacity as a holy woman of some age, and a culmination of a life of devotion and parish status.[32] Guild membership would have afforded Kempe increased funeral provision, prayers to be said for her soul, and the potential for having her name entered on to a Bede Roll to be read out at Requiem masses and obits, thus inscribing her continuous presence in the memory of the community. Her membership, then, symbolises her own preparation for heaven at the same time as she prepares her *Book* as both a memorial of her spiritual life and a generative legacy for the future.

The accounts of Kempe's overseas pilgrimages to northern Europe are recounted in Book II when she is about sixty-five years old and reflect on events in the preceding years. The immediacy and, thus, the authenticity of this narration rests upon its dictation in close temporal proximity to the events themselves and engenders a more reflective process of composition and heightened verisimilitude that makes it a distinctive text to Book I. Barry Windeatt has suggested that Book II is 'less visionary and inward than Book I, with more of the outward concerns of a travel memoir', further positing that 'the production of the later text ... emerged from some division of labour' between Kempe and her priest amenuensis (p. 8). Whilst this may well be the case, that very priest opens Book II with a clear statement of intent: that God's work in Kempe 'schulde be notifyid and declaryd to the pepil', and to show 'sweche grace as owr Lord wrowt in hys sympyl creatur yerys that sche leyd aftyr, not alle but summe of hem, *aftyr hyr owyn tunge*' (p. 385). Furthermore, in addition to 'sweche grace' that the priest affirms underscores the second *liber*, Kempe explicitly explains the absence of detailed place names as owing to her intensified, and concentrated contemplative state in these later years: 'Yf the namys of the placys be not ryth wretyn, late no man merveylyn, for sche stodyid mor abowte contemplacyon than the namys of the placys, and he that wrot hem had nevyr seyn hem, and therfor have hym excusyd' (p. 401).[33] Whilst the tonal quality of Book II is indeed distinct, perhaps recorded more hastily in the interest of time, it is nevertheless underpinned by an implicit reckoning of bereavement and senescence, edified by her ascetic travel through the wider environment. Such a reckoning is hinted at by the cold, long nights and time spent in a suspended lacuna, waiting and resting, contemplating God through those tribulations and moments-in-between, in the *timeplace* of her journey into the elements.

Ther schal no wedyr ne tempest noyin the

Book II presents the natural world as at once a place of hostility and protection, utilised by Kempe as a means of experiencing and articulating worldly tribulation as she completes her geographical and mortal journey.[34] Enhanced by allusions to the isolation in nature of the Desert Fathers and anchoritic modes of contemplation, her relationship with the natural world is intensified. Jonathan Hsy has noted the multiple operations within Book II that its focus on travel permits: 'The *Book*'s resonance as travel writing becomes most apparent as we witness the spectacular collision of hagiographical, mercantile, and maritime motifs: "tempestys", "perellys", "merveyls", and seaborne prayers, all narrated along the way to the Hanseatic port of "Danske in Duchelond", or Danzig'.[35] The intensified presence of the natural world is signalled in the second chapter of Book II as she recalls her son's request for guidance on whether to travel to England by 'lond er be watyr' from Germany, as 'he trustyd meche in hys moderys cownsel' (p. 389).[36] Having received divine locution that either method would result in his arriving 'in saf-warde', and having abandoned the ship they had hired because of rising 'tempestys', travelling 'be lond wey' instead, the son and his wife arrive safely, as prophesied (p. 390). The story operates as a structural means of affirming Kempe's holy privilege, trusted in her older years as an earthly conduit to the Holy Ghost, as the son attests, and also as a narrative foreshadowing of the growing importance that the power of the elements will hold for her subsequent experience. That the son is noted straight after to have shortly died is also appropriated as a sign of verification, bearing witness to his safely 'coming home' into heavenly life: 'So gostly and bodily it myth wel ben verifiid – "He schal comyn hom in safte" – not only into this dedly lond, but also into the lond of levyng men, where deth schal nevyr aperyn' (p. 390). Such a juxtaposition of the 'dedly lond' of earth with the heavenly 'lond of levyng men' resonates with the aforementioned Empedoclean hermeneutic of the elemental motion of love and strife to describe Kempe's alternately harmonious, and dissonant, interactions with nature and the *ordo creationis*. When God's loving presence is tangibly perceived, Kempe is reconciled in the elements.

This paradigm can be seen further during the voyage to Germany, which notably begins in the holy 'Passyon Weke', when 'God sent hem fayr wynde and wedyr that day and the Fryday' (p. 396). By the Saturday, and on Palm Sunday, however, conditions become so perilous that the ship's company fear shipwreck: there are 'swech stormys and tempestys that thei wendyn alle to a ben perischyd. The tempestys weryn so grevows and hedows that thei myth not rewlyn ne governe her schip. Thei cowde no bettyr chefsyawns than comendyn hemself and her schip to the governawns of owr Lord' (p. 396). With the ship given over to divine captaincy, Kempe considers her seafaring fears to be legitimate, decrying to God that he had promised that she would 'nevyr perischyn neithyr on londe ne in watyr ne wyth no tempest' (p. 396).[37] In a moment of natural and spiritual catastrophe, her faith is tested, but she is chastised by God for her doubts: 'Why dredist the? Why art thu so aferd? I am as mythy her in the see as on the londe' (p. 397). Evoking the parable of Jesus calming the storm on the Sea of Galilee, the power of the divine is revealed through the power of the elements.[38] Now assured of his omnipresence, Kempe learns that God inhabits nature, existent everywhere – like Haraway's *ongoingness* – as an integrant of the natural world, *in* the sea, and *on* the land. It is no coincidence, then, that the ship docks on the Norwegian coast on Good Friday, where the company abides for the three days of Easter, receiving the Eucharist on board on Easter Monday in a moment of reconciliation with divine creation. As a quasi-church and symbol of the human-divine negotiation of the treacherous waters, the ship is transformed into a vessel of synchronicity between the natural and Christian worlds.[39]

Like the perils of the sea, the crude terrain of the earth, indifferent to human comfort, is a source of persistent tribulation for Kempe's aged body, and she struggles to keep up with her guide on the journey by foot from Stralsund to Wilsnack with 'gret labowr' (p. 402). On the eve of Corpus Christi, and after a frightening encounter with a curiously unthreatening yet armed man in the woods, she is eventually forced to stop walking after falling ill. As well as adhering to Romance tropes of the forest and actual pilgrim narratives of the dangers of travelling through woods, this strikingly resonates with David Wallace's observation that Book II 'observes a temporality more ordered and sequenced than the more random recollections of Book I ... much more akin to the narrativity of romance than to the more static forms of contemplative literature; the trajectory of Book II in fact models a basic structure of romance, what Susan Wittig termed ... the "exile-and-return-motifeme"'.[40] The auspiciousness of the date on the Christian calendar is again convergent with the ensuing need to take refuge from the elements, which by now have brewed into a summer storm. Yet the relentless 'leevyn [lightning], thundyr, and reyne' are recounted as heaven-sent since the inclement conditions prevent their continuing on: 'Sche was ful glad thereof, for sche was ryth seke, and sche wist wel, yf it had ben fayr wedyr, the man that went wyth hir wolde not abedyn hir, he wolde a gon fro hir' (p. 403). Finding rudimentary shelter in a 'lityl ostage fer fro any towne', Kempe rests without bedding and just a 'lityl strawe', safe in her rural lodging yet separated from the earth by only a sprinkling of dried stalks and equal only to the animals who shelter in similar conditions. As a quasi-anchoritic cell, the 'ostage' provides a place of refuge, and a time – a *timeplace* – in which she can contemplate and reflect, and in which space exists the quiet making-with nature that is only silently present, but present nevertheless, in Book II. This close existence with the simplicity of the natural world, which simultaneously threatens and protects her, and in which God has shown himself to be immersed, engenders a dichotomy of raw, earthly understanding and spiritual elevation as she is climactically carried in a wain to see the 'precyows blod' of Wilsnack.

So inextricably connected are the environmental conditions in Book II with Kempe's spiritual health that the pattern is repeated on the way to Aachen when she is abandoned by John, her guide. Isolated and alone, she is approached by some 'lewyd' priests who call her an 'English sterte' (p. 406). The term, meaning a tail, and also nakedness, refers to the popular slur employed on the Continent which intimated that the English had tails, and underpins the emphasis in the second book on the necessity of Kempe's material abasement for her edification.[41] This trope is developed immediately after, when she is accepted into a party of poor folk who beg for food in each town. Outside the towns and away from civilisation, the group strip naked and pick lice from their bodies and clothes. Since Kempe is aghast at the prospect of naked humiliation, she endures the 'vermyn' that have infested her, too, and instead is 'betyn and stongyn ful evyl bothe day and nyght, tyl God sent hir other felaschep' (p. 407). Regarded by Diane Watt as 'being reduced to little more than an animal', Kempe is afflicted with great tribulation, cast down by her base humanity as a simple source in the food chain. The *De Proprietatibus Rerum* of Bartholomaeus Anglicus (before 1203–72) describes 'lous' – or critters, in Haraway's words – as 'worme[s] of þe skynne'. Engendered of 'most [moist], corrupt ayer and vapours þat sweten [sweat] oute bitwen þe felle [skin] and the fleissch by pores', they come from the 'purgaciouns' that 'kynde [nature] casteþ oute': those who are most beset with lice have a body that is 'swiþe f[o]ulle and corrupte'.[42] Categorised as rank and filthy, the microcosmic presence of the fleas on Kempe's body reduces her to a figure of fleshy abjection, and she is forced to confront her own wretched humanity. But immediately after, her arrival in Aachen to see the Virgin Mary's smock and other holy relics signifies a further moment of heightened sanctity in the aftermath of abjection. Not only were the relics shown rarely to pilgrims, just once every seven years, but Kempe's witnessing of them occurs on 'Seynt Margaretys Day' – her own namesake, and the saint to whom her parish church in Lynn is dedicated. Such a symbolic apotheosis was clearly recognised by the so-called Red-Ink Annotator of the manuscript, who has not only coloured the word Aachen for emphasis but has also drawn the Virgin's smock in the margin, calling readers' attention to the holy significance of her transformation in this episode from degradation to divine grace.[43]

On departure from Aachen for London, Kempe journeys with a poor friar into the countryside, as evening falls. Sheltered under a pile of bracken in an outhouse, Kempe's abject dwelling in the midst of a dark wood brings her closer than ever to the raw creation of her divine father:

> Than went thei forth togedyr owt of the towne ageyn the evyn wyth gret drede and hevynes, mornyng be the wey wher thei schuldyn han herborwe that nyt. Thei happyd to comyn undyr a wodys syde, bisily beheldyng yf thei myth spyin any place wherin thei myth restyn. And as owr Lord wolde, thei parceyvyd an hows er tweyn, and in hast thedir thei drowyn, ther was dwellyng a good man wyth hys wife and tweyn childeryn. Than heldyn thei non hostel ne not woide receivyn gestys to her herborw. The seyd creatur saw an hep of brakys in an hows, and wyth gret instawns sche purchasyd grace to restyn hir on the brakys that nyth. The frer wyth gret preyer was leyd in a berne, and hem thowt thei wer wel esyd that thei haddyn the hows ovyr hem. On the next day thei made aseth for her lodgyng, takyng the wey to-Caleysward, goyng wery weys and grevows in dep sondys, hillys, and valeys tweyn days er thei comyn thedyr, sufferyng gret thrist and gret penawns, for ther wer fewe townys be the wey that thei went and ful febyl herberwe. (pp. 411–12)

Despite the crude dwelling, Kempe is 'wel esyd' in the retreat, cognisant of the God-given sticks and twigs of nature's largess and harmonising with her surroundings in a sympoietic 'making-of-kin' with the natural world. Evoking the anchoritic cell once more, this natural enclosure provides opportunity for spiritual reflection in the wilderness, resonant with the Desert Fathers' early Christian practice of *hesychasm*, in stillness, rest, and silent prayer.[44] In this existential moment of isolation Kempe too finds silence and space under a canopy of twigs. The following days of exhausting and dangerous travel through deep sands, hills, and valleys nevertheless connect physical hardship with the 'penawns' of spiritual reward, and while her frail corporeality almost expires, as she 'thowt hir spyryt schulde a departyd fro hir body as sche went in the wey' (p. 412), she arrives safely in Calais in spite of the harsh terrain after a journey of overcoming and 'oneing' with the world in whose naked creation she has survived.

When God challenges Kempe's loss of faith in his omnipresence – 'Why dredist the? Why art thu so aferd? I am as mythy her *in the see as on the lond*' – it is simultaneously reinforced as an environmental presence; a 'sea grounde' in which God exists in mighty perpetuity '*in* the see' (p. 397). Just as she has existed on the brink of human possibility in the events of Book II, so she realises her intrinsic place in a world inhabited by the micro and the macro in a *scala naturae* that is apparently as levelling as it is ordered. In this way she has already anticipated Haraway's call for 'moving relations of attunement', by understanding her earthly co-inhabitants in the woods and the winds and the seas, and by making new stories in the *timeplace* of Book II, in her *owyn tunge*, where the hierarchies of life are persistently reinforced and exploded. Her fear of tempests and of seafaring, the strife of perilous gales and the God-given love of calm winds, the electrical storms which provide welcome respite from travelling, the forest nook and covering of bracken, the unforgiving terrain – these negotiations with the elements of nature show a holy woman inscribed not only into the Holy Trinity Guild at the same time as the creation of this *liber* but simultaneously into a world of peril and natural connectedness. Though Book II might appear, on the surface, as less 'visionary and inward' than Book I, those inward moments occur silently, privately, in the spaces and pauses, and often in the expanse of nature. That the entire *Book* ends with the notation of Kempe's prayers reiterates her understanding of the same temporal stretch and 'mixed assemblage' of existence as Haraway's imagining. Separated off from the end of Book II, the prayers also transcend textual linearity as they travel with her over time: '[t]hys creatur ... usyd many yerys to begynnyn hir preyerys on this maner' (p. 421). The confluence of past, present, and future existence that the prayers imply, resonant with Carolyn Dinshaw's notion of a 'heterogeneous temporal experience', reveals Kempe's mystical dissolution of time and space as an 'asynchronous now'.[45] She imagines the hearts and souls of heaven in a *timeplace* 'wythow[tyn] begynnyng' and 'wythow[tyn] ende'. She lists, non-hierarchically, the components of the universe – the 'dropys of watyr', 'gravel', 'fischys', 'fowelys', 'bestys', 'leevys', 'fedir[s]', 'sterrys' and 'awngelys'.

And she discovers that her praise is infinitely inadequate: 'that I can not don ne may don' (p. 426). Presented in the first person, the prayers are a differently inflected manifestation of Kempe's *owyn tunge* in the *secondus liber*, ending with her gift of prayer to God, the saints, and her readers, and thus a means of assuring her own sympoeisis as designated 'creatur' of the *Book*, now bestowed with a richer understanding of creation, and her own most ordinary, and most extraordinary, place within it. To learn to 'make-with' the world, in Haraway's terms, and fabulate new ways of being that might 'solicit the absent into vivid copresence', is exactly what Kempe creates through her worlding-with Book II.[46] It is a tribute to her lost son and husband, but also to all living things from the past, present, and yet-to-be as she encounters the world anew in ongoingness; in possibility.

Notes

1 Donna J. Haraway, *Staying with the Trouble: Making Kin in the Chthulucene* (Durham, NC, and London: Duke University Press, 2014), p. 58.
2 *The Book of Margery Kempe*, ed. Barry Windeatt (Cambridge: D. S. Brewer: 2004), p. 426. All subsequent references are to this edition and page numbers appear parenthetically in the text.
3 Haraway, *Staying with the Trouble*, pp. 1–3 and p. 128.
4 Ibid., p. 132.
5 On Kempe's prayers see Josephine A. Koster, 'The prayers of Margery Kempe: a reassessment', Chapter 3 above.
6 *MED* s.v. 'nature' (n).
7 On the particularity of Book II see Nicholas Watson, 'The making of *The Book of Margery Kempe*', in Linda Olson and Kathryn Kerby-Fulton (eds), *Voices in Dialogue: Reading Women in the Middle Ages* (Notre Dame: University of Notre Dame Press, 2005), pp. 395–434.
8 On the social shift of Kempe's widowhood see Tara Williams, '"As thu wer a wedow": Margery Kempe's wifehood and widowhood', *Exemplaria*, 21:4 (2009), 345–62.
9 This maturation is also evidenced by Kempe's first entry into the Holy Trinity Guild, probably in 1435, as this chapter later discusses.
10 Liz Herbert McAvoy and Naoë Kukita Yoshikawa, 'The intertextual dialogue and conversational theology of Mechthild of Hackeborn and Margery Kempe', Chapter 2, this volume.

11 Diane Watt, 'Faith in the landscape: overseas pilgrimages in *The Book of Margery Kempe*', in Clare Lees and Gillian R. Overing (eds), *A Place to Believe in: Locating Medieval Landscapes* (Philadelphia: Pennsylvania State University Press, 2006), p. 183.
12 See *Galen, Works on Human Nature: Vol 1, Mixtures (De Temperamentis)*, ed. P. N. Singer and Philip J. van der Eijk (Cambridge: Cambridge University Press, 2018), esp. pp. 49–51.
13 Jeffrey Cohen and Lowell Duckert (eds), *Elemental Ecocriticism: Thinking with Earth, Air, Water and Fire* (Minneapolis: University of Minnesota Press, 2015), p. 11.
14 On Kempe's life cycle see Laura Kalas, *Margery Kempe's Spiritual Medicine: Suffering, Transformation and the Life-Course* (Cambridge: D. S. Brewer, 2020), esp. pp. 183-210 and pp. 211–21.
15 Nicholas Watson has argued that Kempe's son writes Book I not during the month of his death in c. 1432 but in the preceding year during his extended visit. See 'The making of *The Book of Margery Kempe*', p. 399.
16 *Ibid.*, p. 405; Diana R. Uhlman, 'The comfort of voice, the solace of script: orality and literacy in *The Book of Margery Kempe*', *Studies in Philology*, 91 (1994), 50–69. On the oral history of the *Book* see Katherine J. Lewis, Chapter 6, this volume.
17 Liz Herbert McAvoy addresses the issue of Kempe's age and textual production in '"[A] péler of holy cherch": holiness, authority and the wise woman in *The Book of Margery Kempe*', in Anneke B. Mulder-Bakker (ed.), *The Prime of Their Lives: Wise Old Women in Pre-Industrial Europe* (Leuven, Paris, and Dudley: Peeters, 2004), pp. 17–38. David Wallace regards Book II as more ordered and sequenced than Book I. See *Strong Women: Life, Text, and Territory, 1347–1645* (Oxford: Oxford University Press, 2011), p. 85.
18 Sebastian Sobecki, *The Sea and Medieval English Literature* (Cambridge: D. S. Brewer, 2008), p. 135.
19 There is some dispute as to whether the Bologna church is dedicated to the St Vitalis of Milan or to St Vitale, whose body was discovered together with that of St Agricola by St Ambrose in Bologna in 393. The Vitalis of Book II is undoubtedly Vitalis of Milan, since his feast day is 28 April. Nonetheless, the legends of both St Vitalises were clearly well known in the areas through which Kempe travelled in Italy.
20 Chapter 42 notes how Kempe decided to return home to England 'Whan tyme of Estern er ellys Paske was *come and go*' (p. 211; my emphasis). She had returned to Norwich by 'Trinite Sunday', which Windeatt notes fell on 25 May 1414 (p. 218).
21 Medieval Rome was home to myriad relics and tombs of early martyrs. Pilgrim-guides such as *The Stacions of Rome* provided information

about the places to visit. See *The Stacions of Rome, and the Pilgrims Sea-voyage*, ed. F. J. Furnivall (London: Camden Society, 1867). The most famous church of St Vitalis is the early Christian Basilica of San Vitale at Ravenna, erected on the purported site of his martyrdom. Kempe visited Bologna in 1413 and would have undoubtedly walked along the main thoroughfare of the Via San Vitale, on which the Church of St Vitalis and Agricola stands. She could have passed through Ravenna en route to Venice from Bologna.

22 Jacobus de Voragine, *The Golden Legend: Readings of the Saints*, intro. Eamon Duffy (Princeton and London: Princeton University Press, 2012), p. 67.

23 Advocates Library, Abbotsford MS *Legenda aurea*, p. 182 of digital surrogate. The manuscript's writer is thought to be Osborn Bokenham, c. 1450–75.

24 *Ancrene Wisse: A Corrected Edition of the Text in Cambridge, Corpus Christi College, MS 402 with Variants from Other Manuscripts*, ed. Bella Millett (Oxford: Oxford University Press, 2005), vol. I, part II, lines 1034–5, p. 46. Translation from Bella Millett, *Ancrene Wisse, Guide for Anchoresses: A Translation based on Cambridge, Corpus Christi College, MS 402* (Exeter: University of Exeter Press, 2009), p. 46.

25 *The Writings of Julian of Norwich*: A Vision Showed to a Devout Woman *and* A Revelation of Love, ed. Nicholas Watson and Jacqueline Jenkins (University Park: Pennsylvania State University Press, 2006), p. 159.

26 MED s.v. 'slade' (n): low-lying ground; a valley; hollows; a creek, stream; a channel. *The Writings of Julian of Norwich*, Revelation 14, ch. 51, esp. pp. 273–5.

27 Amy Appleford, 'The sea ground and the London street: the ascetic self in Julian of Norwich and Thomas Hoccleve', *The Chaucer Review*, 51:1 (2016), 49–67, p. 57.

28 Appleford, 'The sea ground', p. 58. On the Christian tradition of underwater immersion for mortification and edification see Alfred K. Siewers, 'Desert islands: Europe's Atlantic archipelago as ascetic landscape', in Benjamin Hudson (ed.), *Studies in the Medieval Atlantic* (New York: Palgrave Macmillan, 2012), pp. 35–64. For literary readings of water see Albrecht Classen, *Water in Medieval Literature* (Lanham: Lexington Books, 2017).

29 King's Lynn Borough Archives, KL/C 38/17. With thanks to Susan Maddock for her assistance with the Holy Trinity Guild account rolls, and Luke Shackell and the King's Lynn Borough Archives.

30 The Holy Trinity Guild ordinances mention 100 shillings as the standard total admission fee. My thanks to Susan Maddock for her generous

help on this matter. See Susan Maddock, 'Society, status and the leet court in Margery Kempe's Lynn', in Richard Goddard and Teresa Phipps (eds), *Town Courts and Urban Society in Late Medieval England, 1250–1550* (Woodbridge: Boydell Press, 2019), pp. 200–19. See also Kalas, *Margery Kempe's Spiritual Medicine*, esp. pp. 213–17.

31 Alice Stopford Green, *Town Life in the Fifteenth Century* (London, 1894), vol. 1, p. 286. From Maddock, 'Society, status and the leet court in Margery Kempe's Lynn', p. 209.

32 Kempe was, for example, summoned to the homes of the dying in Lynn because of the value placed on her prayers and tears. See *BMK*, p. 321.

33 *MED* s.v. 'studīen' (v): To strive, endeavour; direct one's efforts or thoughts; take pains; devote oneself to.

34 The medieval tradition of tribulation texts would have been well known to Kempe. See, for example, *The Chastising of God's Children*, ed. Joyce Bazire and Eric Colledge (Oxford: Blackwell, 1957), and *The Book of Tribulacion*, ed. Alexandra Barratt (Heidelberg: Carl Winter, 1983).

35 Jonathan Hsy, 'Lingua franca: overseas travel and language contact in *The Book of Margery Kempe*', in Sebastian Sobecki (ed.), *The Sea and Englishness in the Middle Ages: Maritime Narratives, Identity and Culture* (Cambridge: D. S. Brewer, 2011), pp. 159–78, p. 177.

36 On the linguistic, mercantile, and business significance of this seafaring episode see Hsy, 'Lingua franca', pp. 172–5.

37 On this episode see Sobecki, *The Sea and Medieval English Literature*, pp. 135–9.

38 See Matthew 8.23–7, Mark 4.35–41, and Luke 8.22–5.

39 David Wallace has noted the reciprocal identification with ships and churches in the Middle Ages, comparing the church nave with its wooden-beamed roof as often evoking a ship; and a ship becoming a church on the high seas. See *Strong Women*, pp. 91 and 93. On the iconography and art of such resonances see V. A. Kolve, *Chaucer and the Imagery of Narrative: The First Five Canterbury Tales* (London: Edward Arnold, 1984), pp. 315 and 317.

40 Wallace, *Strong Women*, p. 85. On Romance tropes of the forest see Corinne Saunders, *The Forest of Medieval Romance: Avernus, Broceliande, Arden* (Cambridge: D. S.Brewer, 1993).

41 *MED* s.v. 'stert' (n). (1): the tail of an animal; naked; the English; a derogatory and salacious term for an Englishwoman. On the background of the slur see P. Rickard, 'Anglois Coué and L'Anglois Qui Couve', *French Studies*, VII, 48–55.

42 John Trevisa, *On the Properties of Things: John Trevisa's Translation of Bartholomaeus Anglicus' 'De Proprietatibus Rerum'*, vol. 2, ed. M. C. Seymour (Oxford: Clarendon Press, 1975), p. 1239.
43 British Library, Additional MS 61823, fol. 1153. On the Red Ink Annotator see Kelly Parsons, 'The Red Ink Annotator of *The Book of Margery Kempe* and his lay audience', in Kathryn Kerby-Fulton and Maidie Hilmo (eds), *The Medieval Professional Reader at Work: Evidence from Manuscripts of Chaucer, Langland, Kempe, and Gower* (Victoria English Literary Studies, University of Victoria, 2001), pp. 143–216.
44 'But thou when thou shalt pray, enter into thy chamber, and having shut the door, pray to thy Father in secret', Matthew 6.6. On Kempe's anchoritic aspects see Liz Herbert McAvoy, '"Closyd in an hows of ston": discourses of anchoritism and *The Book of Margery Kempe*', in Liz Herbert McAvoy and Mari Hughes-Edwards (eds), *Anchorites, Wombs and Tombs: Intersections of Gender and Enclosure in the Middle Ages* (Cardiff: University of Wales Press, 2005), pp. 182–94; and Margaret Hostetler, '"I wold thu wer closyd in an hows of ston": re-imagining religious enclosure in *The Book of Margery Kempe*', *Parergon*, 20:2 (2003), 71–94.
45 Carolyn Dinshaw, *How Soon Is Now? Medieval Texts, Amateur Readers, and the Queerness of Time* (Durham, NC, and London: Duke University Press, 2012), p. 5.
46 Haraway, *Staying with the Trouble*, pp. 126–33.

IV

Performative encounters

12

Writing performed lives: Margery Kempe meets Marina Abramović

Sarah Salih

> My transformation is of fire to song
> then song to words, then telling all to scribes
> who do their craft with ink swept dark and long
> across the thirsty parchment which imbibes
>
> The love that pulled my life into its shape.[1]

To write her *Book* the ageing Margery Kempe had to re-create in words a life of embodied and often 'unspekabyl' devotion.[2] As Rebecca Krug comments: 'It is remarkable, surprising, and in no way simply an aspect of the "times" that Margery Kempe – possibly illiterate and definitely in need of scribes to write for her – came to compose the story of her spiritual life.'[3] Margery's contemplative life was self-sufficient; she enjoyed 'holy spechys and dalyawns', (p. 44) 'hyr felyngys and hir revelacyons' for 'xx yer and mor' (p. 46) before she committed to having them written. The *Book* has long been recognised as a self-authorisation that writes Margery as holy woman and saint.[4] Krug sees the *Book* as a personal self-reckoning, arguing that it was Margery's 'revisionary reflexion and self-construction', 'the means by which she re-understood and re-envisioned both her self and the books she had read'.[5] The identification of the *Book* as self-formation tool is surely true, and yet it is also an urgent address to an exterior audience. Margery had cited the *Life* of Marie d'Oignies to defend her own crying, so she knew that a written record could establish an authoritative interpretation of a holy woman's controversial behaviour (pp. 292–4). Anthony Goodman argues that her recognition that 'the profiles of two contrasting "Margerys", the charlatan and the visionary, [had] become firmly embedded in Lynn lore' prompted her to attempt 'to topple the image of the deceitful Margery' with a book that defended her good name.[6] Rory Critten argues, specifically, that the incident of 1434, when Margery in London was confronted with the legend of her alter ego, the 'fals feynyd ypocrite in Lynne' who 'sett awey the reed heryng and ete the good pike' (pp. 416–17) spurred her to revive the dormant project of writing the *Book* to regain control of her reputation.[7] The *Book*, then, aimed to fix for the record the truth of Margery, which the performed character of her embodied life had put into question. Her marital arrangements, diet, clothing, friendships had all been scrutinised and criticised. Her devotional practices were ephemeral and thus vulnerable to forgetting and misremembering, and often sufficiently obscure to permit, indeed to invite, misinterpretation and controversy.

When Margery took the decision, after half a lifetime of revelations, cryings, and pilgrimages, to start an entirely new enterprise, the writing of her feelings, she made a commitment to new skills and methods, complementing her lifetime of embodied, noisy, and baffling performance with textual analysis. The map is not the territory; the archive is not the performance. During the time that she was working on the present Book 1 she was also caring for the ageing and infirm John Kempe; his descent into dementia must have sharpened Margery's own awareness of mortality and of the fragility of memory. Meanwhile, her caring responsibilities disrupted her devotional regime and kept her at home (pp. 331–2). She recruited, probably, her son and then her confessor to help her, both of whom had their own interest in memorialising her as a holy woman, rather than the annoyance that the *Book* records less sympathetic observers finding her.[8] With their support the performer became her own critic and archivist.

Margery thus turned writer in order to establish an authoritative record of her career as performer. Claire Sponsler discusses the influence of drama on Margery's devotions and the 'remarkably demonstrative and histrionic' quality of her piety; Jesse Njus shows her 'tearful spectatorship' to be both an imitation of the Virgin and Mary Magdalene and a response demanded of the audience of Passion plays.[9] Laura Varnam argues that Margery's improvised religious life required continual 'performance of extraordinary piety modeled on religious imagery'.[10] Of particular interest is Nanda Hopenwasser's identification of Margery as a 'performance artist' who 'exhibits herself body and soul to the scrutiny of observers'; though my argument diverges from Hopenwasser's identification of Margery as a 'naïve' 'comic figure' written with 'irony' by the 'more sophisticated' writer Kempe, I continue her deliberately anachronistic comparison of Margery to contemporary performance artists, and her interest in audience response.[11] Such contemporary artists often distinguish their work from that of the theatre, yet the dividing line between theatre and performance art is contestable in the contemporary world and was probably never operative in medieval Christian performance.[12] Margery belonged to a culture which performed piety and staged sacred drama. Drama, liturgy, procession and informal devotional activities were all components of what Gail McMurray Gibson names the 'theater of devotion': religious services included dramatic elements such as the burial and raising of the crucifix from the Easter Sepulchre; private meditations such as psalm recitals might involve aspects of impersonation, when the reader consciously speaks 'in the person of Christ, in the person of the church', or in the person of King David.[13] To see Margery as a performer or actor is not to denigrate her piety as merely theatrical but to focus on those aspects of it that are founded in, in Rebecca Solnit's phrase, her 'vital body in action'.[14]

Here I focus on Margery's vital body by imagining an encounter with another performer of the bodily, the contemporary artist Marina Abramović, prompted by Abramović's recent participation in a series of retrospective events and publications: the 2010 MoMA, New York, show *The Artist Is Present*, with accompanying catalogue and documentary film, followed by an autobiography, *Walk through Walls*.[15] Her self-mythologising work documenting and memorialising her life in performance is as important to this comparison as the performance itself; like Margery, she continually repeats and recapitulates, before turning in later life to fix the record. The two women share a commitment to performing the self, displaying the female body in youth and age, provoking and exploiting shame. They not only tolerate but actively court divided, hostile, and baffled reactions, and use the ensuing controversy to bolster their claims for their art. Diane Watt in Chapter 1 finds that *The Book of Margery Kempe* 'resonates in curious ways' with women pilgrims and writers up to seven centuries earlier; I argue here that Margery equally curiously resonates with a woman performer and writer seven centuries later.

Medieval holy women and contemporary women performers such as Abramović meet through the bridge of the nineteenth-century hysteric. Luce Irigaray's 'La Mystérique' pioneered the comparison of mystic and hysteric, a comparison taken up, questioned, and examined by medievalists.[16] Amy Hollywood understands the mystical-hysterical body as the focal point of a host of other people's anxieties: 'The mystic, crying out in anguish as God departs from her soul, becomes a mystically marked, hysterical body. ... women bear the weight, in and on their anguished bodies, of human mortality and of the hope for redemption.'[17] Rebecca Schneider continues the chain as she connects the hysteric to the performance artist as women whose bodies screen the faultlines of their society: 'Nineteenth-century hysterics have today become well known for their performative re-enactments of the Symbolic Order upon their physical bodies in a display of tics and twitches, scratches, glitches, breaks. ... Hysteria was either a pathology or a political symptom of the unruly detail – or both, in the more complex terms of the "two-way street".'[18] Marla Carlson, comparing performance artists directly to medieval saints and mystics, would concur: 'Faced with the challenge of expression within a repressive cultural economy, some women perform outside the realm of rational discourse.'[19] I do not claim that mystical performance is the same phenomenon as hysteria, as performance art, but that the remarkable similarity of their contours permits encounters amongst them. Their likeness is a functional kinship, not just a pseudomorphic resemblance.[20] Though actual historical connections between these forms of performance are partial and indirect, the structural and functional similarities are consequential. Similar problems can generate similar responses, even in the absence of conscious citation. Their overt goals of salvation, healing, artistic achievement are as different as can be, but all demand attention to the difficulties of disciplining bodies, of reaching a stable relation between self and other.

The performing bodies of the mystic, the hysteric, the artist are open and porous: the performers are nodes in a network of actors, humans, institutions, processes, things. Subjectively, the performance is an experience of extremity, of reaching for the limits of the self;

to the observer they are difficult, often horrific, bodily spectacles. Not all performers are women, but women tend to be the most visible and paradigmatic occupants of such positions: the domain of the 'mystérique', argues Irigaray, 'is the only place in the history of the West in which woman speaks and acts so publicly'.[21] Their art is collaborative, needing an audience's witness. Their bodies speak of larger forces, but their messages are obscure, at the very edge of what can be articulated at all: hence they are attended by flocks of specialist interpreters, the hagiographers and confessors, psychoanalysts and journalists, critics and curators, who are necessary complements to their activity. Thus the individual performers form relationships with the predominantly masculine institutions – the Church, the hospital, the gallery – that frame and regulate their activities. Certain spaces are marked out as appropriate for these breaches of normal decorum; in so far as these are protests and dissents, they are licensed. Margery, as John Arnold argues, 'talked *within* power, within the accepted strategies power permits for the regulation of its subjects' positions and responsibilities'.[22] Yet they are marginal and often troubling spectacles and their performers undergo real danger, hostility, and suffering: they commit to actually sacrificial acts.

The right to interpret the performances is distributed, and sometimes contested, amongst the network of performers and commentators. The difference between the mystic and the hysteric, Hollywood argues, is that the hysteric is understood to be unable to access the meaning of her behaviour; holy women, meanwhile, 'struggled to maintain the authority to *interpret* that experience [of rapture] against the competing claims of male medical and ecclesial authorities'.[23] Philip of Clairvaux, for example, described the silent, enraptured Elisabeth of Spalbeek violently throwing her body around, a spectacle that the clerical interpreter then explains as a performance of the Passion: 'sche berith ouer hirselfe euen forwarde dyuers tymes, as sche were drawen with vyolens as men do with thefes and mensleers that are pullyd and luggyd ful vyolently with othere mennes handes, representynge oure Lorde Jhesu wordes that hee seyde to hym, "yee come to take me as a thefe with swerdes and battys."'[24] Margery may have known this text, but evidently decided against surrendering so much interpretative control, a strategy that brought its own risks.[25] Whereas, in the Western tradition, men's representations of women constitute art, women who represent themselves are open to accusations of narcissism, insincerity, impropriety. The performance artist Carolee Schneemann found 'I was allowed to be an image but not an image-maker creating her own self-image'.[26] Margery and Abramović, writing their own books about their performances, are also readers and curators of the self-image they have made.

Both women give narrative accounts of themselves that supplement their embodied behaviours. Margery repeatedly told her story in confession; introducing herself to Richard Caister and recruiting him to her support network, she 'schewyd hym al hyr maner of levyng fro hyr chyldhod' (p. 114). Abramović, in a 2010 video performance, *Confession*, staged a parodic-yet-real whole-life confession to a donkey, to whom 'I began to confess … all the flaws and mistakes of my whole life, starting from my childhood and extending to that day. After about one hour, the donkey decided to walk away, and that was it. I felt a little bit better' (p. 305). Abramović's echo of Margery's phrase is surely coincidental, but the likeness of their projects is real: the books, within which they recount their confessions, are summative retellings of lifetime commitments to self-representation. Performance art, inherently ephemeral, is known through unstable memory: as Fraser Ward argues 'to the extent that performances, like other relatively ephemeral practices, generate a community of memory (whether or not that is even the memory of people who were present), they may also generate a community of error'.[27] Both women contest what they consider to be erroneous memories of their performances. When Margery and Abramović write about their performances, they textualise and record something that at its point of origin was bodily, transient, and often non-verbal, ensuring that their own preferred interpretations are remembered.

Abramović's art cites a patchwork of spiritual traditions, working sometimes with Tibetan Buddhist monks, sometimes with Australian Aborigines, but substantially, as Lydia Brawmer recognises, she draws on the 'unmistakable forms of religious imagery and iconography' of Christian tradition, particularly in the performances that constitute Christlike, saintlike acts of sacrifice and love.[28] As a child she 'learned about all the different saints' (p. 6) from her pious grandmother, and later implicitly and explicitly re-performs some practices of the holy women of the European past. In a 2009 photo and video sequence, *The Kitchen*, Abramović posed as St Teresa of Avila, levitating in a convent kitchen (p. 306). In her live works, she rediscovers what medieval ascetics knew, that 'pain was something like a sacred door to another state of consciousness' (p. 89), and challenges audiences to witness the extremes that it permits.[29] A 1975 performance, *Thomas Lips*, used the techniques of devotional asceticism: 'As I whipped myself, my blood flew everywhere. The pain was excruciating at first. And then it vanished. The pain was like a wall I had walked through and come out on the other side. After a few minutes I lay on my back on blocks of ice that had been laid on the floor in the form of a cross.' (p. 75) Abramović, indeed, is more enthusiastic about using ascetic practices to modify consciousness than is Margery, who, I have previously argued, works with the idea of bodily asceticism rather than wholly committing to it.[30] In *The House with the Ocean View* in 2002 Abramović performed a version of anchoritism, 'to see if it is possible to use simple daily discipline, rules, and restrictions to purify myself' (p. 263). She lived for twelve days on display in an installation in a New York gallery, silent and fasting, while viewers came to watch her. The performance sacralised mere bodily life – sitting, sleeping, drinking water – by exposing it to focused attention, as well as being an exercise in bodily discipline and endurance.

Repetition and re-performance, setting up continual encounters of past and present, are central to both women's practices. Margery's re-enactments of the lives of Christ, the Virgin, Mary Magdalene and Margaret of Antioch, Marie d'Oignies and Bridget of Sweden are, in Richard Schechner's terms, restored behaviour, a category of activity particularly conducive to ritual: 'Because the behavior is separate from those who are behaving, the behavior can be stored, transmitted, manipulated, transformed. The performers get in touch with, recover, remember, or even invent these strips of behavior and then rebehave according to those strips.'[31] Devotional texts such as Nicholas Love's *Mirror of the Blessed Life of Jesus Christ* provided a ready-made framework of biblical 'scripted visions' for Margery's contemplative avatar to step into.[32] Margery makes re-behaviour central to her practice. On pilgrimage she re-enacts her social ostracism in front of the legate who had instructed her 'to sytten at the mete in hys presens as sche dede in hys absens and kepyn the same maner of governawns that sche kept whan he was not ther' (p. 154). Repetition is also a long-standing technique of Abramović's art: of her 1973 performance *Rhythm 10*, combining live and recorded action, she comments: 'I'd succeeded in creating an unprecedented unity of time present and time past' (p. 61). She has a consistent interest in re-performance, pioneering protocols for re-performing her own and other artists' work (pp. 278–81). She developed performances entitled *Biography* and *Biography Remix* that performed histories of her life of performance, continually retelling her story (p. 273). As she performed *The Artist Is Present*, other performers re-performed some of her earlier works.[33] A re-retrospective re-reperforming some of the same work is scheduled to run at London's Royal Academy of Arts in 2023: Tim Marlow, the RA's artistic director, confirmed that: 'Her concern at the moment is as much looking forward to the legacy of how performance art can exist when the performer is no longer around. Her main concern is how her own work will be reperformed, as theatre is, as music is, in the future.'[34] Margery too sought unity of time present and time past through repetitive action: her 'crying', as Carolyn Dinshaw argues, is temporal disruption that 'absorbs the temporalities of past, present, and future into a panoramic *now*'.[35] Each crying then takes its place in a sequence of cryings that stitches Margery's mundane linear life to the eternal present of heaven.

Although Margery experienced cryings for only ten of the forty-odd years covered by the *Book*'s narrative, they are a central concern of the narrative. They began in Jerusalem, on the site of Calvary, when Margery's visionary witness to the crucifixion overcame her consciousness and bodily control:

> And therfor, whan sche knew that sche schulde cryen, sche kept it in as long as sche mygth and dede al that sche cowde to withstond it er ellys to put it awey, til sche wex as blo as any leed, and evyr it should labowryn in hir mende mor and mor into the tyme that it broke owte. And whan the body myth ne lengar enduryn the gostly labowr, but was ovyrcome wyth the unspekabyl lofe that wrowt so fervently in the sowle, than fel sche down and cryed wondyr lowde. And the mor that sche wolde labowryn to kepe it in er to put it awey, mech the mor schulde sche cryen and the mor lowder. And thus sche dede in the Mownt of Calvarye, as it is wretyn beforn. (pp. 165–6)

Margery's crying exhibits her lack of ownership of her own body, making visible her usually invisible hosting of Christ within her, producing the fascinating and uncanny spectacle of her as puppet, animated by greater forces. She is performer but also a symptom, neither alone in her body nor in control of it. Her subjective experience of the cryings is of struggling against the unspeakable love rising within her, and finally giving in to it, giving up the boundaries of herself to this thing within her that is not her. Margery's body screens a host of other forces and narratives; this exploitation of passivity is a technique she shares with Abramović.

Abramovic's iconic 1974 performance, *Rhythm 0*, consisted of her body, a table full of objects ranging from flowers to a gun, and an invitation to the audience to do whatever they liked with the combination, thus exposing her to the risks of sexual humiliation and assault, bodily harm, maybe even death.[36]

> Abramović's performance of *Rhythm 0* resulted in her enduring multiple acts of violence. Although the piece did not prescribe that her clothes be cut from her body, they were. She was also pierced with the thorns of the rose and had her throat cut and her blood drunk, in addition to having the loaded gun placed in her hand and held to her head. ... audience interactions with Abramović were gendered and sexualized ... photographs show one man in particular pulling open Abramović's shirt and revealing her breasts, pulling her face down to his and kissing her cheek, and standing with his hands on either side of her head while Abramović lies on a table wrapped in chains with a butcher knife positioned between her legs.[37]

The artist offers her body as a screen, exposing what the audience brought to the room: 'I was a puppet – entirely passive' she wrote (p. 69). For herself, this passivity is a discipline: 'an extraordinary and paradoxical effort of will (roughly, the willed abandonment of will)', as Ward argues.[38] Such abandonment is an intense and temporally limited enactment of the lifelong practice of monastic obedience, and a version of the self-annihilation sought by mystical extremists such as Marguerite Porete, whose Simple Soul 'has not retained any will, but has fallen and come to a state of wishing for nothing, and this knowing nothing and this wishing for nothing have excused and freed her'.[39] Abramović's abandonment of even the will to survive orchestrates the actions of her audience, draws them into exposing the desires they were concealing. The performance centres on the horrifying and uncanny spectacle of a human body behaving as if there were no human there, so that Abramović came to resemble 'an inanimate object with a secret life', as Lara Shalson suggests.[40] Margery screams while Abramović is silent, but neither of them is available to discuss the extraordinary encounter they have set in motion. The audience, Abramović writes, fled when she reclaimed her voice to announce the scheduled end of the performance (p. 70). The passivity of the human performer liberates the latent possibilities of the objects – the flowers, the perfume, the knife and the chains all get to do what is within them – but also positions the human audience as unknowing objects, puppets of the performance who find themselves performing actions they had never anticipated.

Margery's performance likewise turns an analytical gaze back on the audience, challenging them, then assessing them by how they respond to this passive female body which is screening God's desires. Audience response, as with *Rhythm 0*, is visceral, divided between protective appreciation and aggressive hostility. At the temple in Jerusalem the friars, expert interpreters of holy performance, appear to understand the spectacle of the crying as Margery does, as visible evidence of salvific love. Margery calls on clerical authority in her claim that the Franciscans who ran the pilgrim tours at the Holy Sepulchre appreciated the performance: 'the Frerys of the Tempyl mad hir gret cher and yovyn hir many gret relykys, desiryng that sche schuld a dwellyd stille amongs hem, yyf sche had wold, for the feyth thei had in hir' (p. 174). The friars, then, opportunistically talent-spotted Margery as she wept her way around their tour of the holy sites. Presumably they recognised her performance of love and sorrow as an event that might complement their tour and enhance the site, and that could be re-performed on a regular schedule if she could be persuaded to stay longer.

But the performance is divisive: less experienced spectators have responses of pity, horror and disgust that are more appropriate to a spectacle of violence: 'summe seyd it was a wikkyd spiryt vexid hir; sum seyd it was a sekenes; sum seyd sche had dronkyn to mech wyn; sum bannyd hir; sum wisshed sche had ben in the havyn; sum wolde sche had ben in the se in a bottumles boyt; and so ich man as hym thowte. Other gostly men lovyd hir and favowrd hir the mor' (p. 165). This often-cited passage has some oddities. Given the context, Margery's performance is not that obscure. The *Stations of Jerusalem* establish that demonstrative weeping was a normal and expected response to the site:

> And lewd men than ther eyghen wepe,
> That teres fell under ther fete.[41]

In Jerusalem, at the site of Calvary, a devout pilgrim crying out, sinking to the ground, spreading her arms is quite easily legible as mourning and re-enacting the crucifixion, taking on the roles both of Christ as she spreads her arms in crucifixion pose and of mourners as she wails; it is odd, then, that the performance should cause so much bafflement.[42] And it is odd that Margery, enraptured as she is by her direct access to the sacred at the climax of her longed-for pilgrimage, should have the attention to spare to hear and record such a very specific set of comments. Her retrospective position as both critic and performer forces an impossible narrative situation of a consciousness split between a visionary of her own interior and an out-of-body observer; knowing both how unspeakable love felt rising within her, and how she looked as blue as lead to the onlookers.

Both books use such polarised audience responses to explore how the performers and their performances can be at once privileged and marginalised. Margery is an insider, a mayor's daughter, and a burgess's wife, who deliberately alienates her neighbours and marginalises herself. Abramović recounts early privilege and later success, international commissions, prizes and grants, but also documents the hostility of critics who denounce her as 'an exhibitionist and a masochist' (p. 67), and predictable ridicule from the cultural mainstream. When *The House with the Ocean View* was cited in *Sex and the City*, she complains, 'despite my fasting and serious intent to change consciousness … the performance and I were mocked' (p. 269). Yet she licensed the citation, and recalls several occasions when she responded to hatred and ridicule by doubling down on whatever people found objectionable. *Rhythm 0* was her response to 'scandalized' critics who said she 'belonged in a mental hospital' (p. 67). Margery, likewise, persists with behaviours that she knows rouse hostility. She sometimes temporises, backtracking on white clothes and softening her cries, but, like Abramović, she turns hostile responses into fuel for her continued vocation, sucking up shaming and seeking 'mor schame for hys lofe' (p. 219). 'Shame is a very strong emotion', says Abramovic, in relation to *Delusional*, a live performance in which she ate a raw onion in the company of four hundred rats (p. 220), and Margery would agree; she continually exposes herself to shame and faces it down. '[T]ransformational shame … is performance', argues Eve Kosofsky Sedgwick: in this analysis, shame creates an agonising, involuntary identification with another; the performer exposing herself to shaming forces her audience to share that shame.[43] Margery builds the inevitable hostility of audiences subjected to such experiences into an avant-gardist claim for her art. Although the *Book* addresses 'synful wrecchys' in general (p. 41), her art is inherently divisive. Nicholas Love argued that affective contemplation of the Passion was broadly accessible to 'symple creatures þe whiche as childryn hauen nede to be fedde with mylke of ly3te doctryne', but the visceral discomfort of some of Margery's audience indicates the difficulty of looking through the writhing body to the Passion enactment.[44] Margery's art often afflicts the comfortable, such as her pilgrim companions; she looks back at her audience as they watch her; she logs their reactions to make the spectacle a test of the audience's piety and discrimination. She deploys shock and provocation, and seizes on disgust and incomprehension as a badge of honour, as might a contemporary artist excoriated in the *Daily Mail*. Only the perceptive minority, the friars and other holy men, appreciate her performance; those who do not thereby reveal their obtuseness and their inadequacy as spectators. The predictably contentious responses to the crying are built into Margery's analysis of the practice.

In the *Book*, Margery retrospectively reviewed the full history of her reiterated cryings. The cries begin in Jerusalem, in 1414, and continued for ten years, taking them up to 1424 (p. 276).[45] At the time of first drafting the *Book* in c. 1431 she was probably thinking about the cryings in the light of the controversy of c. 1420, when a visiting friar objected to her crying interrupting his sermons and excluded her from church. In the early 1430s her cryings were still so controversial that even the man who was to become her second scribe, probably Robert Spryngolde, was concerned about 'so evel spekyng of this creatur and of hir wepyng' (p. 48). The progress of the *Book* thus depended on his coming to terms, via the example of Marie d'Oignies, with the scandal of the cryings; hence theorising them became a key theme of the *Book*, and was recognised as such by the Carthusian Red Ink Annotator.[46] Margery's description of the crying that annoyed the friar echoes very closely the account of the first crying in Jerusalem: 'Sche kept hir fro crying as long as sche myth, and than at the last sche braste owte wyth a gret cry and cryid wondyr sor' (p. 287). Each crying is an embodied memory of Jerusalem and a re-behaviour of the first crying. Conversely, the responses described to the very first crying are probably a summary of the reception history of the whole ten years of crying, placed at the originary scene.

During the controversy Margery and her defenders took their stand on the involuntary nature of the cryings: her friends apologise for her, saying 'have hir excusyd. Sche may not withstand it' (p. 288). For Margery the authenticity of the cryings is guaranteed by their being something which is done to her, of which she is the vehicle, rather than the origin. Conversely, it seems, some of her detractors suspected that the cryings were inauthentic because they were theatrical, under Margery's conscious control, and performed in order to attract attention. Margery's authenticity is staked on her puppethood, which requires the performance to be repeated whenever the right stimulus appears. Her lack of volition is put to the test when a couple of friendly priests set up an experiment: they take her out of town to a deserted church to see whether a crying would occur in the absence of an audience. It does, of course, and the priests can witness that, when their prayers reach the appropriate trigger point, Margery experienced the usual overload of love and consequent breakdown of bodily control: 'sche myth not kepyn it prevy, but brast owt in boistows wepyng and sobbyng, and cryid as lowde er ellys lowder as sche dede whan sche was amongys the pepil at hom' (p. 360). This slightly comic scene presents Margery as an automaton, who goes into rapture on cue when her buttons are pressed; but that is the necessary outcome of conceiving her performance as being fundamentally that of a woman struggling and being overcome, acted upon by other forces. This, Margery insists, had always been the case; the cryings had always been involuntary, always subject to misunderstanding, but had been authorised at source by the Jerusalem friars. To approve of the cryings is to join the friars as the more perceptive, more devout category of reader.

Margery's performances, in life, were usually framed by religious ceremonies; characteristically, she complemented, or, as less sympathetic observers might feel, interrupted, the service with her outbursts, leaving, for example, a priest hovering over her with the Host waiting until she was calm enough to receive it (p. 274). That context enhanced the divisiveness of the performances: whilst it enabled some to read her performance as devotional, others evidently felt that their own sermon or meditation or pilgrimage had been ambushed by Margery's claim to all the attention in the room. The audience for her performances – everyone in Lynn, in Norwich's Trinity Sunday procession, on the Jerusalem pilgrimage – was very wide, non-selective, and involuntary, more like the audience for civic cycle drama than a literary readership. The *Book* does not expect its readers to be divided in the way that the audience for the live performances were (though the critical history has in fact shown some replication of the responses of Margery's critics); it interpellates an audience of 'synful wrecchys' (p. 41) seeking comfort who are implicitly aligned with the more pious and expert audiences of the spectacle.[47] At Mount Grace the *Book* found a readership of informed specialists who could appreciate Margery and her collaborators' reframing of her performances as part of the textual and emotional community of those who read and followed Richard Rolle, Marie d'Oignies, Bridget of Sweden, an intertextual network logged by Red Ink (p. 443, p. 447). The random live audience of a few thousand people who witnessed a woman crying out was superseded by a self-selecting readership of a few dozen, who read about a woman who cried out in witness to her visions of Christ.[48] Yet an element of performance may have persisted in the reading experience. The *Shorte Treatyse* extracts from the *Book* include plenty of weeping, understood, as Allyson Foster argues, as a 'private form of devotion', but carefully excise the cryings, extracting, for example, Margery's compassion for beaten children and animals from between accounts of her crying, 'so lowde and so wondyrful that it made the pepyl astoynd' (p. 431, p. 163).[49] The Mount Grace readers, however, may have been interested in performance. Jessica Brantley shows that the Carthusian devotional miscellany BL MS Add. 37049 prompts its readers to perform as they read: many of its texts can be treated as lyric, or as 'closet drama, a dramatic text that exists for the page rather than for the stage'.[50] Red Ink's commentary, a 'spontaneous and genuinely emotional', 'personal response', both appreciates aspects of Margery's performance and is itself a potential script for the next reader.[51] His comment on Margery's falling and roaring that 'father M. was wont so to doo' confirms that he had a connoisseurial appreciation of her cryings (p. 323). Other of his annotations raise the possibility that the Mount Grace monks' reading of the *Book* included moments of enactment. His annotations share in Margery's prayers, 'And thu, gloriows Qwen', mark up a particularly dramatic exchange between Margery and Archbishop Bowet, affirm Margery's endurance, 'trew it is blyssyd lord', and speak back to Margery herself, confirming the message of her ring, 'Ihc est amor tuus' (p. 448, p. 446, p. 449, p. 444). The annotations mark moments when readers might speak out to re-perform the life of Margery Kempe, taking her as the vehicle for their own encounters with the divine. Like Abramović she created a documentary record that might also function as a script for future generations to encounter and imitate their lives, so that the performances might outlive the performing body.

Notes

I am grateful to Laura Varnam, Laura Kalas, and Lawrence Warner for constructive and enthusiastic feedback on this chapter.

1 Sarah Law, 'Now I am old I do not cry so much', in *Ink's Wish* (Norwich: Gatehouse Press, 2014), p. 35.
2 *The Book of Margery Kempe*, ed. Barry Windeatt (Cambridge: D. S. Brewer, 2004), p. 166; this edition henceforth cited parenthetically.
3 Rebecca Krug, *Margery Kempe and the Lonely Reader* (Ithaca: Cornell University Press, 2017), p. 5.
4 E.g. Sarah Beckwith, 'Problems of authority in late medieval English mysticism: language, agency, and authority in the *Book of Margery Kempe*', *Exemplaria*, 4 (1992), 171–99; Katherine J. Lewis, 'Margery Kempe and saint making in late medieval England', in John H. Arnold and Lewis (eds), *A Companion to The Book of Margery Kempe* (Cambridge: D. S. Brewer, 2004), pp. 195–216.
5 Krug, *Kempe and the Lonely Reader*, p. 7.
6 Anthony Goodman, 'Margery Kempe', in Alastair Minnis and Rosalynn Voaden (eds), *Medieval Holy Women in the Christian Tradition c.1100–c.1500* (Turnhout: Brepols, 2010), pp. 217–38, p. 235.
7 Rory Critten, *Author, Scribe and Book in Late Medieval English Literature* (Cambridge: D. S. Brewer, 2018), p. 81.

8 *Ibid.*, p. 90; Sebastian Sobecki, '"The writing of this tretys": Margery Kempe's son and the authorship of her book', *Studies in the Age of Chaucer* (2015), 257–83, strengthens the case for identifying the 'Englyschman' and the 'prest' (p. 47) as, respectively, the younger John Kempe and Robert Spryngolde.

9 Claire Sponsler, 'Drama and piety: Margery Kempe', in Arnold and Lewis (eds), *Companion*, pp. 129–44, p. 130; Jesse Njus, 'Margery Kempe and the spectatorship of medieval drama', *Fifteenth-Century Studies*, 38 (2013), 123–51, p. 125.

10 Laura Varnam, 'The crucifix, the pietà, and the female mystic: devotional objects and performative identity in *The Book of Margery Kempe*', *Journal of Medieval Religious Cultures*, 41:2 (2015), 208–37, p. 213.

11 Nanda Hopenwasser, 'A performance artist and her performance text: Margery Kempe on tour', in Mary A. Suydam and Joanna E. Ziegler (eds), *Performance and Transformation: New Approaches to Late Medieval Spirituality* (New York: St Martin's Press, 1999), pp. 97–131, pp. 100, 104–5, and 108.

12 Rebecca Schneider, *Performing Remains: Art and War in Time of Theatrical Reenactment* (London: Routledge, 2011), pp. 128–37, contests performance's disavowal of theatre.

13 Gail MacMurray Gibson, *Theater of Devotion: East Anglian Drama and Society in the Late Middle Ages* (Chicago: University of Chicago Press, 1989); Eamon Duffy, *The Stripping of the Altars: Traditional Religion in England, c. 1400–c. 1580* (New Haven: Yale University Press, 1992), p. 30; Jesse Njus, 'What did it mean to act in the middle ages?: Elisabeth of Spalbeek and *imitatio christi*', *Theatre Journal*, 63:1 (2011), 1–21, pp. 4–5; Fiona Somerset, 'Speaking in person', forthcoming in Louise D'Arcens and Sif Rikhardsdottir (eds), *Medieval Literary Voices* (Manchester: Manchester University Press); thanks to Fiona for sharing prior to publication.

14 Rebecca Solnit, *Wanderlust: A History of Walking* (London: Verso, 2001), p. xiv.

15 Marina Abramović, 'The artist is present', www.moma.org/learn/moma_learning/marina-abramovic-marina-abramovic-the-artist-is-present-2010/ [accessed 22 July 2020]; *Marina Abramović: The Artist Is Present*, dir. Matthew Akers and Jeff Dupre (2012); Marina Abramović with James Kaplan, *Walk through Walls: A Memoir* (London: Fig Tree, 2016), henceforth cited parenthetically.

16 Luce Irigaray, 'La Mystérique', in *Speculum of the Other Woman*, trans. Gillian C. Gill (Ithaca: Cornell University Press, 1985), pp. 191–202; Amy Hollywood, *Sensible Ecstasy: Mysticism, Sexual Difference and the*

Demands of History (Chicago: Chicago University Press, 2002), offers a detailed analysis of twentieth-century theorists' interest in mysticism.
17 Hollywood, *Sensible Ecstasy*, p. 18.
18 Rebecca Schneider, *The Explicit Body in Performance* (London: Routledge, 1997), p. 115
19 Marla Carlson, *Performing Bodies in Pain: Medieval and Post-Modern Martyrs, Mystics, and Artists* (London: Palgrave Macmillan, 2011), p. 80.
20 Amy Knight Powell explains pseudomorphism as 'misleading comparisons based on formal similarities where there is no similarity of artistic intent', see *Depositions: Scenes from the Late Medieval Church and the Modern Museum* (New York: Zone Books, 2012), p. 11.
21 Alison More, 'Convergence, conversion, and transformation: gender and sanctity in thirteenth-century Liège', in Elizabeth L'Estrange and More (eds), *Representing Medieval Genders and Sexualities in Europe: Construction, Transformation, and Subversion, 600–1530* (Farnham: Ashgate, 2011), pp. 33–48, compares the holy men of Liège to the better-known holy women; Nancy Caciola discusses why women are more likely than men to be inspired and possessed in *Discerning Spirits: Divine and Demonic Possession in the Middle Ages* (Ithaca: Cornell University Press, 2006), pp. 130–75; Irigaray, 'La Mystérique', p. 191.
22 John H. Arnold, 'Margery's trials: heresy, lollardy and dissent', in Arnold and Lewis (eds), *Companion*, pp. 75–93, p. 91.
23 Hollywood, *Sensible Ecstasy*, p. 249, p. 247.
24 Jennifer N. Brown, *Three Women of Liège: A Critical Edition of and Commentary on the Middle English Lives of Elizabeth of Spalbeek, Christina Mirabilis, and Marie d'Oignies* (Turnhout: Brepols, 2008), p. 31.
25 Margery knew of Marie d'Oignies (pp. 292–3), whose life circulated alongside this account of Elizabeth in two manuscripts of the Latin texts as well as the Middle English MS Douce 114; Brown, *Three Women*, p. 13.
26 Quoted in Carlson, *Performing Bodies in Pain*, p. 84.
27 Fraser Ward, *No Innocent Bystanders: Performance Art and Audience* (Hanover, NH: Dartmouth College Press, 2012), p. 120.
28 Lydia Brawner, 'The artist is present: performing the icon', *Women & Performance: A Journal of Feminist Theory*, 23:2 (2013), 212–25, pp. 215 and 225.
29 Jerome Kroll and Bernard Bachrach, *The Mystic Mind: The Psychology of Medieval Mystics and Ascetics* (New York: Routledge, 2005), pp. 27–9, outlines the potential of ascetic behaviours to bring about altered states of consciousness.

30 Sarah Salih, 'Margery's bodies: piety, work and penance', in Arnold and Lewis (eds), *Companion*, pp. 161–76.
31 Richard Schechner, *Between Theater and Anthropology* (Philadelphia: University of Pennsylvania Press, 1985), p. 36.
32 See Barbara Newman, 'What did it mean to say "I saw"? The clash between theory and practice in late medieval visionary culture', *Speculum*, 80:1 (2005), 1–43, pp. 30–3, on Margery's commitment to the tradition of scripted vision.
33 See Abigail Levine, 'Being a thing: the work of performing in the museum', *Women & Performance: A Journal of Feminist Theory*, 23:2 (2013), 291–303, and Brawner, 'The artist is present' for two re-performers' accounts of the experience.
34 Mark Brown, 'Marina Abramović's naked living doorway to be recreated at RA', *Guardian* (3 September 2019).
35 Carolyn Dinshaw, *How Soon Is Now: Medieval Texts, Amateur Readers, and the Queerness of Time* (Durham, NC: Duke University Press, 2012), p. 114.
36 A replica of the table of objects, and photographs from the performance, are displayed at Tate Modern, London.
37 Lara Shalson, *Performing Endurance: Art and Politics since 1960* (Cambridge: Cambridge University Press, 2018), p. 49.
38 Ward, *No Innocent Bystanders*, p. 119.
39 Margaret Porette, *The Mirror of Simple Souls*, trans. Edmund Colledge, J. C. Marler, and Judith Grant (Notre Dame: University of Notre Dame Press, 1999), p. 67.
40 Shalson, *Performing Endurance*, p. 75.
41 'The Stations of Jerusalem', in *Codex Ashmole 61: A Compilation of Popular Middle English Verse*, ed. George Shuffelton (Kalamazoo: Medieval Institute Publications, 2008), TEAMS Middle English Text series http://d.lib.rochester.edu/teams/text/shuffelton-codex-ashmole-61-stations-of-jerusalem, lines 113–14 [accessed 22 July 2020]
42 Carol Meale, '"This is a deed bok, the tother a quick": theatre and the drama of salvation in the *Book* of Margery Kempe', in Jocelyn Wogan-Browne, Rosalynn Voaden, Arlyn Diamond, et al. (eds), *Medieval Women: Texts and Contexts in Late Medieval Britain: Essays for Felicity Riddy* (Turnhout: Brepols, 2000), pp. 49–68, p. 59, argues that here Margery performs Mary Magdalene, rather than Christ, but, like Elisabeth of Spalbeek, she might be playing multiple roles.
43 Eve Kosofsky Sedgwick, *Touching Feeling: Affect, Pedagogy, Performativity* (Durham, NC: Duke University Press, 2003), p. 38.
44 Nicholas Love, *The Mirror of the Blessed Life of Jesus Christ*, ed. Michael G. Sargent (Exeter: University of Exeter Press, 2004), p. 10.

45 Dates according to the chronology in the *Annotated Edition*, pp. vii–viii.
46 Kathryn Kerby-Fulton, 'Annotations and corrections in the *Book of Margery Kempe*: cruxes, controversies and solutions', in Kathryn Kerby-Fulton, Maidie Hilmo, and Linda Olson (eds), *Opening Up Middle English Manuscripts: Literary and Visual Approaches* (Ithaca: Cornell University Press, 2012), pp. 234–9, p. 238.
47 Eluned Bremner, 'Margery Kempe and the critics: disempowerment and deconstruction', in Sandra J. McEntire (ed.), *Margery Kempe: A Book of Essays* (New York: Garland, 1992), pp. 117–35, pp. 123–6, discusses the likeness of some twentieth-century critical positions to those of Margery's enemies within the *Book*.
48 Lynn's population has been estimated at 4,691 in 1377; Anthony Goodman, *Margery Kempe and Her World* (London: Pearson Education, 2002), p. 15; witnesses to Margery's performances during her travels could easily have added up to a further thousand. At the Dissolution, Mount Grace housed 17 monks and three novices; W. M. Brown, 'History of Mount Grace', *Yorkshire Archaeological and Topographical Journal*, 7 (1882): 473–94, p. 479.
49 Allyson Foster, 'A *Shorte Treatyse of Contemplacyon*: the *Book of Margery Kempe* in its early print contexts', in Arnold and Lewis (eds), *Companion*, pp. 95–112, p. 98.
50 Jessica Brantley, *Reading in the Wilderness: Private Devotion and Public Performance in Late Medieval England* (Chicago: University of Chicago Press, 2007), p. 282.
51 Kelly Parsons, 'The Red Ink Annotator of the *Book of Margery Kempe* and his lay audience', in Kathryn Kerby-Fulton and Maidie Hilmo (eds), *The Medieval Professional Reader at Work: Evidence from Manuscripts of Chaucer, Langland, Kempe, and Gower* (Victoria: University of Victoria English Literary Studies, 2001), pp. 143–216, p. 151.

13

Recreating and reassessing Margery and Julian's encounter

Tara Williams

Margery Kempe, who met with a mixed reception during her life, has found a robust afterlife in modern drama. The diversity of the playwrights – including a Fox Business Network host, a historical novelist, a Tony award winner, a writer for the television shows 'Billions' and 'Nurse Jackie', a Catholic priest, and the Queynte Laydies – points to a broad and persistent interest in Margery and her *Book*. That interest also extends to writers of poetry and prose, and each genre offers its own rich possibilities for approaching the medieval text. Plays are well suited to explore dialogue, which functions as a recurrent mode within the *Book*; Margery speaks with many divine, clerical, and lay figures. One of those conversations has especially fascinated dramatists: Margery's visit with Julian of Norwich. The two women's lives were radically different, but they share intriguing commonalities as visionaries who became the first known women writers in English. It is easy to imagine that they had much to discuss, and several plays do just that, seeking to 'resurrect the historic moment where – as writings record – Margery met Julian'.[1] There seems to be an urge to reanimate these figures, to put them in the same physical space so that we can see and hear them perform their historic encounter.

Each script gives Margery and Julian's relationship a narrative arc and develops it through private exchanges between the women. *Marge & Jules*, a two-person play written by the Queynte Laydies and the most recent example considered in this chapter, highlights these features before the first scene begins. The title implies a close friendship, and the synopsis describes a mutual intimacy that emerges through dialogue:

> In a world where sin and punishment govern their lives, two remarkable women discover different ways of living their faith. Interpreting the Bible is a dangerous thing to do – especially for a woman – but Margery and Julian find silence harder still. Filled with her conviction that God is love, not a voice of punishment, Julian shows Margery how to lift the weight of guilt from off her shoulders. In return, Margery reminds Julian what it is to have an earthly existence.
> ... As spiritual enlightenment meets the darker stories of life in the Middle Ages, these women confess all; talking faith, life, after-life, semantics, erotics and the mysteries of the Man they love.[2]

The contemporary nicknames in the title and the allusion to Jesus as 'the Man they love' signal to the audience that they will be able to relate to 'Marge' and 'Jules' and their concerns while also reinforcing that the characters share (and will enact) a connection specific to the two of them.

Marge & Jules rewards scholarly attention, as do other dramatic retellings of Margery's and Julian's lives. This chapter posits that the modern plays can also illuminate scholarly treatments of the *Book*, a reversal of the more familiar dynamic. The scripts' investment in Margery and Julian's encounter brings to light a similar investment in the scholarship: both creative medievalism and medievalist criticism can exhibit a desire for a transhistorical form of female friendship. The interest in dramatising the women's private dialogue parallels the scholarly predilection to put their texts into conversation.[3] Some works in both genres also share an assumption that the meeting involved a special connection, with Julian's and Margery's identities as women at the heart of it. Among scholars that assumption rarely appears as a central claim, but instead surfaces as a brief comment – as when Karma Lochrie characterises the episode with Julian as 'the most famous' of 'a variety of glimpses into spiritual friendship among women in her *Book*' or Liz Herbert McAvoy describes it as 'female-focused, non-hierarchical', and fundamentally different from other 'encounters with representatives of ecclesiastic authority' – within interpretations that are thoughtful and persuasive overall.[4]

The plays, too, are interpretations. They take a playful approach to their subjects, fusing modern and medieval elements. As they reimagine Margery and Julian's encounter in those terms, however, the twentieth- and twenty-first-century texts produce a more insular and more conservative depiction than the fifteenth-century *Book* presents. The scripts' anachronistic and yet familiar view of the relationship prompts us to revisit the medieval text and reflect on how modern assumptions and desires may also have influenced scholarly readings. In what follows I suggest that foregrounding Margery and Julian's meeting – and their genders – is at odds with the *Book*'s emphases on Julian's authority and the range of Margery's network. Few critics have examined the details of the textual evidence or how the encounter compares to Margery's many others with religious and secular figures in public, private, and visionary spaces.[5] Attending to that wider context as well as to the language in the Norwich episode reveals that the conversation with Julian best fits the pattern of Margery's meetings with religious authorities rather than with those whom she calls friends.

Dramatic encounters

Regardless of which woman is the primary focus, most of the scripts cast Julian as wise and calm and Margery as impetuous and naive – she is in crisis, or at least in desperate need of advice and affirmation. Their friendship functions as a mentorship and usually culminates in an insight for Margery, as when she begins writing her book in *Marge & Jules* or, as we will see below, returns to her family in *Creature*. In every case the women's connection is developed through dialogue; the opportunity to recreate their discussion may be one reason why this subject has lent itself to the dramatic genre. I will consider the plays in chronological order, beginning with James Janda's *Julian: A Play Based on the Life of Julian of Norwich*, then Dana Bagshaw's *Cell Talk: A Duologue Between Julian of Norwich and Margery Kempe*, Heidi Schreck's *Creature*, and finally the Queynte Laydies' *Marge & Jules*.[6] Jacqueline Jenkins studied representations of the anchorhold in plays about Julian, including the first two I consider here; my analysis draws on her foundational work, but I am primarily interested in the representations of Margery and Julian's relationship and how those can inform our reading of the same episode in the *Book*.[7]

Because Julian is the only speaker in Janda's play, it seems like an exception to the relationship-through-dialogue paradigm. The production notes characterise *Julian* as 'a poem celebrating the life and love of Julian' and the Prologue identifies it as 'a dramatic monologue'.[8] Despite the apparently exclusive focus on Julian and her *Showings*, which is quoted at several points, Margery has a significant presence. After describing Julian's position in history, the prologue concludes: 'Another interesting woman of that age was Margery Kempe. She also left us a manuscript, her biography ... As the play opens, Julian has been listening to Margery Kempe' (p. 16). Julian's first words establish that setting:

> Yes, Margery, I understand.
> There are tempests
> and storms,
> and howling winds,
> and hail and ice,
> but they too shall pass –
>
> The Holy Church – a what?
>
> A ship of fools?
>
> But Margery,
> if you image it a ship –
>
> I beg your pardon,
> I was not listening?
>
> A 'leaking' ship
> of fools –
>
> Yes, Margery, I have seen
> a few fine paintings
> depicting it as such –
>
> No –
>
> But –
>
> That is quite true,
> none has depicted it
> as a 'leaking' ship –
>
> You are quite right,
> none has done thus –
> I?

> I see it more
> as a nest –
>
> Yes, a nest – (pp. 19–20)

This monologue reads like half of a dialogue. It includes ten dashes that indicate interruptions or pauses for response from Margery, as well as four questions and two repetitions of language from her (unheard) answers. The stage directions indicate that, although Margery is silent, she is visible for over a hundred lines before departing.

Those lines include a striking reference to female community. Julian calls the Holy Spirit 'she', and then assures Margery:

> Yes, I am careful.
> I'd never say 'her' to confuse
> a priest or bishop –
> only to women such as we –
>
> Yes. That is our joke. (p. 21)

Julian's subsequent speeches are mostly addressed to herself or the audience, yet Margery remains the original interlocutor. In this play explicitly devoted to representing Julian's life and voice, the relationship and exchanges with Margery are the crucial modes through which Julian encounters the world.

The imagined dialogue of *Julian* becomes a performative encounter in *Cell Talk*. As the subtitle indicates, it is a 'duologue' between Margery and Julian, the only characters. Bagshaw's preface explains that the script 'explores what led to that first meeting when Margery was thirty-seven and Julian sixty-seven, as well as subsequent meetings that might have occurred over the next ten years' and 'focuses on the relationship between the two women'.[9] Here that relationship is based on their common experiences as women and supportive exchanges that contrast with the ineffectual intervention by a male priest. Margery talks about her sin (that which remains unnamed in the *Book*) and how confession has not helped, then muses, 'But perhaps it would help to tell another woman instead' (p. 12). She reveals that, with the help of a 'witch', she ended a pregnancy after a rape. 'And out came this, this tiny creature', Margery says, 'Horrible and ugly and blue / And writhing' (p. 13). Julian responds, 'It happened once to me, you know / When I, like you, was very young

/ I too lost a baby'; she goes on to talk about a husband and another child who died in the Black Death, concluding, 'In truth, I think this experience is what led me to my showings' (p. 15).

Shortly afterwards, Margery shifts from 'Dame Julian' to 'Mother Julian' (p. 16), suggesting an increased intimacy. This moment is one of several that show change and complexity in their relationship. When Margery explains that she has come to Julian because of her expertise, Julian answers, 'I have been sitting in this cell meditating on my own showings for over thirty-five years now, / I certainly cannot expect to understand yours in one telling' (p. 9). The play allows for an understanding between them that develops over time, and not always smoothly. Although the two are usually in agreement, Margery declares during their second meeting, 'you fill me with such anger when you seem to have all the answers' (p. 24). They laugh together throughout, and, near the end of the play, Julian observes, 'Ah, we've had a good cackle, haven't we Margery?' (p. 47). As in Janda's *Julian*, a shared sense of humour signals their bond.

Schreck's *Creature* takes Margery rather than Julian as the primary subject; however, it demonstrates the same key features by focusing on their relationship and using dialogue extensively. As the title reveals, *Creature* emphasises Margery's creaturely life. The early scenes show her struggling with desires for sex and food along with the demands of motherhood and wifehood. Julian (as Juliana of Norwich) first enters via her text, which a priest hands to Margery. Juliana later reaches out to Margery as a voice emerging from a pile of hazelnuts:

JULIANA. Look at me.
MARGERY. *(with a mouthful of herring)* What?
JULIANA. Over here. Look at this little thing over here that was created.
MARGERY. What are you?
JULIANA. A hazelnut. What are you?
MARGERY. A woman.[10]

While Margery is enmeshed in her earthly life, Juliana appears unencumbered by a physical body. As a hazelnut she takes on the shape of one of her revelations; when she tries to explain that revelation, however, Margery is distracted by the sound of a baby crying and Juliana-as-hazelnut 'exits, disappointed' (46).

Even more than the previous examples, *Creature* highlights the differences between the women, suggesting that Julian is further along in her spiritual development. Margery interacts with a variety of characters, including her husband, a priest, a nurse, a demon, and a young man, but only Juliana is able to coax Margery into a new way of seeing the world and her position within it. When the two meet in person in the penultimate scene, Juliana becomes Margery's mentor, and the interpolation of her showings into the script maps out a path forward for Margery. This scene, entirely composed of dialogue between the women in the anchorhold, is the longest in the play. They talk about a wide range of topics, from pomegranates and cats to visions and temptations. The conversation ends with Juliana asking Margery to recall and meditate on her mother's face:

> Do you see her eyes? Do you see how tenderly they look at you? ... Do you see how more than anything in the world she wishes no harm ever to come to you? Do you see how her eyes hold onto you in your entirety? Do you see that you are enclosed within her gaze and do you see that her gaze is actually a world, an entire world of its own, the very world in which you are enfolded and embraced?
>
> ...
>
> Try to remember that face when you are thinking of God. (pp. 72–3)

The maternal gaze, like the hazelnut, encapsulates the created world; the image also recalls Julian's theology of Jesus as mother. The associations between divinity and motherhood allow Margery to think of her own motherhood as compatible with rather than antithetical to a spiritual life. In the final scene she returns home and holds her son for the first time, appearing to embrace him as both a human child and a reminder of Christ's manhood and suffering.

In *Marge & Jules*, by contrast, the women's journeys are mutually informative and – in a particularly nuanced and successful narrative arc – their exchanges lead Margery to undertake her book.[11] The performance opens with Julian praying alone, interrupted by a frantic Margery so eager to connect that she attempts to enter the space through a window. 'Why are you here?' Julian asks. 'You must help me!' Margery exclaims. Julian offers Margery insight into the nature of God as well as the typical advice and reassurance; however, Julian also shares the story of her own near-death experience and Margery comforts her in turn. Their dialogue becomes a true exchange, in which one woman shares a confidence and the other responds supportively (going beyond Bagshaw's depiction, in which Julian's revelations about her own life meet only with curious requests from Margery for more details). The staging makes their connection easily legible to a modern audience: the women embrace, they walk hand-in-hand, Julian fixes Margery's hair, and Margery tells a story about her husband while she and Julian lie in parallel pews as if at a slumber party.

From the outset Margery expresses her desire to write. Julian periodically records Margery's words, like the memorable image of being chopped as small as meat for the pot, which appears twice in the *Book*.[12] By the end, with Julian's encouragement, Margery embarks on the project that will become her *Book*. She asks Julian to write for her and begins dictating, 'When I was 20 ...'. This allusion to Margery's authorship is unusual; most plays incorporate references only to Julian's text, implying that she is more learned and sophisticated. As Margery departs in the closing scene, Julian voices a famous line from the *Showings*, 'All shall be well'. She inspires and enables Margery to write, but the play establishes both women as religious authorities and authors.

In all of these plays the relationship between the women is a significant focus: in *Cell Talk* and *Marge & Jules* it is the main subject; in *Julian* it is the impetus for the monologue that lasts the length of the script; and in *Creature* it is the means by which the central conflict is resolved. We learn about their relationship through their shared conversations, not through one woman's or a third person's report; we see their private interactions, not public or group encounters. In choosing this form the plays re-create the experience of reading this portion of the *Book*, which positions the readers as witnesses to Margery and Julian's encounter. The text describes how Margery 'schewyd' her experiences as Julian listened, then represents her responses directly (p. 120). Whereas Julian's showings are visual, Margery's religious experiences – both visionary and earthly – often take the form of conversations.[13] By re-creating Margery and Julian's relationship through dialogue, the twentieth- and twentieth-first-century plays are adopting Margery's medium even when they focus on or privilege Julian's voice.

Dramatising the encounter invites the audience to flesh out their sense of what happened centuries ago, rendering it livelier and more fully imagined. At the same time performance carries the danger of reproducing an emphasis on embodiment and reinforcing assumptions that women's spirituality falls naturally into that mode. Janda combats that impression by focusing on language and theology, and the other scripts also associate Julian with those themes; however, Margery often functions as a counterpoint. The plays mark her struggles with desire as not only human but also specific to her roles as a woman and wife. What these scripts do not capture is the full range of exchanges and experiences in which Margery engages across the other ninety-eight and three-quarter chapters of the *Book*. When the meeting with Julian takes centre stage, it becomes untethered from that substantial context and more easily transferred by the text or the audience into other narratives about female spirituality or friendship.

Female religious figures like Bridget of Sweden, Marie d'Oignies, Angela of Foligno, and Elizabeth of Hungary provide important precedents or contexts for the *Book*, but Julian is the closest in location and language. She is also the only one whom Margery encounters in person. In the next section I examine how the *Book* positions that visit, looking at the same features that are so prominent in the later representations – the connection and dialogue between the women – to consider how the *Book* approaches those elements in the context of the many other meetings and exchanges that it chronicles.

'Holy dalyawns'

The most balanced dramatic depictions of Margery still present her as troubled and in need of help. The *Book*, on the other hand, suggests that Margery strategically seeks approval and authority and that her visit to Julian represents an opportunity on both fronts. Margery moves within networks of religious authorities, supporters, and women, and the 'holy dalyawns' with Julian is a point where these networks intersect (p. 123). Nonetheless the *Book* positions their meeting most firmly within the genre of Margery's encounters with religious authorities. She is interested in Julian not because of her gender but because of her visionary authority and Margery is in search not of comfort or friendship but of another seal of approval to add to a steadily growing list.

Margery and Julian's meeting is recorded in Chapter 18 of eighty-nine in the first book. That chapter begins with Margery's visit to a White Friar in Norwich, then the Lord instructs her to visit Julian. The descriptions of these visits are comparable in length, and the section on the women's encounter is shorter than we might expect, given how much interest it has generated. It occupies just over thirty lines in the manuscript, beginning a third of the way down one page (fol. 21r) and concluding two-thirds of the way down the following page (fol. 21v). The framing of this moment suggests its connection to rather than distinction from other encounters in the same textual and geographical proximity. The meeting with Julian is one of a series in Norwich: Christ directs Margery to visit the vicar of St Stephen's, then a Carmelite friar, and finally Julian. The vicar – Richard Caister – is not only the first but also arguably the most significant. Christ tells Margery to go to 'the Vykary of Seynt Stefenys and sey that I gret hym wel, and that he is an hey chossyn sowle of myn, and telle hym he plesyth me mech wyth hys prechyng and schew hym thy prevytes and myn cownselys swech as I schewe the' (p. 113). A detailed description of the meeting follows, including what Margery wore, where they sat, and what they each said. The chapter closes with a preview of how prominently the vicar will figure in Margery's life: he 'evyr held wyth hir and supportyd hir ayen hir enmys', acting as her confessor and defender (p. 116).

The meeting with the vicar occupies Chapter 17; the meetings with the friar and Julian are covered in the first half of Chapter 18 and are more similar to each other than to the previous encounter. The prompts to the visits include parallel language: 'go to a Whyte Frer in the same cyte of Norwych, whech hyte Wyllyam Sowthfeld' (p. 117) and 'gon to an ankres in the same cyte, whych hyte Dame Jelyan' (p. 119). The friar is 'good' and 'holy' and Julian is an 'expert' who can offer 'good cownsel' (pp. 117 and 120) – language that, as I discuss below, underscores her authority – but neither receives the high praise that the vicar did directly from Christ. Margery's portions of the exchanges are presented largely as summary, rather than in the earlier detail, and William and Julian both respond positively, offer counsel, and address Margery as 'Syster'. In fact

William uses 'syster' three times to Julian's one, although Laura Saetveit Miles suggests that the term has a different impact coming from a woman.[14]

The brevity of the descriptions suggests that they are typical rather than unusual, and the sentence immediately following reinforces that: 'Thys creatur schewyd hyr maner of levyng to many a worthy clerke, to worshepful doctoryrs of divinyte, bothe religiows men and other of seculer abyte, and thei seyden that God wrowt gret grace wyth hir and bodyn sche schuld not ben aferde – ther was no disseyte in hir maner of levyng' (p. 123). The phrasing recalls Margery's motivation to share her visions with Julian 'to wetyn yf ther wer any deceyte in hem' (p. 120) and is followed by a digest of the authorities' responses that resonates with Julian's comments. She prayed for God to 'grawnt yow perseverawns' (p. 122); the authorities 'cownseld [Margery] to be perseverawnt' (p. 123). Julian exhorted Margery to 'feryth not the langage of the world, for the mor despyte, schame, and repref that ye have in the world, the mor is yowr meryte in the sygth of God' (p. 122); the authorities worry that Margery 'had so many enmys and so mech slawndyr, that hem semyd sche myte not beryn it wythowtyn gret grace and a mygty feyth' (p. 123). The *Book* suggests that Julian is not only in line with these religious and lay authorities but also one of them, and that the visit with Julian is part of a pattern of visits that affirm Margery's visions and conduct. Sarah Rees Jones explored the *Book*'s investment in male clerical authority, going so far as to posit that it was 'written by clergy, for clergy, and about clergy';[15] I see that investment as encompassing religious authority more broadly, including Julian, who, as a laywoman-turned-visionary-authority, is well positioned to assess and validate Margery's visions.

Excepting Julian from these categories, singling her out as unusual because of her gender (as creative and scholarly responses tend to do), reflects our modern preoccupations rather than those of the fifteenth-century text.[16] The *Book* understands Julian as authoritative in a way that later readers have largely overlooked: it casts her not as a female friend but as one of the 'other [authorities] of seculer abyte' and invites us to consider how she fits into the overall constellation of authorities. She is not the highest authority globally or locally; however, her lay and visionary authority complements the clerical authority of the vicar and white friar, adding an important dimension to the approvals that Margery garners in Norwich. The *Book* makes this point explicitly, explaining that Margery revealed her visions to Julian 'for the ankres was expert in swech thyngys and good cownsel cowd yevyn' (p. 120). This is the only appearance in the *Book* of 'expert', denoting someone who has attained wisdom through experience or study (and corresponding to Julian's portrayals in modern drama).[17] As her own texts attest, Julian's expertise derives from both the visions she experienced and the intense study she devoted to explicating them. In this episode the *Book* offers insight into perceptions of female theologians and mystics during Margery's lifetime and the ways in which they might confer authority on others. Although Julian offers general approval of Margery's way of life, it is on the subject of visions that her assessment carries most weight. Her endorsement does not end Margery's quest for approval; instead, it – like the other endorsements Margery lines up from religious and lay authorities – contributes to that ongoing project.

Of course no two meetings are exactly the same. One sentence from (and about) Julian and Margery's encounter seems to have been the most generative for dramatists and suggestive for scholars: 'Mych was the holy dalyawns that the ankres and this creatur haddyn be comownyng in the lofe of owyr Lord Jhesu Crist many days that thei were togedyr' (p. 123). Both 'dalyawns' and 'comownyng' can refer to different levels of connection and carry sexual connotations. 'Dalyawns', often paired with 'spechys' in the *Book* and glossed as 'conversation', can signify spiritually edifying exchanges, but also small talk, flirtation, or sexual union.[18] 'Comownyng', often glossed as 'talking' or 'fellowship', can denote sexual intercourse as well as spiritual communion;[19] Margery vividly describes her disgust for 'fleschly comownyng' with her husband (p. 62). Such language is not singular or characteristic of Margery's relationship with Julian (or John). Examining other usages allows us to see how their 'holy dalyawns' and 'comownyng' fit into a larger pattern in the *Book* and to understand the nature of their connection more precisely.

Both 'dalyawns' and 'comown' first appear in the Proem. It describes Margery's close connection to Christ, alluding to the 'spechys and dalyawns whech owr Lord spak and dalyid to hyr sowle', and then previews how 'oftentymes, whel sche was kept wyth swech holy spechys and dalyawns, sche schuld so wepyn and sobbyn that many men wer gretly awondyr' (p. 44). These lines establish 'dalyawns' as a special and holy intimacy, paired with and achieved through private dialogue. It renews Margery's devotional fervour and those who are not privy to the experience wonder at its spectacular effects. After Margery begins writing about these experiences, the scribe with whom she was working dies and she approaches a priest for whom she has 'gret affeccyon' and 'comownd wyth hym of this mater' (p. 47). 'Comown' here suggests intense discussion about an issue of personal and religious significance. The consequences of this discussion unfold over several years, with the priest promising to transcribe the manuscript but delaying and then refusing. Ultimately, he agrees to try again; she prays for him, he trusts in her prayers, and 'it was mych mor esy ... And so he red it ovyr beforn this creatur every word, sche sumtym helpyng where ony difficulte was' (p. 49). Although the *Book* does not repeat the term, we might read this moment as a shift from Margery 'comown[ing] wyth hym' to the two of them 'comown[ing]' together. This outcome – the *Book* itself – becomes possible only when they collaborate.

'Dalyawns' recurs several times in the context of Margery's relationship with Christ, hinting at a deep intimacy; she describes 'heryng and undirstondyng this swet dalyawnce in hir sowle as clerly as on frende schulde spekyn to another' (p. 377). In Chapter 13 she is accused for the first time of being a Lollard but is restored by the 'holy spech and dalyawns of owyr Lord Jhesu Cryst bothe afornoon and aftyrnoon' as well as an 'ardowr of lofe, whych was kyndelyd wyth the holy dalyawns of owyr Lord' (pp. 96–7).[20] She reports 'dalyawnce[s]' with Christ at several points during her pilgrimage to Jerusalem, including when she nearly falls from her ass after seeing the city (p. 161), weeps at Mount Calvary (p. 169), visits Mary's grave (p. 171), and sees where Christ was born (p. 172). Christ also uses the word to describe their encounters, reminding Margery that 'thow mayst not han terys ne swych dalyawns but whan God wyl send hem the' (p. 99). Perhaps because they are at divine instigation and not under her control, Margery includes 'dalyawns[es]' when laying out her experiences for examination by religious authorities, including the archbishop of Canterbury (p. 111), a 'Frer Menowr' in Assisi (p. 180), and her confessors (p. 362). During her series of Norwich visits, she uses 'dalyed' or 'dalyawns' four times when describing her experiences to Richard

Caister (pp. 114–16) and reveals the 'ful many holy spechys and dalyawns that owyr Lord spak to hir sowle' to Julian (p. 120).

The *Book* records other divine figures who 'daly' with Margery, including God (p. 190), Mary (p. 134), and St Jerome (p. 210).[21] In Chapter 87 she lists five saints with whom she has visionary conversations, explaining that 'sche cowde understond be her maner of dalyawns whech of hem it was that spak unto hir' (p. 378). However, the term is not restricted to divine figures or visions. When she spent fourteen days in York, 'many good men and women ... weryn ryth glad to heryn hyr dalyawns' (p. 242). The archbishop's clerks later warn him that 'the pepil hath gret feyth in hir dalyawnce' (p. 250).[22] 'Comown' occurs in similar contexts. 'On a tyme a worschepful lady sent for hir, for cawse of comownyng' and praised Margery liberally (p. 321). The nuns at Denny also 'oftyntymys sent for the sayd creatur', and Christ commands her to 'comfortyn the ladiis that desyryc to comownyn wyth hir' (p. 362). On the journey back from Rome such 'comownyng' had paid off: other pilgrims gave Margery money 'in-as-meche as sche had in comownyng telde hem good talys' (p. 215). Through her religious instruction she forged a connection with this group.

Other occurrences more closely approach the nature of Margery and Julian's meeting, with two people connecting through religious conversation. Several chapters before that meeting, Margery describes her joy at being criticised 'for reprevyng of synne, for spekyng of vertu, for comownyng in scriptur whech sche lernyd in sermownys and be comownyng wyth clerkys' (pp. 97–8). Here the 'comownyng' occurs both with religious texts and with religious authorities, the latter enabling the former. Margery comes across a monk who initially 'despysed hir and set hir at nowt' but, 'thorw hir dalyawns' comes to have great affection for her (p. 90). On a later visit she sees that he has followed her counsel to forsake his sins and is now a sub-prior; their 'dalyawns' thus initiates a relationship that not only deals with intimate religious conversations but also extends over some period of time.[23] Margery's encounter with an English priest in Rome features each key term twice. When they first meet, 'be holy dalyawns and communycacyon sche felt wel he was a good man' (p. 206). Later, at a multilingual dinner designed to demonstrate whether her German-speaking confessor can understand Margery, she and the English priest begin by 'dalying and comownyng in her owyn langage, Englysch' (p. 207). Their shared language reinforces the shared understanding established earlier. When she returns to England from Rome, Margery stops in Norwich to see Richard Caister again and 'thei dalyed in owr Lord a good while' (p. 216). This dalliance seems to encompass Christ as well as the two of them, pointing beyond a conversation to a shared religious experience that recalls Julian and Margery's 'dalyawns' and 'comownyng in the lofe of owyr Lord Jhesu Crist' (p. 123).

With a few notable exceptions the connotations are positive for these key terms. The Proem sets the foundation for later uses, establishing that 'dalyawns' and 'comown' convey a complex range of relationships built through verbal exchanges between figures who share emotions, interests, or experiences. It also shows the desire for connection as a powerful motivation for and within the *Book*.[24] Modern readers have picked up on this theme – Margery's desires figure prominently in the plays, as we have seen, and in the critical history – but have positioned intimacy primarily in the context of affective piety, sexual desire, or female friendship. Those contexts exist in the *Book*,[25] but the Proem demonstrates that 'dalyawns' and 'comowning' can occur within or result from a broader spectrum of connections. Margery's 'comown[ing]' with the scribe complicates the 'affeccyon' she initially felt (p. 47), creating tension and distance before they find a way to bring together her visionary experiences and his clerical authority to complete the *Book*. Christ and Margery have an enduring intimacy, but with a firm hierarchy: he chooses to dally 'to hyr sowle' and uses that process to 'tech' and guide her (p. 44). The description of Margery and Julian's encounter as 'dalyawns' and 'comownyng' reveals that they had a meaningful exchange but does not necessarily imply that they became friends. The uses of these terms throughout the *Book* suggest instead that the connection with Julian is one of many that Margery makes through her visions and travels.

Rebecca Krug observes that the *Book* 'traces [Margery's] repeated experiences of isolation and loss of fellowship as well as her successes in finding new friends and companions'. Krug also points out that Margery's 'efforts ... are largely concerned with finding *male* friends'.[26] Her negative exchanges with laywomen have received more attention than the positive ones; in one often-mentioned example from the same chapter that describes the visit with Julian, a widow bars Margery from her home after Margery instructs the widow to replace her confessor with an anchorite.[27] At Christ's direction Margery has a letter written and sent to the widow, asserting that she 'schuld nevyr han the grace that this creatur had' and that 'thow this creatur come nevyr in hir howse, it plesyd God ryt wel' (p. 126). It may be tempting for modern readers to see this as a stereotypically feminine squabble, but that would replicate the dynamic we create when singling out the meeting with Julian: an emphasis on the relationships between women, interpreted in terms of modern rather than medieval conceptions of gender. Margery's strong sense of individual authorisation from Christ brings her into conflict with various figures in the *Book*. At the same time she builds a strong and widespread network of supportive relationships with women as well as men, laypeople as well as clerics.

The text describes Margery's personal connections with women in terms quite different from the holy dalliances. Some are noted only in passing; as Margery prepares to travel to Santiago, for example, she receives money from 'a woman, a good frend to this creatur' (p. 221). Others are chronicled at greater length, such as the one with Margaret Florentine.[28] This relationship develops over the course of Chapters 31 and 38 and the two women spend significant time together, meeting in Assisi and travelling together to Rome. Because of the language barrier, their opportunities for conversation are limited, but they forge a shared understanding through 'syngnys', 'tokenys', and their 'fewe comown wordys'. Margaret honours and serves Margery at their dinners together, leaving her feeling both 'cheryd' and 'cherisched' – the latter usage denotes esteem as well as affection and is rare within the *Book*, pointing to an unusually close relationship (p. 201).

This context confirms that Margery and Julian's visit more closely resembles Margery's meetings with like-minded religious authorities than those with her female friends. By building different interpretations of their relationship, however, modern drama equips us to re-examine its depiction in the *Book*. We can recognise how the encounter contributes to the diverse and international networks that Margery builds through her many conversations as well as to the status that Julian carries as a recognised visionary and expert; Margery becomes more strategic and less isolated, and Julian becomes more authoritative. The 'holy dalyawns' is no longer singular, but it is no less significant.

Notes

Many thanks to Laura Kalas and Laura Varnam for their thoughtful guidance on this chapter and of this volume, and to Jessica Barr, Suzanne Edwards, Lynn Shutters, and Barbara Zimbalist for their helpful comments on an earlier draft of the piece.

1 The Queynte Laydies, 'Marge and Jules', www.queyntelaydies.com/marge-and-jules/ [accessed 11 July 2019].
2 The Queynte Laydies, 'Marge and Jules'.
3 As Karma Lochrie points out, that predilection existed 'even before it was known that Kempe visited the anchoress during her lifetime', see *Margery Kempe and Translations of the Flesh* (Philadelphia: University of Pennsylvania Press, 1991), p. 224. Although we have come a long way from those comparisons, as well as the mid-twentieth-century assessments of Margery as a second-rate Julian, the two women writers are still frequently paired together. The examples are too numerous to cite and include my own previous work, *Inventing Womanhood: Gender and Language in Later Middle English Writing* (Columbus: Ohio State University Press, 2011), chapter 4.
4 Karma Lochrie, 'Between women', in Carolyn Dinshaw and David Wallace (eds), *The Cambridge Companion to Medieval Women's Writing* (Cambridge: Cambridge University Press, 2003), pp. 70–88, p. 75, and Liz Herbert McAvoy, *Authority and the Female Body in the Writings of Julian of Norwich and Margery Kempe* (Cambridge: D. S. Brewer, 2004), p. 198. Some critics perceive Margery's connection with Julian to be unusual because they see Margery as having few relationships with human women; others (like McAvoy) perceive it as unusual because they see Margery's relationships with male religious authorities as mostly contentious.
5 Among the exceptions are Laura Saetveit Miles, 'Queer touch between holy women: Julian of Norwich, Margery Kempe, Birgitta of Sweden, and the Visitation', in David Carrillo-Rangel, Delfi I. Nieto-Isabel, and Pablo Acosta-Garcia (eds), *Touching, Devotional Practices, and Visionary Experience in the Late Middle Ages* (New York: Palgrave Macmillan, 2019), pp. 203–35, and Naoë Kukita Yoshikawa, '*Discretio Spirituum* in time: the impact of Julian of Norwich's counsel in the *Book of Margery Kempe*', in E. A. Jones (ed.), *The Medieval Mystical*

Tradition in England: Exeter Symposium VII. Papers Read at Charney Manor, July 2004 (Cambridge: D. S. Brewer, 2004), pp. 119–32.

6 This list represents the plays of which I am aware that treat Margery and Julian's connection substantially. John Wulp's 'The Saintliness of Margery Kempe' (1958) does not feature Julian as a character, www.johnwulp.com/the-saintliness-of-margery-kempe [accessed 11 July 2019]. Elizabeth MacDonald adapted her book *Skirting Heresy* into a play performed at King's Lynn in 2018; I was unable to see that performance or obtain a script, but Margery's relationship with Julian is not a major emphasis in the book.

7 Jacqueline Jenkins, 'Playing Julian: the cell as theater in contemporary culture', in Sarah Salih and Denise N. Baker (eds), *Julian of Norwich's Legacy* (New York: Palgrave Macmillan, 2009), pp. 113–29.

8 J. Janda, *Julian: A Play Based on the Life of Julian of Norwich*, with production notes and stage directions by Bing D. Bills (New York: Seabury Press, 1984), pp. 11 and 15. Hereafter cited parenthetically.

9 Dana Bagshaw, *Cell Talk: A Duologue between Julian of Norwich and Margery Kempe* (London: Radius, 2002), p. 4. Hereafter cited parenthetically. Recent performances under the title *Cell Talk: 1410* include Cupertino, CA, in 2013, the North Stoke Julian Festival in 2016, and The Hague in 2018.

10 Heidi Schreck, *Creature* (New York: Samuel French, 2011), p. 45. Hereafter cited parenthetically.

11 Because this script is unpublished, my analysis is based on the performance I saw in the chapel of University College, Oxford, on 6 April 2018.

12 *The Book of Margery Kempe*, ed. Barry Windeatt (Cambridge: D. S. Brewer, 2004), pp. 69 and 278. Hereafter cited parenthetically by page number.

13 On the rhetorical nature of the *Book* see Barbara Zimbalist, 'Christ, creature, and reader: verbal devotion in *The Book of Margery Kempe*', *Journal of Medieval Religious Cultures*, 41:1 (2015), 1–23. For a reading of Margery's internal conversations informed by cognitive science see Corinne Saunders and Charles Fernyhough, 'Reading Margery Kempe's inner voices', *postmedieval*, 8 (2017), 209–17.

14 Miles, 'Queer touch between holy women', pp. 207–8.

15 Sarah Rees Jones, '"A peler of holy cherch": Margery Kempe and the bishops', in Jocelyn Wogan-Browne et al. (eds.), *Medieval Women: Texts and Contexts in Late Medieval Britain* (Turnhout: Brepols, 2000), pp. 377–91, p. 391. I disagree with Jones's conclusion but find the assessment of the *Book*'s investment in religious authority productive.

16 This preoccupation has long history; we could make a similar argument about the early print versions of the text, which often marked her gender by rendering her name as Juliana (as *Creature* does much later).

17 *MED* s.v. 'expert' (ppl., adj., and n).
18 *MED* s.v. 'daliaunce' (n).
19 *MED* s.v. 'communing' (ger).
20 Cf. pp. 200, 208, 273, 332, 377, 397, 402, and 418.
21 When Christ withdraws from Margery, the devil 'dal[lies] unto hir wyth cursyd thowtys, liche as owr Lord dalyid to hir beforntyme with holy thowtys' (p. 282); this co-optation of 'dalyawns' underscores Margery's suffering.
22 Cf. pp. 328, 359, and 410.
23 Cf. pp. 223 and 225.
24 Wendy Harding suggests that these multivalent terms underscore the 'subversive potential' of Margery's practices, see 'Body into text: *The Book of Margery Kempe*', in Linda Lomperis and Sarah Stanbury (eds), *Feminist Approaches to the Body in Medieval Literature* (Philadelphia: University of Pennsylvania Press, 1993), pp. 168–87, p. 177.
25 See, for example, Kathy Lavezzo, 'Sobs and sighs between women: the homoerotics of compassion in *The Book of Margery Kempe*', in Louise Fradenburg and Carla Freccero (eds), *Premodern Sexualities* (New York: Routledge, 1996), pp. 175–98, and Laura Varnam, 'The crucifix, the pietà, and the female mystic: devotional objects and performative identity in *The Book of Margery Kempe*', *The Journal of Medieval Religious Cultures*, 41:2 (2015), 208–37.
26 Rebecca Krug, *Margery Kempe and the Lonely Reader* (Ithaca: Cornell University Press, 2017), pp. 174 and 205; emphasis in original.
27 Clementine Oliver goes so far as to suggest that Margery 'seems to have disliked secular women' ('Why Margery Kempe is annoying and why we should care', in Jason Glenn (ed.), *The Middle Ages in Texts and Textures: Reflections on Medieval Sources* (Toronto: University of Toronto Press, 2011), pp. 323–31, p. 325. Lavezzo, 'Sobs and sighs', Varnam, 'The crucifix, the pietà, and the female mystic', and Varnam, Chapter 7 above, are among the exceptions.
28 See Anthony Bale and Daniela Giosuè, Chapter 9 above.

Select bibliography

Manuscript and early print

British Library Additional 61823

Here begynneth a shorte treatyse of contemplacyon taught by our lorde Jhesu cryste, or taken out of the boke of Margerie kempe of lyn[n] (London: Wynkyn de Worde, 1501 [STC 14924]).

'A Short Treatyse of Contemplation taught by our Lord Jesu Christ, or taken out of *The Book of Margery Kempe*, Ancress of Lynn', *The Cell of Self-Knowledge: seven Early English Mystical Treatises printed by Henry Pepwell mcxxi*, ed. Edmund G. Gardner (London: Henry Pepwell, 1521 [STC 20972]).

Primary texts

Ancrene Wisse: A Corrected Edition of the Text in Cambridge, Corpus Christi College, MS 402 with Variants from Other Manuscripts, ed. Bella Millett (Oxford: Oxford University Press, 2005).

Ancrene Wisse, Guide for Anchoresses: A Translation Based on Cambridge, Corpus Christi College, MS 402, by Bella Millet (Exeter: University of Exeter Press, 2009).

The Anglo-Saxon Missionaries in Germany, trans. and ed. C. H. Talbot (London: Sheed and Ward, 1954).

Augustine, *De Trinitate*, 1.1: *The Trinity*, in *Works of Saint Augustine: A Translation for the 21st Century*, vol. 5, 2nd edition, trans. Edmund Hill, ed. John E. Rotelle (Hyde Park, NY: New City Press, 1991).

Bagshaw, Dana, *Cell Talk: A Duologue between Julian of Norwich and Margery Kempe* (London: Radius, 2002).

Birgitta of Sweden, *Life and Selected Revelations*, ed. Marguerite Tjader Harris; trans. Albert Ryle Kezel; intro. Tore Nyberg (New York: Paulist Press, 1990).

The Booke of Gostlye Grace of Mechtild of Hackeborn, ed. Theresa A. Halligan (Toronto: Pontifical Institute of Mediaeval Studies, 1979).

The Boke of Gostely Grace, edited from Oxford, MS Bodley 220 with Introduction and Commentary, ed. Naoë Kukita Yoshikawa and Anne Mouron with assistance of Mark Atherton, Exeter Medieval Texts and Studies (Liverpool: Liverpool University Press, forthcoming 2022).

The Book of Margery Kempe 1436: A Modern Version, trans. W. Butler-Bowdon (London: Cape, 1936).

The Book of Margery Kempe, ed. Sanford Brown Meech and Hope Emily Allen, EETS OS 212 (London: Oxford University Press, 1940).

The Book of Margery Kempe, ed. Barry Windeatt (Cambridge: D. S. Brewer, 2000, reprinted 2004, 2006).

The Book of Margery Kempe, trans. Anthony Bale (Oxford: Oxford University Press, 2015).

The Book of Tribulacion, ed. Alexandra Barratt (Heidelberg: Carl Winter, 1983).

Boniface, *Die Briefe des heiligen Bonifatius und Lullus*, ed. Michael Tangl, MGH Epistolae Selectae 1 (Berlin: Weidmann, 1916) www.dmgh.de/de/fs1/object/display/bsb00000534_00361.html?sortIndex=040%3A010%3A0003%3A010%3A00%3A00.

The Chastising of God's Children, ed. Joyce Bazire and Eric Colledge (Oxford: Blackwell, 1957).

Codex Ashmole 61: A Compilation of Popular Middle English Verse, TEAMS Middle English Text Series, ed. George Shuffelton (Kalamazoo: Western Michigan University Medieval Institute Publications, 2008).

Elizabeth of Hungary, Two Middle English Translations of the Revelations of St Elizabeth of Hungary, ed. Sarah McNamer (Heidelberg: Universitätsverlag C. Winter, 1996).

The English Correspondence of Saint Boniface, trans. Edward Kylie (London: Chatto and Windus, 1911) http://elfinspell.com/MedievalMatter/BonifaceLetters/Letters30-38.html#Aethelbert.

Epistolae: Medieval Women's Latin Letters, ed. Joan Ferrante https://epistolae.ccnmtl.columbia.edu/letter/354.html.

Felix Fabri, *Evagatorium in Terrae Sanctae, Arabiae et Egypti peregrinationem*, ed. Konrad Dietrich Hassler, 3 vols (Stuttgart: Sumtibus Societatis Literariæ Stuttgardiensis, 1843–49), vol. 1, pp. 309–11.

Felix Fabri (ca. AD 1480–1483), trans. Aubrey Stewart, 2 vols. (London: Palestine Pilgrims' Text Society, 1893–96), vol. 1, part 2, pp. 378–82.

The Fifteen Oes (Westminster: William Caxton, 1491), Bibliographic identifier 20195. In EEBO https://data.historicaltexts.jisc.ac.uk/view?pubId=eebo-99836861e&terms=Caxton%20The%20Fifteen%20Oes.

Galen, *Works on Human Nature: Vol 1, Mixtures (De Temperamentis)*, ed. P. N. Singer and Philip J. van der Eijk (Cambridge: Cambridge University Press, 2018).

Jacobus de Voragine, *The Golden Legend: Readings of the Saints*, intro. Eamon Duffy (Princeton and London: Princeton University Press, 2012).

Jacques de Vitry, *The life of Marie d'Oignies*, trans. Margot H. King (Toronto: Peregrina, 1989).

Janda, J., *Julian: A Play Based on the Life of Julian of Norwich*, with production notes and stage directions by Bing D. Bills (New York: Seabury Press, 1984).
Julian of Norwich, *The Writings of Julian of Norwich: A Vision Showed to a Devout Woman and A Revelation of Love*, ed. Nicholas Watson and Jacqueline Jenkins (University Park: Penn State University Press, 2006).
Law, Sarah, *Ink's Wish: Poems for Margery Kempe* (NP: Amethyst Press, 2017; first published Gatehouse Press, 2014).
The Lay Folks Mass Book: Or the manner of hearing mass, with rubrics and devotions for the people, in four texts, in English according to the use of York, from manuscripts of the Xth to the XVth century, ed. Thomas F. Simmons, EETS OS 71 (London: N. Trübner and Co., 1879).
The Liber Celestis of Bridget of Sweden, Vol. 1, ed. Roger Ellis, EETS 291 (Oxford: Oxford University Press, 1987).
Love, Nicholas, *The Mirror of the Blessed Life of Jesus Christ*, ed. Michael G. Sargent (Exeter: University of Exeter Press, 2004).
Mechthild of Hackeborn, *Liber Specialis Gratiae*, ed. Dom Ludwig Paquelin, in *Revelationes Gertrudianae ac Mechtildianae*, 2 vols (Paris: H. Oudin, 1875–77), vol. II, pp. 1–422.
Mechthild of Hackeborn, *The Book of Special Grace*, trans. and intro. Barbara Newman (New York: Paulist Press, 2017).
Mechthild of Magdeburg, *The Flowing Light of the Godhead*, trans. Frank J. Tobin (New York: Paulist Press, 1998).
Mechthild von Magdeburg, *Das fließende Licht der Gottheit, Nach der Einsiedler Handschrift in kritischem Vergleich mit der gesamten Überlieferung*, 2 vols, ed. Hans Neumann with Gisela Vollmann-Profe (Munich: Artemis, 1990/1993).
A Mirror to Devout People (Speculum Devotorum), ed. Paul J. Patterson, EETS OS 346 (Oxford: Oxford University Press, 2016).
The Myroure of Oure Ladye, ed. John Henry Blunt, EETS ES 19 (London: N. Trübner, 1973).
The Norton Anthology of Literature by Women: The Traditions in English, ed. Sandra M. Gilbert and Susan Gubar, 3rd edition (New York: W. W. Norton, 2007).
The Norton Anthology of English Literature, volume A, edited by Stephen Greenblatt et al., 9th edition (New York: W. W. Norton, 2012).
On the Properties of Things: John Trevisa's Translation of Bartholomaeus Anglicus' 'De Proprietatibus Rerum', ed. M. C. Seymour (Oxford: Clarendon Press, 1975).
Porete, Marguerite, *Le mirouer des simples ames: Speculum simplicium animarum, Corpus Christianorum: Continuatio Mediaeualis*, vol. 69, ed. Romana Guarnieri (Turnhout: Brepols, 1986).
Porete, Marguerite, *The Mirror of Simple Souls*, trans. E. L. Babinsky (Mahwah, NJ: Paulist Press, 1993).
Porete, Marguerite, *The Mirror of Simple Souls*, trans Edmund Colledge, J. C. Marler, and Judith Grant (Notre Dame: University of Notre Dame Press, 1999).

The Prymer or Lay Folks' Mass Book, ed. Henry Littlehales, EETS OS 105 (London: Kegan Paul, 1895).
The Red Register of King's Lynn, ed. Holcombe Ingleby (King's Lynn: Thew and Son, 2 vols, 1919–22).
A Revelation of Purgatory, ed. and trans. Liz Herbert McAvoy (Cambridge: D. S. Brewer, 2017).
Schreck, Heidi, *Creature* (New York: Samuel French, 2011).
'The Stations of Jerusalem', in *Codex Ashmole 61: A Compilation of Popular Middle English Verse*, ed. George Shuffelton (Kalamazoo: Medieval Institute Publications, 2008) http://d.lib.rochester.edu/teams/text/shuffelton-codex-ashmole-61-stations-of-jerusalem.
The Stacions of Rome: and the pilgrims sea-voyage, ed. F. J. Furnivall (London: Camden Society, 1867).
Three Women of Liège: A Critical Edition of and Commentary on the Middle English Lives of Elizabeth of Spalbeek, Christina Mirabilis and Marie d'Oignies, ed. Jennifer Brown (Turnhout: Brepols, 2008).
Vitae Willibaldi et Wynnebaldi Auctore Sanctimoniali Heidenheimensi, ed. Oswald Holder-Egger, MGH Scriptores 15.1 (Hanover: Hahn, 1887) www.dmgh.de/de/fs1/object/display/bsb00000890_00114.html?sortIndex=010%3A050%3A0015%3A010%3A01%3A00andsort=scoreandorder=descandcontext=Vitae+Willibaldi+et+WynnebaldianddivisionTitle_str=andhl=falseandfulltext=Vitae+Willibaldi+et+Wynnebaldi+.

Secondary texts

Abramović, Marina, with James Kaplan, *Walk through Walls: A Memoir* (London: Fig Tree, 2016).
Akel, Catherine S., 'Familial structure in the religious relationships and visionary experiences of Margery Kempe', *Studia Mystica*, 16 (1995), 116–32.
Ammannati, Francesco (ed.), *Religion and Religious Institutions in the European Economy, 1000–1800* (Florence: Firenze University Press, 2012).
Amtower, Laurel, *Engaging Words: The Culture of Reading in the Later Middle Ages* (New York: Palgrave, 2000).
Andersen, Elizabeth, Henrike Lähnemann, and Anne Simon (eds), *A Companion to Mysticism and Devotion in Northern Germany in the Late Middle Ages* (Leiden and Boston: Brill, 2014).
Appleford, Amy, 'The sea ground and the London street: the ascetic self in Julian of Norwich and Thomas Hoccleve', *The Chaucer Review*, 51:1 (2016), 49–67.
Arnold, John H., and Katherine J. Lewis (eds), *A Companion to The Book of Margery Kempe* (Cambridge: D. S. Brewer, 2004).
Atkinson, Clarissa W., *Mystic and Pilgrim: The Book and the World of Margery Kempe* (Ithaca: Cornell University Press, 1985).
Bale, Anthony, 'Richard Salthouse of Norwich and the scribe of *The Book of Margery Kempe*', *The Chaucer Review*, 52 (2017), 173–87.

Barr, Helen, and Anne M. Hutchinson (eds), *Text and Controversy from Wyclif to Bale: Essays in Honor of Anne Hudson* (Turnhout: Brepols, 2005).
Beattie, Cordelia, 'Married women's wills: probate, property, and piety in later medieval England', *Law and History Review*, 37:1 (2019), 251–69.
Beckett, Katharine Scarfe, *Anglo-Saxon Perceptions of the Islamic World* (Cambridge: Cambridge University Press, 2003).
Beckwith, Sarah, 'Problems of authority in late medieval English mysticism: language, agency, and authority in *The Book of Margery Kempe*', *Exemplaria*, 4 (1992), 171–99.
Beebe, Kathryn, *Pilgrim and Preacher: The Audiences and Observant Spirituality of Friar Felix Fabri (1437/8–1502)* (Oxford: Oxford University Press, 2014).
Bell, David N., *What Nuns Read: Books and Libraries in Medieval English Nunneries* (Kalamazoo: Cistercian Publications, 1995).
Bettancourt, Roland, *Byzantine Intersectionality: Sexuality, Gender and Race in the Middle Ages* (Princeton: Princeton University Press, 2020).
Bhattacharji, Santha, *God Is an Earthquake: The Spirituality of Margery Kempe* (London: Darton, Longman, and Todd, 1997).
Bettancourt, Roland, 'Tears and screaming: weeping in the spirituality of Margery Kempe', in Kimberley Christine Patton and John Stratton Hawley (eds), *Holy Tears: Weeping in the Religious Imagination* (Princeton: Princeton University Press, 2005), pp. 229–41.
Bowers, Terence N., 'Margery Kempe as traveler', *Studies in Philology*, 97:1 (2000), 1–28.
Bridenthal, Renate, Claudia Koonz, and Susan Mosher Stuard (eds), *Becoming Visible: Women in European History* (Boston: Houghton Mifflin, 1977).
Brown, Peter (ed.), *A Companion to Medieval English Literature and Culture, c.1350–c.1500* (Oxford: Blackwell, 2007).
Brucker, Gene A., *The Civic World of Early Renaissance Florence* (Princeton: Princeton University Press, 1977).
Bryan, Jennifer, *Looking Inward: Devotional Reading and the Private Self in Late Medieval England* (Philadelphia: University of Pennsylvania Press, 2008).
Caciola, Nancy, *Discerning Spirits: Divine and Demonic Possession in the Middle Ages* (Ithaca: Cornell University Press, 2006).
Carlson, Marla, *Performing Bodies in Pain: Medieval and Post-Modern Martyrs, Mystics, and Artists* (London: Palgrave Macmillan, 2011).
Carrillo-Rangel, David, Delfi I. Nieto-Isabel, and Pablo Acosta-Garcia (eds), *Touching, Devotional Practices, and Visionary Experience in the Late Middle Ages* (New York: Palgrave Macmillan, 2019).
Carruthers, Mary J., and Elizabeth D. Kirk (eds), *Acts of Interpretation: The Text in Its Contexts 700–1600, Essays on Medieval and Renaissance Literature* (Norman: Pilgrim Books, 1982).
Chappell, Julie A., *Perilous Passages: The Book of Margery Kempe, 1534–1934* (New York: Palgrave Macmillan, 2013).

Classen, Albrecht, *Water in Medieval Literature* (Lanham: Lexington Books, 2017).
Cohen, Jeffrey, and Lowell Duckert (eds), *Elemental Ecocriticism: Thinking with Earth, Air, Water and Fire* (Minneapolis: University of Minnesota Press, 2015).
Collins-Hughes, Laura, 'Review: In "the saintliness of Margery Kempe", a comically restless mystic', *New York Times*, 1 August 2018, www.nytimes.com/2018/08/01/theater/the-saintliness-of-margery-kempe-review.html.
Critten, Rory, *Author, Scribe and Book in Late Medieval English Literature* (Cambridge: D. S. Brewer, 2018).
D'Arcens, Louise, and Sif Rikhardsdottir (eds), *Medieval Literary Voices* (Manchester: Manchester University Press, forthcoming).
D'Arcens, Louise, with Juanita Feros Ruys (eds), *Maistresse of My Wit: Medieval Women, Modern Scholars* (Turnhout: Brepols, 2004).
de Man, Paul, 'Autobiography as de-facement', *Modern Language Notes*, 94:5 (1979), 919–30.
DiBattista, Maria, and Emily O. Wittman (eds), *The Cambridge Companion to Autobiography* (Cambridge: Cambridge University Press, 2014).
Dinshaw, Carolyn, *Getting Medieval: Sexualities and Communities, Pre- and Postmodern* (Durham, NC: Duke University Press, 1999).
Dinshaw, Carolyn, *How Soon is Now? Medieval Texts, Amateur Readers, and the Queerness of Time* (Durham, NC, and London: Duke University Press, 2012).
Dinshaw, Carolyn, with David Wallace (eds), *Cambridge Companion to Medieval Women's Writing* (Cambridge: Cambridge University Press, 2003).
Duffy, Eamon, *The Stripping of the Altars: Traditional Religion in England, c. 1400–c. 1580* (New Haven: Yale University Press, 1992).
Erler, Mary C., *Women, Reading and Piety in Late Medieval England* (Cambridge: Cambridge University Press, 2002).
Farley, Mary Hardman, 'Her own creatur: religion, feminist criticism, and the functional eccentricity of Margery Kempe', *Exemplaria*, 11 (1999), 1–21.
Foucault, Michel, 'Of other spaces', trans. Jay Miskowiec, *Diacritics*, 16:1 (1986), 22–7.
Foucault, Michel, *On the Order of Things* (London and New York: Routledge, 2002; first published 1966).
Fradenburg, Louise, and Kathy Lavezzo (eds), *Premodern Sexualities* (New York: Routledge, 1996).
Galloway, Andrew (ed.), *The Cambridge Companion to Medieval English Culture* (Cambridge: Cambridge University Press, 2011).
Glasscoe, Marion (ed.), *The Medieval Mystical Tradition in England: Papers Read at Dartington Hall, July 1984* (Cambridge: D. S. Brewer, 1984).
Glasscoe, Marion (ed.), *The Medieval Mystical Tradition in England: Exeter Symposium V: Papers Read at the Devon Centre, Dartington Hall, July 1992* (Woodbridge: D. S. Brewer, 1992).

Glasscoe, Marion (ed.), *The Medieval Mystical Tradition in England, Ireland and Wales, Exeter Symposium VI, Papers Read at Charney Manor, July 1999* (Cambridge: D. S. Brewer, 1999).

Glenn, Jason (ed.), *The Middle Ages in Texts and Textures: Reflections on Medieval Sources* (Toronto: University of Toronto Press, 2011).

Gluck, Sherna Berger, and Daphne Patai (eds), *Women's Words: The Feminist Practice of Oral History* (New York and London: Routledge, 1991).

Goodman, Anthony, *Margery Kempe and Her World* (London: Pearson Education, 2002).

Haraway, Donna, *Staying with the Trouble: Making Kin in the Chthulucene* (Durham, NC, and London: Duke University Press, 2016).

Heng, Geraldine, *The Invention of Race in the European Middle Ages* (Cambridge: Cambridge University Press, 2018).

Hirsh, John C., *Hope Emily Allen: Medieval Scholarship and Feminism* (Norman, OK: Pilgrim Books, 1988).

Hirsh, John C., 'Author and scribe in The Book of Margery Kempe', *Medium Aevum*, 44 (1975), 145–50.

Hirsh, John C., 'Hope Emily Allen, the second volume of *The Book of Margery Kempe*, and an adversary', *Medieval Feminist Forum: A Journal of Gender and Sexuality*, 31:1 (2001), 11–17.

Hollis, Stephanie, *Anglo-Saxon Women and the Church: Sharing a Common Fate* (Woodbridge: Boydell Press, 1992).

Holloway, Julia Bolton, Joan Bechtold, and Constance S. Wright (eds), *Equally in God's Image: Women in the Middle Ages* (New York: Peter Lang, 1990).

Hollywood, Amy, *Sensible Ecstasy: Mysticism, Sexual Difference and the Demands of History* (Chicago: Chicago University Press, 2002).

Holmes, Catherine, and Naomi Standen (eds), *The Global Middle Ages*, Past & Present, 238 (Oxford: Oxford University Press, 2018).

Hostetler, Margaret, '"I wold thu wer closyd in an hows of ston": re-imagining religious enclosure in *The Book of Margery Kempe*', *Parergon*, 20:2 (2003), 71–94.

Hsy, Jonathan, '"Be more strange and bold": kissing lepers and female same-sex desire in *The Book of Margery Kempe*', *Early Modern Women*, 5 (2010), 189–99.

Hsy, Jonathan, *Trading Tongues: Merchants, Multilingualism, and Medieval Literature* (Columbus: Ohio State University Press, 2013).

Innes-Parker, Catherine, and Naoë Kukita Yoshikawa (eds), *Anchoritism in the Middle Ages* (Cardiff: University of Wales Press, 2014).

Irigaray, Luce, *Speculum of the Other Woman*, trans. Gillian C. Gill (Ithaca: Cornell University Press, 1985).

James, Daniel, *Doña María's Story: Life, History, Memory, and Political Identity* (Durham, NC, and London: Duke University Press, 2000).

Johnson, Lynn Staley, 'The trope of the scribe and the question of literary authority in the works of Julian of Norwich and Margery Kempe', *Speculum*, 66 (1991), 820–38.

Jones, E. A. (ed.), *The Medieval Mystical Tradition in England: Exeter Symposium VII. Papers Read at Charney Manor, July 2004* (Cambridge: D. S. Brewer, 2004).

Kalas, Laura, *Margery Kempe's Spiritual Medicine: Suffering, Transformation and the Life-Course* (Cambridge: D. S. Brewer, 2020).

Kalas, Laura, *see also* Williams, Laura Kalas.

Kane, Bronach C., *Popular Memory and Gender in Medieval England: Men, Women and Testimony in the Church Courts, c. 1200–1500* (Woodbridge: Boydell Press, 2019).

Kerby-Fulton, Kathryn, and Maidie Hilmo (eds), *The Medieval Professional Reader at Work: Evidence from Manuscripts of Chaucer, Langland, Kempe, and Gower* (Victoria: University of Victoria English Literary Studies, 2001).

Kerby-Fulton, Kathryn, Maidie Hilmo and Linda Olson (eds), *Opening Up Middle English Manuscripts: Literary and Visual Approaches* (Ithaca: Cornell University Press, 2012).

Kim, Dorothy, 'Critical race and the middle ages', *Literature Compass*, 16.9–10 (2019) https://doi.org/10.1111/lic3.12549.

Klapisch-Zuber, Christiane, *Women, Family, and Ritual in Renaissance Italy* (Chicago: University of Chicago Press, 1985).

Knowles, David, *The English Mystical Tradition* (London: Burns and Oates, 1961).

Kroll, Jerome, and Bernard Bachrach, *The Mystic Mind: The Psychology of Medieval Mystics and Ascetics* (New York: Routledge, 2005).

Krug, Rebecca, *Margery Kempe and the Lonely Reader* (Ithaca and London: Cornell University Press (2017).

Lacan, Jacques, *Écrits*, trans. Bruce Fink (New York: Norton, 2006).

Lees, Claire. A., and Gillian. R. Overing (eds), *A Place to Believe In: Locating Medieval Landscapes* (Pennsylvania: Penn State University Press, 2006).

Legassie, Shayne Aaron, *The Medieval Invention of Travel* (Chicago: University of Chicago Press, 2019).

Lejeune, Philippe, *On Autobiography*, ed. Paul John Eakin, trans. Katherine Leary (Minneapolis: University of Minnesota Press, 1989).

Lejeune, Philippe, *Signes de vie: Le pacte autobiographique 2* (Paris: Seuil, 2005).

L'Estrange, Elizabeth, and Alison More (eds), *Representing Medieval Genders and Sexualities in Europe: Construction, Transformation, and Subversion, 600–1530* (Farnham: Ashgate, 2011).

Lewis, Gertrud Jaron, *By women, for Women, about Women: The Sister-Books of Fourteenth-Century Germany* (Toronto: Pontifical Institute of Mediaeval Studies, 1996).

Lochrie, Karma, *Margery Kempe's Translations of the Flesh* (Philadelphia: University of Pennsylvania Press, 1991).

Lomperis, Linda, and Sarah Stanbury (eds), *Feminist Approaches to the Body in Medieval Literature* (Philadelphia: University of Pennsylvania Press, 1993).

Maddock, Susan 'Mapping Margery Kempe's Lynn', *The Annual: The Bulletin of the Norfolk Archaeological and Historical Research Group*, 26 (2017), 3–11.
McAvoy, Liz Herbert, *Authority and the Female Body in the Writings of Julian of Norwich and Margery Kempe* (Cambridge: D. S. Brewer, 2004).
McAvoy, Liz Herbert, and Diane Watt (eds), 'Women's literary culture and late medieval English writing', special issue of *The Chaucer Review*, 51 (2016).
McEntire, Sandra J. (ed.), *Margery Kempe: A Book of Essays* (New York and London: Garland, 1992).
McNamer, Sarah, *Affective Meditation and the Invention of Compassion* (Philadelphia: Pennsylvania University Press, 2010).
Meier-Ewart, Charity, 'A Middle English version of the *Fifteen Oes*', *Modern Philology*, 48 (1971), 359–60.
Minnis, Alistair J. (ed.), *Late-Medieval Religious Texts and Their Transmission: Essays in Honour of A. I. Doyle* (Woodbridge: D. S. Brewer, 1994).
Minnis, Alistair J., with Rosalynn Voaden (eds), *Medieval Holy Women in the Christian Tradition c.1100–c.1500* (Turnhout: Brepols, 2010).
Mitchell, Marea, *The Book of Margery Kempe: Scholarship, Community, and Criticism* (New York: Peter Lang, 2005).
Moore, Kathryn Blair, *The Architecture of the Christian Holy Land: Reception from Late Antiquity through the Renaissance*, (Cambridge: Cambridge University Press, 2017).
Morrison, Susan Signe, *Women Pilgrims in Late Medieval England: Private Piety as Public Performance* (London: Routledge, 2000).
Mulder-Bakker, Anneke B. (ed.), *The Prime of Their Lives: Wise Old Women in Pre-Industrial Europe* (Leuven, Paris, and Dudley: Peeters, 2004).
Newman, Barbara, *From Virile Woman to WomanChrist: Studies in Medieval Religion and Literature* (Philadelphia: University of Pennsylvania Press, 1995).
Newman, Barbara, 'What did it mean to say "I saw"? The clash between theory and practice in late medieval visionary culture', *Speculum*, 80:1 (2005), 1–43.
Njus, Jesse, 'What did it mean to act in the middle ages?: Elisabeth of Spalbeek and *imitatio christi*', *Theatre Journal*, 63:1 (2011), 1–21.
Norris, Robin, Rebecca Stephenson, and Renée Trilling (eds), *Feminist Approaches to Anglo-Saxon Studies* (Tempe: Arizona Center for Medieval Studies, forthcoming).
Oen, Maria H. (ed.), *A Companion to Birgitta of Sweden and Her Legacy in the Later Middle Ages* (Leiden: Brill, 2019).
Olson, Linda, and Kathryn Kerby-Fulton (eds), *Voices in Dialogue: Reading Women in the Middle Ages* (Notre Dame: University of Notre Dame Press, 2005).
Owen, Dorothy M., *The Making of King's Lynn: A Documentary Survey of Lynn* (Oxford: Oxford University Press, 1984).
Passerini, Luigi, *Gli Alberti di Firenze* (Florence: Cellini, 1869).

Patton, Kimberley Christine and John Stratton Hawley (eds), *Holy Tears: Weeping in the Religious Imagination* (Princeton: Princeton University Press, 2005).

Pfaff, Richard W., *The Liturgy in Medieval England: A History* (Cambridge: Cambridge University Press, 2012).

Powell, Amy Knight, *Depositions: Scenes from the Late Medieval Church and the Modern Museum* (New York: Zone Books, 2012).

Renevey, Denis, with Christiania Whitehead (eds), *Writing Religious Women: Female Spiritual and Textual Practices in Late Medieval England* (Cardiff: University of Wales Press, 2000).

Renevey, Denis, and Naoë Kukita Yoshikawa (eds), 'Convergence / divergence: the politics of late medieval English devotional and medical discourses', Special Issue, *Poetica*, 72 (2009).

Riehle, Wolfgang, *The Middle English Mystics*, trans. Bernard Standring (London: Routledge and Kegan Paul, 1981).

Rosenfeld, Jessica, 'Envy and exemplarity in *The Book of Margery Kempe*', *Exemplaria*, 26:1 (2014), 105–21.

Ross, Ellen M., 'Spiritual experience and women's autobiography: the rhetoric of selfhood in *The Book of Margery Kempe*', *Journal of the American Academy of Religion*, 59 (1991), 527–46.

Ross, Robert C., 'Oral life, written text: the genesis of *The Book of Margery Kempe*', *The Yearbook of English Studies*, 22 (1992), 226–37.

Salih, Sarah, 'Two travellers tales', in Christopher Harper-Bill (ed.), *Medieval East Anglia* (Woodbridge and Rochester: NY: Boydell Press, 2005), pp. 318–31.

Salih, Sarah, and Denise N. Baker (eds), *Julian of Norwich's Legacy* (New York: Palgrave Macmillan, 2009).

Sauer, Hans, Joanna Story, and Gaby Waxenberger (eds), *Anglo–Saxon England and the Continent* (Tempe: ACMRS, 2011).

Saunders, Corinne, 'Writing revelation: *The Book of Margery Kempe*', in Tamara Atkin and Jaclyn Rajsic (eds), *Manuscript and Print in Late Medieval and Early Modern Britain: Essays in Honour of Professor Julia Boffey* (Cambridge: D. S. Brewer, 2019), pp. 147–66.

Saunders, Corinne, and Charles Fernyhough, 'Reading Margery Kempe's inner voices', *postmedieval*, 8 (2017), 209–17.

Scanlon, Larry (ed.), *The Cambridge Companion to Medieval English Literature, 1100–1500* (Cambridge: Cambridge University Press, 2009).

Schneider, Rebecca, *The Explicit Body in Performance* (London: Routledge, 1997).

Schneider, Rebecca, *Performing Remains: Art and War in Time of Theatrical Reenactment* (London: Routledge, 2011).

Scott-Stokes, Charity, *Women's Books of Hours in Medieval England* (Cambridge: D. S. Brewer, 2006).

Sedgwick, Eve Kosofsky, *Touching Feeling: Affect, Pedagogy, Performativity* (Durham, NC: Duke University Press, 2003).

Sobecki, Sebastian, *The Sea and Medieval English Literature* (Cambridge: D. S. Brewer, 2008).
Sobiecki, Sebastian (ed.) *The Sea and Englishness in the Middle Ages: Maritime Narratives, Identity and Culture*, ed. Sebastian I. Sobecki (Cambridge: D. S. Brewer, 2011).
Sobiecki, Sebastian, '"The writyng of this tretys": Margery Kempe's son and the authorship of her book', *Studies in the Age of Chaucer*, 37 (2015), 257–83.
Spearing, A. C., *Medieval Autographies* (Notre Dame: University of Notre Dame Press, 2012).
Spencer-Hall, Alicia, *Medieval Saints and Modern Screens: Divine Visions as Cinematic Experience* (Amsterdam: Amsterdam University Press, 2018).
Staley, Lynn, *Margery Kempe's Dissenting Fictions* (Philadelphia: Pennsylvania State University Press, 1994).
Stoever, Jennifer Lynn, *The Sonic Color Line: Race and the Cultural Politics of Listening* (New York: New York University Press, 2016).
Strocchia, Sharon T., *Nuns and Nunneries in Renaissance Florence* (Baltimore: Johns Hopkins University Press, 2009).
Strohm, Paul (ed.), *Middle English* (Oxford: Oxford University Press, 2007).
Suydam, Mary A., and Joanna E. Ziegler (eds), *Performance and Transformation: New Approaches to Late Medieval Spirituality* (New York: St Martin's Press, 1999).
Swanson, R. N., 'Prayer and participation in late medieval England', *Studies in Church History*, 42 (2006), 130–9.
Szarmach, Paul E. (ed.), *An Introduction to The Medieval Mystics of Europe* (Albany: State University of New York Press, 1984).
Thompson, Paul, with Joanna Bornat, *The Voice of the Past: Oral History*, fourth edition (Oxford: Oxford University Press, 2017).
Thurston, Herbert, 'Margery the astonishing', *The Month*, 168 (1936), 446–56.
Varnam, Laura, 'The crucifix, the pietà, and the female mystic: devotional objects and performative identity in *The Book of Margery Kempe*', *Journal of Medieval Religious Cultures*, 41:2 (2015), 208–37.
Varnam, Laura, 'The importance of St Margaret's church in *The Book of Margery Kempe*: a sacred place and an exemplary parishioner', *Nottingham Medieval Studies*, 61 (2017), 197–243.
Varnam, Laura, '#TeamMargery: collaboration, compassion, and creativity', https://drlauravarnam.wordpress.com/2018/04/29/teammargery-collaboration-compassion-and-creativity/.
Voaden, Rosalynn, *God's Words, Women's Voices: The Discernment of Spirits in the Writing of Late-Medieval Women Visionaries* (Woodbridge and Rochester, NY: York Medieval Press, 1999).
Voaden, Rosalynn (ed.), *Prophets Abroad: The Reception of Continental Holy Women in Late-Medieval England* (Cambridge: D. S. Brewer, 1996).
Wallace, David, *Strong Women: Life, Text, and Territory, 1347–1645* (Oxford: Oxford University Press, 2011).

Watt, Diane, *Medieval Women in Their Communities* (Toronto: University of Toronto Press, 1997).
Watt, Diane, *Medieval Women's Writing: Works by and for Women, 1100–1500* (Cambridge and Malden: Polity, 2007).
Watt, Diane, *Women, Writing and Religion in England and Beyond, 650–1100* (London: Bloomsbury, 2019).
Webb, Heather, *The Medieval Heart* (London: Yale University Press, 2010).
Williams, Laura Kalas, 'The *swetenesse* of confection: a recipe for spiritual health in London, British Library, Additional MS 61823, *The Book of Margery Kempe*', *Studies in the Age of Chaucer*, 40 (2018), 155–90.
Williams, Laura Kalas, '"Slayn for goddys lofe": Margery Kempe's melancholia and the bleeding of tears', *Medieval Feminist Forum: A Journal of Gender and Sexuality*, 52:1 (2016), 84–100.
Williams, Laura Kalas, *see also* Kalas, Laura.
Williams, Tara, '"As thu wer a wedow": Margery Kempe's wifehood and widowhood', *Exemplaria*, 21:4 (2009), 345–62.
Williams, Tara, *Inventing Womanhood: Gender and Language in Later Middle English Writing* (Columbus: Ohio State University Press, 2011).
Winston-Allen, Anne, *Convent Chronicles: Women Writing about Women and Reform in the Late Middle Ages* (University Park: Pennsylvania State University Press, 2004).
Wogan-Browne, Jocelyn (ed.), *Medieval Women: Texts and Context in Early Medieval Britain* (Turnhout: Brepols, 2000).
Wogan-Browne, Jocelyn, with Rosalynn Voaden, Arlyn Diamond, et al. (eds), *Medieval Women: Texts and Contexts in Late Medieval Britain: Essays for Felicity Riddy* (Turnhout: Brepols, 2000).
Yoshikawa, Naoë Kukita, *Margery Kempe's Meditations: The Context of Medieval Devotional Literature, Liturgy, and Iconography* (Cardiff: University of Wales Press, 2007).
Yoshikawa, Naoë Kukita (ed.), *Medicine, Religion and Gender in Medieval Culture* (Cambridge: D. S. Brewer, 2015).
Zimbalist, Barbara, 'Christ, creature, and reader: verbal devotion in *The Book of Margery Kempe*', *Journal of Medieval Religious Cultures*, 41:1 (2015), 1–23.
Zumthor, Paul, 'Autobiography in the Middle Ages?', trans Simon Sherry, *Genre*, 6 (1973), 29–48.

Online resources

Kim, Dorothy, YouTube channel to accompany Chapter 10: www.youtube.com/channel/UCx5MHU6qbvfadJrzlnqWH2Q (accessed 14 September 2021).
The Margery Kempe Society: https://themargerykempesociety.wordpress.com (accessed 14 September 2021).

Select bibliography

'Margery Kempe Studies in the 21st Century' conference: https://margerykempeconference.wordpress.com (accessed 14 September 2021).

Marina Abramović, *The Artist Is Present*: www.moma.org/learn/moma_learning/marina-abramovic-marina-abramovic-the-artist-is-present-2010/ (accessed 14 September 2021).

Medieval English Dictionary: https://quod.lib.umich.edu/m/middle-english-dictionary/dictionary (accessed 14 September 2021).

Oxford English Dictionary: www.oed.com (accessed 14 September 2021).

Watt, Diane, 'Margery Kempe', *Oxford Bibliographies Online* www.oxfordbibliographies.com/view/document/obo-9780199846719/obo-9780199846719-0034.xml (accessed 14 September 2021).

Index

References to figures are in bold

A Revelation of Purgatory 35, 46, 57
Abramović, Marina 13, 261, 264–70
Alan of Lynn 12, 47–8, 60n.22, 60n.25, 129, 170, 174–5
  see also Warnekyn, Alan
Alberti, Margherita degli 12, 187–200, 293
Alberti family 189–99
Allen, Hope Emily 5, 7, 17n.19, 45–6, 51, 57, 67, 102–4, 114
annotators (of the *Book*) 150, 179, 223, 249, 270, 272
  see also Red Ink Annotator
autobiography 10, 11, 83–95, 101–15, 121

Bartholomaeus Anglicus 248
Beaufort, Joan 47, 186
Benedictines 65
Bishop's Lynn 47, 65, 101, 163–80, **165**
  see also King's Lynn
Boke of Gostely Grace, The 10, 44–8, 58, 142, 154
  see also Mechthild of Hackeborn
Bonaventure 43

Boniface 9, 24, 34
Book II of *The Book of Margery Kempe* 13, 48, 64, 135n.10, 234–51
Bridget of Sweden 29–30, 43, 45–7, 49–51, 66, 83, 106, 188–91, 194–5, 265, 272, 286
British Library, Additional 37049 152–3, 272
British Library, Additional 61823 8, 64, 102–3, 114
de Brunham, John 12, 163–9, 171, 173
de Brunham family 168–71
Butler-Bowdon, William 103–4

Caister, Richard 128–9, 152, 264, 287, 290–2
Carmelites 47–8
Carthusians 45, 50, 223–4
Catherine of Siena 29, 45–50, 190, 198
Cell Talk, Dana Bagshaw 282–3
chthulucene 235
Creature, Heidi Schreck 283–4
crying (Margery Kempe's) 53–6, 66, 70–1, 115, 149–50, 198, 205–28, 243, 266–73, 290

Index 311

Danzig 37, 48–9, 178, 236, 245
daughter-in-law (Margery Kempe's) 48–50, 239
diagnosis (of Kempe) 113–15
Digital Humanities 218–22
Dominicans 12, 45
Dorothy von Montau 45

Elisabeth of Spalbeek 263
Elizabeth of Hungary 44, 286
emotions 4, 8, 123, 141–56, 292
Empedocles 237, 246
encounter, theorisation of 3–6

Fabri, Felix 213–15, 217–18, 223
female friendship 140–7, 186–8, 191–2, 200, 279, 285, 288, 292–3
Fifteen Oes, The 66, 68
Florence 12, 187–90, 192–8
Florentyne, Margaret 4, 12, 30, 145, 187–8, 192–4, 197–9, 293
  see also Alberti, Margherita degli
Foucault, Michel 2–3, 15, 129
Franciscans 12, 189, 216–18, 222

Germany 24, 28, 45, 48, 50, 110, 186, 239, 245–9
Gertrude of Helfta 50
Global Middle Ages 6, 16n.18, 228

Haraway, Donna 13, 234–5, 237, 247–8, 250–1
heart, the 141–5, 147, 149–50, 152–6
Helfta 44–5, 50–1, 57, 142
Henderson, Rebecca 156
Hildegard of Bingen 50
Hilton, Walter 43, 208
Hodoeporicon 9, 24, 31–9
Holland, Joan 12, 165
Holy Land 27, 30–1, 236, 266–71, 290

Holy Trinity guild 126, 164, 177–8, 237, 243–4, 250
Hugeburc of Heidenheim 31–9
hysteria (and mysticism) 262

imitatio Christi 54, 92, 209, 266–9
Incendium Amoris 43
Irigaray, Luce 262–3
Isidore of Seville 238

Jacobus de Voragine 240
Jerusalem 12, 33, 36–7, 66, 205–28, 266–71, 290
Julian, Julian Janda 280–3
Julian of Norwich 13, 83, 87, 91–2, 113, 145, 153, 186, 242–3, 278–9, 292–3

Kempe family, of Lynn 171–2, **172**
Kempe, John 96n.1, 139n.72, 171–2, 179, 236, 251, 260, 284–5, 289
King's Lynn 47, 65, 101, 163–80, **165**
  see also Bishop's Lynn

Lacan, Jacques 86, 92
Lay Folks Mass Book, The 71–2
Leicester 38, 145, 149, 185–6, 225
Lejeune, Philippe 10, 83, 87–8, 105–6
Liber specialis gratiae 10, 44–8
Lok family, of Lynn 169–70
Lollardy 29, 38, 70, 143, 225
London 1–2, 15
Love, Nicholas 265, 270

de Man, Paul 11, 87–8, 105–7, 112–13
Marge & Jules, Queynte Laydies 278–9, 284–5
Marie d'Oignies 44, 83, 208, 259, 265, 270, 272, 286
Mechthild of Hackeborn 11, 44–58, 142, 144, 153–5

Mechthild of Magdeburg 90–1
Mediterranean 12, 212, 220
Meech, Sanford Brown 104, 114, 163
Mirror of the Blessed Life of Jesus Christ, The 265, 270
Mount Grace 64, 68, 223, 272–4
Myroure of oure Ladye, The 46

natural world 234–43, 245–50
St Nicholas's chapel, Lynn 172–3
Norfolk 26, 101, 112, 163–80
Norwich 13, 65, 146, 152, 167, 177, 287, 290, 292

Passion, the 53–5, 66, 68, 147, 152, 195, 209–11, 263, 270
performativity 144, 150–2, 259–73, 278–94
Pike Gate 1–3
pilgrimage 24–39, 208–9, 236–7, 244, 247–8
Porete, Marguerite 91, 267
prayers (Kempe's) 63–77, 110, 151–3, 197, 250–1

Red Ink Annotator 150–1, 249, 270, 272
  see also annotators
Renaissance 12, 187, 197–200
Roldán, Doña María 124–8, 131–3
Rolle, Richard 158n.36, 272
Rome 12, 25–39, 109–11, 128, 146–7, 186–8, 190–200, 236, 240, 291–3

Sacred Heart 11, 142, 149
Salthows (or 'Salthouse'), Richard 64–5, 67–8, 72–5

Santiago de Compostela 30, 36, 225, 236, 293
scribe(s) 36, 48–50, 64–6, 68, 72–5, 84, 90, 93–4, 110, 114, 122, 130, 150, 235–6, 239, 270, 290, 292
Short Treatyse of Contemplation taught by our Lord Jesu Christ, or taken out of The Book of Margery Kempe, Ancress of Lynn, A 272
Speculum devotorum 46
Spryngolde, Robert 65, 129–30, 150, 176–7, 270
Southfield, William 287–8
Stagel, Elsbet 84
Stations of Jerusalem, the 209–13, 269
Stimulus Amoris 43–4, 47
Syon Abbey 45–50

tears *see* crying

Venice 37, 199, 240
Virgin Mary 6, 66, 69–70, 75, 111, 146, 248–9, 265, 291
St Vitalis 240–3

Warnekyn, Alan 12, 47–8, 60n.22, 60n.25, 129, 170, 174–5
  see also Alan of Lynn
weeping *see* crying
white women tears 225–8
Wyreham, John 175

YouTube, Margery Kempe channel 8, 12, 218, 220–2

EU authorised representative for GPSR:
Easy Access System Europe, Mustamäe tee 50,
10621 Tallinn, Estonia
gpsr.requests@easproject.com